Have Japanese Firms Changed?

Palgrave Macmillan Asian Business Series Centre for the Study of Emerging Market Series

Series Editor:

Harukiyo Hasegawa is Professor at Doshisha Business School, Kyoto, Japan, and Honourable Research Fellow at the University of Sheffield's School of East Asian Studies, where he was formerly Director of the Centre for Japanese Studies.

The Palgrave Macmillan Asian Business Series seeks to publish theoretical and empirical studies that contribute forward-looking social perspectives on the study of management issues not just in Asia, but by implication elsewhere. The series specifically aims at the development of new frontiers in the scope, themes and methods of business and management studies in Asia, a region which is seen as key to studies of modern management, organisation, strategies, human resources and technologies.

The series invites practitioners, policy-makers and academic researchers to join us at the cutting edge of constructive perspectives on Asian management, seeking to contribute towards the development of civil societies in Asia and further afield.

Titles include:

Glenn D. Hook and Harukiyo Hasegawa (*editors*)
JAPANESE RESPONSES TO GLOBALIZATION IN THE 21st CENTURY
Politics, Security, Economics and Business

Hiroaki Miyoshi and Yoshifumi Nakata (*editors*)
HAVE JAPANESE FIRMS CHANGED?
The Lost Decade

Diane Rosemary Sharpe and Harukiyo Hasegawa (*editors*)
NEW HORIZONS IN ASIAN MANAGEMENT
Emerging Issues and Critical Perspectives

Sten Söderman (*editor*)
EMERGING MULTIPLICITY
Integration and Responsiveness in Asian Business Development

Oliver H.M. Yau and Raymond P.M. Chow (*editors*)
HARMONY VERSUS CONFLICT IN ASIAN BUSINESS
Managing in a Turbulent Era

Tan Yi
THE OIL AND GAS SERVICE INDUSTRY IN ASIA
A Comparison of Business Strategies

Palgrave Macmillan Asian Business Series
Series Standing Order ISBN 978-1-4039-9841-5

You can receive future titles in this series as they are published by placing a standing order. Please contact your bookseller or, in case of difficulty, write to us at the address below with your name and address, the title of the series and the ISBN quoted above.

Customer Services Department, Macmillan Distribution Ltd, Houndmills, Basingstoke, Hampshire RG21 6XS, England

Have Japanese Firms Changed?

The Lost Decade

Edited by

Hiroaki Miyoshi
Professor of Graduate School of Policy and Management,
Doshisha University

and

Yoshifumi Nakata
Professor of Graduate School of Policy and Management,
Doshisha University

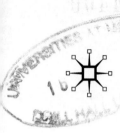

First published 2011 by
PALGRAVE MACMILLAN

Palgrave Macmillan in the UK is an imprint of Macmillan Publishers Limited,
registered in England, company number 785998, of Houndmills, Basingstoke,
Hampshire RG21 6XS.

Palgrave Macmillan in the US is a division of St Martin's Press LLC,
175 Fifth Avenue, New York, NY 10010.

Palgrave Macmillan is the global academic imprint of the above companies
and has companies and representatives throughout the world.

Palgrave® and Macmillan® are registered trademarks in the United States,
the United Kingdom, Europe and other countries.

ISBN: 978–0–230–25021–5 hardback

This book is printed on paper suitable for recycling and made from fully
managed and sustained forest sources. Logging, pulping and manufacturing
processes are expected to conform to the environmental regulations of the
country of origin.

A catalogue record for this book is available from the British Library.

Library of Congress Cataloging-in-Publication Data

Have Japanese firms changed? : the lost decade / edited by Hiroaki
Miyoshi And Yoshifumi Nakata.
    p. cm.
    ISBN 978–0–230–25021–5 (alk. paper)
    1. Industries – Japan. 2. Industrial management – Japan. 3. Industrial
policy – Japan. 4. Japan – Economic conditions – 1989– 5. Japan – Economic
policy – 1989– I. Miyoshi, Hiroaki, 1960– II. Nakata, Yoshifumi, 1955–
III. Title.

HC462.95.H388 2011
338.70952—dc22   2010034186

10 9 8 7 6 5 4 3 2 1
20 19 18 17 16 15 14 13 12 11

Printed and bound in Great Britain by
CPI Antony Rowe, Chippenham and Eastbourne

Contents

List of Illustrations		vii
Preface		xi
Notes on Contributors		xiii

1 Introduction 1
Hiroaki Miyoshi and Yoshifumi Nakata

2 The Evolution of Japan's Semiconductor Industry 14
Searching for Global Advantage
Clair Brown and Greg Linden

3 The Japanese Enterprise Software Industry 41
An Evolutionary and Comparative Perspective
Robert E. Cole and Shinya Fushimi

4 The Evolution of Japan's Human-Resource Management 70
Mitsuo Ishida and Atsushi Sato

5 Have Japanese Engineers Changed? 88
Yoshifumi Nakata and Satoru Miyazaki

6 Strategic Alliances in the Japanese Economy 109
Types, Critiques, Embeddedness, and Change
James R. Lincoln and Emily W. Choi

7 R&D Management in Japanese Manufacturing Firms 137
Technology Trade, R&D Outsourcing, and Joint R&D
Akihiko Kawaura and Dai Miyamoto

8 Foreign Direct Investment and Management in Japan 161
The Impact of Japanese Corporations' Foreign
Direct Investment Strategies on Managerial Decisions
and Corporate Performance in Japan: An Analysis Based
on Corporate-Level Microdata
Jun Ma

9 Why Do Japanese Companies File Patents in China? 191
Empirical Findings from Japanese Firm-level Data
Yoshifumi Nakata and Xingyuan Zhang

10   **Changing Ownership and Governance Innovation**   218
Japanese Enterprises in Transition
Asli M. Colpan, Takashi Hikino, and Toru Yoshikawa

11   **Why Do Japanese Companies Issue Stock Options?**   247
Behind the Introduction of Stock Options in Japan:
Theory of Shareholder Sovereignty vs. Theory of
Managerial Sovereignty
Hiroaki Miyoshi and Takeo Nakao

12   **Automotive Technology Policy in Japan**   273
Masanobu Kii, Hiroaki Miyoshi, and Masayuki Sano

13   **Science and Technology Policy**   292
Tateo Arimoto

Index   309

Illustrations

Figures

2.1 Home substitution index for semiconductor sales,
    1992–2000   20
3.1 Software sales between system integrator (SI) firms
    X and Y and their customers   60
4.1 Markets, organizations, and wage decisions in
    Japan and the US   74
4.2 A schematic depiction of the interrelation among
    organizational structure, performance management,
    and personnel management   80
5.1 An international comparison of labor productivity and
    professional jobs as a fraction of all jobs (2005)   93
5.2 Engineering innovativeness determination model   95
5.3 Changes in motivation to work   103
5.4 The fraction of all aspiring college students who
    aspire to major in science or engineering fields   105
6.1 Strategic alliances connect horizontal and vertical *keiretsu* 122
6.2 Observed durations of horizontal and vertical
    keiretsu effects on R&D and non-R&D alliances   128
7.1 R&D spending by Japanese firms per research
    employee (million yen)   138
7.2 Ratio of the value of all Japanese technology
    exports to the value of all technology imports   140
7.3 Fraction of technology exports going to Asia,
    Europe and North America   141
7.4 Fraction of corporate R&D expenditures
    disbursed for external R&D activities   143
7.5 Shifts in distribution by R&D location   146
8.1 Fraction of foreign-expanding Japanese corporations
    adopting each of the seven possible foreign-expansion
    patterns between 1994 and 2003   169
9.1 Growth of Chinese patent applications for
    foreign inventions   196
9.2 Growth of Chinese patent grants for foreign inventions   196
9.3 Growth of technology transfer in China   199

10.1	Structural change in Japanese corporate governance	221
10.2	Change in ownership structure of Japanese firms	223
10.3	Relative influence of governance and strategy factors on ROA in STP1	236
10.4	Relative influence of governance and strategy factors on ROA in STP2	237
12.1	Relationship between battery price and EV sales volume ($\alpha_0=3.32$)	285
12.2	Relationship between battery price and EV sales volume ($\alpha_0=3.41$)	286
12.3	Sensitivity of battery price to changes in parameter values	288
13.1	Schematic diagram of an *innovation ecosystem*	303
13.2	The global innovation ecosystem	305

Tables

2.1	Changes in industry leadership, 1980–2007	16
2.2	Top-10 chip companies' sales by region, 2005 (as a percentage of global semiconductor revenue)	21
2.3	Paths for emerging companies	24
2.4	High-commitment and high-innovation HRM systems	28
2.5	Chinese chip-packaging facilities of leading Japanese companies	34
2.6	Chinese design centers of leading Japanese companies, 2005	35
3.1	Top ten worldwide system integrator market share leaders in 2005	44
3.2	Revenue and computing market share for the top ten consulting and system integration providers in Japan, 2006–2007	45
3.3	IT deployment and migration in a major Japanese manufacturing firm	54
3.4	Methods of building information systems	56
4.1	A comparison of personnel system reforms in Japan and in the US	78
5.1	Weekly hours worked for engineers (male/female total)	90
5.2	Patent applications: An international comparison	
	(A) Numbers of patent applications in 2005	92
	(B) Patent applications per 1000 researchers	92

5.3   Numbers of surveys distributed and returned   96
5.4   Factors and elements used in data analysis   97
5.5   Factors that influence performance
       (demonstration of ability)   99
5.6   Elements identified as enhancing engineer performance   100
5.7   Changes in jobs and the workplace environment   102
6.1   Domestic and international R&D strategic alliances
       by period   112
7.1   Categorization of firms during the sample period   144
7.2   Ratio of R&D expenditures to sales, by firm
       R&D category   145
7.3   R&D outsourcing decisions and utilization rates   149
7.4   Joint R&D activities in Japan: 1998–2004   151
7.5 (a) Factors influencing whether or not a company pursues
         domestic joint R&D initiatives (left half); factors
         influencing the extent of a company's utilization of
         domestic joint R&D initiatives (right half)   154
7.5 (b) Factors influencing whether or not a company
         pursues *overseas* joint R&D initiatives (left half); factors
         influencing the extent of a company's utilization of
         overseas joint R&D initiatives (right half)   155
8.1   Foreign-expansion-pattern dummy variables
         (collectively denoted $\{D_{i,t-1}\}$ in equations (8.1) and (8.2))   168
8.2 (a) Managerial-decision variables related to personnel
         allocations (collectively denoted $\{R_{i,t}\}$ in
         equations (8.1) and (8.2))   170
8.2 (b) Managerial-decision variables related to
         domestic R&D activities (collectively denoted $\{R_{i,t}\}$
         in equations (8.1) and (8.2))   170
8.2 (c) Managerial-decision variables related to inter-firm
         transactions (collectively denoted $\{R_{i,t}\}$ in equations
         (8.1) and (8.2))   171
8.3 (a) Control variables describing corporate attributes
         (collectively denoted $\{X_{i,t-1}\}$ in equations
         (8.1) and (8.2))   171
8.3 (b) Control variables describing regional dependence of
         corporate exports and imports (collectively
         denoted $\{X_{i,t-1}\}$ in equations (8.1) and (8.2))   171
8.4   Statistical properties of variables   172
8.5   Conclusions of model regarding the impact of FDI on
         the composition of the domestic workforce (1)   174

8.6	Conclusions of model regarding the impact of FDI on the composition of the domestic workforce (2)	176
8.7	Conclusions of model regarding the impact of FDI on research and development and on inter-firm transactions (3)	178
8.8	Conclusions of model regarding the impact of FDI on corporate added value	183
9.1	Patent applications for inventions in China by Japanese parent companies	198
9.2	Descriptive statistics, 1995–2003 (N=436)	206
9.3	Estimated results for patent application	207
9.4	Impact of patent reforms on patent applications	209
9.5	Dynamic panel GMM estimates	211
10.1	Pearson correlation coefficients	231
10.2	GLS regression results on ROA (STP1)	233
10.3	GLS regression results on ROA (STP2)	234
10.4	Incremental contribution of the explanatory variables	239
11.1	Predictions of the theories of shareholder and managerial sovereignty	256
11.2	Definitions, calculation procedures, and statistical properties of dependent and independent variables	261
11.3	Expected signs of correlations between size of stock-option packages and explanatory variables	265
11.4	Results of regressions on the size of stock-option packages	266
12.1	Parameters used to simulate the impact of more-widespread use of EVs	284

Preface

This book presents the fruits of research conducted under the *Synthetic Research on Technology, Enterprise and Competitiveness* program, a member of the *Twenty-first Century COE (Centers of Excellence) Program* sponsored by MEXT (Japan's Ministry of Education, Culture, Sports, Science and Technology) and housed at Doshisha University's Institute for Technology, Enterprise and Competitiveness (ITEC). The *Twenty-first Century COE Program* is aimed at creating world-class research and education hubs in Japanese universities, and ITEC was chosen in 2003 as one of 26 hubs within the field of social science.

ITEC has fostered the *Synthetic Studies on Technology, Enterprise, and Competitiveness* project with a particular focus on two pedagogical goals. The first is a fusing of the soft and hard sciences: social scientists are organized together with physical scientists and engineers into common educational and research units, and work jointly to pursue research questions addressing phenomena such as 'technology' and 'innovation' that encompass both the sciences and the humanities. The objective is to instill in researchers an entirely new set of values that transcend the boundaries of the traditional social sciences. The second goal is to instigate international collaboration. ITEC extends far beyond the confines of Doshisha University, conducting joint research projects – including frequent exchanges of research personnel – with other Japanese universities, corporations, and government institutions, as well as with overseas research institutions, including the Centre for Business Research (CBR) at Cambridge University in the UK and the Center for Work, Technology and Society (CWTS) at the University of California at Berkeley. The authors of this book include researchers, as well as members of corporations and government agencies, invited by ITEC to collaborate on research projects.

Although ITEC pursues an extensive variety of research questions under the common theme of 'the competitiveness of Japanese corporations', the present volume represents a summary of work to date addressing a central unifying question: *Have Japanese firms changed?* To the authors of the research works contained herein, who graciously agreed to summarize their research with particular attention toward this one central theme, we extend our heartfelt gratitude.

There are a number of people we wish to thank for their invaluable support, both of this book and of the growth of ITEC. In particular,

Professor Harukiyo Hasegawa of Doshisha University, the General Editor of Asian Business & Management at Palgrave Macmillan, gave us the opportunity to publish the results of our research. Professor David Hugh Whittaker of the University of Auckland, the former director of ITEC, provided valuable comments and suggestions on several chapters in this book. We acknowledge the substantial contributions of Professors Eiichi Yamaguchi and Tetsushi Fujimoto of Doshisha University, the ITEC Deputy Directors, to the development of ITEC. Finally, we are grateful to our publisher, Palgrave Macmillan, and in particular to our editor, Virginia Thorp, and our editorial assistant, Paul Milner, for keeping us on track toward the publication of this book.

In conclusion, we launch this volume in the fervent hope that it speeds the world's researchers and practitioners alike toward a better understanding of Japanese corporations and the Japanese economy.

Hiroaki Miyoshi
Director of the Institute of Technology, Enterprise
and Competiveness at Doshisha University

Yoshifumi Nakata
Director-General of the Institute of Technology, Enterprise
and Competiveness at Doshisha University

Contributors

Tateo Arimoto is Director-General of the Research Institute of Science and Technology for Society (RISTEX) and Deputy Director-General of the Center for R&D Strategy (CRDS) in the Japan Science and Technology Agency (JST). He has been intensely involved in the crafting of Japanese science and technology policy. Previously, he served as Director General of the Science and Technology Policy Bureau in Japan's Ministry of Education and Science. He held the position of Deputy Director General for Science and Technology Policy, a Cabinet Office. As Director-General of RISTEX, he now oversees an ambitious effort to foster innovation to address social challenges. His recent publications include 'Innovation Policy for Japan as a Front Runner', in D. Hugh Whittaker and Robert E. Cole (eds), *Recovering from Success: Innovation and Technology Management in Japan* (Oxford, 2006) and 'International Competitiveness of Japan and Science and Technology Policy-Structure Change of Science and Technology', in Y. Kuwahara and Fujio Niwa (eds), *MOT for the 21st century and Technology Management*.

Clair Brown is Professor of Economics and Director of the Center for Work, Technology and Society, IRLE at UC Berkeley. Brown is a past Director of the Institute of Industrial Relations (now the Institute for Research on Labor and Employment) at UC Berkeley, and a past OMRON fellow at Institute for Technology, Enterprise and Competitiveness (ITEC), Doshisha University, Kyoto. She has published research on many aspects of the labor market, including high-tech workers, labor market institutions, firm employment systems and performance, the standard of living, wage determination, and unemployment. The industries she has studied in the field include semiconductors, automobiles, consumer electronics, telecommunications, and high-tech start-ups. Brown directed the human resources group of the Sloan Semiconductor Program at UC Berkeley. Their research analyzed the labor market for engineers, and how semiconductor companies create and capture value. Her books include *American Standards of Living, 1919–1988* (Blackwell, 1994), *Work and Pay in the United States and Japan* (with co-authors), *Economic Turbulence* (with co-authors), and *Chips and Change: How Crisis Reshapes the Semiconductor Industry* (with Greg Linden). Currently Brown is directing an NSF-funded survey of US firms that documents their domestic jobs and global location of functions.

Emily W. Choi is a doctoral candidate at the Walter A. Haas School of Business at UC Berkeley. Her research focuses on strategic alliances and entrepreneurial firms. Currently, she is studying strategic alliance activities in the software industry. She is a recent recipient of the Ewing M. Kauffman Foundation Dissertation Fellowship. She holds a Master of International Management from Thunderbird School of Global Management, an MBA in Supply Chain Management from Arizona State University, and a BA in East Asian Studies from Washington University in St. Louis. Prior to her doctoral studies, she held senior management positions at IBM, E2open and Apple Computer.

Robert E. Cole has researched and published extensively in the fields of organizational change, quality and knowledge management. His most recent book, co-edited with D. Hugh Whittaker, is *Recovering from Success: Innovation and Technology Management in Japan*. His most recent publication is 'Automotive Quality Reputation: Hard to Achieve, Hard to Lose, Still Harder to Win Back: The Case of U.S. and Japanese Auto Quality' (*California Management Review* 50 (Fall 2009): 67–93) (with Michael Flynn). Cole is Professor Emeritus of Walter A. Haas School of Business and the Department of Sociology at UC Berkeley, and has been a visiting researcher at ITEC, Doshisha University from 2004 to the present.

Asli M. Colpan is Associate Professor of Corporate Strategy and holds the Mizuho Securities Chair at the Graduate School of Management, Kyoto University. She is also Adjunct Associate Professor of the Kyoto Consortium for Japanese Studies at Columbia University. Her research interests include corporate strategy, corporate governance, and especially the evolution of large enterprises in industrial and emerging economies. Her work has been published in such journals as *Industrial and Corporate Change, Journal of Management Studies* and *Asian Business & Management*. She is also a co-editor of *The Oxford Handbook of Business Groups* (with Takashi Hikino and James R. Lincoln), Oxford University Press, 2010.

Shinya Fushimi is general manager of strategic IT business planning at Mitsubishi Electric Corporation, Tokyo. He started his career as a researcher of Mitsubishi Electric, and then served various management positions in R&D, sales, marketing, and engineering. He received the BS, MS, and PhD degrees in computer science from The University of Tokyo. From 2006 to 2007 he was with the Sloan Master's Program at the Graduate School of Business at Stanford University, where he received a master's degree in business management. He also conducted research on the Japanese software industry at Shorenstein Asia-Pacific Research Center, Stanford University, from 2007 to 2008.

Takashi Hikino is Associate Professor of Industrial and Business Organization at the Graduate School of Economics and the Graduate School of Management at Kyoto University. His recent publications include *Big Business and the Wealth of Nations* (co-edited with Alfred D. Chandler and Franco Amatori), *Policies for Competitiveness: Comparing Business-Government Relationships in the 'Golden Age of Capitalism'* (co-edited with Hideaki Miyajima and Takeo Kikkawa), *The Global Chemical Industry in the Age of the Petrochemical Revolution* (co-edited with Louis Galambos and Vera Zamagni), and *The Oxford Handbook of Business Groups* (co-edited with Asli M. Colpan and James R. Lincoln).

Mitsuo Ishida is Professor of Industrial Relations on the Faculty of Social Studies at Doshisha University. His research interests cover comparative human resources management and labor relations research among the US, the UK, Germany and Sweden. He has also researched automotive labor relations in Japan, the US, and Germany. His recent Japanese publications include *Work, Remuneration and Management in Japanese Automotive Companies* (co-authored with Y. Tomita and N. Mitani), *Comparative Human Resources Management between Japan and USA* (co-authored with J. Higuchi), and *GM's Experiences and Lessons for Japan* (co-edited with K. Shinohara).

Akihiko Kawaura is Professor of Economics at the Graduate School of Policy & Management, Doshisha University. Before joining Doshisha University in 2005, he was affiliated with Otaru University of Commerce between 1995 and 2005. His professional experience includes assignments with the United Nations Economic and Social Commission for Asia and the Pacific (Bangkok) and the World Bank (Washington, DC) as staff economist. His research interests lie in the area of public choice, economic development, and law and economics. His recent publications include 'Public resource allocation and electoral systems in the U.S. and Japan', in *Public Choice*, 115(1–2) (April 2003) and 'Institutional Change in Japan: Theories, Evidence, and Reflections' (with S. J. LaCroix), in M. Blomstrom and S. J. Lacroix (eds), *Institutional Change in Japan*.

Masanobu Kii is Associate Professor of Environmental Policies and Planning on the Faculty of Engineering, Kagawa University in Japan. He worked at the Institute for Transport Policy Studies (2000–2003), the Japan Automobile Research Institute (2004–2008), and the Research Institute of Innovative Technology for the Earth (2008–2009) before joining Kagawa University in 2009. He has conducted various types of policy impact analysis in transport sector, including fuel economy regulation, public transport policy, and urban land use planning. His research interests include sustainability of energy and environment systems. His recent publications include 'An Integrated Evaluation Method of Accessibility, Quality of Life, and Social Interaction' (*Environment and Planning B*, 2007) (with co-authors), 'Impact Assessment of Fuel-Efficient Technologies for Passenger Vehicle' (*Energy and Resources*, 2007) (with co-authors) (in Japanese), and 'Multiagent Land-Use and Transport Model for the Policy Evaluation of a Compact City' (*Environment and Planning B*, 2005).

James R. Lincoln is the Mitsubishi Professor of International Business and Finance at the Walter A. Haas School of Business of UC Berkeley. He is a former Associate Dean for Academic Affairs (2005–2008) of the Haas School and former Director of UC Berkeley's Institute for Research on Labor and Employment (1997–2002). He is the author (with Michael Gerlach) of *Japan's Network Economy: Structure, Persistence, and Change*, and (with Arne Kalleberg) *Culture, Control, and Commitment: A Study of Work Organizations and Work Attitudes in the U.S. and Japan*. He co-edited (with Asli M. Colpan and Takashi Hikino) *The Oxford Handbook of Business Groups* in 2010. He is also the author of numerous scholarly articles on international business and various other topics in organization and management.

Greg Linden is Research Associate at the Institute for Business Innovation, a research unit at the Haas School of Business, UC Berkeley. His current work includes the analysis of global value chains, with an emphasis on the ability of firms to shape industry outcomes. In addition to more than a dozen academic publications, Linden co-authored *Chips and Change: How Crisis Reshapes the Semiconductor Industry*. The book resulted from a multi-year study of the globalization of semiconductor design. Early results of the study, which was supported by the Alfred P. Sloan Foundation and Doshisha University, were published through the Brookings Institution and the National Academy of Engineering. Linden has also worked as a consultant on projects in Asia to develop industrial policy for high-tech industries. His research interests include the competitive dynamics of the electronics industry, collaboration in the semiconductor industry, the emergence of global competitors from industrializing countries, and the effect of foreign direct investment on economic growth.

Jun Ma is Professor of Management on the Faculty of Economics, University of Toyama, Japan. His research interests include human-resource management and the economics of organization. His recent papers include 'Analysis of Unemployment During Transition to a

Market Economy: The Case of Laid-off Workers in the Beijing Area' (*Far Eastern Studies*, 7: 41–64, 2008) (co-authored with Hiroko Imamura and Guo-Qing Zhao), 'Entrepreneurship, Innovation and Growth of Venture Businesses in Japan' (*Far Eastern Studies*, 5: 15–33, 2006), and 'The "Seniority" in Promotion and Wage Systems of the Japanese Firm: An Empirical Analysis on Personnel Data' (*Japanese Journal of Labour Studies*, 46: 45–56, 2004 in Japanese).

Dai Miyamoto is a lecturer in the Department of Economics at Japan's Ryutsu Keizai University. His research areas and interests lie in the fields of labor economics, human-resource management, and industrial relations. His recent articles include 'Paying for Success: Performance-related Pay Systems and its Effects on Firm Performance in Japan' (*Asian Business & Management*, 2007) (with Junpe Higuchi) and 'Determinants of R&D Outsourcing at the Japanese Firms: Transaction Cost and Strategic Management Perspectives' (*International Journal of Humanities and Social Sciences*, 2007).

Satoru Miyazaki is a post-doctoral fellow at ITEC at Doshisha University. His main research areas are in human-resource management and labor economics. His recent articles include 'Increasing Labor Flexibility in Japan: The Role of Female Workers in Manufacturing', in C. Brown, B. J. Eichengreen, and M. Reich (eds), *Labor in the Era of Globalization* (with Yoshifumi Nakata), 'Non-working Nurses in Japan: Estimated Size and its Age-cohort Characteristics' (*Journal of Clinical Nursing*, 17: 3306–3316, 2008) (with Yoshifumi Nakata), and 'Has Lifetime Employment become Extinct in Japanese Enterprise?' (*Asian Business & Management*, 6(S1): S33–S56, 2007) (with Yoshifumi Nakata).

Hiroaki Miyoshi is Director of ITEC at Doshisha University, as well as Professor at the Graduate School of Policy and Management at Doshisha University. He worked at a major private sector think tank for ten years, conducting research and making policy recommendations on a broad range of issues as a senior researcher, before joining Doshisha University in 2003. His research interests include public economics and transport economics. His recent publications include *Knowledge Asset Management and Organizational Performance* (co-edited with Y. Shozugawa, in Japanese), *Technological Innovation in the Automotive Industry and Economic Welfare* (co-edited with M. Tanishita, in Japanese), 'Factors Associated with Safety of Passenger Cars (IATSS Research, 2008)(with M. Tanishita)', and 'Policy Problems Relating to Labor Immigration Control in Japan', in Roger Goodman *et al.* (eds), *Global Japan: The Experience of Japan's New Immigrants and Overseas Communities*.

Takeo Nakao is Professor of Economics on the Faculty of Economics at Doshisha University. He was a visiting scholar at the University of Michigan's Department of Economics in 1978–1979, at UCLA's Department of Economics in 1979–1980, at the Harvard Yenching-Institute at Harvard University in 1983–1984, and at the School of Public Health at UCLA in 1996–1997. He was also a research fellow at the International Institute of Management in Berlin, Germany in 1984–1985. His research interests include the behavior of firms in oligopolies, and his publications have appeared in such journals as *Review of Economics and Statistics*, *Journal of Industrial Economics*, *Quarterly Journal of Economics*, *Bell Journal of Economics*, and *Canadian Journal of Economics*. He is also a co-author of *Main Stream in Industrial Organization* (Leiden: Martinus Nijhoff, 1986).

Yoshifumi Nakata is Professor of Human Resource Management at the Graduate School of Policy and Management at Doshisha University. He also serves as Director-General of ITEC at Doshisha University. From 2003 to 2008 he directed *Synthetic Research on Technology, Enterprise and Competitiveness*, a Centers of Excellence Program created by Japan's Ministry of Education. Among his recent publications are 'Increasing Labor Flexibility in Japan: The Role of Female Workers in Manufacturing', in C. Brown, B. J. Eichengreen, and M. Reich (eds), *Labor in the Era of Globalization* (with Satoru Miyazaki), 'Non-working Nurses in Japan: Estimated Size and its Age-cohort Characteristics' (*Journal of Clinical Nursing*, 17: 3306–3316, 2008) (with Satoru Miyazaki), and 'Has Lifetime Employment become Extinct in Japanese Enterprise?' (*Asian Business & Management*, 6(S1): S33-S56, 2007) (with Satoru Miyazaki).

Masayuki Sano is a consultant and founder of Libertas Terra Co., Ltd., a consulting firm specializing in energy and environmental issues. He has been director at a major private think tank in the past five years, and supervised a variety of research projects mostly sponsored by governmental organizations. He currently serves as a consultant to the Japan Automobile Manufacturers Association Inc. (JAMA). From 2006 to 2009 he was a visiting fellow at ITEC, Doshisha University. His research interests include energy and environmental issues in the world road transportation sector. His recent publications include 'Genealogy of Automotive Technology Innovation and Technology Policy in Japan', in H. Miyoshi and M. Tanishita (eds), *Technological Innovation in the Automotive Industry and Economic Welfare* (in Japanese).

Atsushi Sato is Professor on the Faculty of Lifelong Learning and Career Studies, Hosei University, Tokyo. Before joining Hosei University in 2008, he was affiliated with the Japan Institute for Labour Policy and Training (formerly the Japan Institute for Labour Policy) and the Graduate School of Policy and Management at Doshisha University. His research areas and interests lie in the field of industrial sociology and human resource management. His recent publications in Japanese include *World of White-collar Worker: Spectrum of Work and Career* (Japan Institute of Labour, 2001), *Sociology of Work* (co-edited with H. Sato), and *Transformation of Performance Management and Human Resource Management.*

Toru Yoshikawa is Associate Professor of Management at Lee Kong Chian School of Business, Singapore Management University. His main research interest is corporate governance, especially its relation to corporate strategy and performance in large publicly listed firms and in family-owned firms. His research has been published in such journals as the *Academy of Management Journal, Strategic Management Journal, Organization Science, Journal of Management, Organization Studies,* and *Journal of Business Venturing.*

Xingyuan Zhang is Professor of Economics and Econometrics at Okayama University, Japan. He spent his graduate school days at Kobe University and received a PhD in economics in 1998. His research interests are corporate innovation and patent strategies. His recent publications include 'Bayesian and Non-Bayesian Analysis of Gamma Stochastic Frontier Models by Markov Chain Monte Carlo Methods' (*Computational Statistics,* 20(4), 2005) and 'Productivity Analysis of IT Capital Stock: The U.S.–Japan Comparison' (*Journal of the Japanese and International Economies,* 17, 2003).

1
Introduction

Hiroaki Miyoshi and Yoshifumi Nakata

A nation or region suffering from ten or more years of economic stagnation is often said to have entered a 'lost decade'. The term has been used to describe the US during the Great Depression, the UK after World War II, Latin America in the 1980s, and, most recently, the experience of Japan in the years between the collapse of the 'bubble economy' around 1991 and the nation's eventual reemergence around 2002–2003. The central research question we ask in this book is: *How did Japanese corporations and government institutions evolve during Japan's lost decade?*

The structure of this book

The next ten chapters of this book examine how Japanese firms evolved during the lost decade. We begin by exploring this theme in the context of two specific high-tech industries, namely, the semiconductor industry (Chapter 2) and the software industry (Chapter 3). The following eight chapters consider changes in Japanese firms from four distinct perspectives: **(1)** the evolution of human-resource management systems, which in Japanese companies were traditionally based on the lifetime employment system (Chapters 4 and 5); **(2)** the evolution of relationships among businesses, which in Japanese companies were traditionally based on the *keiretsu* structure (Chapters 6 and 7); **(3)** the evolution of foreign investment initiatives and other global strategies by Japanese firms, with a particular focus on the rapidly developing East Asian region (Chapters 8 and 9); and **(4)** the evolution of Japanese corporate governance, which had traditionally been characterized as *contingent governance* (Aoki, 1994) (Chapters 10 and 11).

The final two chapters of this book examine how Japan's government policies evolved during the lost decade. The years of the lost decade

witnessed several drastic reforms in Japan's government sector, implemented primarily by the Hashimoto cabinet, and we review in particular the evolution of Japanese industrial technology policy (Chapter 12)
and of Japanese science and technology policy (Chapter 13), which constitute two critical pillars supporting corporate innovation activities.

This book in relation to the literature on Japan's lost decade

Before summarizing the unique features of this book, we must first survey the existing literature on Japan's lost decade, which already boasts
several remarkable studies examining changes in Japan's corporate and
government sectors during this period.

Works addressing specific areas of change include Aoki *et al.* (2007),
which discussed the evolution of corporate governance in Japanese
firms, and Amyx (2006), which reviewed the evolution of Japan's financial sector. The work of Aoki *et al.* (2007) examines how the Japanese
approach to corporate governance has changed in the post-bubble
era. This book offers a unique empirical exploration of how, and why,
Japanese firms have reshaped their corporate governance arrangements,
leading to greater diversity among firms and new 'hybrid' forms of corporate governance. Amyx (2006) discusses the Japanese banking crisis
and concludes that the distinctive feature of the Japanese experience
was the unusually long delay between the emergence of the bad-loan
problem and the government's aggressive intervention to address it.

Other works, including Katz (2002), Whittaker and Cole (2006), and
Hook and Hasegawa (2006), offer more comprehensive discussions of
recent and future changes in Japan's private and public sectors, as we
seek to do in this volume. Katz (2002) discusses the struggle between the
forces of reform and the forces of resistance in Japan. This work dissects
Prime Minister Koizumi's role in the process, explains why Japan is in so
much trouble today, and suggests what needs to be done, both now and
in the future. Whittaker and Cole (2006) examine the challenges faced by
Japan's high-tech companies, including the successful emulation of some
of their key practices by foreign competitors and the emergence of new
competitive models linked to open innovation and modular production.
The work of Hook and Hasegawa (2006) is an analysis and evaluation
of Japanese responses to globalization. This study constructs a three-
dimensional structure, linking issues of politics and security with issues
of economics and business, addressing both internal and external factors,
and ultimately shedding light on Japan's globalization in its totality.

In comparison to these previous works, this book is unique in the following three ways.

First, eight of the 12 chapters in this book (Chapters 2, 3, 5, 6, 7, 9, 12, and 13) discuss changes in the systems and strategies of Japanese firms together with contemporaneous changes in Japanese government policy, focusing primarily on *technology* enterprise and policy, the traditional basis for the strong competitiveness of Japanese corporations. This is the key feature of this book, and one which differentiates it from all previous studies except that of Whittaker and Cole (2006).

Next, this book includes many quantitative analyses. All of the studies mentioned above, with the exception of that of Aoki *et al.* (2007), are qualitative discussions, based on theories or outcomes of field studies. In contrast, in seven of the 12 chapters in this book (Chapters 5–11), we conducted econometrical analyses using extensive microdata – such as that provided by the *Basic Survey of Japanese Business Structure and Activities* conducted by Japan's Ministry of Economy, Trade and Industry (METI) – and used the results of these analyses as a basis for objective discussions of evolving patterns in Japanese firms. While Japanese researchers have often used extensive microdata, such as that provided by the *Basic Survey*, in recent studies, these data have not always been known to foreign researchers. We hope that the introduction of such microdata on Japanese firms will be one of the major academic contributions made by this book.

Finally, this study includes several cross-national studies. Chapters 2 and 3 report on comparative analyses of Japanese and US firms in two high-tech industries – the semiconductor industry and the software industry. Similarly, Chapter 4 discusses trends in human-resource management systems in Japan and the US. These three chapters reveal multiple ways in which Japanese firms hewed close to – as well as other ways in which Japanese firms differed significantly from – US and European firms during the lost decade.

A detailed overview of this book

We will now provide a brief summary overview of each chapter in this book.

Chapters 2 and 3 discuss changes in Japanese business practices in two high-tech industries: the semiconductor industry (Chapter 2) and the software industry (Chapter 3). For more than 30 years, a strong commitment to the semiconductor ('chip') industry has been an important strategic element for Japan's electronics leaders. After capturing global leadership from the US in the 1980s, Japan's chip firms saw their position erode in the decade that followed, as US firms dominated new product markets, Japan's domestic economy stagnated, and new competitors, especially from South Korea, challenged Japan's dominance of the memory chip market. Chapter 2, 'The Evolution of Japan's Semiconductor Industry: Searching for Global Advantage', by Clair Brown and Greg Linden, explores the important steps taken by Japan's semiconductor companies to reverse their decline, including organizational restructuring, technology alliances, and offshore investment. The authors also discuss important structural weaknesses that remain in Japan's semiconductor industry, including excess capacity, a hostile environment for start-ups, and human-resource management systems that constrain flexibility and globalization. They conclude that Japanese chip firms must continue to restructure both their organizations and their human-resource systems, and must use the resources available in the dynamic economies of the Asia-Pacific region to become more globally competitive.

Chapter 3, 'The Japanese Enterprise Software Industry: An Evolutionary and Comparative Perspective', by Robert E. Cole and Shinya Fushimi, addresses the question of how and why, despite initial similarities, the US and Japanese software industries evolved in such different directions. IBM dominated the early development of the computer industry, providing the dominant product architecture and the business model for software. Thereafter, even as most US producers (with the exception of IBM) came to specialize in hardware in the 1980s, Japanese producers retained software as a major business. In many cases, major Japanese computer firms created captive software firms. These firms became experts at churning out code to strict contractor specifications through the development of 'software factories'. This vertical business model led to low profits but secure business relationships among members of a *keiretsu* family and its customers. This contrasted with the path taken in the US, which witnessed the emergence of many new start-up firms developing innovative and profitable software products for the broad corporate or consumer market. Around the turn of the twenty-first century, the emergence of open architecture and networks in the US allowed system integrator firms to compare a large variety of software and hardware and choose 'best-in-class' solutions to meet the needs of individual customers. Eventually, Japanese firms also started to reap the benefits of new designs, with firms diversifying their system integration providers. However, a prototypical example demonstrates that the vertical system, with its long-term relationships, continues to survive, albeit in more specialized arenas. These changes can be characterized as indicating increasing, but still limited, convergence with US practices. Even though the pressures for Japanese firms to move toward more open solutions are growing, the authors of Chapter 3 suggest that change will come gradually, because long-established business relationships in Japan change slowly, and because many managers, unwilling to question current business processes, tend to assume that all current practices confer competitive advantage.

Chapters 4 and 5 discuss changes in Japanese business from the perspective of human-resource management. In the face of head-on global competition, how did Japan's human-resource management evolve through a 'lost decade' to arrive at its current state? If we compare Japanese human-resource management systems to those of the US, how are they similar – and how do they differ? Chapter 4, 'The Evolution of Japan's Human-Resource Management', by Mitsuo Ishida and Atsushi Sato, examines these research questions through case studies in the electronics industry and elsewhere. According to these studies, personnel-system reforms in Japanese companies were inspired by the concept of 'pay-for-performance', an umbrella term encompassing a range of personnel-management techniques that emphasize work results over personal ability. A critical backdrop underlying these shifts has been a larger paradigm shift from thinking of personnel in *organizational* terms to thinking of personnel in *market-based* terms. The authors also indicate that human-resource management systems in Japan and the US are converging on a common structure, although important differences remain. In short, a striking feature of corporate governance both in Japan and in the US has been that firms focused on designing organizational performance management systems with high sensitivity and responsiveness to the movement of markets, and then developed rules for applying resources (people, money, and things) in ways that followed naturally from these systems. The authors conclude that the two key principles of human-resource management systems that operate in harmony with, and contribute to, organizational performance management systems are *roles* and *performance*.

Chapter 5, 'Have Japanese Engineers Changed?', by Yoshifumi Nakata and Satoru Miyazaki, analyzes the impact of human-resource management reforms in Japan on employees, focusing on engineers, who have been the driving force behind postwar economic growth in Japan. In this analysis, Nakata and Miyazaki investigate how the personal characteristics and work environments of Japanese engineers affect their work performance. The authors begin by assessing the innovativeness and productivity of Japanese engineers as compared to engineers in other countries. They then attempt to clarify the relationship between the personal characteristics of engineers, such as ability and motivation, and the corporate and workplace environments in which those engineers operate, and they analyze the impact of all of these factors on innovativeness. More specifically, the authors ask: what factors, and what interrelationships among those factors, determine engineering innovativeness? They review data on the changing workplace and corporate environments faced by Japanese engineers, and they identify a set of factors as the key contributors to engineer performance: longer working hours, changing workplace culture and the deterioration of personal relationships, diminishing motivation, and the mid-to-long-term deficit of young engineers entering the workforce. The authors then use their 'Engineering Innovativeness Determination Model' to assess how these changes might impact engineers' innovativeness and the factors that determine it. Finally, they ask how the negative influences of the changing environment might be mitigated, discuss what types of responses might be necessary and effective, and propose practical countermeasures. The authors conclude with a set of five proposed policy responses: (1) the introduction of a working-hour system for engineers, designed to stimulate continual learning and active self-improvement; (2) improved fairness in performance-based treatment, particularly in compensation; (3) improved balance between the performance evaluation of individual engineers and the teamwork evaluation of their groups; (4) a carefully calibrated relationship between short-term and long-term strategies; and (5) a transition toward more engineer-friendly labor unions.

Chapters 6 and 7 discuss changes in Japanese business from the perspective of inter-corporate relationships. Chapter 6, 'Strategic Alliances in the Japanese Economy: Types, Critiques, Embeddedness, and Change', by James R. Lincoln and Emily Choi, presents an overview and interpretive analysis of the changing nature of the Japanese strategic alliance. The authors consider both international and domestic alliances, although their emphasis is on domestic partnerships. They argue that the domestic Japanese economy in the past was 'underallianced' relative to the extensive participation of Japanese firms in partnerships with foreign firms. This is particularly true if we consider only private-sector match-ups initiated by two or more previously unrelated firms – that is, if we exclude government-sponsored consortia and *keiretsu*-based alliances. The authors find that Japanese companies appear, for a variety of institutional and cultural reasons, to have had some difficulty partnering with strangers and competitors. This has led to the formation of fewer synergistic and otherwise constructive cooperative arrangements within Japan than Japanese companies arguably need. The authors conclude that this pattern is changing, however, and that there is evidence that the rate of domestic alliances among Japanese firms is accelerating, particularly when the focus of the alliance is technology and innovation.

Chapter 7, 'R&D Management in Japanese Manufacturing Firms: Technology Trade, R&D Outsourcing, and Joint R&D', by Akihiko Kawaura and Dai Miyamoto, discusses changes in inter-corporate R&D relationships among Japanese firms. Most Japanese innovations in the twentieth century were *closed* innovations, in which firms conducted all R&D within their own organizations. In contrast, the *open* innovation paradigm, which incorporates external knowledge and wisdom into the R&D process, is attracting much attention today as a new form of innovation, and the authors examine R&D management by Japanese firms from the perspective of this shift in outlook. First, the authors analyze aggregate corporate R&D data, and find that the behavior of Japanese corporations started to shift in the 1990s, when companies began to seek opportunities to combine their own internal R&D efforts with external innovation resources. Then, using information on *individual* manufacturers from the years 1995–2004, the authors investigate Japanese firms' utilization of external R&D resources in the 1990s, and seek to answer two questions: first, whether or not companies chose to outsource R&D – and, if so, to what extent – and, second, which factors facilitated joint R&D initiatives with other companies. The principal conclusions are as follows. First, internal R&D activities are found to facilitate external R&D initiatives, implying that in-house and external R&D activities complement one another. This is consistent with the view that internal R&D nurtures a firm's ability to evaluate external R&D partners and to assimilate the fruits of external R&D efforts. Moreover, the impact of a firm's internal R&D on the extent to which it exploited external R&D grew steadily in magnitude toward the end of the sample period. This suggests that the Japanese companies began to attain higher levels of synergy between the two types of R&D in the second half of the 1990s. Second, large firms tend to exploit external R&D resources through their corporate group networks. A related finding is that significant shareholding by a parent company in a subsidiary tends to assist the subsidiary in conducting R&D outsourcing, but not in conducting joint R&D. This may stem from the greater information requirements that a firm must meet before it can identify a desirable partner for joint R&D. This asymmetric role of parent companies in external R&D activities is an area for further research.

Chapters 8 and 9 discuss changes the management strategies of Japanese corporations. Chapter 8, 'Foreign Direct Investment and Management in Japan: The Impact of Japanese Corporations' Foreign Direct Investment Strategies on Managerial Decisions and Corporate Performance in Japan – An Analysis Based on Corporate-Level Microdata', by Jun Ma, presents a panel analysis, based on corporate microdata, conducted to investigate the impact of Japanese corporations' foreign direct investment (FDI) strategies on executive decisions back in Japan – including human-resource allocations, R&D initiatives, and transactions between corporations – as well as on corporate performance. In brief, the results of this analysis are as follows. The FDI strategies of Japanese corporations from the 1990s onward remained largely unchanged from the strategies of the 1980s, and primarily followed a global strategic model. More specifically, manufacturing centers were shifted to lower-cost regions in order to pursue efficiencies on a worldwide scale, but R&D was concentrated in corporate headquarters to maintain high quality, and corporations made aggressive inroads into high-value-added regional markets. In order to execute this global strategy, Japanese corporations pursued an executive methodology that we might term 'concentrate and select', which involved strengthening the international business-development and R&D capabilities of corporate headquarters in Japan, while simultaneously spinning off manufacturing departments as subsidiary firms, and establishing more-tightly-interconnected relationships with subsidiaries and corporate affiliates. The author concludes that this style of executive decision-making did contribute to improved financial performance for corporations as a whole, but the 'closed' R&D strategy did not necessarily improve corporate financial performance.

Chapter 9, 'Why Do Japanese Companies File Patents in China? Empirical Findings from Japanese Firm-level Data', by Yoshifumi Nakata and Xingyuan Zhang, discusses intellectual property strategies in Japanese business. This chapter analyzes why multinational enterprises file patents in China, and, in particular, what factors lie behind the recent surge in Chinese patents filed by these multinational enterprises. The authors conducted an empirical investigation of applications for Chinese patents made by Japanese parent companies to study the correlation between FDI and patenting practices. Analyzing a firm-level data set covering Japanese parent companies owning one or more affiliates in China, the authors found that Japanese parent firms that engaged in more FDI in a given period were more likely to apply for Chinese patents during that period. However, after the second revision to China's patent laws in 2000, there was a sudden uptick in patent applications by, and a corresponding uptick in patents granted to, Japanese companies operating subsidiaries in China. The Chinese patent law reform, needless to say, had a significant positive impact on the number of patent applications filed by Japanese companies. But the authors' findings support the view that the surge in patent applications by Japanese companies resulted more from a strategic shift toward increasing technology transfer to China than from a desire on the part of parent companies to protect their products against imitations from local competitors.

Chapters 10 and 11 discuss changes in Japanese firms from the perspective of corporate governance. In contrast to corporate governance systems in the UK and the US, which grant stockholders the ultimate right to control firms, in Japan a system of *contingent governance* (Aoki, 1994), which incentivizes managers to work hard to avoid shareholders, has been predominant. However, as globalization intensified in the 1990s, Japanese corporations began frequently to introduce corporate governance techniques from the UK and the US. Chapter 10, 'Changing Ownership and Governance Innovation: Japanese Enterprises in Transition', by Asli M. Colpan, Takashi Hikino, and Toru Yoshikawa, presents regression analyses of panel data conducted to examine the impact of these new corporate governance systems – representing the interests of stockholders – on ROA (return on assets). The authors examined Japanese enterprises both before and after 1997, the year in which several reform measures designed to enhance shareholder value were legislated and implemented in practice by Japanese firms. Paradoxically, the empirical results seem to indicate that the explanatory power of corporate governance variables did not rise after 1997. The authors conclude that the profitability of Japanese firms has continued to be determined primarily by strategic choices representing the sphere of managerial discretion, and that these characteristics have become more prominent in the governance-oriented time period after 1997.

Chapter 11, 'Why Do Japanese Companies Issue Stock Options? Behind the Introduction of Stock Options in Japan: Theory of Shareholder Sovereignty versus Theory of Managerial Sovereignty', by Hiroaki Miyoshi and Takeo Nakao, analyzes the factors that underlie a Japanese corporation's decision to introduce stock options, which aim to promote shareholder-conscious management by strengthening the link between executive compensation and firm performance. The major firms listed on the first section of the Tokyo Stock Exchange have large numbers of shareholders, and the fraction of shares controlled by large shareholders is not particularly high. In addition, it is quite common for a firm's board of directors – whose primary interest should be to maximize shareholder profit – to comprise top managers in the firm, since board and management functions are highly overlapping in Japanese business. Therefore, it is reasonable to suspect that managers might prioritize maximizing their own utility over maximizing the profit of the firm when designing the stock option packages that they (the managers) themselves receive. The authors define the *theory of managerial sovereignty* to refer to the hypothesis that managers elect to introduce stock options in order to maximize their own utility, and the *theory of shareholder sovereignty* to refer to the hypothesis that shareholders choose to introduce stock options in order to enhance managerial incentives to improve corporate value and to reduce agency costs. They conclude, based on a regression analysis, that the theory of managerial sovereignty describes the introduction of stock options by Japanese firms more accurately than the theory of shareholder sovereignty. Chapters 10 and 11 together suggest the possibility that governance reforms in Japanese business may well be superficial, failing to bring about any substantial changes.

Chapters 12 and 13 discuss changes in Japanese government policies regarding industrial technology and regarding science and technology. Chapter 12, 'Automotive Technology Policy in Japan', by Masanobu Kii, Hiroaki Miyoshi, and Masayuki Sano, discusses industrial technology policy, focusing on the automotive industry, a key industry in Japan. Japanese automotive technology policies have traditionally been crafted by a system that combines industrial associations with advisory committees. Under this system, regulatory standard levels are calibrated to the base technological level expected to exist at the time the regulations go into effect. The authors first explain that regulatory standards in Japan have been strengthened multiple times throughout the postwar era, but that the underlying system in place today has remained largely unchanged. Next, after reviewing the present status of the global warming problem, the authors describe a simulation model used to assess conditions necessary for the spread of electric vehicles (EVs), and observe that small changes in the values of pricing parameters can have significant influence on the efficacy of government policies to promote the spread of new technologies. Based on these analyses, the authors suggest two directions for future automotive technology policies. First, if we wish to mitigate the global warming crisis by stimulating the development of technology for – and more-widespread market availability of – new-energy vehicles, then taxes or incentives proportional to the volume of CO_2 emitted will be more effective tools than technical regulations. Indeed, if Japan attempts to respond to the global warming crisis by imposing new regulations crafted through its traditional system of industrial associations combined with advisory committees, it will be difficult to achieve any sort of future consensus, because of the large disparities in technological capability to develop new-energy vehicles that exist among today's automakers. Second, the authors suggest that, when it comes to new technologies such as EVs and fuel cell vehicles, policies to promote the spread of technologies must always keep in mind the underlying technological uncertainties.

Chapter 13, 'Science and Technology Policy in Japan', by Tateo Arimoto, considers Japanese science and technology policy. The author begins by reviewing the history of Japanese science and technology policy in the postwar era, focusing particularly on technological trade friction between Japan and the US and on the resulting transformation in Japanese policies in the late 1980s. This review culminates in a discussion of the Science and Technology Basic Law, enacted in Japan in 1995; the author examines the significance of this legislation for public investments in science and technology and for reforms in Japan's research systems. The author then explains that a worldwide trend in recent years, catalyzed by the rapid globalization of economic and scientific activity, has been a shift away from science and technology policies and instead toward *innovation* policies; this observation sets the stage for a discussion of the concepts of 'innovation ecosystems', designed to foster sustainable innovation for both economic and societal value, both nationally and globally, and of a 'global innovation ecosystem', which could help to combat global problems in areas such as climate change, energy, clean water and the environment, and infectious diseases, while maintaining continued economic and societal growth. The author concludes by emphasizing the critical importance of international cooperation and more-integrated governance of science and technology policy.

The lessons of this book

If we revisit, after reviewing the analyses of the 12 chapters in this book, the central question we seek to address – *Have Japanese firms changed?* – our answer must be an unequivocal *yes*. There is no question that management practices in Japanese firms changed in myriad ways during the lost decade, including executive strategies, corporate governance, human-resource management, and inter-corporate relationships. The unambiguous conclusion is that Japanese firms *do* have the power to change. Moreover, government policies in support of corporate activities exhibited gradual change throughout this period as well, and can be expected to continue to evolve in the future.

On the other hand, if we shift the focus of our question and ask whether Japanese firms, on top of making *formal* changes, also changed in any *substantive* ways that might lead to improved future outcomes, we are forced to accept a decidedly less sanguine conclusion. Although management strategies have changed, we find no evidence that these changes brought more profits. Although personnel systems shifted to pay-for-performance structures, employee morale seems to have *declined*, not improved. Although new forms of governance are increasingly common, managers still retain near-absolute decision-making authority. Although R&D systems are moving toward a more open paradigm, market environments, and the particular features of individual firms, remain the key factors determining R&D strategies.

Were we seeking to answer a rhetorical question? Are there other questions we should be asking next? If asked how Japanese firms have changed, we will happily report the results of our studies. But if asked how these changes have *strengthened* Japanese firms, we must admit to having no clear answers; nor can we clearly identify which of the changes observed in Japanese firms were unique to the Japanese context. In view of these ambiguities, we must conclude that we have not yet fully understood the substance of the changes experienced by Japanese firms during the lost decade. Were these changes different from the changes experienced in previous eras? Were the changes brought on by common factors, or did they arise from a variety of disparate sources? In either case, could the factors that provoked change in Japanese firms lead to similar changes in other countries?

If nothing else, our research advances us to a point from which we can begin to ask a new round of questions. To zero in more closely on the fundamental essence of the changes in Japanese firms, we must first place the experiences of Japanese firms within a comparative contextual framework; this, in turn, forces a more thoroughgoing examination of the relationship between corporate behaviors and cultural norms. Ultimately, the most fulfilling possible accomplishment we could hope to achieve with this book would be to identify the critical directions for the next generation of research.

References

Amyx, J. (2006) *Japan's Financial Crisis: Institutional Rigidity and Reluctant Change*, Princeton: Princeton University Press.

Aoki, M. (1994) 'The Contingent Governance of Teams: An Analysis of Institutional Complementarity', *International Economic Review*, 35(3): 657–676.

Aoki, M., Jackson, G., and Miyajima, H. (2007) *Corporate Governance in Japan: Institutional Change and Organizational Diversity*, Oxford: Oxford University Press.

Hook, G. D. and Hasegawa, H. (2006) *Japanese Responses to Globalization: Politics, Security, Economics and Business*, Basingstoke: Palgrave Macmillan.

Katz, R. (2002) *Japanese Phoenix: The Long Road to Economic Revival*, Armonk: M. E. Sharpe.

Whittaker, D. H. and Cole, R. E. (2006) *Recovering from Success: Innovation and Technology Management in Japan*, New York: Oxford University Press.

2

The Evolution of Japan's Semiconductor Industry
Searching for Global Advantage

Clair Brown and Greg Linden

Introduction

Semiconductors, also known as integrated circuits or 'chips', are one of the primary enablers of the technological revolution that has spread from the electronics industry to nearly every corner of the modern world. This chapter analyzes how the Japanese semiconductor (electronics) industry captured global leadership in the mid-1980s, and then lost it by the mid-1990s. Japanese electronics firms struggled to find new sources of advantage in a globalized electronics industry, as new competitors in Taiwan and South Korea, and later China, accounted for a growing share of output.

We explore how Japan's semiconductor companies have undertaken restructuring and reform along several dimensions. Some of the changes, including organizational restructuring, technology alliances, and expansion of their value chains into low-cost countries, have been deeper than other changes, such as those in human-resource management and support for start-ups, which can be seen as minor modifications. These changes are still underway, and they have taken on added urgency with the global recession that began in 2008. To recover their competitiveness, Japanese chip firms must continue their restructuring and become more globally integrated.

The chapter begins with a review of the factors behind Japan's rise in the semiconductor industry, and the circumstances, particularly in Japan itself, that contributed to its loss of leadership to the US. We focus in particular on the roles of the government and of alliances. We contrast Japan and the US in two important areas that affect innovation and global competitiveness: how the development of start-ups is relatively constrained in Japan, and how the human-resource management systems used in Japanese firms tend to make those firms more inward-looking and more resistant to change. Then we discuss how Japan's electronics companies have been restructuring since the mid-1990s and the outlook for the future.

Japan's rise

Japan's rise to prominence in the semiconductor industry was widely chronicled and analyzed in the 1980s. A consensus emerged around a few key factors. Perhaps first among these was government support. In the 1960s, powerful government agencies demanded tough terms, including technology transfers, from foreign companies such as IBM and Texas Instruments that wanted access to the growing Japanese market (Prestowitz, 1988: Chapter 2). In the 1970s, Japan's government pursued an active policy of subsidizing research and promoting cooperation between its fiercely competitive business groups that helped them to close the technology gap with US firms in chips and related technologies (Fransman, 1990). Import protection of the Japanese market and an overvalued dollar were other factors that helped Japanese producers reach economies of scale in production (Flamm, 1996). Japanese firms also benefited from access to capital on more favorable terms than were available to US rivals, which helped them to pursue costly long-term strategies (Borrus, 1988; Warshofsky, 1989).

The main product on which the Japanese firms rose to market dominance was dynamic random-access memory (DRAM), the memory chips used in computer hardware, a technology area in which the Japanese government was anxious to establish national autonomy. In the 1970s, Japanese companies such as Fujitsu and Hitachi were competing with IBM, whose internally produced memory chips were a key source of advantage for its successful System/370 mainframe computer system (Fransman, 1995).

The considerable capital investment required to deploy cutting-edge process technology could be justified by the large demand for memory chips, which accounted for 15–20 per cent of semiconductor revenues during the late 1980s.[1] The long production runs of a single design permitted learning about and improving the process, raising yield (the percentage of defect-free die on a wafer), and lowering unit cost. Japanese companies excelled in the process-oriented business of memory production. A 1987 report by a US Defense Science Board task force reported that, of 25 major semiconductor products and processes considered, Japanese companies were better in 12, US companies were ahead in only five, and there was rough parity in five more.[2] By the mid-1980s, the best Japanese producers were achieving yields of 70–80 per cent, while the best US firms were in the 50–60 per cent range (Prestowitz, 1988: Chapter 2). The reliability of Japanese memory chips was also higher (*ibid.*). US memory producers saw their market share fall from 75 per cent in 1980 to just over 25 per cent in 1986, while that of Japanese producers rose from 24 to 65 per cent during the same period (Borrus, 1988: Figure 7–1).

The shift in the memory market was reflected in the industry as a whole (see Table 2.1). The position of the industry leaders changed dramatically between 1980 and 1990, a decade during which industry revenue expanded almost fivefold. The initial rise of Japanese producers is mirrored by the fall of US producers. In 1980, Texas Instruments (TI) was the leader, and six US companies in the top ten accounted for 43 per cent of the market compared to three Japanese companies with 14 per cent. In 1990, the top two chip suppliers (NEC and Toshiba) were Japanese, with five Japanese companies in the top ten accounting for

Table 2.1   Changes in industry leadership, 1980–2007

1980		1990		2000		2007	
Total Market $9.4 billion		**Total Market $44.6 billion**		**Total Market $197.1 billion**		**Total Market $273.9 billion**	
Texas Instr.	14 %	NEC	8 %	Intel	15 %	Intel	12 %
National Semi	7 %	Toshiba	7 %	Samsung	5 %	Samsung	8 %
Motorola	7 %	Intel	7 %	NEC	5 %	Toshiba	4 %
Philips Semi	7 %	Hitachi	7 %	Texas Instr.	5 %	Texas Instr.	4 %
Intel	6 %	Motorola	6 %	Toshiba	4 %	Infineon[d]	4 %
NEC	6 %	Texas Instr	6 %	STMicro.	4 %	STMicro.	4 %
Fairchild Semi	5 %	Fujitsu	5 %	Motorola	4 %	Hynix[a]	3 %
Hitachi	4 %	Mitsubishi	4 %	Micron	3 %	Renesas[b]	3 %
Toshiba	4 %	National Semi	4 %	Hyundai	3 %	AMD	3 %
Mostek	4 %	Philips	3 %	Hitachi	3 %	NXP[c]	2 %

Notes:
a) Hynix: formerly Hyundai Semiconductor.
b) Renesas: formerly the logic-chip divisions of Hitachi and Mitsubishi.
c) NXP: formerly Philips' semiconductor division.
d) Infineon's share also reflects sales of its majority-owned memory-chip spin-off Qimonda.

Source: Brown and Linden (2009: Chapter 1).

31 per cent, while four US companies totaled only 23 per cent of the market.

However, by 2000 industry leadership had once again undergone dramatic shifts. Intel had grown to dominate the industry, and Samsung edged out NEC for second place. Three Japanese companies in the top ten accounted for 12 per cent of the market. In 2007, Intel maintained its industry leadership, and the two Japanese chip companies in the top ten had only 7 per cent of the market.

The response of global competitors

We see that Japan's reversal of fortune reflects both the rise of global competitors, especially Intel in the US and Samsung in South Korea, as well as the decline of the Japanese companies. In this section we summarize industry and government responses in the US and South Korea.

As the US chip industry became aware of Japan's rise, it pursued non-market strategies in concert with the government. In 1977, five leading US chip producers joined together to form the Semiconductor Industry Association (SIA), which gave the industry a more unified voice for lobbying the government. In 1985, the SIA filed an unfair-trading petition claiming that Japan was continuing to protect its market in violation of inter-government semiconductor agreements reached in 1982 and 1983. This, along with dumping actions on specific types of chips, helped pressure Japan to agree in 1986 to even more drastic measures, although US penetration of the Japanese market remained limited (Prestowitz, 1988). In 1987, the US imposed $300 million in penalties on Japanese imports to bring further pressure for the enforcement of existing agreements.

On the macroeconomic level, US government policy was also helpful, leading to the 1985 Plaza Accord to devalue the dollar relative to the yen. Over the following two years, coordinated central bank action helped lower the exchange value of the dollar against the yen by 51 per cent.

The US government also helped the industry by relaxing antitrust laws that affected inter-firm cooperation and by providing half the $200 million annual budget for the research consortium SEMATECH formed by 14 US chip companies in 1987 to improve manufacturing technology (Ham *et al.*, 1998). After an uneven start, SEMATECH made advances in equipment development, a key to developing manufacturing technology (Grindley *et al.*, 1994). SEMATECH's model of horizontal and vertical cooperation was based on the earlier successful collaboration believed to have contributed to the Japanese success in the chip industry (Fransman, 1990).

US firms also responded to the Japanese crisis by exiting the DRAM market, which faced severe overcapacity. Intel, which had invented the memory chip, exited the memory market in 1986 in order to concentrate on microprocessors. Meanwhile, dozens of fabless (design only) start-ups were founded in the US to take advantage of two important technological advances: design automation software for designing custom digital logic chips, and contract (or *foundry*) production.

Meanwhile, in high-volume memory chips, leadership was taken from Japanese firms by a Korean producer, Samsung, which followed a relentless investment strategy straight out of the Japanese playbook in its pursuit of market share. Samsung was a Japan-style industrial conglomerate capable of funding its own R&D, and the government played a relatively small role in its ascent, apart from supporting an information-sharing alliance between Samsung and the two other Korean memory producers, LG and Hyundai (both now part of Hynix). By the mid-1990s, after a decade of effort, Samsung had captured the top spot in memory production, which it has held ever since.

Taiwanese firms have also grown as memory producers, but the island's flagship chip producers are its foundries. Taiwan's importance in the chip industry is sometimes understated, because foundries are not included in global sales rankings to avoid double counting. If TSMC, the leading foundry, had been listed in the 2007 ranking (Table 2.1), it would have been seventh, and the next largest foundry, UMC, would have been twentieth. Their combined sales in 2007 amounted to 5 per cent of total chip industry revenue.

How Japan stumbled

The relative decline of Japan's chip industry owes much to circumstances in Japan itself. These include a deterioration of the investment climate, overemphasis on quality, and overdependence on the domestic market. Another factor, Japan's weak environment for start-up ventures, is addressed in the following section.

One of Japan's biggest obstacles to maintaining market leadership was a decline in investment in new factories brought on by the bursting of Japan's asset bubble in the early 1990s.[3] Much as occurred in the US in 2008, the end of the earlier Japanese real estate bubble led to a credit crunch in which it was much harder to raise funds. As Japanese firms reduced their capital equipment spending in 1992, Korean firms raised theirs. Japan's share of global capital equipment purchases continued to fall, while the combined share of South Korea and Taiwan rose (Macher *et al.*, 1999). Steady renewal of production capacity is a minimal requirement for maintaining or raising DRAM market share.

Ironically, the emphasis on quality and reliability that brought Japanese firms to the top of the memory-chip industry was part of their undoing. The problem was that the primary application markets for memory shifted from mainframes, where long-term reliability was highly valued, to personal computers and consumer products, where low prices seemed more important than reliability because of shorter product life spans (Cole and Matsumiya, 2007). Japanese DRAM engineers continued to use costly customized equipment to produce chips that exceeded product requirements when non-Japanese chip producers were pursuing more standardized solutions (Yunogami, 2006). This overemphasis on quality reflected the characteristics of the human resource management system that we discuss below.

Beyond memory, Japanese chip makers clung to a broad portfolio of chips while producers elsewhere were pursuing specialization, as exemplified by the processor-centric strategy of Intel and the DSP-centric strategy of Texas Instruments. A great many medium-size US chip companies, which account for about half the places in the global Top 50, were founded after 1980 and specialize in specific types of analog or digital-logic chips.

Japan's market share was also undermined by the domestic focus of its chip firms. All the leading Japanese chip producers of the 1990s were vertically integrated with systems divisions. This was a strength when it came to promoting sales opportunities within business group networks, and Japanese companies were able to rely on high prices in Japan to subsidize price-based competition overseas (Prestowitz, 1988). But this strength became a major weakness when the Japanese economy itself, which had roared ahead at more than 3 per cent per year in the 1980s, slid into a decade of much slower growth in the 1990s.

Japanese systems companies were strong global competitors in mainframe computers, but not in personal computers, the major global growth market of the 1990s. The Japanese market was relatively slow to adopt the PC platform, partly because of the difficulty of inputting Japanese characters. In 1995, the number of PCs per capita in Japan was roughly one-fifth that in the US.[4] Instead of general-purpose PCs, Japanese business users had favored specialized equipment like dedicated word processors.

The idiosyncrasies of Japan's domestic market had implications for memory chips as well.[5] Memory chips have subtle but important differences of configuration (for example, number of bits per storage unit, power supply), which require significant engineering effort to rede-sign. The DRAM requirements of Japan's consumer electronics makers, which were the priority for their captive chip divisions, were incompat-ible with those of PC makers in the rest of the world.

To explore this dependence on the domestic market, we constructed a 'home substitution index' (Figure 2.1), which shows the excess of home market sales over the home market's share of total global sales.[6] For Europe, Asia-Pacific (namely, Taiwan and South Korea), and the US, the home substitution index (HSI) was lower in 2000 than in 1992, because these countries' foreign sales had grown faster than their domestic sales. In sharp contrast, Japan's reliance on chip sales within Japan was slightly *higher* in 2000 than in 1992, and Japan's chip consumption declined as a share of the world market, from 32 per cent in 1992 to 23 per cent in 2000.[7] US share of global chip consumption rose slightly from 30.8 per cent to 31.3 per cent over this period, while US depend-ence on its own domestic market began low and fell even lower.

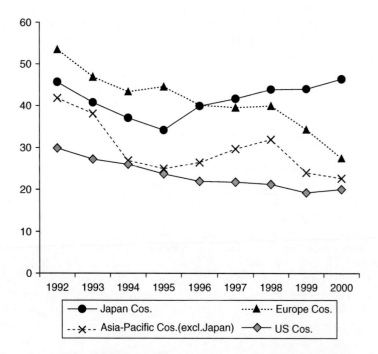

Figure 2.1   Home substitution index for semiconductor sales, 1992–2000
Source: Brown and Linden (2009: Figure 1.2).

The decline in Japan's HSI in the early-1990s was driven by a boom in the memory market that allowed Japanese suppliers to expand overseas. As their memory market share declined during the later years of the graph, they lost share faster overseas than in Japan. Japan's HSI for non-memory chips alone fell slightly, from 57 in 1992 to 51 in 2000.

Table 2.2, which shows the regional breakdown of sales by the top ten chip companies in 2005, provides an updated view of home-market dependence. While most of these companies earn the bulk of their revenue in the Asia-Pacific region because of the importance of Taiwan and China for electronics manufacturing, the three Japanese firms earned between 57 per cent and 63 per cent of their revenues from sales to Japanese customers, at a time when the Japan market accounted for a declining share of world consumption. By 2005, Japan's market size had fallen to 22 per cent (and the US to 18 per cent) as Asia-Pacific (mostly China) grew to 45 per cent of the world market.

Another area in which Japan's chip industry has lagged behind the rest of the world – and particularly the US – is the growth of start-up

Table 2.2 Top-10 chip companies' sales by region, 2005 (as a percentage of global semiconductor revenue)

2005 rank	Company	Americas (%)	Europe and Mid. East (%)	Japan (%)	Asia-Pacific (%)
1	Intel	19.6	21.0	9.5	49.9
2	Samsung Electronics	28.7	19.9	16.4	35.0
3	Texas Instruments	14.2	19.6	15.3	50.9
4	Toshiba	6.2	4.3	62.7	26.8
5	STMicroelectronics	16.5	33.5	3.4	46.6
6	Infineon Technologies	24.6	37.7	4.8	32.9
7	Renesas Technology	6.2	9.3	58.9	25.6
8	NEC Electronics	12.3	12.2	56.5	19.1
9	Philips Semiconductor	9.5	25.2	4.3	61.1
10	Freescale	26.6	20.4	5.1	48.0
	Top 10 companies	18.0	20.5	19.9	41.6
	All others	17.5	12.0	23.3	47.2
	All companies	17.7	16.1	21.6	44.5

Source: Brown and Linden (2009: Table 1.5).

ventures. New enterprise creation can be an important source of innovation and growth, although it is one that, to date, Japan has decided to
support more in word than in action.

Lack of support for start-ups

Start-ups can help an economy to develop new technology and exploit
new business opportunities where long-established companies may
fail, but Japan's economy is relatively inhospitable to high-tech start-up
ventures. In the US, Taiwan, and China, policies that support start-
ups, along with the global circulation of highly motivated engineers
to obtain education and jobs, have been a vital part of the innovation
process in the semiconductor industry (Saxenian, 2006).

In the fiscal year ending March 2004, Japan had well over 50 companies with electronics revenues of more than US$1 billion, but none
of them were established more recently than 1968.[8] The most recently
established semiconductor firm among them was Rohm (1958). By contrast, the US is home to many electronics companies that are much
younger and have grown to considerable size, such as Dell (1984), Cisco
Systems (1984), and Solectron (1977). Among the top 20 US semiconductor companies in 2004, all of which have revenue greater than US$1
billion, three were founded in the 1960s (including Intel), six in the
1980s, and two (Nvidia and Broadcom) in the 1990s.

The difference in the role of smaller companies in the innovation
process in the US and Japan is highlighted by the fact that, in the US
in 2004, companies with fewer than 250 employees accounted for 9 per
cent of manufacturing R&D spending and had an R&D-to-sales ratio
of 7.5 per cent,[9] whereas, in Japan, firms with up to 300 employees
accounted for only 4 per cent of manufacturing R&D spending and had
an R&D-to-sales ratio of only 2.2 per cent.[10]

In both Japan and the US, major semiconductor and electronics producers undertake a great deal of R&D, and only a small portion of the
ideas generated are ever commercialized. We learned in our interviews
in Japan and the US that about 70 per cent of the ideas will never be
developed because:

- the company lacks the resources to pursue all the available ideas;
- some ideas are not related to the company's core capabilities;
- some ideas compete with the company's existing products; or
- the potential market appears too small, and thus the company's high
  overhead costs make the project unprofitable.

The primary business model for new semiconductor companies is the fabless model, in which the company designs and markets its own chips but outsources the manufacturing to another company, most frequently a 'foundry' that specializes in manufacturing chips for others. According to the Fabless Semiconductor Association's report on publicly traded fabless companies in 2005, 84 US companies accounted for 64 per cent of global fabless revenue.[11] The second-highest concentration of fabless companies was in Taiwan, with 62 companies and 17 per cent of revenue. Fabless companies were scarce in Japan, with three listed companies (MegaChips, RealVision, and Thine Electronics) accounting for just over 1 per cent of global fabless revenues.

A high-level and comprehensive national report on the state of start-ups (Study Group, 2008) reflects Japan's concerns that the country is losing out, especially to the US, on developing innovation in high-tech industries because of lack of a supportive environment for start-ups, especially in relations with large Japanese enterprises and in operating in domestic labor and financial markets. Our findings from 2004–2006 fieldwork at start-ups in Tokyo, Yokohama, Kyushu, and Osaka[12] are consistent with this report. In general Japanese start-ups face four major difficulties: (1) acquiring management and marketing skills, since there are a limited number of executives with start-up experience; (2) finding customers, since large Japanese companies prefer established suppliers; (3) recruiting engineers, who don't want to lose the status and security provided by a large company; and (4) securing early-stage financing, although this has improved in recent years.[13]

A variety of types of start-ups exist in Japan, and they can be characterized by their independence from, or their ties to, large companies. Table 2.3 presents a taxonomy of start-ups, based on their ties to large companies, which decrease from left to right.

A common method of creating new companies in Japan is for a large company to assign a developed technology to a wholly-owned *corporate division or subsidiary* that remains under corporate control. We consider these divisions or wholly-owned spin-offs to be paths to commercialization, rather than truly innovative organizations, because they typically involve a late stage of product development, and their employees are still under the large company's umbrella and protected from failure, and so have only low-powered incentives. The employees are also prevented from sharing in high returns from the innovation in the event of a success. An example of this type of company is Hitachi's Mu Solutions, which was set up as an in-house (*shanai*) venture company (fully owned but with separate management team) to commercialize wireless data

Table 2.3 Paths for emerging companies

	Corporate division or subsidiary	independent spin-out	cooperative venture	independent start-up	Silicon Valley
Patent Rights					
controlled by big company	X	X	X		
controlled by small company		X	X	X	X
Executive Team					
Can return to big company	X				
Independent from big company		X	X	X	X
Early Stage Resources					
majority finance from big company	X				
in-kind support[a] from big company	X	O	X	O	O
founders' funding and sales		O	O	X	O
early-stage venture funding					X
Examples	Hitachi Mu Solutions	FabSolutions	THine IPFlex	MegaChips	Rakuten RealVision

Notes:
a) in-kind support can include agreement to purchase output.
X = defining characteristic; O = may or may not be present.

tags. After Mu Solutions became a supplier to a large company, Hitachi dissolved the venture into other business units to facilitate total systems integration.[14]

The *independent spin-out* model, which represents a more autonomous type of corporate spin-out, is rare in Japan. When a parent company has a technology that it chooses not to develop, the engineers who worked on the technology leave to start a new company that receives an exclusive technology license and only partial funding from the parent company. An example is Fab Solutions, which markets an advanced system for process control in semiconductor manufacturing. Four engineers from NEC were allowed to take the business private in 2002. They obtained two rounds of venture funding and were included in a 2004 list of 'Top Emerging Start-ups',[15] but appear to have gone out of business, underscoring the riskiness of new ventures.

The *cooperative venture* involves an independent start-up that enters a strategic alliance with a larger company, which provides up-front resources in return for a share of the licensing fees or a share of output. The large company will usually be part of the venture company's supply chain (for example, an equipment supplier or potential customer). This relationship overcomes some of the problems facing venture companies in Japan, because the model has the advantage of providing better resources and, in the case of downstream cooperation, better access to customers. In the components sector, THine Electronics was founded in 1991 as a joint venture with its customer Samsung Electronics, and the founders were able to buy out Samsung's share in 1997. A younger semiconductor start-up, IPFlex, received a minority investment in 2003 from Fujitsu, which provided fabrication services and development assistance.

Difficulty in securing early-stage financing has led to the self-funded *independent start-up* model used by many young Japanese companies in the electronics industry. Initial funding is provided by the founders, who sell services to generate cash flow while a new product is being developed. For example, start-up semiconductor firms in Japan often sell chip design services while developing their own chip. This was the model followed by MegaChips, a fabless semiconductor company founded in 1990 and listed on the Tokyo Stock Exchange in 2000.

Although this model (funding R&D with services) can succeed, it is a slow path to innovation. Independent start-ups suffer from inadequate early-stage funding and from lack of access to large Japanese companies as customers. The services business, which has limited growth potential, requires as much as 80 per cent of the managers' and engineers' time, which slows down the development of an innovative product.

An important but rare variant is the *Silicon Valley model* where the start-up adopts a high-risk, high-return strategy of commercializing innovative technology with funding from venture capitalists instead of using the cash flow from services. This model, pursued by visionary firms like Internet company Rakuten and the fabless start-up RealVision, is slowly becoming more common in Japan. However, most venture-funded start-ups in Japan are less ambitious than those in the US. Companies like Sony and Matsushita operate corporate venture capital subsidiaries, but so far most of their investments are outside Japan. Silicon Valley's venture capital model, which targets opportunities for high, rapid growth with a low success rate, is not congruent with Japanese economic institutions and culture, in which failure carries a heavy penalty, such as the inability to obtain bank financing for a new venture for ten years after a business failure.

For start-ups to flourish, the Japanese environment for start-ups must shift in a way that is congruent with social and business norms. Given the many constraints on entrepreneurs in Japan, we advocate an evolutionary transition toward the right-hand side of the table along the following lines:

- Corporations with technologies they are reluctant to develop in-house should consider supporting independent start-ups, where the new company receives a clear license to the technology and 'seed funding' from the large company.
- Young companies pursuing an *independent start-up* model should consider a more ambitious business plan to be funded by venture capital, possibly including funds from non-Japanese investors.
- Large Japanese companies, for their part, must become more willing to cooperate with start-ups, which can be an excellent source of new technology through acquisition or purchase of components.
- Build networks of executives in a national or regional registry who can help start-ups obtain access to and structure joint ventures with the large companies where they have contacts, and can also provide management advice to inexperienced start-up executives.
- Reduce the obstacles to worker mobility: make pensions more portable, with earlier vesting, and with fewer years required for a partial payout; and reduce workers' costs of instability by paying unemployment insurance directly to unemployed workers rather than only to companies to subsidize retaining workers.

Although the Japanese government has already taken important steps to remove regulatory constraints facing start-ups, including liberalizing stock options and abolishing minimum capital requirements, additional regulatory change is needed. According to a World Bank ranking (http://www.doingbusiness.org), starting a new company in Japan has become easier and less expensive in recent years. For example, the administrative steps required for registering a new firm fell from 11 in the 2004 report to eight in 2008, which is still above the OECD average of six. The cost of a start-up, expressed as a percentage of gross national income per capita, has fallen from 10.5 per cent to 7.5 per cent, also above the OECD average of 5.1 per cent.

Valuable support for emerging companies is given by government agencies (and sometimes by the private sector) at a growing number of 'incubators' that provide office space, business services, and IT infrastructure. Local and/or prefectural governments are best positioned to evaluate the start-ups that apply for incubator support. The national government should subsidize local government incubator efforts, rather than directly supporting individual start-up companies. METI (The Ministry of Economy, Trade and Industry) has a potential conflict of interest when supporting start-ups that might eventually challenge large companies.

A successful start-up sector would be complementary to the large firms. Start-ups, with their low overhead, rapid decision-making, and high-powered incentives, can develop and commercialize technologies that might have been ignored by existing companies. Without a dynamic start-up community, the Japanese industrial engine is missing an important source of innovation.

Another area in which Japan and the US show marked differences is human resource management, although in this case the US system is not clearly superior to the Japanese system.

Japan and the US: Labor market norms define constraints

We begin by describing two idealized types of high-performance human-resource management (HRM) systems: a *high-commitment* system (Baron and Kreps, 1999: Chapter 9) and a *high-innovation* system (Brown, 2006; Katz, 1997). These model systems are representative of the actual HRM systems used by many high-tech companies. We focus on four major component parts of the HRM system: job assignment ('what to do'), skill development and communication flows ('how to do it'), and compensation and promotion ('reward for doing it'). Table 2.4 summarizes the key characteristics of our two idealized systems.[16]

The *high-commitment HRM system* is designed to elicit high effort and responsibility from loyal employees who have the knowledge, skills, and judgment required by the company. The traditional top-tier Japanese organizations use a high-commitment internal labor market system, in which workers enter the company directly from school and move up well-defined job ladders with specific pay scales and responsibilities.

High-commitment HRM works well when knowledge is tacit and/or proprietary (specific to the company), as well as cumulative or slowly depreciating. Under these conditions, much learning is done on the job, and experience is valuable. The loss of an engineer who quits is seen as a net asset loss to the company. The company can plan for the skills

Table 2.4   High-commitment and high-innovation HRM systems

	High commitment	High innovation
GOALS	– Long-term jobs to create required knowledge and foster commitment	– Project-oriented hiring with state-of-art knowledge from mobile talent pool
Worker mobility	– Seen as a net loss	– Seen as cost-effective
CHARACTERISTICS		
Knowledge	– Experiential, cumulative job-related knowledge used	– University and classroom training used
Technology depreciation	– Slow	– Rapid
External sources of knowledge	– Customers and suppliers; public documents (journals, patents)	– Networks of colleagues, peers; conference papers, open source materials
HRM COMPONENTS		
Job assignment	– Chosen to develop broad skill set, flexible assignments – Contributions to team tasks as well as individual task	– Chosen to exploit narrow specialization – Work done individually or sequentially within team
Skill development	– Planned by project manager – OJT supplemented by formal classroom training	– Individual development through professional groups and access to technology (jobs) – Required proprietary knowledge learned on the job
Communication flows	– Open flow internally – Gatekeepers for external knowledge – Structured flows with suppliers, customers – Weak IP protection training	– Internal Chinese walls – Individual use of external networks (public, private) – Structured flows with suppliers, customers – IP protection emphasized

Table 2.4   Continued

	High commitment	High innovation
Compensation & promotions	– Performance-based pay to reward ongoing efforts – Small differentials within cohort – Steady promotions (some variance in speed) – Steep age-earnings profile with low variance	– Bonus for project milestones with individual rewards for specific targets – Large pay differentials based on market opportunities – Promotion of those selected to become executives – Relatively flat experience-earnings profile with large variance

required over time, since the company is in charge of the development of workers' skills and knowledge through job assignments, which determine on-the-job training combined with some formal classroom training. Since job assignment is the primary way that workers develop skills, project assignments reflect skills being developed as well as skills being used. Engineers can be flexibly deployed across projects, and can be quickly reassigned when needed, since they have been broadly trained and such movements are accepted in order to meet company needs. Engineers tend to go to other engineers on the team or in the division to discuss problems they are solving, and only secondarily turn to scientific journals or public documents. Contact with people outside the company to discuss problems is rare, unless it is a specific part of the job assignment (Appleyard *et al.*, 2006).

Because the company expects low employee turnover, an open flow of information within and across levels of the organization is encouraged. Communications external to the company are typically structured so that specific people are in charge of specific information flows (for example, gatekeepers stay abreast of external knowledge and disseminate relevant knowledge to colleagues; specific team members communicate with specific suppliers or customers on relevant parts of the project). Required company documentation of projects reflects what other teams will need to know down the road, with the assumption that project members will be readily available for consultation. Training of engineers on how to protect the company's intellectual property (IP) from people outside the company may be weak or nonexistent, since engineers are assumed not to communicate outside the company's official knowledge network, which is well defined.

In addition to effort and project performance, incentives reward loyalty and relationship building within the company and with its partners. Compensation includes performance-based pay to reward ongoing effort, although the differentials among engineers with the same experience are kept small in order to minimize competition among team members and to promote team effort. Promotion is used to signal future contributions; however, all workers advance up the ladder (with some variation in speed) as they gain experience. A steep age–earnings profile rewards workers for experience, and younger workers do not mind the transfer of income to the older workers, since all workers eventually receive this transfer, and it reflects the life cycle demands of their families.

The *high-innovation HRM system* supports rapid innovation by using a mobile talent pool connected to informal global knowledge networks. Engineers are typically hired because their skills and knowledge are required for a specific technology or product being developed. The company wants engineers to remain at least for the tenure of the project. Once hired, the company signals to engineers their future with the company by assignments to follow-up projects, including development of some engineers as managers and executives. Engineers can be let go, or are encouraged to leave, by being put on dead-end projects, such as maintenance of legacy technology. This approach fits well when knowledge is rapidly depreciating and knowledge across generations of technology is only partially cumulative, so that experience is less important than state-of-the-art knowledge learned at a university or lab. Additional formal classroom training and 'need to know' proprietary company knowledge are taught when required for the project ('just-in-time training'). Overall, the mobility of engineers is seen as cost effective because the company can hire its required skills and does not have to retrain experienced workers.

In the high-innovation system, engineers are in charge of their career development, and must rely upon their professional associations and networks, as well as learning on their own, to maintain and expand their skills and knowledge. To the extent possible, engineers carefully choose their jobs (and projects) in order to develop their skills and knowledge over their careers. Knowledge exchange with colleagues outside the company is an important source of information about new technologies and products being developed, as well as about job opportunities. Engineers are assumed to be interacting with colleagues from other companies, and are taught what types of information they may share. The flow of information even *within* the company is restricted in order to protect company IP.

Compensation rewards the individual engineer's skills and talents. The experience–earnings profile reflects the market opportunities of the engineers. Incentives reward project work, often with bonuses for project milestones, rather than skill development or institution building. Individual effort is rewarded by compensation for specific goals, often related to sales or value to the customer.

Compared to high-commitment HRM, high-innovation HRM depends more on the external labor market and less on internal rules for determining pay and promotion. Knowledge workers are evaluated and rewarded for their application of knowledge to specific projects and customer problems. For example, at IBM Research, employees are rewarded for their ability to generate solutions to specific customer problems, and research managers are rewarded for delivering solutions to business units (Chesbrough, 2003: Chapter 5). Companies are more concerned with project performance than with long-term careers for their workers. To acquire the knowledge required for a new technology or business model, companies often prefer to hire new graduates rather than to retrain their experienced engineers. For example, IBM hired software engineers and systems engineers while laying off semiconductor engineers in the mid-1990s as they changed their business model toward services and no longer had indefinite control of IP as a long-run goal (*ibid.*).

In summary, the high-commitment HRM system provides a stable, well-trained, and loyal workforce that can be flexibly deployed and whose costs over time are predictable; the high-innovation HRM system provides flexibility in hiring and laying off workers, whose availability and costs are much harder to predict over time.

The evolution of Japan's HRM systems

In general, large multinational corporations in developed countries tended to use variants of high-commitment HRM systems during the second half of the twentieth century (Jacoby, 1998). However, since the mid-1980s, and even before, the HRM systems in high-tech companies worldwide have incorporated more aspects of high-innovation systems, especially in compensation. US high-tech companies began transforming their high-commitment HRM systems into high-innovation systems in the 1980s (Cappelli, 1999). In contrast, large Japanese companies made only minor modifications to their high-commitment systems.

Major Japanese manufacturing companies have been able to retain a high-commitment HRM system for regular workers by making modifications that provide more flexibility in total headcount. They have accomplished this primarily by increasing their reliance on nonregular workers, while reducing the proportion of female regular workers. Female regular employees fell from 23 per cent of manufacturing workers in 1992 to 16 per cent in 2002, while female nonregular employees increased from 14 per cent to 17 per cent. Male nonregular employees increased from 4 per cent to 7 per cent of manufacturing workers, while male regular employees remained at 60 per cent (Nakata and Miyazaki, 2007). Since the mid-1990s, major Japanese manufacturing companies, including those in electronics, have reduced their numbers of regular workers, which some observers have interpreted as abandoning the lifetime employment system. However, major computer and IT equipment manufacturers adjusted their regular employment for a given change in demand only slightly more during the long recession than they did in the 1980s, and employment adjustments were highly unresponsive to underlying changes in labor demand during both periods (*ibid.*).

Japanese semiconductor companies, including those within multi-product electronics companies such as Toshiba and NEC as well as the newer stand-alone semiconductor companies Renesas and Elpida, continue to use a high-commitment HRM system modified to include more performance-based pay for individuals in both base pay and semi-annual bonuses. Traditionally, bonuses amounted to five or six months' pay and depended primarily on company performance, with a small component reflecting individual achievement. The new bonus systems are based primarily on individual performance evaluations, with total bonuses reflecting company performance so that annual earnings for some (sometimes a majority of) workers can actually fall.[17] As a result, the variance of pay within each cohort of engineers hired as new university graduates has increased (Tsuru *et al.*, 2003).

The new emphasis on performance-based pay in Japanese companies can cause morale problems if workers disagree with their evaluations and are discontent with their bonuses. Given the limited job mobility in the Japanese labor market, disgruntled workers cannot easily move to another (and often better) job if they disagree with their supervisor's performance evaluation. In the US, labor market mobility is an important mechanism for ensuring that performance-based pay is working correctly. Without other job opportunities, the worker has little power and cannot use the marketplace to challenge the supervisor's evaluation. For this reason, we expect professional workers in Japan to view performance-based pay less favorably than their US counterparts.

Major Japanese semiconductor and electronics companies must be careful in modifying their high-commitment HRM systems. In the absence of institutions that support a mobile labor market, such as adequate unemployment insurance, portable retirement systems (both private and public), and social acceptance of job hopping, and in the presence of strong social norms that favor stability and frown upon breaking a relationship for private gain, the transition to a more mobile labor market is not one that will be made easily. However, during Japan's long recession, many young Japanese found their labor market and career expectations unfulfilled; consequently, many became more mobile, as well as more global, than their parents in their labor market behavior. In our fieldwork, we observed more willingness by younger Japanese to travel and work in China and Taiwan, as well as to have colleagues from those countries work in Japan. This younger generation's experiences and revised expectations may be the foundation for new labor institutions that are congruent with both societal norms and global talent circulation (Saxenian, 2006).

Restructuring Japan's semiconductor industry

In recent years, Japanese companies have restructured and reformed in several dimensions in an effort to strengthen their position within the global semiconductor industry. In this section we review the changes they have made: expanding their value chains into lower-cost economies, and developing technology alliances and restructuring their companies at home. We also summarize the less-sweeping modifications to HRM systems and to the regulations of start-ups that we discussed earlier.

Japanese semiconductor companies have been slower than their US rivals to take advantage of opportunities to relocate operations to lower-cost regions in Asia, even though such areas are closer to home than they are for US companies. This reflects the Japanese preference for keeping manufacturing and research (and jobs) in Japan, as well as language and cultural differences.

In the 1990s, Japanese companies set up chip assembly operations in China (Table 2.5), and NEC even entered two joint fab ventures

Table 2.5 Chinese chip-packaging facilities of leading Japanese companies

Year launched	Parent company (Name when started)	City
1993	NEC	Beijing
1994	Matsushita	Shanghai
1994	Toshiba	Wuxi
1996	Renesas (Hitachi)	Suzhou
1997	Fujitsu	Nantong
1998	Renesas (Mitsubishi)	Beijing

Source: Press reports.

promoted by the Chinese government. These foreign investments allowed Japanese firms to take advantage of lower costs as well as to develop a presence in the large and rapidly growing Chinese market, although Japanese (and US) firms found that building chip fabrication and assembly plants in China, which now accounts for about one third of the world semiconductor market, did not establish the market presence that they had anticipated. In 2007, Toshiba was ranked No. 3 worldwide but No. 5 in China, while Renesas, ranked No. 8 worldwide, did not appear in China's top 10.[18]

Japanese companies have also set up offshore design centers in China (Table 2.6) rather than India, the preferred destination for US companies. China offers Japanese firms greater geographical and linguistic proximity than India, a nation in which only Sanyo has opened a wholly-owned design center. Other Japanese companies, including Elpida and NEC Electronics, hired Indian outsourcing companies to run dedicated design centers for them.[19]

Although joint research in the 1970s by Japan's semiconductor companies contributed to their rise in the industry, the firms worked independently during the bubble years of the late 1980s. However, the costly transition to 300mm wafers in the following decade motivated Japan's semiconductor companies to begin to conduct joint research again (Ham *et al.*, 1998). In 1996, the launch of Selete, a private equipment evaluation consortium, and ASET, a publicly funded research consortium, revived the trend of broad cooperation by Japanese chip companies, which deepened considerably in the ensuing years.

In addition to extending their cooperation to new broad-based research projects, such as Asuka and Mirai,[20] Japanese chip companies

Table 2.6 Chinese design centers of leading Japanese companies, 2005

2005 Rank by global sales	Parent company (Name when started)	City (Year launched)
4	Toshiba	Shanghai (1994)
7	Renesas (Hitachi)	Suzhou (1995)
7	Renesas (Mitsubishi)	Beijing (1995)
13	NEC	Beijing (1998)
13	NEC	Shanghai (2000)
19	Fujitsu	Shanghai (2003)
33	Sanyo	Shenzhen (2002)

Source: Brown and Linden (2009: Table 4.2).

have entered a number of narrower arrangements. In 2002, Sony and Toshiba agreed to co-develop a 90nm process that could be used for the Cell processor under development for Sony's PlayStation 3. The following year, Sony arranged to pay 30 per cent of the cost of Toshiba's 12-inch fab to guarantee capacity. In 2005, NEC Electronics (the former semiconductor division of NEC) entered into an agreement with Toshiba and Sony to develop a 45nm fabrication process. In 2007, Sony sold its interest in the fab back to Toshiba and ended its process R&D, but Toshiba and NEC extended their cooperation to 32nm.

Japan's semiconductor companies have been in transition as they experiment with radical restructuring, by spinning off and combining chip operations, and with new business models, particularly the use of foundries by both integrated and fabless companies. In 1999, the memory operations of Hitachi and NEC were combined to form a new company called Elpida, which absorbed Mitsubishi's memory division in 2003. Also in 2003, the non-memory chip divisions of Hitachi and Mitsubishi were combined to form Renesas Technology, which cooperated with Matsushita over several technology generations. Among Japan's other major chip producers, Fujitsu put its flash operations into a joint venture called Spansion with US firm AMD, and, as mentioned above, Sony co-invested with Toshiba to produce the multicore Cell processor for its PlayStation 3 game consoles. NEC and Fujitsu have spun off their chip divisions, in 2002 and 2008, respectively, as separate units that must finance and account for their own success or failure. Then, in late 2009, it was announced that Renesas Technology and NEC Electronics would merge as of April 2010 to form Renesas Electronics, with new capital supplied by parent firms Hitachi, NEC, and Mitsubishi Electric.[21]

The way forward

The transition to a stronger, more consolidated Japanese chip industry is not yet complete. For example, relatively little has been done to reduce excess capacity. In 2005, a joint foundry project was proposed, with the participation of five of the largest chip producers. The idea was ultimately rejected, and several companies, not all associated with the project, went on to build separate 300mm fabs, each with relatively low capacities that cannot take advantage of the potential economies of scale. Only Toshiba's large 300mm fab used to fabricate flash memory was able to take advantage of scale economies.

Another area of concern, for both the large firms and for the struggling start-up sector, is the labor market. As mentioned above, Japan's electronics companies have been slower than their US rivals to adjust their high-commitment HRM systems. Japan's low labor mobility, which reflects risk aversion and the preference for long-term relationships, keeps lifetime employment available to a declining proportion of male workers, while female workers are used as a buffer stock. As the proportion of the workforce with lifetime employment in major companies continues to decline, we expect that labor market norms will change – especially as those who entered the labor market during Japan's long recession and landed fewer good regular jobs become a larger share of the labor force. These workers appear to be more mobile and more global in their outlook than more senior workers, and will be more accepting of changes in HRM systems. The weakening of the lifetime employment system, increased mobility, and changes in government policy are important steps for supporting start-ups in Japan and for integrating Japan into the global talent circulation.

We expect these changes will come slowly. One of Japan's strengths, and one of its weaknesses, is making changes in a slow and careful manner that builds consensus. Although Japanese companies change less quickly than their US rivals, we have seen that they do eventually change in response to global competition and market pressures. Japan's next economic upturn, and the renewed growth of the chip industry, will provide the opportunity to return to profitability and to create new product markets both at home and abroad. The expansion of Japanese manufacturing and design operations in Asia indicates that Japan may finally be able to take advantage of the rapid growth of regional talent and product markets. We believe that Japan's future depends upon its ability to play a key role in the integration and development of regional Asian markets, which requires that Japan's companies and Japanese society become more global in their outlook and behavior. We see signs of this happening, and we believe that the rate at which Japanese electronics and semiconductor companies continue to make changes that facilitate this regional leadership role will determine Japan's global competitive advantage over the next 20 years.

Acknowledgments

This chapter draws (with permission) from the authors' book *Chips and Change: How Crisis Reshapes the Semiconductor Industry* (Brown and Linden, 2009), and all rights to the materials from *Chips and Change* remain with MIT Press. This research has been funded by the Institute for Technology, Enterprise and Competitiveness (ITEC)-COE Program at Doshisha University, the Alfred P. Sloan Foundation, and the Institute for Research on Labor and Employment at UCB. We are grateful to Ben Campbell, Bob Doering, David Ferrell, Michael Flynn, Gartner Dataquest, Dave Hodges, Rob Leachman, Yoshifumi Nakata, Semiconductor Industry Association, Chintay Shih, Gary Smith, Bill Spencer, Strategic Marketing Associates, Tim Tredwell, Eiichi Yamaguchi, Takashi Yunogami, C.-K. Wang, and Hugh Whittaker for their valuable contributions. Melissa Appleyard, Hank Chesbrough, Robert Cole, Jason Dedrick, Rafiq Dossani, Deepak Gupta, Martin Kenney, Ken Kraemer, Frank Levy, James Lincoln, Lindsay Lowell, Jeff Macher, Noboru Maeda, Dave Mowery, Tom Murtha, Yong Paik, Tim Sturgeon, Mon-Han Tsai, as well as participants at the Berkeley Innovation Seminar and the Doshisha ITEC Seminar series provided thoughtful discussions that improved the chapter. The authors are responsible for all errors.

Notes

1. Based on data from Gartner Dataquest.
2. Reported in Young (1992: 269).
3. We are grateful to Professor Robert Leachman for helpful discussions on this point.
4. 'Teenagers help start belated PC boom in Japan', Reuters, 16 August 1995.
5. We are grateful to Professor David Hodges for elucidating this point for us.
6. $HSI = \dfrac{\left[\left(\% \text{ of Sales in 'Home' Region}\right) - \left('\text{Home' Market as }\% \text{ of World Market}\right)\right]}{\text{Foreign Markets as }\% \text{ of World Market}} \times 100$

   See Brown and Linden (2009) for details.
7. Based on Semiconductor Industry Association data (see https://www.sia-online.org/downloads/shares.pdf, accessed in March 2008). The global share of Japan's market peaked in 1988 at 40 per cent.

8. Calculated by the authors based on the listing by Electronic Business, http://www.edn.com/article/CA630171.html?partner=eb.
9. Calculated from National Science Foundation Science and Engineering Indicators, 2004, Table 4–5.
10. Calculated from Statistics Bureau data downloaded in March 2005 from http://www.stat.go.jp/data/kagaku/2003np/index.htm. See also Whittaker's excellent study (2009) of Japanese entrepreneurs.
11. Calculated from data provided by the Fabless Semiconductor Association.
12. Our fieldwork was conducted with Eiichi Yamaguchi, whose insights helped shape our thinking. This section is based upon Brown, Linden, and Yamaguchi (2005).
13. METI data accessed via the Venture Enterprise Corporation (http://www.vec.or.jp/) shows that the share of venture capital going to firms within five years of their establishment was between 50 and 60 per cent of all Japanese venture funding from 2000 through 2005. This is a higher share than in the US.
14. Personal communication, November 2008.
15. 'Silicon Strategies' 60 emerging start-ups', Silicon Strategies, 6 April 2004.
16. These HRM systems build upon Brown *et al.* (1997), which compares three types of systems, termed SET-Career Ladders (Japan), SET-Post and bid (US), and JAM (US), which are primarily for managing production workers. The two SET systems are high-commitment systems. The analysis presented here focuses on knowledge workers, and brings the analysis of HRM systems up to the mid-2000s.
17. Interviews with engineer executives at two high-tech companies provided details of their bonus restructuring, which resulted in reduced earnings for many workers, in the summer of 2006 in the Kansai area.
18. Based on data from Table 1 in 'China's Impact on the Semiconductor Industry, 2008 Update', PricewaterhouseCoopers, available at http://www.pwc.com/us/en/technology-innovation-center/china-semiconductor.jhtml
19. Yoshiko Hara, 'Japan taps into "glocalization"', *EE Times*, 19 June 2006.
20. 'Asuka' was a five-year, privately funded development program for 100nm and 70nm process technology launched in 2000 by Fujitsu, Hitachi, Matsushita, Mitsubishi Electric, NEC, Oki, Rohm, Sanyo, Sharp, Sony, and Toshiba. South Korea's Samsung was also affiliated. 'Mirai' was a seven-year project to develop five process modules for 70nm and 50nm technology using government labs, with the same companies participating.
21. 'NEC, Renesas Agree on Funding for Chip Merger', WSJ.com, 17 September 2009.

References

Appleyard, M., Brown, C. and Sattler, L. (2006) 'An International Investigation of Problem-Solving Performance in the Semiconductor Industry', *Journal of Product Innovation Management*, 23(2):147–167.
Baron, J. and Kreps, D. (1999) *Strategic Human Resources: Frameworks for General Managers*, Hoboken: Wiley.
Borrus, M. (1988) *Competing for Control: America's Stake in Microelectronics*, Cambridge, MA: Ballinger Publishing.

Brown, C. (2006) 'Managing Creativity and Control of Knowledge Workers,' in D. H. Whittaker and R. Cole (eds), *Recovering from Success: Innovation and Technology Management in Japan*, 145–165, New York: Oxford University Press.

Brown, C. and Linden, G. (2009) *Chips and Change: How Crisis Reshapes the Semiconductor Industry*, Cambridge, MA: MIT Press.

Brown, C., Linden, G., and Yamaguchi, E. (2005) 'The Role of Japanese Start-ups in High-Tech Innovation', ITEC Policy Brief, March (http://www.itec.doshisha-u.jp/03_publication_03_policy_main.html)

Brown, C., Nakata, Y., Reich, M., and Ulman, L. (1997) *Work and Pay in the United States and Japan*, New York: Oxford University Press.

Cappelli, P. (1999) *The New Deal at Work: Managing the Market-Driven Workforce*, Boston: Harvard Business School Press.

Chesbrough, H. (2003) *Open Innovation*, Boston: Harvard Business School Press.

Cole, R. and Matsumiya, T. (2007) 'Quality as an Obstacle to Innovation: Too Much of a Good Thing?', *ITEC Working Paper Series* 07–08 (June) (http://www.itec.doshisha-u.jp/03_publication/01_workingpaper/2007/07–08-FINAL-Cole-Matsumiya-itecwp.pdf).

Flamm, K. (1996) *Mismanaged Trade? Strategic Policy and the Semiconductor Industry*, Washington, DC: Brookings Institution Press.

Fransman, M. (1990) *The Market and Beyond: Cooperation and Competition in Information Technology Development in the Japanese System*, Cambridge: Cambridge University Press.

Fransman, M. (1995) *Japan's Computer and Communications Industry: The Evolution of Industrial Giants and Global Competitiveness*, Oxford: Oxford University Press.

Grindley, P., Mowery, D.C., and Silverman, B. (1994) 'SEMATECH and Collaborative Research: Lessons in the Design of High-Technology Consortia', *Journal of Policy Analysis and Management*, 13(4): 723–758.

Ham, R. M., Linden, G., and Appleyard, M. M. (1998) 'The Evolving Role of Semiconductor Consortia in the US and Japan', *California Management Review*, 41(1): 137–163.

Jacoby, S. M. (1998) *Modern Manors*, Princeton: Princeton University Press.

Katz, R. (ed.) (1997) *The Human Side of Managing Technological Innovation*, New York: Oxford University Press.

Macher, J. T., Mowery, D. C., and Hodges, D. A. (1999) 'Semiconductors' in D. C. Mowery (ed.), *US Industry in 2000: Studies in Competitive Performance*, Washington, DC: National Academy Press.

Nakata, Y. and Miyazaki, S. (2007) 'Has Lifetime Employment Become Extinct in Japanese Enterprise? An Empirical Analysis of Employment Adjustment Practices in Japanese Companies', *Asian Business & Management*, 6(S1): 33–56.

Prestowitz, C. V. Jr. (1988) *Trading Places: How We Allowed Japan to Take the Lead*, New York: Basic Books.

Saxenian, A. (2006) *The New Argonauts: Regional Advantage in a Global Economy*, Cambridge, MA: Harvard University Press.

Study Group of Creation and Development of Start Ups (2008) Creation and Development of Start Ups for Innovation in the Japanese Economy, Final Report, April. Available at http://www.meti.go.jp/english/report/data/startups Finalreport.pdf.

Tsuru, T., Abe, M., and Kubo, K. (2003) 'Pay Structures and the Transformation of Japanese Firms: An Empirical Analysis of Performance and Pay Using Personnel Data' (in Japanese), *The Economic Review*, 54(3): 264–285.

Warshofsky, F. (1989) *The Chip War: The Battle for the World of Tomorrow*, New York: Charles Scribner's Sons.

Whittaker, D. H. (2009) *Comparative Entrepreneurship: The UK, Japan, and the Shadow of Silicon Valley*, New York: Oxford University Press.

Young, R. (1992) 'Structural and Ideological Mismatch: A Study of U.S.-Japan Competition in the High Technology Food Chain', Manuscript, San Diego: UC San Diego.

Yunogami, T. (2006) 'Technology Management and Competitiveness in the Japanese Semiconductor Industry', in D. H. Whittaker and R. Cole (eds), *Recovering from Success: Innovation and Technology Management in Japan*, New York: Oxford University Press.

3
The Japanese Enterprise Software Industry
An Evolutionary and Comparative Perspective
Robert E. Cole and Shinya Fushimi

Introduction: Issues and background

Software is the main driver of information technology and is critically linked to communications and computers. Hardware increasingly
depends on software for its functionality, and software needs hardware
to express its capabilities. Software is critical both as an industry itself
but also as an infrastructure enabling all other industries. It drives the
spread of information and communications industries and the Internet
in increasingly knowledge-based economies. An understanding of how
the two largest economies, Japan and the US, have organized their enterprise software activities is central to an understanding of the dynamism
of both economies.

Contemporary observations on the US and Japanese software industries reveal significant differences in firm strategy, organizational structure, and processes. To be sure, there are those who stress similarities
among leading users of IT (Rapp, 2002) but the dominant image is one
of differences. What are some of the differences to which we refer? They
include, but are not limited to: a large packaged software sector in the
US and a weak one in Japan, more horizontal markets for software products in the US versus more vertical markets in Japan, a greater role for
firms producing software products in the US versus services in Japan,
a greater role for start-ups in the US versus the continuing dominance
of large incumbents in Japan, a stronger emphasis on quality in the
software development process in Japan versus innovation and time to

market in the US, and a more consolidated market for system integrators in Japan than in the US. How do we account for these differences?

These differences, many of which are interrelated, are all the more remarkable in view of the fact that, at the start of the computer revolution some 50 years ago, there were important similarities in strategy, structure, and processes. Nevertheless, first-mover advantages, different institutional practices, and the interests and strategies of powerful actors drove the evolution of the two industries in quite different directions. Our task in this chapter is to trace what became increasingly divergent evolutionary paths, given some common starting points, and to provide some accounting for these differences. At the same time, we identify punctuated pressures for convergence over the last 60 years. Dosi and Kogut (1993: 249–260) point us toward an understanding of these contradictory movements by describing a cycle of divergence in the organizational structure and processes of common national industries due to the introduction of new organizing heuristics, followed by gradual convergence resulting from the diffusion of these new heuristics across national borders, with the process repeating itself over time.

Because of the breadth of the software industry, we have chosen to focus on two linked segments in Japan, namely, those computer manufacturers and their subsidiaries that deliver *system integration services* for *enterprise software* to their corporate clients. The strong need for system integration services is driven in part by the heavy use of customized enterprise software, especially in Japan. Most Japanese corporate software is still for mainframes and mid-range computers, and large firms account for most software use. Customized software for corporate users accounts for 85 per cent of the total Japanese software market (Ministry of Economy, Trade and Industry (METI, 2007a); see also Rapp, 2002: 48). We aim to show that the prominence of this sector and of its functions is key to understanding the lack of a strong packaged software industry in Japan as well as the persistence of incumbents over time and the corresponding relative absence of strong venture capital/ start-up activities.

The remainder of this chapter is organized as follows. The second section provides an introductory description of the system integration market in the US and Japan. The third section reviews the emergence of the computer industries, and the subsequent rise of the software sector, in both Japan and the US, aiming to capture both differences and similarities. In the fourth section, we turn to the rise of factory models of software development and examine their differing impact in Japan and the US.

The fifth section describes the transformative developments around the turn of the century that imposed strong pressures for Japan's convergence with global practices. These pressures arise from the emergence of open architecture and open networks. The sixth section takes up the strikingly different ways in which US and Japanese firms build their information systems. Japanese firms have a much higher propensity to develop their own software or to order custom software as compared to US firms, which are more open to packaged solutions.

The seventh section details how system integration firms deliver customized solutions to their customers, highlighting the continued importance of *keiretsu* boundaries in Japan. In the eighth section, we analyze the impact of the dominance in Japan of customized software for international software trade and examine why it is so difficult to grow the packaged software market in Japan. Finally, in our concluding section, we explore the pressures on Japanese firms to move more toward packaged and semi-custom solutions in the future.

The system integration market

By *system integrators* we refer to those firms which specialize in planning, design, implementation, and project management to join together component subsystems into a whole and ensure that these subsystems work together in a seamless fashion. In the IT world, this often involves customization of innovative software applications from different vendors. System integration may involve the process of configuring newly acquired applications software to fit into a company's technology infrastructure and business processes. It may be as basic as filling out the Bill of Materials (BOM) for Enterprise Resource Planning (ERP) or as complex as the integration of an ERP solution into a firm's existing IT system.

As the mainframe computing needs of large organizations grew more complex in the 1980s, corporate IT capabilities came under increasing pressure, both technologically and from rising costs. Internal development capabilities, and particularly the ability to keep pace with fast-moving technology, were called into question. As a result, US firms began to explore external support. To meet this need, established companies delivering system solutions, such as Computer Sciences Corporation and EDS, as well as four of the big eight accounting firms, came to offer system integration services. Delivery of these services requires close cooperation with the client firm (Steinmueller, 1996: 39–40).

In the case of Japan, the major computer/software vendors in the 1970s adopted, and continue to follow to this day, the business model of the

IBM mainframe era. Initially, this was to sell both hardware and software to client companies. Later, this evolved to selling custom application systems, wrapped in hardware and software, and then to augment this initial contract by a series of deals, continuing as long as possible, for maintenance, administration, and upgrades. This makes vendors primarily information-services providers rather than product companies. In the 1990s, these firms (including units within large firms) came to be called system integrators. Japanese information service firms numbered under 1000 in 1985; that number jumped to 7000 by 1990. The number of firms then declined and flattened out for a number of years before starting to rise again in 1997 and ultimately reaching just under 8000 by 2002. Sales of information service firms, however, showed steady growth from 1985 on, rising some 800 per cent above 1985 levels by 2002. System integration firms accounted for about 43 per cent of total information service revenues in that year (JPSA, 2007: 19–20).

Table 3.1 shows the top ten worldwide system integrators in terms of market share. When we compare the top two US firms, Accenture and IBM (ranked one and two, respectively) with the top two Japanese firms (ranked three and six, respectively), we find that the bulk of sales of the two Japanese firms were in Japan, while IBM and Accenture focused more on global markets.

Table 3.2 reports revenues and share of the computing market, in 2006 and 2007, for the top ten consulting and system integration firms in the

Table 3.1 Top ten worldwide system integrator market share leaders in 2005

Rank	Vendor	Headquarters of vendor
1	Accenture	US
2	IBM	US
3	Fujitsu	Japan
4	Lockheed Martin	US
5	CSC	US
6	Hitachi	Japan
7	SAIC	US
8	SAP	Germany
9	Capgemini	France
10	Northrup Grumman	US

Source: Torto, 2006.

Japanese market. Fujitsu had the highest revenue, with $4.9 billion in 2007 and a market share of 15.8 per cent. By comparison, Accenture, the leading US system integrator, had global system integration revenues of $6.3 billion in 2005. There has been growing concentration over the last 15 years in the global system integration market (OECD, 2002: 122). The Japanese system integration market, remarkably, is the most consolidated of all the worldwide regional markets, with an estimated 73 per cent of total system integration market share held by the top ten providers (Karlsson, 2008). Compared to other world regions, potential new entrants to the Japanese system integration market face larger barriers to entry (OECD, 2002: 122).

Table 3.2 also lists estimates of total market revenue for the Japanese system integration sector in 2006 and 2007. For 2006, this was estimated to be $29.7 billion. To get a sense of the role of this sector in the total IT service industry, we draw on data from METI's *Survey on*

Table 3.2 Revenue and computing market share for the top ten consulting and system integration providers in Japan, 2006–2007

Rank	Vendor	2006 Revenues	2007 Revenues	2006–2007 Growth (%)	2007 Market Share (%)
1	Fujitsu	4,849	4,938	1.8	15.8
2	NEC	4,146	4,311	4.0	13.8
3	Hitachi	3,668	3,913	6.7	12.5
4	IBM	3,466	3,555	2.6	11.4
5	Nomura Research Institute	1,067	1,220	14.3	3.9
6	NTT Data	1,021	1,052	3.0	3.4
7	Toshiba	987	1,047	6.1	3.3
8	Fuijsoft	986	965	–2.2	3.1
9	Mitsubishi Electric	866	882	1.9	2.8
10	Nihon Unisys	657	858	30.7	2.7
	Other Service Vendors	8,007	8,547	6.8	27.3
	Total Market	29,720	31,289	5.3	100.0

Source: Karlsson, 2008.
Units: millions of dollars.

the Status of Specific Service Industry for 2006 (METI, 2007b). The entire industry reported revenues of $143.8 billion in 2006. Fully 28 per cent of that total is accounted for not by software-development revenues but by revenues from data-processing services (METI, 2007b). If we eliminate this latter portion, then system integration services impressively account for some 29 per cent of all software-development revenues.

Early development

We turn now to the early stages of the commercial computer industry in Japan and the US. The origins of the US computer industry during and immediately after World War II lay in military and scientific activities. By the 1950s, interest turned toward business objectives. In the period from 1950 to 1965, software was not a separate business for computer companies, but rather a service provided by these companies to sell their hardware. Consistent with this approach, software was a product whose costs were bundled with computer prices (Steinmueller, 1996: 19). Many of the new companies in this field, including IBM, Burroughs, Remington Rand, and NCR, originated as business service firms who came to understand that more and better software sold more computers.

The early development of the Japanese computer industry followed a similar pattern, minus the military origins, and with a lag. Strong interest in the new computer industry by commercial companies did not take place until the mid-to-late 1950s by what were to become the three major players: Fujitsu, NEC, and Hitachi (see Fransman, 1995: 130–137). These were all telecommunication companies and dedicated suppliers to NTT, the telephone monopoly. As such, they had secure businesses that made them somewhat slow, especially Fujitsu, to venture into this new world of computing, with its new ways of thinking about information collection, analysis, and deployment.

As a dominant first mover, IBM (with 70 per cent of the global value of computer sales in 1956 and 62 per cent even as late as 1971) was both the model to be followed and the target for Japanese hardware manufacturers. This induced important commonalities between the US and Japanese industries in this mainframe era. Particularly with the creation and release of the IBM 360/370 series in 1964, IBM product architecture became the *de facto* architecture for the emergent global industry; this architecture delivered, for the first time in the history of the young industry, a family of computers with backward and upward compatibility, which minimized the need to develop new software for each new computer. Firms throughout the world were now playing by IBM rules. That meant they were making devices, writing software, manufacturing clones, and running time-share centers, all within the computing environment that IBM defined (Ferguson and Morris, 1993: 15). The launch of the System 360 family of computers in 1964 established the first broad installed base of computers with a single operating system, thereby enabling independent software vendors to market the same product to a variety of users.

A third factor stimulating software sales by independent software vendors was IBM's decision to unbundle software from hardware pricing. Following a 1956 consent decree, IBM – fearing further antitrust action by the US Department of Justice – decided to unbundle software from hardware pricing. This 1968 announcement led to a momentous shift that provided a firm launch for the already nascent independent software industry. Initially there was rapid growth of new and existing companies producing IBM-compatible software, especially application software. Early on, computer vendors provided tools for application development. There was consequently an enormous growth of user-developed application software in the US in the 1960s. Those firms developing their own software for their own proprietary uses, however, had little incentive to sell that software to others. Consequently, in the US there also arose strong independent software vendors (ISVs) for whom software was a business. It is during the years 1965–1970 that we witness the real beginnings of the US independent software vendor industry (Steinmuelller, 1996: 17–24).

Gradually, US computer hardware companies came to believe that their ability to understand and solve user problems was limited, and that they should instead specialize in hardware. The 1980s witnessed a sharp decline in software and service revenues as a percentage of total revenues for computer firms. A number of computer companies, such as DEC, abandoned the vertical market strategies which had established them as leaders in providing integrated hardware and software for selected industries. Instead, companies concluded they could gain more by concentrating on hardware innovation, leaving software development to others. IBM, however, was an exception to this development, in that it did not experience a diminishing share of revenues from software production. IBM focused on those software products that strongly raised the level of hardware demand, such as those products that stimulated the sales of computational or mass storage hardware (Steinmueller, 1996: 17, 30–35, 45).

The Japanese were just as much prisoners of IBM's architecture as their US competitors. The Japanese struggled mightily, and eventually rather successfully, to catch up with IBM's performance by the late 1970s. Inspired by IBM's global success, which was attributed to economies of scale, scope, and vertical integration, the leading Japanese computer vendors organized as vertically integrated firms (Fransman, 1995: 148–149). Consistent with IBM, but unlike other US computer firms, the Japanese computer vendors sought to keep software central to their mission, either through internal software divisions and/or captive subsidiaries. The way in which they went about this, however, was quite distinctive.

Following IBM somewhat belatedly, Japanese computer vendors formally unbundled software from hardware in 1977. This spurred the creation of spin-offs from user companies which were early leaders in new uses of computing (steel-industry spin-offs were an early example, followed in the early 1990s by financial-sector spin-offs). These user firms spun off their management information systems (MIS) divisions, because they were becoming too expensive for the parent company. The new subsidiaries continued to do work for the parent company, hire new engineers for programming, and complete other tasks, but paid lower wages than the parent firm. Starting in the 1970s, Japanese computer vendors took an active role in developing software for users, quite the opposite of the overall trend in the US. This required the employment of large numbers of system engineers, who were often dispatched for extended periods to the data-processing departments of client firms. These client firms became dependent on their services. As demand increased, those dispatched employees were assigned to separate internal divisions of the computer vendors or spun off as external captive subsidiaries (Baba *et al.*, 1996: 116).

The captive software firms of the major computer vendors were invariably members of their parent firm's vertical *keiretsu*. Some computer vendors, such as NEC and Fujitsu, preferred to organize much of their software development capabilities in internal divisions (although they eventually established software subsidiaries as well), while others, such as Hitachi, emphasized the creation of captive subsidiaries. In both cases, the target customers were typically the parent firm, other members of the corporate group, and their customers and suppliers. This led to the formation of vertical markets. The links between computer vendors, their software development activities (either by internal divisions or captive subsidiaries), and user firms tended to be long term and stable, especially in the mainframe era. Ronald Dore has used the term 'relational management' to describe these distinctive contractual links (Dore, 1987: 173–192).

The computer-maker spin-offs and user spin-offs grew expert and quite accustomed to churning out code to strict contractor specifications. They chose low-profit but secure business relationships within the *keiretsu* family instead of more risky, but potentially higher-profit, activities developing innovative software products for the broad corporate or consumer market. Of course, since they were often under the control of their corporate parents, they had little choice (compare Hamilton, 1993: B4).

What were the initial origins of these vertical divisions? In the early 1960s, the Ministry of International Trade and Industry sponsored multiple alliances between selected fledgling Japanese companies and overseas producers as a means for Japanese firms to catch up technologically. As a result, each of these emergent computer firms had a different source for their operating systems. Hitachi became allied with RCA, and then became IBM-compatible when RCA exited the market in 1971; NEC became allied with Honeywell and was not IBM-compatible; Toshiba became allied with RCA and then General Electric; Mitsubishi Electric became allied with TRW; and Fujitsu was on its own and later became IBM-compatible (Rapp, 2002: 49).

The operating systems of IBM-compatible producers were able to run a new customer's existing IBM programs. However, the operating systems of even IBM-compatible producers were sufficiently different that the application programs written for one system would not run on the operating system of other IBM-compatible competitors, much less on the operating systems of non-IBM-compatible producers. Computer firms made little effort to ensure interoperability, given their objective of ensuring that customers stayed locked in for maintenance, upgrades, application development, and system integration. It was these relationships that were later to solidify into the current vertical divisions of the computer and software markets, locking major corporations and their vertical *keiretsu* into selected proprietary hardware and software systems.

Factory models of software development

Initially, both IBM – as the dominant US player – and the large Japanese mainframe companies were confronted with the challenge of organizing software development. By the 1970s, considerable discontent had developed among US producers and users over the patchwork-quilt nature of the industry and the problems this created for software development, including lack of standardization, poor productivity and quality, cost overruns, and failures to meet new product launch dates. In what follows we draw heavily on Cusumano's analysis (1991, 2004) of responses to these challenges.

The software factory model was based on efforts to apply to software the strategy, tactics, and practices used in hardware manufacturing. Software development in the early years of the industry utilized programmers operating more as creative artists than as disciplined production workers engaged in a standardized development process with standardized tools and methods. As a result, costs were high and quality low.

In the US, firms like IBM, General Electric, and AT&T made notable efforts in the 1960s to apply concepts and practices developed in manufacturing to software. IBM, as the most successful firm engaging in software development, faced the challenges of managing software development earlier than most. Yet IBM, even as late as 1970, lacked a firm-wide coordinated system for development, quality assurance, and maintenance. In the absence of centralization, each of the company's worldwide development centers was free to develop its own tools and methods, thus defeating standardization efforts.

Gradually, these problems came into focus, and IBM sought to address them using much of the language of what was to be called (although not by IBM) the *software factory*. For example, efforts were made in the late 1960s and 1970s to develop general-purpose tools rather than product-specific tools, and efforts in the late 1970s were directed toward organizational and technological integration. A variety of process innovations were instituted as well, including top-down hierarchical design (Cusumano, 2004: 101). Further efforts were made in the late 1980s to standardize internal hardware and software architectures and interfaces, thus enabling greater reusability of systems and tools, as well as whole programs. Japanese software managers often claimed to have been inspired by IBM's efforts to impose structure and discipline in the software development process.

The System Development Corporation (SDC) made the most concerted effort to impose the factory model on software in the US, devoting several years to planning and experimentation in the 1970s as it sought to put its software factory into practice. SDC opened its software factory in December 1976, with the experiment coming to an end after just three years. Many reasons have been put forward to explain its failure. In particular, according to Cusumano (1991: 136, 157–160), the factory fell short in managing requirements, specifications, and changes, in creating design and verification tools, and in enabling more systematic reuse of software. Underlying these weaknesses was a mismatch between the company's product line, which emphasized innovation for a variety of customers, and the standardization focus appropriate for a software factory. This made it difficult for SDC to focus on process improvement. The emphasis of US firms on products and of Japanese firms on process innovation is a paradigmatic distinction which has long been observed in comparisons of US and Japanese manufacturing (Mansfield, 1988).

Nonetheless, there were important positive legacies of these efforts in design, quality assurance, and project management, as manifested in particular in US defense and space programs. A well-known offshoot of the software factory concept emerged in the founding of the Software Engineering Institute (SEI) at Carnegie Mellon University by the US Department of Defense in 1984. The Institute's objective was to codify and disseminate best practices in software development. Cusumano notes that most of the practices recommended by SEI arose from IBM's experiences at creating operating systems and complex applications. SEI became particularly well known for its delineation of the stages of maturity for software development practices.

In spite of these legacies, the Americans fell short of fully implementing the software factory concept. The explanation for this seems to lie primarily in the emphasis on product innovation and time to market. These emphases eventually served US producers well, leading to the creation of a vibrant ISV sector specializing in hugely successful packaged software businesses. This strategy was possible in the software industry because, in contrast to manufacturing, process improvement – while important in the software *development* process – is a non-issue in software *production*. That is to say, software, unlike hardware, is not manufactured. The costs of producing the first copy of an information-related good can be substantial, but the cost of replication is minimal (compare Shapiro and Varian, 1999: 3).

The Japanese began their efforts at creating software factories just a few years after IBM had begun to organize its own software operations. The major Japanese computer manufacturers – Fujitsu, NEC, Toshiba, Hitachi, and Mitsubishi Electric – all made long-term commitments to building software factories. The overriding objective of these Japanese software factories was not to make products to be sold on the open market, but rather to customize software for internal divisions or corporate parents, who then sold the resulting product to corporate end-users as part of an integrated hardware and software solution.

For these companies, creating software factories meant, above all, the strategic management and integration of software development, along with the realization of economies of scale among related projects (for example, through reuse of software modules). On a tactical level, this meant emphasizing incremental innovation in feature design, a strong focus on getting user needs built into the initial design specifications, standardized development techniques, common training programs, reusable component libraries, computer-aided support tools, and adherence to strong quality control policies and practices driven by a 'quality-first mentality' (compare Cusumano, 2004: 8).

Most importantly, the Japanese showed a commitment to creating software factories that went well beyond US activities in terms of the resources allocated to these efforts. Consequently, Japanese software factories made considerable progress, as measured by their strong quality and productivity performance relative to international competitors (Cusumano *et al.*, 2003).

The leading Japanese captive software firms, and the software divisions of corporate vendors, were largely organized into 'software factories' whose mission was to develop custom IBM or IBM-compatible mainframe software for the large computer hardware vendors and their large end-user corporate customers. These 'products' met the needs of these corporate customers for software systems and customized applications which supported their existing organizational practices. In prioritizing these objectives, enterprise software in Japan came to be seen not as an independent industry, but more exclusively as infrastructure support for large corporations. Software came to be treated as more of a service than a product. Just like IBM, the objective of large Japanese software producers was to use the creation of software to sell hardware (mainframes) and services (for example, maintenance). Stability and performance of core functions, rather than innovation, were the hallmark of these software systems.

Nonetheless, even the Japanese fell well short of creating the ideal software factory, in large part because of the difficulty of conforming to advanced software specifications in a dynamic market with rapidly changing customer needs and technologies.

The rise of open architecture and its impact on the corporate enterprise market

At the turn of the twenty-first century, the major challenge for Japanese software providers arose from emergent technologies based upon open architecture. This challenge was twofold. First, there were open hardware architectures, leading to a downsizing from mainframe computing and a reduction in the total cost of system development. Second, there were open *software* architectures, leading more companies to enter the IT services market and enabling users to mix-and-match products. This is seen in the impact of Sun Microsystems' object-oriented software, Java, starting in the early 2000s. Java had a huge impact on software development; it eliminated the risk of vendor lock-in, enabling customers to assemble 'best-of-breed' solutions. More recently, the impact of open software architectures has been evident in the accelerating adoption of Open Source Systems (OSS), including Linux, Apache, and PostgresSQL.

The problem for established Japanese software leaders was that their dominance in the mainframe era was based on long-term vertical partnerships, rooted in closed, proprietary systems, among business partners, often including even retailers. The mainframe vendors followed an 'enclosure' strategy, in which they sought to have exclusive ownership of the entire value chain for their particular customer base. Their machines had proprietary hardware and software and proprietary interfaces with peripheral equipment, and computer vendors and their subsidiaries sought to provide customized applications for their customers (Kokuryo, 1997). These tight linkages among business partners were, in fundamental ways, incompatible with the opportunities created by the emerging open-network era. Yet, understandably, the dominant firms were slow to abandon the basis for their past success and to embrace the uncertainty of open-platform systems. Practically speaking, open architectures now allowed system integration companies to use a large variety of software and hardware to design systems based on each customer's specific needs. This was an enormous change from the mainframe era, with its proprietary systems based on technological incompatibility.

Open architecture enables *any* software company with the requisite design capabilities to enter the market. This development helped break the 'vendor lock-in' system and accelerated the pace of outsourcing. Proprietary IT technology within a given company came to contribute less to that firm's competitive advantage than it had in the mainframe era. This led to severe competition in the system integration market, eventually leading to more equal relationships between system integrators and end-users and ultimately to cost reductions (Cole and Matsumiya, 2006: 9). Under these circumstances, users gradually found it easier to change vendors for a given layer of, or even all of, their IT system when they became dissatisfied with existing services. To be sure, these changes came much more slowly to Japan than to the US. By now, however, they have worked their way through a good part of the Japanese economy. Consider the case study of a major manufacturing firm's deployment of its current IT system (Table 3.3).

Table 3.3 IT deployment and migration in a major Japanese manufacturing firm

Business function	Vendor(s)
R&D	IBM → UGS + Fujitsu
Manufacturing design	Unisys → UGS + Fujitsu
Manufacturing system	Hitachi → Partially went to NEC
Finance	IBM + SAP[a]
Sales overseas (Main Markets)	IBM

Note:
[a]IBM was responsible for implementing, and continues to maintain, the SAP system.
Source: E-mail communication from Hideyuki Yamagishi, Oracle Japan Corporation, 16 October 2008.

We see in Table 3.3 the result of replacing mainframes and legacy applications with open servers and migrations to different vendors for different specialized applications. This is a major change from the mainframe era, when end-user firms were likely to have only one hardware and software vendor which served as a long-term partner. Today many firms have a number of specialized long-term partners. If the advantages of a competitor become large enough, firms are increasingly prepared to change partners. To be sure, many firms still depend on one single system integration vendor to build and maintain core and mission-critical systems (for example, mega banks). These firms may use other system integration vendors to develop relatively 'light systems' (for example, e-mail, web, payroll, and human-resource management systems).

Methods of building information systems

We can broaden this discussion to address fundamental methods of building information systems. We begin with some definitions. Packaged software, narrowly defined, consists of those software products aimed at the mass market which require very little after-sales support. Network effects tend to be strong, with the firms developing and distributing such products operating on a 'printing press' model. If a firm can develop hit products, the rewards are very large. Packaged software is tradable software licensed to users by the software creator and holder of the copyright. The industry, early in its history, produced a 'shrink-wrapped' product, but this evolved over time, and firms now use a variety of new distribution methods and channels. More specifically, distribution moved from a 'bunch of tapes' to CDs, and then to DVDs; today, software is often downloaded from the Internet.

The narrow definition of packaged software, however, grows largely out of observations of the consumer mass market and fails to do justice to the actual practices associated with packaged software in the enterprise market. For the enterprise market, we might instead view packaged software as a software product in which the majority of the functionality – say 80 per cent – is pre-built. That leaves 20 per cent to be customized during implementation. Packaged software is generally cheaper per user than highly customized software, and much easier and less expensive to maintain and upgrade. When it is time to upgrade, the vendor only needs to write the change once, and then distribute it *en masse* to all its customers. The economies of scale are enormous, and they are one reason why charging high maintenance fees can be so profitable.

Customized software, by contrast, involves an end-user firm entrusting customized software development to a partner (often a system integration company), which develops the customized product based on the client's needs. In a world of pure customization, the vendor would do something different for every customer. Unlike packaged software, where the copyright is retained by the developer, in the case of customized software the copyright for the developed software is often agreed to be shared with the client firm (JPSA, 2005: 6). While more expensive than packaged software, customization can deliver exactly the functionality desired by the end-user.

How do Japan and the US compare in their utilization of these activities? We first examine corporate end-user data from 2004, commissioned by Japan's Ministry of International Affairs and Communications and tabulated in Table 3.4. The most striking feature of these data is the large percentage of Japanese firms (54 per cent) reporting that they develop their own software or order custom software, versus only 16 per cent of the US firms surveyed. This represents a huge difference in business practices. On the other hand, a total of 43 per cent of Japanese firms used some form of packaged software, versus 78 per cent of US firms.

Data from METI's *Survey on the Status of Specific Service Industry* (*tokutei saabisu sangyou jittai chousa*) for 2006, as reported by the Japan Information Technology Service Industry Association (JISA), cover only the activities of Japanese software firms for which software development is the primary business activity. If we exclude data-processing and internal software-development activities, we find that 86.3 per cent of

Table 3.4   Methods of building information systems

	Packaged software with little customization(%)	Customized packaged software(%)	Internally developed or custom-ordered software(%)
Japan	17	26	54
US	29	49	16

Source: Ministry of International Affairs and Communications (2003), Appendix: 340.

sales are accounted for by customized software development, versus just 13.6 per cent (a 6.3 to 1 ratio) coming from software product sales (JISA, 2008: 4). From these data we conclude that the Japanese market relies heavily on customization, with packaged software products playing a minor role.

Customization

How do the leading firms organize their activities in the customized software sector and who are their customers? What follows is a proto-typical example of the organizational structure, practices, and ration-ale of the 'Big Five' Japanese enterprise software players, based on our field observations. These players, as noted earlier, are Hitachi, NEC, Fujitsu, Mitsubishi Electric, and Toshiba. Our prototypical example will not exactly describe any one of the five firms, but instead represents an 'ideal type'.[1] As one software specialist confirmed, 'major Japanese software firms resemble one another in structure and practices'.[2] As in many Japanese industries, the leading software firms have a full range of matched product offerings. The extensive use of the term 'sogo' (gen-eral or full-line) in Japanese captures these strong tendencies (Kokuryo, 1997: 6). That is to say, at the firm level, there is relatively modest spe-cialization in software product offerings among the Big Five. Such com-parable coverage by competitors is not absent in the US, particularly in fields such as human resources and financial software, where regula-tory requirements induce a similarity in offerings, but the phenomenon is more pervasive in Japanese industry.

We begin our description of our prototypical Company X with a dis-cussion of its Product Group A. Group A is a software 'product center' for the system integration business. Although it is often formally organ-ized and referred to as a 'business unit', its 'products' (such as database management software, application development tools, and job management software) are intended to be used only within Company X's system integration projects. Group A is ostensibly a profit center, but in reality is managed as a *cost* center of the system integration business unit to which it reports.

The rationale for this reporting relationship is that the enterprise software developed by Company X is plugged into large, complex custom solutions for specific customers. These inputs are coordinated and combined by the system integration business unit. The solutions in question are typically vertically integrated solutions (for example, Operating System + Database + Applications + Hardware). In this sense, the business application 'product' developed by Group A is only one component (one independent module) of this larger complex solution. Nonetheless, these components are referred to as 'products', because this term encompasses critical components of the system that have been already 'productized'. To say that a component has been 'productized' is to say that it has been made operational and put into use elsewhere, and thus that the development time and cost of building that module will be reduced. These components are also referred to as 'products' because the firm wants to have the same set of 'products' that IBM and other competitors provide. The firm also wants to follow current industry fashions by making statements like 'our version 1.xx supports the Service-Oriented-Architecture concept'.

In other words, to make an ideal product at low cost in this 'software factory' approach, firms avail themselves of commonly used software components as independent modules, which they call 'products'. These modules are then deployed for use in multiple end-user products to provide economies of scale. It is critical that these components are smoothly integrated into the larger custom solution.

The contrast with IBM is quite striking. IBM's software group has brought to market many innovative packaged software products, tools, and middleware, which the software group passes over to the Global Business Services (GBS) group to be taken as starting points; the GBS then adds to these products a range of value-added services associated with their customization work for end-users. These products, like the DB2 database, compete directly with the products of other enterprise software firms, such as those from Oracle and Microsoft. And yet the GBS group also partners with those same enterprise software companies as part of its stated commitment to provide customers the best possible solution to meet their needs. In other words, IBM's GBS unit offers its end-users both IBM products *and* products from IBM's competitors in its efforts to deliver optimal solutions to customers. As a result, the software group cannot be sure of sales from global services unless they have cutting-edge products.[3]

Company X's Group A, on the other hand, is primarily oriented toward meeting the needs of its System Integration Business Unit, which, in turn, is responsible for integrating a total, complex, custom solution. Thus the System Integration Business Unit is Group A's primary, and sometimes exclusive, customer. As a result, business applications – which in the US may be marketable stand-alone products such as order entry modules for an ERP system, application development software tools, or even entire ERP and database systems – tend to be seen quite differently in Japan. For the Japanese firms producing these applications, they are typically non-marketable components aimed at contributing to a complete solution package to be sold to an end-user. The system integration business unit provides a vertically integrated solution. As a consequence, the 'products' created by Group A, customized as they are for a specific end-user, are typically not marketed to other customers. Indeed, Group A has neither a strong marketing arm nor an aggressive sales force aimed at the external market. Software groups operating in this fashion have few incentives to produce innovative software which would be competitive on the open market. That said, there are differences among the Big Five. For example, Hitachi and Fujitsu's versions of Product Group A are notably more aggressive in marketing their products to other system integrators.

Company X also contains software Group B. Group B's revenues are (typically) much smaller than those of Group A. Group B is a true software product business unit, and operates as a profit center with relative autonomy. In some system integration firms, Groups A and B are in the same business unit. Although Group B is a profit center, it does not market its products to the external market, nor to the consumer mass market. Rather, it markets its products – enterprise software – to the Group As of other major system integrators. The unstated assumption is that it would be futile to try to sell directly to end-user corporations. This is in striking contrast to much software sales activity in the US. Group B does have some marketing and sales capabilities, but they are not strong. In contrast, US companies making innovative business applications, such as Oracle, have succeeded in the US and Japan by prioritizing sales functions.

The huge challenge facing Group B is that it is trying to sell its products to system integrators at other companies which typically offer a full range of their own Company X products. Thus, unless Group B can develop a new breakthrough product or greatly improve an existing one, it is very difficult to make sales to other system integrators. These other system integrators are customers, and these customers have every incentive to use their own products for their own end-user customers. Moreover, even if Group B can develop a successful product, the other system integrators will quickly act to 'cover its hit'. They will also do everything they can to persuade the end-user to buy a related product from them, even if its functionality is more limited, or to wait until an equivalent product becomes available.

This brings us to an interesting feature of this system from a Western perspective. The pivotal role of system integrators in Japan is such that software vendors rarely succeed – for the reasons just discussed – in marketing enterprise software directly to large corporate end-users. While successful cases do occur, the end-user corporations are usually heavily dependent on their long-term system integration partners to guide them in their IT selection choices. Heads of IT departments are, on average, relatively weak in Japan, as seen by looking at the proportion of firms with a full-time Chief Information Officer (CIO) position. It would be hard to find a single US firm with revenues over $500 million which did not have a CIO in 2008,[4] and yet Mitsubishi Research Institute software specialists estimate that only some 30–40 per cent of large Japanese firms had full-time CIOs in 2008.[5] In a 2005 publication, the Japan Personal Computer Software Association (JPSA) refers to 'the absence or inadequacy of Japanese CIOs', noting the overdependence of CIOs on system integration vendors when it comes to decision-making (JPSA, 2005: 33). Another survey reported that, whereas 51 per cent of US CIOs state that they participate in designing corporate strategy, only 13 per cent of Japanese CIOs could make similar claims (Ministry of International Affairs and Communication, 2003, Appendix: 340). Rapp claims that, in the highest-performing Japanese firms, CIOs play a critical role in ensuring that IT is fully integrated into business strategy (Rapp, 2002: 27). This may be the case in the highest-performing firms, but the data suggest it is hardly the norm among large firms.

Because most high-level Japanese managers lack confidence in their abilities to evaluate IT choices, they rely instead on their system integrators, who – thanks to the long-term nature of the relationship – know every detail of their business processes and can guarantee a smooth implementation process without disruptions.[6] System integrators thus have a strong incentive to look for software solutions which prioritize stability over innovation, namely, software systems which ensure few disruptions or quality problems.

In summary, we can say that, in Japan, customization work is the central activity of system integration firms, and is done in collaboration with in-house teams and, in some cases, external software vendors. In Japan, much more than in the US, there is overwhelming acceptance among corporate managers that large-scale business applications like ERP require extensive customization, despite the added costs this imposes. From the perspective of a Japanese system integration vendor, the ultimate form of a product (hardware or software) is one which is fully customized for a specific customer, and this is exactly what customers have come to expect and demand. Software producers, inextricably tied to hardware firms, seem to have fully internalized the user mentality epitomized by Japanese hardware managers.

Figure 3.1 summarizes the relationships we have described in terms of sales results. System-Integration Firm X represents a prototypical system integration firm. Its Product Group A is focused primarily on supplying software components to its System Integration Business Unit, which in turn integrates those components into complete solutions for its customers. In a relatively small number of cases, efforts are made to sell directly to Company Y's system integration unit. Success is not common, but, when efforts are successful, Company X's system integration unit proceeds as follows. Instead of attempting to sell directly to Company Y's system integration business unit, Company X instead tries to influence Y's end-user customers to use enterprise application Z. If successful, the end-users come to prefer Z, and tell System Integrator Y to use it in their system integration projects; Company X's actual sales are to System Integrator Y. Meanwhile, a much smaller Product Group

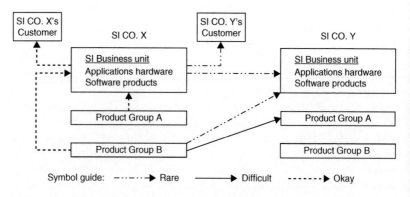

Figure 3.1   Software sales between system integrator (SI) firms X and Y and their customers

B sells software products primarily to Company X's system integration business unit, but also tries to accomplish the difficult task of selling its outstanding products to Product Group As within other system integration vendors.

We add here a few additional observations regarding the customization of enterprise software from a US perspective. As noted above, customizing a business package like ERP is often very expensive and complicated. Customization usually involves altering the code to meet a specific company need. Some business packages have very generic features, such that a great deal of customization occurs in most implementations. Alternatively, all US enterprise products, like Oracle's ERP, have increased configuration options which obviate the need for customization in some areas. Rather than changing the source code, setting configuration options is more a process of setting variables or parameters to meet specific customer needs, such as setting up payment terms or the length of customer records.

The creation of best-practice capabilities embedded in enterprise software systems is based on the modeling of specific business processes among 'lead users' and then the creation of a standardized best-practice model for such things as order-entry systems. A common view among US software vendors is that customization is a main cause of cost overruns in software development and tends to increase the costs of long-term maintenance and upgrades. In this view, all too often customizations are made to satisfy a perceived need for company-specific functionality, even though more than adequate methods and processes already exist in standard software routines. Indeed, a number of researchers in the US cite the avoidance of customization as one of the critical success factors in successful ERP implementations (Lorenzo *et al.*, 2009: 160). While long-term relationships with system integrators certainly exist in the US, it is also the case that customization work is often undertaken on a time- and materials-basis, rather than as a long-term partnership activity.

In summary, much research over the last decade has documented the diminishing significance of *keiretsu* in the Japanese economy, using as performance measures the diminished role of interlocking stock ownership and boards of directors (Lincoln and Gerlach, 2004). In Chapter 6 of this volume, James Lincoln and Emily Choi report that, in recent years, strategic technology alliances in the electronics industry are less reliant on *keiretsu* ties. In the world of enterprise software, however, *keiretsu* networks continue to have a powerful influence on trading relationships among enterprises.

Packaged software

The OECD's 2002 examination of the global market for packaged software includes three types of packaged software: applications software (roughly 50 per cent of the worldwide market), system infrastructure software (32 per cent), and software development tools (19 per cent). The leading software products in each category, as measured by market share, are, for applications, cross-industry business ERP systems; for system infrastructure software, operating systems; and for software development tools, database management systems.

Packaged software, defined as marketable software dispensed with a license, is, by definition, commercialized and capable of being extensively replicated and exported. There are a variety of quite complicated issues regarding how we measure software imports and exports. Nonetheless, official data from business associations and governments can give us a rough idea of Japan's global competitiveness in software. In the year 2000, according to data from a leading industry association, the value of measurable application software (broadly defined) exported from Japan was only 5.1 billion yen, compared to application software imports for the same year totaling 297.5 billion yen (JPSA, 2005: 23). In 2004, the leading ERP supplier in Japan was the German firm SAP, accounting for 56 per cent of the large-firm corporate market in Japan; Microsoft dominated the operating system market, while Oracle, IBM, and Microsoft had about 75 per cent of the database market in 2005. Overall, foreign firms are dominant in lower layers (operating systems, databases, and other middleware) and in some portions of upper layers (for example, ERP).[7] While the domestic Japanese markets of most advanced manufacturing industries are dominated by Japanese firms, this is clearly not the case in software.

Steinmueller suggests that the US software industry's advantage in packaged software, not only over Japan but over the rest of the world, lies in its first-mover advantage, an advantage enabled by government R&D policy and the early development of computer science education at leading US universities. The importance of software for national defense resulted in generous US government support for basic and applied research in software, as well as support for reconfiguring computer education at the university level (Langlois and Mowery, 1996: 53–85; Steinmueller, 1996: 42). The US advantage was also greatly facilitated by existing institutional arrangements, including a vibrant venture capital industry, and universal applications of contract law, securities law, employment law, and intellectual property law. All associated institutional practices came with a set of uncommitted professional 'outsiders' who stood ready to help new software entrepreneurs. This gave birth to a vast array of innovative start-up firms supported by a very active venture capital community (Rtischev and Cole, 2003; 146–148).

The contrast with Japan is stark. In the mainframe era, value added was overwhelmingly contributed by hardware; the government gave generous support to hardware vendors. As Japan entered the era of open systems, more and more of value added was contributed by software. Nevertheless, government bureaucrats continued to see Japan's success as rooted in manufacturing hardware. Consequently, government support policies remained fixated on supporting hardware development in large existing firms. In 2004, METI's budget for IT-related policies totaled some 150 billion yen, with software-related items accounting for only 5 per cent of that total. By contrast, hardware-related R&D (especially device-related) took up 75 per cent of the budget (JPSA, 2005: 16).

Japan boasts very few computer science departments in its national universities, with most having not been established until the 1980s. The quality of instruction in these departments has been recognized to be well below US and European standards. The relatively small number of software engineers in Japan have not been well used or valued in an environment in which the primary software engineering activities revolve around customization (see Baba *et al.*, 1996: 122). Finally, unlike in the US, Japan had few uncommitted professional outsiders and resources. Instead, we see strong adherence to existing organizations and networks, buttressed by structural barriers inhibiting new, competing organizations and networks (Rtischev and Cole, 2003).

Beyond these macro observations, we can still ask why it is so difficult to grow the packaged software market in Japan, given the seeming cost advantages over the customization model. After all, with successful packaged software products, firms can amortize development costs over a large base of users. That large base of users, combined with minimal reproduction costs, is a recipe for high profits among the winners. Nonetheless, the data suggest that incentives for developing packaged software in Japan are quite weak. We can examine this matter first from the perspective of corporate users.

According to survey results accumulated by Mitsubishi Research Institute, corporations are reluctant to adopt packaged software in the applications-software layer for three main reasons. The most-cited reason is the perceived inconsistency between the process routines required of packaged software applications and existing business processes. The second most common reason firms gave was insufficient quality, and the third was loss of control. The latter is a reference to the fact that packaged software products do not come with source codes, and thus opportunities for modification are limited.[8]

With regard to the perceived inconsistency between the process routines required for packaged software and existing business processes, managers fear additional costs arising after the purchase of packaged software. These costs come from the perceived need to customize software products to conform to existing organizational practices, rather than changing the organizational practices to conform to the software requirements. Nezu points to the fierce resistance encountered by those seeking to introduce organizational change to accommodate routines required by software packages (Nezu, 2002: 21–22). In a study of US and Japanese executives conducted by NTT Data, 65 per cent of US respondents indicated a willingness to reform organizational practices to comply with IT system operations, whereas only 42 per cent of comparable Japanese executives were willing to do so (Cole, 2006: 120).

Rapp (2002: 26) argues that, in the highest-performing firms both in Japan and the US, organizational adjustments flow from strategic decisions and improvement activities, not from IT deployment. That is, decisions are made for their own sake, rather than because of opportunities created by IT (Rapp, 2002: 26). But this is a rather formulaic and limited view of how and why changes do or do not occur in organizations. Surely *both* factors can, and should, be potential drivers of change; firms benefit from 'needs pull' adoption as well as 'technology push' adoption of new organizational practices. To rely on only one source limits the drivers of change and innovation. In earlier field research on a large, successful manufacturing firm, we found that Japanese managers often assumed their current organizational processes conferred competitive advantage to the firm. Specifically, these managers uncritically assumed that *all* current practices were conferring competitive advantage, rather than critically examining which did and which did not (Cole, 2006).

Consistent with the observations of Nezu cited above, managers are often unwilling to consider the possibility that some of the required process routines embedded in software applications could actually improve productivity. Decisions about whether to adopt software as is or to customize are often left to lower-level managers, many of whom have strong incentives to maintain the status quo and/or to optimize the local organization (*genba*) at the expense of the larger organization (Cole, 2006: 105–126). It seems quite possible that many US firms suffer from precisely the opposite affliction, namely, an uncritical assumption that new process routines required by new software must necessarily be best practices.

We can also examine the barriers to growth for the packaged software sector from the perspective of software developers. Research among JPSA members found that these barriers include the weakness of distribution networks (including the difficulty of selling directly to large end-user companies), the difficulty of developing markets, the difficulty of understanding and accommodating diverse user needs, the speed of technological changes, and the difficulty of establishing competitive pricing (JPSA, 2005: 29).

There appears to be insufficient incentive for larger firms in Japan to invest in the production of high-quality packaged software, judging by the modest R&D expenditures of those firms as a percentage of sales revenues (JPSA, 2005: 30). In discussing this matter, the JPSA notes that the investment of capital in software-related venture companies in Japan is one-fourteenth that of Europe and one-thirtieth that of the US (JPSA, 2007: 30). A reasonable explanation for this phenomenon can be found in the overwhelming bias of Japanese end-users for customized software and a further bias toward working with long-term partners rather than upstart newcomers. While the latter bias is far from absent in the US, it takes on even more power in Japan's vertically organized society (Rtischev and Cole, 2003). In understanding these outcomes, we must remember our earlier conclusion that the dominant Big Five software vendors have relatively little incentive to invest in uncertain new packaged software development when they have a secure revenue stream from customizing, integrating, maintaining, and upgrading services for their long-term corporate customers.

Conclusion

What is apparent from this discussion is that the concept of software as a product, or, more to the point, software as a *business*, is not very well developed in Japan relative to the size and strength of Japan's overall economy. To be sure, there are long-term trends indicating the growth of packaged software, and there are pockets of success, particularly in recent years, among producers of packaged software for small and medium-sized firms. But, for large firms, vertical markets and customized software continue to dominate. Given this dominance, we can say that enterprise software in Japan is primarily an infrastructure-support industry. While there are high costs associated with this approach, there are also many advantages – in particular, that solutions are precisely tailored to end-user needs. For software developers, however, these markets are low-return markets compared to the increasing returns that can be generated by successful semi-custom or packaged software firms. Large software firms have chosen instead a low-risk model, with low but predictable returns from the custom software business based on serial deals for maintenance, administration, and updates. These are 'gifts that keep on giving'.

What about the future? In a 2006 web survey of 1078 IT professionals at large firms concerning enterprise applications, some 61 per cent reported that they were currently developing software from scratch (fully customized), with only 19 per cent reporting the use of commercial off-the-shelf (COTS) packaged software; 54 per cent reported using semi-customized package software (multiple answers were allowed in this survey). When asked about future expectations, however, and with only a single response allowed, only 31 per cent of respondents expected to develop their own software from scratch in the future, and only 10 per cent reported that they expected to rely on packaged software. Instead 55 per cent expected to use a semi-customized packaged software solution as their primary solution. This might well point the way to the future (MIJS, 2007).

The current pressures for this new direction arise from firms trying to minimize the growth of their IT investments. Aggregate investment in IT has been relatively flat in recent years. Moving away from the costly approach of building software solutions from scratch can make a big contribution to holding down IT investment. Still another solution on the horizon is 'cloud computing', which, by potentially giving final users direct access to software stored on the Internet, could diminish the size of IT departments and the role of system integrators. The long-term growth of semi-customized packaged software solutions will depend on whether or not firms grow more willing to reevaluate the utility of their current business processes. The unwillingness of many managers to question current business processes – and their tendency instead to assume that all current practices confer competitive advantage – is a major obstacle to progress toward semi-customized packaged software solutions.

That said, despite the initial divergences between the US and Japanese software industries – which resulted primarily from the first-mover advantages enjoyed by the US at the birth of the software industry – various technological developments over the last 60 years have created strong pressure for convergence. Three of the most important of these developments were **(1)** the development of the IBM architecture; **(2)** the introduction of the Windows standard; and more recently, **(3)** the adoption of open architectures and open networks. The Japanese software industry's use of IBM as a model, however, later put that industry out of step with the evolution of a strong new product-oriented venture sector in the US – a sector comprised of firms targeting horizontal markets. Large Japanese system integration firms focused instead on providing services and products (modules) aimed at their narrow base of customers. Heavy customization, despite its high costs, gave large Japanese end-user firms exactly the functionality they desired. Moreover, powerful institutional forces in Japan led computer firms to adapt the IBM model – developing their own software – to the *keiretsu* system, thereby furthering divergence. Nonetheless, more recently, in a historic reversal that brings the US software industry closer to the Japanese model, US computer firms such as Hewlett Packard have greatly increased their focus on software and services; Hewlett Packard now calls itself the sixth-largest software company in the world. Conversely, Oracle has acquired Sun Microsystems, a hardware company. In short, and in accordance with the observations of Dosi and Kogut (1993), we see continued pressures for both divergence and convergence, and it is not always Japanese firms which are moving toward US practices.

Acknowledgments

We are indebted to Shinji Takai, Doshisha University, Hideyuki Yamagishi, Oracle, Japan, and Josh Greenbaum, Principal at Enterprise Applications Consulting, as well as to Gen Oyama and Kazuhiro Sekiguchi of Mitsubishi Research Institute, for their views and suggestions. We alone are responsible, however, for the analysis included in this chapter.

Notes

1. The term 'ideal type' is used here in the Weberian sense. An ideal type is based on the characteristics and elements of a given phenomenon, such as organizational structure, but is not meant to correspond to all characteristics of any one particular case. The term is not meant to refer to a perfected version of the phenomenon in question.
2. E-mail communication from Prof. Shinji Takai, Doshisha University, 3 September 2008.
3. E-mail communication from Josh Greenbaum, Enterprise Applications Consulting, 24 October 2008.
4. *Ibid.*
5. Interview with Gen Oyama and Kazuhiro Sekiguchi of Mitsubishi Research Institute conducted by Shinya Fushimi on 18 June 2008.
6. *Ibid.*

7. *Ibid.*
8. *Ibid.*

References

Baba, Y., Takai, S., and Mizuta, Y. (1996) 'The User-Driven Evolution of the Japanese Software Industry: The Case of Customized Software for Mainframes', in D. Mowery (ed.), *The International Computer Software Industry*, New York: Oxford University Press.

Cole, R. (2006) 'Software's Hidden Challenges', in D. H. Whittaker and R. E. Cole (eds), *Recovering From Success: Innovation and Technology Management in Japan*, New York: Oxford University Press.

Cole, R. and Matsumiya, T. (2006) 'Capturing Value from Technology and Challenges to Past Successes: The Case of NTT DATA', *ITEC Working Paper Series* 06–01 (March): 1–39.

Cusumano, M. (1991) *Japan's Software Factories*, New York: Oxford University Press.

Cusumano, M., MacCormack, A., Kemerer, C. F., and Crandall, W. (2003) 'Software Development Worldwide: The State of the Practice', *IEEE Software*, 20(6): 28–34.

Dore, R. (1987) *Taking Japan Seriously*, Stanford: Stanford University Press.

Dosi, G. and Kogut, B. (1993) 'National Specificities and the Context of Change: The Coevolution of Organization and Technology', in B. Kogut (ed.), *Country Competitiveness*, New York: Oxford University Press.

Fransman, M. (1995) *Japan's Computer and Communications Industry*, New York: Oxford University Press.

Ferguson, C. and Morris, C. (1993) Computer Wars, New York: Times Books.

Hamilton, D. (1993) 'U.S. Companies Rush in to Fill Japanese Software Void', *Wall Street Journal*, (7 May: B4).

JISA (2008) *IT Services Industry in Japan, 2006*, Tokyo: Japan Information Technology Service Industry Association.

JPSA (2007) '*Heisei 16 nendo pakkeeji sofutowea shijou kakudai kenkyūkai katsudou houkokusho*' (Package Software Market Expansion Research Forum Activity: Fiscal Year 2004 Report), Tokyo: Japan Personal Computer Software Association.

Karlsson, S. (2008) *DATAQUEST INSIGHT: Top 10 Consulting and System Integration Providers, Market Share in Computing, Worldwide, 2007*, Stanford: Gartner.

Kokuryo, J. (1997) 'Information Technologies and the Transformation of Japanese Industry', Paper presented at the Pacific-Asia Conference on Information Systems in Brisbane: 1–15.

Langois, R. and Mowery, D. (1996) 'The Federal Government Role in the Development of the U.S. Software Industry', in D. Mowery (ed.), *The International Computer Software Industry*, New York: Oxford University Press.

Lincoln, J. and Gerlach, M. (2004) *Japan's Network Economy*, Cambridge: Cambridge University Press.

Lorenzo, O., Kawalek, P., and Ramdani, B. (2009) 'The Long Conversation: Learning How to Master Enterprise Systems', *California Management Review*, 52 (Fall): 166.

Mansfield, E. (1988) 'Industrial R&D in Japan and the United States: A Comparative Study', *American Economic Review Papers and Proceedings*, 78 (May): 223–228.

METI (2007a) *2006 Survey on Selected Service Industries*, http://www.meti.go.jp/english/statistics/tyo/tokusabizi/index.html.

METI (2007b) *2006 heisei 18 nen tokutei saabisu sangyou jtttai chousa* (Survey on the Status of Specific Service Industry), Tokyo: The Ministry of Economy, Trade and Industry.

MIJS (2007) MIJS Research Report: Questionnaire Concerning Enterprise Applications, Tokyo: Made in Japan Software Consortium.

Ministry of International Affairs and Communications (2003) *Kigyou keiei ni okeru IT katsuyou chousa* (Survey on Practical Use of IT in Company Management), Tokyo: The Ministry of International Affairs and Communications.

Nezu, R. (2002) 'Perspectives and Strategies for Japanese Industry', paper presented at the Conference on Prospects for Core Industries in Japan and Germany, Berlin: Fujitsu Research Institute and German Institute for Economic Research.

OECD (2002) *OECD Information Technology Outlook*, Paris: Organisation for Economic Co-operation and Development.

Rapp, W. (2002) *Information Technology Strategies*, New York: Oxford University Press.

Rtischev, D. and Cole, R. E. (2003) 'Social and Structural Barriers to the IT Revolution in High-Tech Industries', in J. Bachnik (ed.), *Roadblocks on the Information Highway*, New York: Lexington Books.

Shapiro, C. and Varian, H. (1999) *Information Rules*, Boston: Harvard Business School Press.

Steinmueller, W. E. (1996) 'The U.S. Software Industry: An Analysis and Interpretive History', in D. Mowery (ed.), *The International Computer Software Industry*, New York: Oxford University Press.

Torto, S. (2006) *Worldwide Systems Integration 2005 Vendor Shares: Top 10 Vendors and Industry for 2005*, Stanford: Gartner.

4
The Evolution of Japan's Human-Resource Management

Mitsuo Ishida and Atsushi Sato

Introduction

In the face of head-on global competition, how did Japan's human-resource management evolve through a 'lost decade' to arrive at its current state? If we compare Japanese human-resource management systems today to the practices that were common at Japan's zenith in the 1980s, what do we find has changed?

To answer this question, we have conducted three investigations: (1) a comparative study of personnel and wage system reforms in the US and Japan; (2) a comparative study of the US and Japanese automotive industries; and (3) a study of the electronics industry.[1]

In this chapter, we begin in the second section with a discussion of personnel and wage system reforms in Japan, based on the first of our three studies. In the third section we discuss some of the conclusions of our study of the electronics industry. The furious pace of technological innovation, and the intensity of global competition, have conspired to bring about major changes in management structure and human-resource management in this industry, and this makes it an ideal setting for the investigations of this chapter. Finally, in the fourth section, we use the results of the analyses of the second and third sections to anticipate future themes in organizational operation and personnel management for Japanese companies.

The status overall: The evolution of personnel systems

Overview

We looked at changes in the personnel and wage systems for union-level employees at nine large representative Japanese firms. From the decade of the 1990s to the decade of the 2000s, personnel system reforms in Japanese companies were inspired by the concept of 'pay-for-performance', an umbrella term encompassing a range of personnel management techniques that emphasize work results over personal ability. Because these pay-for-performance systems evolved simultaneously with various restructurings of each company's business model, there is today no one unique system, but rather a broad range of different systems; nonetheless, if we look at the systems that lie near the center of this range, we find some striking differences with the personnel systems that were standard in the 1980s. We may summarize these differences in four main points:

1. The key concept: a shift in emphasis from ability to get the job done to roles.
2. Employee classifications: A shift from aptitude-based classifications to role-based classifications.
3. Base pay: A shift from age-based seniority pay plus aptitude pay to role-based pay.
4. Personnel evaluations: a shift from ability evaluations, attitude evaluations, and performance evaluations to competency evaluations and performance evaluations.

A critical backdrop underlying these shifts has been a larger paradigm shift from thinking of personnel in *organizational* terms to thinking of personnel in *market-based* terms. Another way to phrase this is to say that, in the last two decades, a certain logical progression has clearly emerged: from markets, to management strategies, to organizational restructuring, to performance management, and finally to personnel and wage management. This new way of thinking led firms to emphasize the notion of employees' *roles* as a means of reconciling the demands of performance management with personnel and wage management systems. The concept of role-based employee classifications, supported by a two-pillar structure of performance evaluations and competency evaluations, allowed firms to translate pricing information – as communicated by the market – into administrative rules within their organizations. It is difficult to overstate the magnitude of this transformation.

The limitations of Japan's system – and how they were overcome

But what provoked such a wholesale transformation? Inasmuch as Japan's personnel system had clearly been highly successful in the 1980s, a critical priority is to identify the inherent factors lurking within the system that led eventually to its revamping. International competition was clearly one driving factor, but there must have been other factors intrinsic to the Japanese system itself. What were these factors? What elements of Japan's personnel systems were deemed by the reformers to enhance Japanese competitiveness – and which elements were seen as hindrances?

The first straitjacket from which Japan's personnel systems needed to escape was the historical dominance of the seniority-based pay system. This paradigm was so firmly entrenched in Japan that, even when the concept of *meritocratic management* (*nouryoku shugi*) infiltrated Japan's large firms in the 1980s, it did so only under the universal assumption that the rules governing the age-versus-pay curve would remain firmly intact, including aptitude-based classifications, operational rules for promotions, the continued existence of age-based pay, operational rules for aptitude-based pay raises, and even personnel appraisals. Ultimately, the net impact of the meritocratic management concept was merely to introduce employee-by-employee gaps in the average age-versus-pay curves, with the magnitudes of the gaps determined by employee merit. But the underlying hypothesis – that age and merit were inextricably linked – remained unchanged. The nature of this seniority-based pay orthodoxy was not something that could be easily changed simply by a little wage engineering. Moreover, maintaining an age-based pay system in a rapidly aging society like Japan would inevitably lead to an unavoidable rise in overall labor costs.

It is no exaggeration to say that the reforms that led to today's pay-for-performance ideas represented as thorough a dismantling as was possible of the seniority-based pay regime. Employee classifications based on aptitude were consolidated into less-granular categories and eventually shifted toward role-based classifications. At the same time, base-pay calculations were revised to eliminate age-based pay and to deemphasize aptitude-based pay in favor of role-based pay. This shift toward a role-based scheme for calculating base pay proceeded in one of two different ways: (1) fixed salary amounts for each role classification, or (2) pay raises based both on zones and on personnel evaluations (the same as the US green card effect).

Underlying these reforms was a fundamental shift in corporate philosophy: the realization that corporations simply could not survive without instituting *market-driven* personnel systems in place of organization-driven personnel systems. The key concepts involved in translating market pricing information into governing rules for an organization were, first, the idea that an organization's performance must be rigorously grounded in a PDCA framework (the abbreviation is for **Plan, Do,** Check, Act) linking goals to actual results, and, second, that the contribution of each employee to the organization's perform-ance must be systematically measured to gauge that employee's role.

What do the US and Japan have in common?

To emphasize the unique features of this transformation in Japan's per-sonnel system, let us now consider some ways in which the US and Japan are similar – and some ways in which they differ.

If the seniority-based pay guidelines had been a straitjacket on Japanese organizations, the opposite problem – an obsessive concern with the whim and caprice of the market – was no less a hindrance to US firms. At the same time that Japan needed reforms to bring the oper-ating principles of its organizations closer in line with the market, US organizations needed to declare greater independence from the market. The reforms that evolved in each case would eventually draw the two countries closer together.

The first point of commonality between the US and Japan was that, in both cases, the crux of the reforms was a repositioning of personnel and wages, closely linked with department-by-department performance management, at the center of corporate governance philosophy.

Consider Figure 4.1. In Japan – for regular employees, if not for non-regular employees – 'moving closer to the market' certainly did not mean getting closer to the *labor* market, but instead meant moving closer to the markets for products and raw materials, as well as to the capital and financial markets. By taking the results of corporate activity in these markets – such as sales volume, profits, and stock prices – as measures of corporate performance, Japan designed a style of organizational governance that was highly sensitive to the product and raw-materials markets, as well as to the capital and financial markets. This then led to an intimate relationship between organizational restructurings and the top-to-bottom management of each department's performance. Moreover, with management principles grounded in the belief that a well-oiled PDCA cycle for regulating each department's performance would be reflected in sales volume, profits, and stock price, it was only logical to base each individual employee's compensation on the extent to which that employee contributed to the attainment of departmental objectives. With an employee's contribution decomposed schematically as *contribution = performance × role*, it became commonly recognized that the proper way to formulate a new personnel model was to base it on a

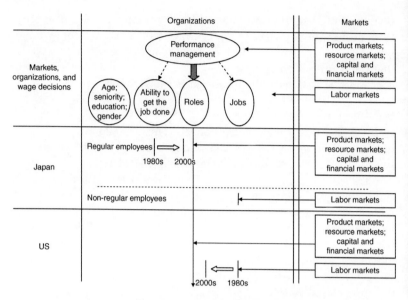

Figure 4.1 Markets, organizations, and wage decisions in Japan and the US

hierarchy of roles. The role became the central organizing principle for a system of personnel and wage management.

On the other hand, in the US, when organizations declared their independence from the market, the impact on the personnel and wage management system would be to establish the greatest possible distance from the labor market – but this was just the *outcome*. The *impetus* for the reforms, as in Japan, came from the attempt to design human-resource management models to support and enhance the performance management systems needed to cooperate with the market. As a result, the reforms proceeded in ways that led away from human-resource management based on job descriptions – away, in other words, from market-based wage determinations. The central feature of the reforms was a style of performance management that emphasized high degrees of sensitivity and responsiveness to the product markets and to the capital and financial markets. Thus, organizations established their independence through a somewhat convoluted process that ensured the preservation of a certain distance from the labor market.

In short, the striking feature of corporate governance in both Japan and in the US was that firms focused on designing performance management systems with high sensitivity and responsiveness to the movement of markets, and then developed rules for applying resources (people, money, and things) in ways that followed naturally from these systems. The two key principles of human-resource management systems that operate in harmony with, and contribute to, performance management systems are *roles* and *performance*. The introduction of a new organizational order, in which base pay would be determined by classifying (grouping) employees according to their *roles*, would be the common unifying feature of the new system designs. The gravity of these performance management systems would shift the focus of human-resource management from ability to get the job done to roles in Japan, and from job descriptions to roles in the US.

A second point of commonality between the US and Japan was the similarity between the systems that evolved in the two cases. First, in Japan, role-based employee classifications became dominant. In the US, job-description-based classifications were consolidated into less-granular categories, and systems moved to the left in Figure 4.1 – that is, away from job-description-based classifications. Next, in Japan, it became common for raises in base pay to be determined both by personnel evaluations and by zone. Meanwhile, in the US, the traditional LR (location in range = green card effect) system, together with pay raises based on personnel evaluations, remained in effect. Thus, the Japanese and US systems for handling pay raises became one and the same, at least in appearance. Finally, in Japan, the formula for personnel evaluations changed from 'ability evaluations + attitude evaluations + performance evaluations' to 'competency evaluations + performance evaluations'. In the US, the traditional formula had been based largely on performance evaluations, but this formula changed to 'performance evaluations + competency evaluations'.

Where do the US and Japan differ?

Despite these similarities, the reform processes in Japan and in the US differed in some key ways. The differences lay in the nature of the societal tensions that arose in the process of moving in the directions discussed above. To put it briefly, the different historical restrictions inherent in the two countries' personnel management systems ensured that the process of converging toward the optimal systems demanded by corporations engendered different societal tensions – tensions which reflect, in each case, the unique characteristics of the two societies.

Japan

The reform process in Japan triggered an evolution in the criteria for determining the treatment of employees in organizations from 'age, work history, gender, and education', to 'ability to get the job done', and finally to 'role', and the societal tensions that arose were simply those attendant on the process of effectively destroying the age-based treatment system that had been in place for many years. On one side of the equation, Japan saw the establishment of more precise methods of managing organizational performance – methods which reflected the market's evaluation of corporate performance – and the implementation of employee-treatment systems, based on *role* classifications, that such methods required. On the other side of the equation, the process was met with emotional voices of societal opposition, asking questions grounded in lifestyle and labor experiences: 'But can people live on that?' 'Can people have children and raise families on that?' 'Are these wages enough to support the development of technical skills?' 'Will corporate loyalty and motivation be preserved?' The tension arose in balancing the two sides of the equation. But societal forces were already in motion that would eventually tend to mitigate these tensions: a rise in the average number of employed persons per household, increasing opportunities for women in the labor force, and an evolution of the corresponding norms and conceptions of social justice.

But even more important than these factors was the fact that the tensions that arose were, above all, tensions *within* organizations – or, to put it more bluntly, tensions between two competing viewpoints within the minds of individual employees themselves, employees at each level of organizational hierarchy responding to issues arising within their level. Here there was room within the organization to talk things through to resolution. Because these resolutions were achieved by discussion, they were arrived at internally, within the organization, without falling prey to external destabilizing factors. For this reason, it was only natural that the ensuing system redesign process would proceed in a comprehensive and sophisticated manner. This point presents a striking contrast to what happened in the US; it would be difficult to overstate the magnitude of the distinction between the US 'chaotic' process and Japan's 'neat and orderly' process for achieving reforms.

Another tension that existed in Japan was that between regular employees and nonregular employees. Although we will not discuss it in detail in this chapter, the treatment of employees who are employed directly but are not covered under standard employment rules (part-time workers, fixed-term contractual employees, and so on) is fundamentally governed by prevailing market wages, according to a system in which pay is determined by job description. Similarly, employees of temporary staffing firms are paid an amount specified in the contract drawn up between the staffing agency and its client company, minus administrative fees and other deductions taken out by the staffing agency. Moreover, the amount specified in the contract is determined in accordance with prevailing market wages for the type of work in question. The widening disparity between the *role*-based pay structure for regular employees and the job-description-based prevailing wage system for other employees has been criticized as a source of inequality, and calls have been made for a 'same work, same wage' system to resolve the inequities. The real tensions in Japan's personnel and wage management systems arise from this fundamental distinction in the treatment of regular employees and nonregular employees. Although we will not discuss the point in detail, to allow the role-based treatment system for regular employees to slide down the slippery slope toward a prevailing market wage system, and certainly to allow the system to slide so far down that slope that it becomes a job-description-based system, would be to undermine a key factor in Japan's international competitiveness. Instead, the key line of attack should be to move in the opposite direction: to move nonregular employees further in the direction of organizational principles, by internalizing nonregular employees – or, more specifically, by establishing role-based classification systems for nonregular employees and by codifying and expanding the routes by which nonregular employees can become regular employees. Governmental and policy leadership on this issue will be essential in the future.

The US

Reforms in the US took the form of organizations standing up to, and declaring independence from, the market, and therein lay the seed of the ensuing tensions. A personnel and wage management system that makes it easy for an organization to reflect prevailing market wages for each job description is a job-description-based-classification system with job-description-based pay, but the compensation system that results from such a structure is not conducive to extracting the maximum benefit possible from an organization's human resources. This fact was both the motivation for the reforms and the cause of the problems that resulted.

The reforms consisted of a shift in the criteria for determining employee treatment from *job description* to *role* and *ability to get the job done*, but underlying the very notion of a *job description* lies the full complexity of the market. For this reason, these reforms could not have been set in place simply by discussions and innovations occurring within organizations. Employee classification settings and wage systems based on *roles* and on *ability to get the job done* contain intrinsically within them the ineradicable devil of prevailing market wages for each job description. Because the system contains within it the unruly devil that is the market, it cannot help being *chaotic*. But this *chaos* was the very strategy that historically underpinned the innovations used to incorporate prevailing market wages back into employee classification and wage systems based on roles and ability to get the job done. These innovations, in turn, represented the large amount of discretionary authority granted to department managers, and their result was the disorderly, unsystematic nature of the structures to which they gave rise.

In short, despite the reputation the US enjoys as the birthplace of human-resource management – or, indeed, perhaps because of that very fact – the lower-class status and weakened authority of personnel departments in US companies, especially as compared to the juggernauts that are the financial and accounting departments, is astonishing. This speaks not to any lack of effort on the part of those personnel departments, but to fundamental structural problems in US capitalism.

The foregoing discussion of similarities and differences between the US and Japan is summarized in Table 4.1.

Table 4.1   A comparison of personnel system reforms in Japan and in the US

	Drawback of existing system	Impetus for change (point of commonality)	Features of reformed system (point of commonality)	Societal tensions (point of contrast)
Japan	Age-based seniority	Performance management	• Role-based employee classifications • Pay raises based both on zones and on personnel evaluations • Competency evaluations and performance evaluations	• Regular employees enjoy the benefits of a comprehensive system, while • All other employees are subject to the vagaries of prevailing market wages
US	Disorder and chaos of the market	Performance management	• Toward classifications based on factors other than job descriptions • Pay raises based on LR and on personnel evaluations • Performance evaluations and competency evaluations	• Large discretionary authority granted to department managers • A wide range of disparate systems; no structural uniformity • Absence of human-resource management in the union sector

Results of a study of the electronics industry

The electronics industry boasts a rapid pace of technical evolution and exhibits perhaps the most exacting global competition of any industry. How have management organizations and human-resource management models evolved in this industry? In this section, we will summarize the results of a case study conducted on a company in the electronics industry, with the goal of illuminating the logical progression from markets, to management strategies, to organizational restructuring, to performance management, and finally to personnel and wage management.

Organizational structures, performance management, and personnel management

Figure 4.2 presents a simple graphical depiction of the organizational structure, the performance management model, and the personnel management model we found at the electronics firm on which we conducted a case study; the discussion below is based on this schematic diagram. Let us begin at the organizational structure level. Here we see the following mindset at work.[2] In a competitive environment, it is best to divide up an organization into units of a certain size and to manage profits at the level of each individual unit, and in order to do this it is best to devolve authority to the level of each individual unit. Here a 'unit' refers either to a collection of business units (BUs) or a collection of geographical regions, either domestic or overseas, that are organized into a conglomeration of subsidiaries or affiliates for the purposes of profit management. In the case of globalization or global management, the choice of these units as the basic managerial elements may be thought of as a technique for emphasizing the company's push to grow its businesses more overseas than domestically. However, because each unit is a part of the overall corporate structure, an organization chart would show the units lying below corporate headquarters and below the overall corporate level.

Top-level corporate management grants the BU managers – who are the leaders of the units – the privilege, and the responsibility, of distributing management resources at the unit level as they see fit. However, what is critical is that the units themselves are composed of a number of performance-management strata and even smaller subunits, which function almost as mini-companies themselves. For example, it is common for the head of a working team to be referred to by underlings as '*shacho*' ('company president'), even though of

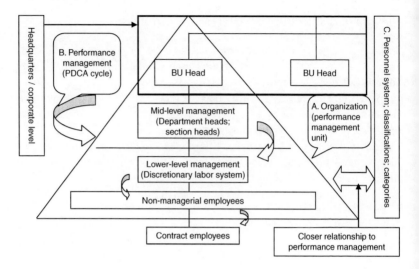

Figure 4.2 A schematic depiction of the interrelation among organizational structure, performance management, and personnel management
Source: Sato (2007: 223).

course the actual company president works in an entirely different office in an entirely different building. Similarly, the existence of various managerial levels, such as BU manager, department manager, section manager, and subsection manager (for employees within the discretionary labor[3] system) may be thought of as an example of hierarchical performance-management strata. In this way, subunits and performance-management strata are gathered together to form larger units, and the work done by employees is managed at the level of each unit.

Thus, let us next consider the performance-management level. In a competitive environment, it is critical to be able to run rapidly through the PDCA cycle, and financial milestones tend to be the most strongly emphasized of all performance-management milestones. The PDCA cycle refers to a process in which a plan is established, its progress is monitored, and assessments are performed at fixed intervals before moving on to the next activity. To be able to churn through this cycle without getting bogged down in delays, critical managerial milestones must be identified. The objective is then simply to attain these milestones, and if this objective is not realized then the milestones themselves are used as clues in identifying the causes of the failure and in determining appropriate remedial measures. To give just one example, in a certain product business unit's headquarters, sales and profits are taken to be the critical milestones, and progress toward realizing these milestones is assessed by establishing milestones for manufacturing, retail, and inventory. These milestones are set separately, each month, for each geographical region, and for each product model.

The importance of managing this PDCA cycle has remained unchanged for many years. However, some important recent modifications must not be overlooked. Examples include (i) a reduced time interval for the progress-management cycle and (ii) emphasis on the attainment of financial milestones as barometers of performance management methods. The former of these was implemented by increasing the frequency of productivity management and by designing a Supply Chain Management (SCM) production system.

On the other hand, the latter is reflected in an increasing tendency in the field of factory-level productivity management to emphasize revenue per yen invested and revenue per yen spent on labor costs in addition to revenue per man-hour worked.

When it comes to achieving a company's critical objectives, there is nothing more important than respecting these managerial milestones. The global competitive environment and the entrenchment of uncertainty make this more difficult. Consequently, any changes made to these managerial milestones will force corresponding modifications in several related managerial areas. Human-resource management and workforce management are certainly no exceptions.

Thus, let us turn next to a consideration of personnel management.

At the human-resource management level, the following mindset emerges. (i) In a competitive environment, rather than making top-level decisions that apply uniformly across an entire company, the most desirable incentive structure is achieved by entrusting personnel matters to individual lines or departments, and then adopting a salary distribution in which pay is linked to the performance of each unit. (ii) To restrain personnel costs and respond rapidly to changing production volumes, it is best to reduce employment of regular employees, and to make up the difference with nonregular employees or indirect hiring.

Let us begin with item (ii). To investigate the logic of indirect hiring, we examined the case of a certain product business unit headquarters. According to our study, the number of workers would be calculated according to the logic 'number of products to produce → quantity of assembly work to be done → number of days operational → average number of hours × number of employees', and the resulting number of workers would be imposed on the factory from the business unit headquarters. However, the need to reduce the total operating budget had begun to sink in, and consequently the number of regular employees could not be increased. The difference was made up by contract employees. The backdrop for this decision was the shifting landscape of managerial milestones, in which traditional considerations of revenue per man-hour worked were being augmented by additional considerations: revenue per yen invested and revenue per yen spent on labor costs (which could be improved by reducing the labor cost for each day worked). Other factors included the shortening of the progress management interval, as reflected in the introduction of the SCM production system, and the reclassification of labor costs as variable costs instead of fixed costs.

On the other hand, item (i) was primarily a change in the personnel and wage management practices for regular employees. First, the criteria for personnel evaluations shifted from an employee's personal characteristics, such as age or number of years worked, to the *role* that the employee played. This was exemplified by the creation of employee classifications, such as 'creative' and 'meister', tied to future potential for growth. Second, role-based evaluation criteria also came to the forefront of the compensation system, and a system for calculating raises based both on zones and on personnel evaluations was introduced. In this system, upper limits were established for the range of pay deemed appropriate for each role; employees whose base pay within the range was high, but whose personnel evaluation was poor, would receive zero raise, whereas employees whose base pay was low but whose personnel evaluation was strong would receive large raises. Third, for managerial employees, a new system for calculating bonus payouts took effect, in which the strength or weakness of the business performance of the department in which a manager worked would be taken into account in addition to the job performance of the manager himself. In addition to this, a 'discretionary labor' system was instituted for measuring the amount of time worked by managerial employees; in this system, the relevant quantity was not the number of hours the employee spent at work, but instead the results that the employee's work produced.

In this way, a new, role-based framework for personnel and wage management took hold, and each unit's business performance came to be reflected in employee compensation; the personnel and wage management system thus became more inextricably linked with performance management and ultimately with the organization itself.

The relationship between performance management and personnel management

To summarize the conclusions of the previous section, in an era of increasing uncertainty the company chose to proceed in the following directions. (i) Divide the organization up into profit-management units. (ii) Within the performance management decision-making process at the unit level, place more emphasis on financial milestones and accelerate the PDCA cycle turnaround. (iii) As a human-resource management technique, introduce a compensation system in which unit-level performance, and employee roles within the unit, are reflected. The overall picture is captured in summary by these general trends.

Further trends that surfaced within this management model include *profit- and cash flow-based business performance management* and a *decentralized, business unit-by-business unit, self-reliant managerial model, including overseas divisions.* Within the personnel management sphere, the logical progression was[4] *identification of profit-management units → performance management (the PDCA cycle) → pay-for-performance personnel management and indirect hiring.*

The point we would like to emphasize is that these trends once again illustrate the underlying theme of this chapter, namely, the relationship between performance management and personnel management. On the one hand, personnel decisions were increasingly devolved to individual departments and lines; on the other hand, discretion over inputs (such as personnel costs and workforce strength) remained low. Given these circumstances, how did line managers – who were expected to deliver improved performance (in sales and profits) – make personnel management decisions?

The situations we observed suggest that performance management is an extremely high priority for line managers. Meanwhile, we received the strong impression that the operating commandment seemed to be 'whatever you do, just don't hire any more regular employees'. Any workforce shortages were to be remedied by nonregular employees or indirect employment. Moreover, these indirect employment decisions seemed to be governed not so much by any explicit workforce–management logic as by the logic of dollar-for-dollar productivity management (revenue per yen invested). With little discretionary input on workforce-strength decisions, line managers came to demand from their underlings a level of commitment and ability that effectively raised expectations for each employee by one rank. Thus, what had traditionally been expected of department managers and section managers was now expected of assistant managers, what had traditionally been expected of subsection managers was now expected of ordinary employees, and – to take it one step further – what had previously been expected of ordinary employees was now expected of contract employees and their leaders. In one instance, ordinary employees were expected to exhibit leadership skills such as managerial abilities and the ability to negotiate with leaders at contract staffing agencies (the tendency, noted above, to refer to team leaders as '*shacho*' is of particular symbolic importance here).

Issues facing Japanese companies

In this final section we would like to anticipate some practical issues facing Japanese companies as the relationship between performance management and personnel management deepens in the coming months and years.

First, as we consider the linear chain of responsibility from business unit head, to manager, and then to assistant manager, an important practical question that must be reassessed is how, and to which levels, to delegate discretionary authority regarding hiring and other personnel matters. As far as line managers are concerned, with increased emphasis on performance management results should come correspondingly increased discretion to make personnel decisions. An intensified push for performance management that nonetheless deprives managers of discretionary input on human-resource decisions may lead to short-term profits, but cannot be a basis for long-term sustained growth. It is no overstatement to say that the fate of the electronics industry depends on improved product development capabilities and the personnel development efforts that enable those capabilities, all the more so in view of the need for 'back-to-back strings of innovative products'[5] and 'the design of a new profit model that does not insist on vertical integration',[6] in the words of executives at representative Japanese electronics manufacturers. In that sense, we must both increase the amount of discretionary input that line managers have on human-resource decisions and heighten the priority afforded to personnel development as a criterion in their personnel evaluations.

A second point is the importance of attempts to reclaim, on the employee side, the shift in personnel management to the demand side. A wave of environmental changes has provided the impetus for further movement toward a strict unit-by-unit profit management structure. On the other hand, from the supply side, a countervailing wave is approaching – namely, the diversification in employee needs. In places where these two waves collide, three practical and/or policy issues are likely to arise: (i) personnel development, (ii) work–life balance, and (iii) retention of talented employees amid increasing trends toward indirect employment. In view of the tendency, discussed in the second section above, for expectations of employees to creep up one full rank, item (i) will require measures to encourage human-resource development in the context of long-term career planning, item (ii) will require measures to provide environments conducive to the coexistence of work and life,[7] and item (iii) will require measures to encourage indirect employment to be converted into direct employment.

Conclusions

As we saw in the previous section, the challenges facing Japanese companies include (1) how to foster human-resource development in an era of performance management and pay-for-performance; (2) how to foster work–life balance, and avoid overwork and burnout, for regular employees; and (3) how to mitigate the gaps in treatment that arise from the increasing prevalence of part-time, short-term, contractual, and indirect hiring.

US and European observers of Japan's employment system (see, for example, Hall and Soskice, 2001) have emphasized Japan's 'coordinated market economy', in contrast to the 'liberal market economy' found in the Anglo-Saxon countries. However, in contrast to the 'consensus' model found in European countries, in the case of Japan, wage decisions are decentralized and made separately by each company; moreover, individualization based on across-the-board personnel evaluations has taken hold to a striking degree. As we saw in our electronics industry case study, the trends toward decentralization and individualization have been tremendously accelerated by organizational reforms and by personnel system reforms based on a pay-for-performance model. Researchers are questioning how, in this Far Eastern country, to design 'fair' work rules based on 'consent'. Do such rules even exist – and is there any practical path toward constructing them?

As is appropriate for a discussion of contrasts with the 'consensus' model, on this point corporate society has been vocal in stressing the importance of *communication*. However, whether we are talking about communication between supervisor and underling, or about communication between different departments, all this communication will amount to little more than shouts into the wind without some kind of systematization and concrete progress toward the establishment of new work rules. The question of how to bind together a cooperative structure at a time of extreme decentralization and individualization will surely draw upon both the wisdom of labor unions and the legislative policy stances of government leaders.

Notes

1. The final conclusions of our comparative study of US and Japanese personnel and wage system reforms may be found in Ishida and Higuchi (2009). The second section of this chapter is a significantly revised version of the final chapter of Ishida and Higuchi (2009). For further details on our comparative study of the US and Japanese automobile industries, we refer the reader to Ishida and Shinohara (2010).

2. The notions of 'managing profits at the level of individual units' and 'devolving authority to the level of individual units' themselves require rigorous definitions, but here we will understand the former to refer to an reference structure in which profits are managed at the levels of business units and domains, while the latter emphasizes the intention of the company to move from a hierarchical organizational model, segregated into strata and optimized for efficient handling of familiar routines in a stable market environment, to a flatter, more decentralized organizational model capable of responding rapidly to changing market needs. Note that a number of recent studies have presented examples of the consolidation of organizations into less-granular categories and of responsible governance (Tsuru *et al.*, 2004: 20–23) and of 'the entrenchment of decentralized responsible governance and the simultaneous evolution of corporate, group, and conglomerate governance' (Inagami *et al.*, 2000: 68) so it is not correct merely to emphasize the devolution of authority to the individual unit level. In any event, there are situations in which the units appropriate for profit management do not coincide with the units appropriate for the efficient functioning of the organization, and we leave the question of how to choose appropriate units as an open research question.

3. 'Discretionary labor' refers to jobs in which the employee's performance is not measured in terms of numbers of hours worked, and in which there is no concept of overtime.

4. Inagami and Whittaker (2005) evaluate three types of reforms instituted at Japanese electronics giant Hitachi – namely, organizational reforms, personnel reforms, and business process reforms – and ask 'to what extent do these reforms convert the corporate culture to a market-centric mindset?' The crux of the reforms was a series of measures designed to leave the firm better positioned to meet the needs of a diversified, globalized marketplace: (i) the enactment of an accelerated decision-making process and a flattening of the organizational hierarchy designed to achieve it; (ii) the creation of 'new virtual companies' that act, from a responsible-governance standpoint, as miniature corporations within the larger corporate framework of the Hitachi group (a transformation that has been likened to 'turning battleships into speedboats'); and (iii) a reorientation of the business process to promote an evolution 'from a manufacturing company to a company that provides solutions'. Reforms to the personnel system were commensurate with this sequence of innovations, and sought to advance the diversification of the workforce while simultaneously remaining grounded in the goal of maximally applying the talents of creative employees (a high-road strategy)

capable of contributing to an increase in intangible corporate assets (Hitachi value). Above all, the goal of applying the talents of creative workers was pursued through a series of systematic reforms: a qualification structure that emphasized clearly demonstrated talents and performance, a wage system that sought to revise seniority-based or age-based pay curves, and a new work system that enabled discretionary labor systems and other flexible means of managing working hours (Inagami and Whittaker, 2005: 140–145).

5. Kunio Nakamura, President of Matsushita Electric Industrial (quoted in Nikkei BP (2005)).
6. Tamotsu Nomakuchi, President of Mitsubishi Electric Corporation (quoted in Nikkei BP (2005)).
7. The history of meager past efforts to introduce work–life balance as a conceptual foundation for corporate policy, the increasingly rigorous work-management system, and the tendency for employees to be expected to perform at levels roughly equivalent to one job title greater than their actual positions – surely these three phenomena are not entirely disconnected from one another. When the fundamentals of the working environment become less and less favorable to employees (for example, as working hours grow longer), the addition of fringe benefits such as a parental-leave system will do little to assuage the concerns of employees that 'the system doesn't work for me, or is too hard to use'. For this reason, measures to improve the fundamentals, including 'rethinking the establishment of milestones' and 'thinking about how work management should work', will surely be an important part of labor–management relations in the future (Sato, 2007).

References

Hall, P. A. and Soskice, D. (2001) *Varieties of Capitalism: The Institutional Foundations of Comparative Advantages*, Oxford: Oxford University Press.
Inagami, T. and Research Institute for Advancement of Living Standards (eds) (2000) *Gendai nihon no cooporeeto gabanansu* (Corporate Governance in Modern Japan), Tokyo: Toyo Keizai.
Inagami, T. and Whittaker, D. H. (2005) *The New Community Firm: Governance and Management Reform in Japan*, Cambridge: Cambridge University Press.
Ishida, M. and Higuchi, J. (2009) *Jinji seido no nichibei hikaku – seika shugi to amerika no genjitsu* (A Comparison of Personnel Systems in the US and Japan – Pay-for-Performance and the Reality of the US), Kyoto: Minerva Publishing.
Ishida, M. and Shinohara, K. (2010) *GM no keiken – nihon e no kyoukun* (The GM Experience: Lessons for Japan), Tokyo: Chuo Keizai.
Nikkei BP (2005) *'Tokushuu: denki no seto giwa'* (Special Issue: Electronics on the Brink), *Nikkei Bijinesu* 21 November 2005: 30–31.
Sato, A. (2006) *'Ima roudou kumiai ni motomerareru monowa'* (What is Required from Labor Unions Now), *Denki Souken Ripooto* May (314): 2–5.
Sato, A. (ed.) (2007) *Gyouseki kanri no henyou to jinji kanri* (Personnel Management and the Transformation of Performance Management), Kyoto: Minerva Publishing.
Tsuru, T. and JEIU (Japanese Electrical and Electronic Information Union) Research Center (eds) (2004) *Sentaku to shuuchuu* (Selection and Focus), Tokyo: Yuhikaku.

5
Have Japanese Engineers Changed?

Yoshifumi Nakata and Satoru Miyazaki

Introduction

In recent years, Japan's status as a nation of abundance, and the comfortable lifestyle of the average Japanese person, have grown ever more dependent on the innovations coming out of Japan's R&D infrastructure – and thus ultimately on Japan's engineers. But the environment in which Japanese companies conduct R&D – and thus the natural operating habitat of the Japanese engineer – has deteriorated in recent years.

A first concern is that engineers are increasingly unable to keep up with the pace of technological advancement and transformation. To respond to the rapid pace of technological change, engineers need to improve their technical skills on a daily basis. Broadly speaking, there are two ways in which engineers develop technical skills: organizational education and training, conducted by companies, and personal development, which engineers do on their own. The long-running poor performance of Japanese companies has left little budgetary leeway for the former. Moreover, a gradual shift in the burden of labor from full employees toward part-time and other non-full employees has strengthened the argument that education and training should not be the responsibility of companies, but should be left to individual workers. Meanwhile, poor corporate performance and the increasing prevalence of non-full employees have saddled full-time engineering employees with additional burdens, including overseeing the work of part-time and contract engineers. Faced with increasing workloads and longer working hours, full-time engineering employees have less time for personal development.

A second concern is the diminishing zest engineers seem to take in their work. Pay-for-performance-based personnel systems gained a foothold in the 1990s and spread rapidly throughout Japanese corporations, but by now there have been many reports that such systems are not producing the types of labor productivity gains they promised. Among the observations that have been proposed to explain this phenomenon are (1) the tendency of pay-for-performance systems to demand quick results, and (2) the problems inherent in the emphasis such systems place on goals in which employee performance is evaluated objectively and in a horizontal manner, cutting across job descriptions. The problems created by pay-for-performance systems are serious for engineers as well; in R&D, for example, results often take many years to emerge, and, when those results *do* become clear, they are often the product of teamwork by an entire R&D group, making objective assessments of each individual's contribution extremely difficult. The inadequacy of such personnel systems in assessing the contributions of engineers leads to a demoralized engineering workforce and a diminished sense of cohesive identity within the corporate organization. Recent studies of engineers' workplace drive and motivation have furnished numerous concrete examples to provide evidence of this negative impact.

A third concern relates to the actual content of the work that gets done – and the transformation in *how* it gets done. As we noted before, the environment in which corporations operate has shifted in major ways in the past years; one result has been a series of corporate restructurings and organizational reforms that, in many cases, have taken engineers away from the type of work they know and love. These types of job changes and reallocations not only render useless the majority of the knowledge and experience that an engineer has accumulated over the years – and which forms the bedrock of his or her technical skills – but also frequently reassign the engineer to a new, unfamiliar job description, with no consideration of his or her interests or abilities. In such situations, the engineer must carry out daily work responsibilities while simultaneously learning a new job, and the working hours for the average engineering position – which had already been longer than in other professions – are stretched even further (see Table 5.1).

Long working hours often lead to short-term productivity gains, but exhibit a number of negative consequences in the medium-to-long term. One which we have already mentioned is the reduced time engineers have for self-education and personal skills development, something which ultimately reduces productivity gains in the medium-to-long term. The other consequence is the worsening of the work–life balance caused by long working hours, which can lead to a deterioration in the foundations of engineers' lives. This type of quality-of-life degradation

Table 5.1 Weekly hours worked for engineers (male/female total, working more than 250 days per year)

Year	34 hours or fewer(%)	35–45 hours(%)	46–59 hours(%)	60 hours or more(%)
1997	0.4	35.0	42.6	21.8
2007	1.3	28.1	46.1	24.3

Source: *Employment Status Survey* (Statistics Bureau, Japanese Ministry of Internal Affairs and Communication).

has been linked to a variety of psychiatric ailments and can result in a breakdown in marital and family relations, the repair of which, in the medium-to-long term, can lead to exorbitant personal and organizational costs.

We anticipate that these various types of changes in engineers' jobs and workplace environments will lead to diminishing productivity for engineers both in the short term and in the medium-to-long term. Needless to say, such negative effects have not been scientifically proven to exist, and, moreover, regarding the mutual interplay among the various effects we have described, we can only make educated guesses. Nonetheless, in view of the present situation, we feel that if Japanese engineers are to continue to achieve high productivity levels, and if Japanese society is to continue to enjoy the abundance that derives from the steady stream of innovations those engineers produce, we must understand the substance of the changes in the engineering environment and the impact that those changes are having on engineers.

Research questions and analytical framework

In this chapter, starting from the underlying premise that the problems discussed above are real and must be addressed, we first assess the innovativeness and productivity of Japanese engineers as compared to engineers in other countries. We then attempt to clarify the relationship between engineers' personal characteristics, such as ability and motivation, and the corporate workplace environments in which those engineers operate, and we analyze the impact of all of these factors on innovativeness. More specifically, we ask: what factors, and what interrelationships among those factors, determine engineering innovativeness? We propose a testable hypothesis to answer this question, which we might call our 'engineering innovativeness determination model', and we demonstrate the applicability of our model to the real world.

We then review data on the changing workplace and corporate environments faced by Japanese engineers, and we use our innovativeness model to assess how those changes might impact engineers' innovativeness and the factors that determine it. Finally, we ask how the negative influences of the changing environment might be mitigated; and we discuss what types of responses might be necessary and effective, and we propose practical countermeasures.

The innovativeness of Japanese engineers: An assessment based on real-world results

One statistic that concisely summarizes the magnitude of Japanese engineers' contribution to global innovation is the number of patents granted to engineers in Japan. In general, engineers secure the rights to new technologies they develop by applying for and registering patents. Here 'new technologies' can refer to new products or to more efficient production methods that reduce consumption of energy or other resources. The number of patents is thus an appropriate measure of engineers' contributions to innovativeness. Moreover, patent counts are an objective, quantitative measure, convenient for comparing engineers in different countries.

How many patents have engineers from each of the world's nations requested to secure rights to new technologies? To compare the productivity and innovativeness of Japan's engineers with those of engineers from the rest of the world, we look at patent applications submitted from around the globe to the world's three largest patent-granting organizations – the European Patent Office, the US Patent and Trademark Office, and the Japan Patent Office. Table 5.2(A) displays patent applications in 2005, categorized by the nationality of the applicant. We see that Japan accounted for more patent applications than any other country, followed by the US, South Korea, and Germany. Japan's two million engineers applied for some 500,000 patents in the space of one year, or an average of about 0.25 patent applications per engineer per year.

How do the nations of the world compare in terms of numbers of patent applications per engineer?[1] We begin by comparing Japan against Germany and the US (we exclude South Korea from this comparison as we were unable to obtain complete data for that case). Table 5.2(B) demonstrates that, not only in 2005 but even as far back as 1991, Japan led the world in this category, followed by Germany and then the US. The number of patent applications per engineer has decreased across the board – owing to changes in the global environment for engineering

Table 5.2   Patent applications: An international comparison
(A) Numbers of patent applications in 2005

Origin of application	Japan	US	South Korea	Germany
European Patent Office	21,470	32,741	3,854	23,789
Japan Patent Office	367,960	23,811	6,845	7,929
US Patent and Trademark Office	71,994	207,867	17,217	20,664
World Total	518,611	333,950	160,983	119,405

(B) Patent applications per 1000 researchers

	Year	Japan	Germany	US
European Patent Office	1991	25.0	43.3	15.3
	2005	30.5	85.7	23.6
Japan Patent Office	1991	684.0	30.4	21.1
	2005	522.0	28.6	17.2
US Patent and Trademark Office	1991	78.6	55.9	90.7
	2005	102.1	74.4	149.8
World Total	1991	954.8	764.8	415.9
	2005	735.7	430.1	240.6

Notes:
1) Due to limitations in our data, we use data on the number of researchers instead of the number of engineers.
2) Because we were not able to obtain data under identical conditions on the number of researchers in South Korea, we have omitted that nation from Table (B).
Sources: Numbers of patent applications: Patent Office Annual Reports (various years). Numbers of researchers: OECD Main Science and Technology Indicators.

and patent applications, such as the fact that there are now more engineers overall than in the early 1990s – but Japan's engineers have continued to exhibit best-in-class performance.

This discussion of patent applications demonstrates that the patent productivity of Japan's engineers is the highest in the world. Nonetheless, numbers of patent applications do not tell the full story regarding international engineering competitiveness; we must also compare productivity in terms of economic value. But it is extremely difficult to measure the economic value of any individual patent, because most products and services grow out of various combinations of multiple different patents, and individual patents generally do not create economic value on their own. Thus, let us instead compare engineers' labor productivity, where 'labor productivity' is computed by dividing the total economic value produced in a company or country by the total number of workers involved in producing that value. In other words, labor productivity is a measure of the average economic value created by a single worker.

The vertical axis in Figure 5.1 measures labor productivity in the manufacturing sector, while the horizontal axis measures the fraction of all manufacturing-sector employees who work in engineering positions.[2] Although Japan lags behind the US in terms of the total value of goods produced per worker in the manufacturing sector, it surpasses Germany, the UK, and France. What is more surprising is that Japan exhibits high labor productivity in its manufacturing sector despite having a smaller ratio of engineers to total workers than any other country. Japan has roughly half as many engineers per total workers as

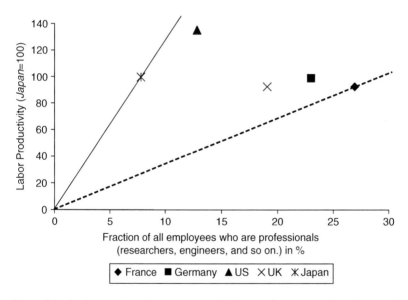

Figure 5.1 An international comparison of labor productivity and professional jobs as a fraction of all jobs (2005, manufacturing sector)

Notes:
1) Most 'professional jobs' are jobs in engineering or the natural sciences.
2) Labor productivity is measured in terms of purchasing power.

Sources: ILO LABORSTA Internet; OECD. Stat Extracts.

the US, but nonetheless manages to achieve only slightly lower labor productivity. Another way to think about this is to note that, if we draw lines from the origin of the graph in Figure 5.1 to the points representing each country, Japan's line has the steepest slope, while France's line is the least steep. This says that, if we define the 'engineering labor productivity' to be the total value (added value) produced by the manufacturing sector divided by the number of engineers, then Japan leads the world in engineering labor productivity, surpassing even the US, while France lies in last place.

In reality, of course, one needs more than just engineers to manufacture products. For this reason, the tables and figures presented here do not directly prove that Japan's engineers have the highest productivity in the world. However, they provide strong circumstantial evidence in support of such a contention. This is the remarkable strength of today's Japanese engineer. Japanese engineers produce large numbers of patents and generate the world's highest levels of economic value, allowing the people of Japan to enjoy an abundant lifestyle and an abundant economy in an abundant society.

The engineering innovativeness determination model

We now turn to a consideration of the factors that contribute to the innovativeness of Japanese engineers, and, in particular, the relationship between the individual characteristics of engineers themselves and the corporate workplace environments in which they operate. We interviewed the managers of personnel and engineering departments at seven large electronics firms; based on the results of these interviews, we developed a model to describe the factors that determine innovativeness – and the interrelationships among those factors. Our 'engineering innovativeness determination model' is presented in graphical form in Figure 5.2 and described in detail below. The model identifies five distinct factors that determine an engineer's innovativeness: ability, motivation, working conditions, workplace environment, and corporate environment.

The upper half of Figure 5.2 depicts the relationships among these five factors, while the lower half represents *performance* (ability exhibited) and *evaluated performance*, two of the *products* of innovativeness. Our model, expressed in this way, postulates that performance and evaluated performance are determined by the five factors in the upper half of the figure. In addition, our model suggests that an engineer's evaluated performance can provide useful feedback regarding that engineer's

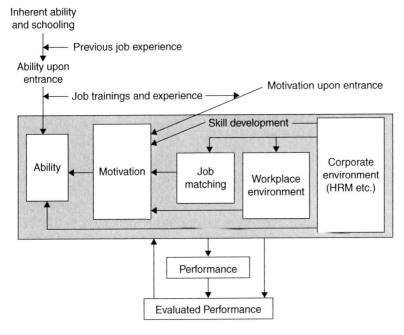

Figure 5.2 Engineering innovativeness determination model

ability, motivation, working conditions, workplace environment, and corporate environment; the results can thus serve to influence the determining factors, and we obtain a cause-and-effect feedback loop.

Data collection and data attributes

To test the engineering innovation model described above, we conducted three surveys of 80 companies and their unions belonging to the Japanese Electrical, Electronic, and Information Union (JEIU); we also conducted on-site in-person listening interviews.

We devised a set of questions necessary to test our model, formulated these questions in the form of surveys targeted at three levels of employees – union-affiliated engineers, engineering group managers, and central-office personnel departments – and distributed and collected our surveys through labor unions in each of our target companies. The surveys were paper forms to be filled out by the employees themselves; we distributed the surveys in February 2008 and collected them between March and April of that year. Table 5.3 details the distribution and response rates for our surveys.

Table 5.3   Numbers of surveys distributed and returned

	Surveys distributed	Surveys returned	Response rate
A. Survey of union members	4,500	3,657	81.3%
B. Survey of managers	1,000	616	61.6%
C. Corporate surveys	80	63	78.8%

In-person interviews were conducted between November 2007 and January 2008 at seven large firms affiliated with the JEIU; together, these seven firms comprise some 40 per cent of the JEIU. These firms employ a variety of advanced human-resource management systems, which, in their degree of penetration and completeness, rank among the most sophisticated in all of Japan's electronics industry.

Data used in our analysis

Questions relating to each of the five factors illustrated in Figure 5.2 were selected from the total set of questions asked in the survey; based on the responses to those questions, we constructed data elements indicating the relative strength of each factor (referred to below simply as 'elements'). These data are tabulated in detail in Table 5.4.

We used two metrics to assess the performance of engineers: **(1)** the number of performance goals attained (an *objective* metric) and **(2)** gut feelings about the engineer's demonstration of ability (a *subjective* metric). We then used a principal component analysis to construct aggregate variables (principal component scores) to determine an overall performance assessment. To assess the number of performance goals attained (metric **(1)**), we used principal component analysis and other methods[3] to construct a measure incorporating four types of data: **(a)** number of patent applications, **(b)** number of requests to lecture outside the company, **(c)** number of other presentations delivered outside the company (such as at academic conferences), and **(d)** number of papers written for journals or other publications, where all data refer to totals over the past three years. To assess gut feelings regarding an engineer's demonstration of ability (metric **(2)**), we use self-evaluations, in which the engineer responded to the question 'I am capable of demonstrating my abilities' using a four-point response scale with responses ranging from 'strongly agree' to 'strongly disagree'.

Table 5.4 Factors and elements used in data analysis

Factor	Element	Description
(1) Ability	Ability as an engineer (on a scale of 1–3)	Your confidence in your technological abilities and the age at which you attained that confidence (0 point: not confident; 1 point: confidence attained after age 30; 2 points: confidence attained before age 30)
	Education (1–5)	Highest level of education completed (high school, associate degree, bachelor's degree, master's degree, or doctorate)
(2) Motivation	Corporate loyalty (1–4)	Your attitudes and opinions regarding the corporation
	Motivation to work (1–4)	How motivated you are to work
(3) Working conditions	Goodness of job match (1–4)	Your own assessment of how well suited you are to your current job
	Overtime work (real number)	How many hours per month you work overtime
	Job discretion (1–7)	How much discretion you have over the way you do your job, the pace at which you work, and your job description
	Importance of work (1–4)	Do you feel your job is important?
(4) Workplace environment	Positive workplace relationships (1–4)	Do you enjoy working with your co-workers?
	Comfortably challenging workplace culture (1–7)	Workplace discussions regarding work or research are active and civil; the workplace culture welcomes new challenges without fear of risk or failure

Continued

Table 5.4   Continued

Factor	Element	Description
(5) Corporate environment	Introduction of pay-for-performance personnel systems (1~2)	Do you use a pay-for-performance model for human-resource management?
	Change in ratio of sales to R&D expenses in the past 5 years (1~3)	Regarding the positioning of R&D activities within the overall executive strategy, in the past 5 years, has the ratio of overall sales to R&D costs changed?
	Trend in corporate performance (real number: consideration of long-term trends in corporate performance)	Average aggregate sales profits for 2002–2006 minus those for 1997–2001
	Market sector (1 of 10 possible sectors)	The primary market sector in which your business sells products (example: 'materials and electronic components')

Factors that enhance engineer performance

Using the metrics described above to assess engineer performance together with the five factors depicted in Figure 5.2, we performed a regression analysis on the data obtained from our surveys of engineers to identify the influence of each of the five factors on the performance of individual engineers. The results of this analysis are tabulated in Table 5.5.

In Table 5.5, a '+' in the right column indicates that a statistically significant[4] positive impact was found, while an empty box indicates that no statistically significant impact was found. From the table, we see immediately that ability, motivation, working conditions, workplace environment, and corporate environment are all factors that have a positive impact on performance. Delving deeper into the elements that comprise each factor, we can identify the specific

Table 5.5 Factors that influence performance (demonstration of ability)

Factor	Element	Impact
(1) Ability	Ability as an engineer	+
(2) Motivation	Corporate loyalty	
	Motivation to work	+
(3) Working conditions	Goodness to work	+
	Overtime work	+
	Job discretion	+
	Importance of work	+
(4) Workplace environment	Positive workplace relationship	+
	Comfortably challenging workplace culture	+
(5) Corporate environment	Introduction of pay-for-performance personnel systems	
	Change in ratio of sales to R&D expenses in the past 5 years	+

Note: In the **Impact** column, '+' denotes a positive impact, while an empty box indicates no statistically significant impact. (The cutoff for determination of statistical significance was set at 10 per cent.) In this analysis, we have eliminated the influence of the following elements: gender and age (personal characteristics), education (ability), market sector (workplace environment), and corporate performance trends (corporate environment).

elements that enhance engineer performance; these are tabulated in Table 5.6.

There were some elements for which we were unable to discern any impact; among these was the introduction of pay-for-performance personnel systems (an element which falls under the 'corporate environment' category). Many of the corporations targeted by our survey have already introduced pay-for-performance personnel systems, but we were unable to determine any impact of these systems on engineer performance.

To summarize the results of our analysis, the engineer innovativeness model that we proposed earlier is highly consistent with real-world data; we have demonstrated that engineer performance is determined

Table 5.6 Elements identified as enhancing engineer performance

---

Ability:
Strong engineering abilities

Motivation:
Strong motivation to work

Working conditions:
Overtime work
Work well-suited to engineers' abilities
Job discretion
Work that contributes significantly to the achievement
    of organizational goals

Workplace environment:
Good personal relationships with supervisors and
    coworkers
Comfortable, challenging workplace culture

Corporate environment:
Increasing investment in R&D

---

by ability, motivation, working conditions, workplace environment, and corporate environment.

The future for Japanese engineers: The changing environment faced by engineers

To summarize the results of the model-verification research discussed in the previous section, engineers who work for Japanese corporations exhibit world-class levels of productivity, the keys to which are the early acquisition of technological skills and favorable working conditions and workplace environments. However, today these favorable techno-logical conditions, working conditions, and workplace environments are undergoing rapid transformations. Intensifying global competition, and the need to respond to the demands of the stock market, are forc-ing corporate executives to focus increasingly on short-term corporate performance; this in turn leads to longer working hours and increased reliance on part-time and contract employees. For full employees in engineering positions, these realities amount to significant changes in working conditions and the workplace environment. On top of all of this, major transformations are beginning to creep into the very society in which corporations operate. These include changing societal attitudes toward the engineering profession – indeed, a society that is turning away from engineering in general – and a corresponding drying-up in the pipeline of next-generation engineers. The future of Japanese engineering *cannot* be simply a continuation of today's status quo.

Changing working conditions

Long working hours for engineers have become endemic – and are growing even longer (recall Table 5.1). The numbers in Table 5.1 represent hours worked per week for all engineers who work more than 250 days per year. Of course, engineers have long exhibited a tendency to work long hours. But those long working hours are growing even longer. In 1997, a majority of both male and female engineers reported overtime work of six or more hours per week (total weekly working hours of 46 hours or more), or more than 24 hours per month. By 2007, the fraction of engineers reporting overtime work had risen significantly – to 70 per cent of male engineers and 60 per cent of female engineers. We are seeing an increase in the number of overtime-working engineers. In addition, the overtime hours are growing longer and longer. The fraction of engineers who report extra overtime work – 20 or more overtime hours per week (or 60 or more total work hours per week), for a total of more than 80 overtime hours per month – is rising rapidly. The transformation is particularly striking in the case of female engineers, who, until recently, had been somewhat exempt from the relentless drive toward ever-longer working hours.

The transformation is having an impact on quality. In the past, long working hours coexisted with high morale, and were largely a volunteer decision on the part of engineers, but that is starting to change. This is illustrated most starkly by the number of survey respondents who agreed with the statement 'I don't have enough time to do my job to my own satisfaction': 61.4 per cent of union members and 59.7 per cent of managers agreed with the statement, indicating that some six in ten Japanese engineers, regardless of job description, are highly dissatisfied with the way they are being forced to work and the performance they are delivering as a result (JEIU, 2008). On top of this, long working hours are causing engineers' assessments of their work–life balance to plummet, leading to yet another negative influence on job satisfaction.

The long working hours that engineers don't want truly are 'unwanted' overtime hours. Today's long working hours are stealing time that engineers could otherwise spend learning; long working hours make it difficult for employees to find time to learn, whether on or off the job. Moreover, the time that senior engineers and supervisors used to spend

Table 5.7   Changes in jobs and the workplace environment

Age of respondent Survey questions	<30 (%)	30–34 (%)	35–39 (%)	40–44 (%)
I do not receive enough guidance to fulfill my daily duties.	70.8	76.3	74.8	70.6
The supervisor who is supposed to give me guidance is too busy to give me enough guidance.	73.7	76.2	77.1	74.6
The environment for training workers in the workplace is vanishing.	53.6	62.0	65.0	61.8

Note: The population surveyed consisted of engineers belonging to the JEIU (Japanese Electrical, Electronic, and Information Union).
Source: JEIU (2008).

providing guidance and assistance to junior engineers (in a form of on-the-job-training) today is vanishing due to the need to attend to other responsibilities (see Table 5.7).

In short, today's long working hours are eating away at the culture that allowed early adoption of technologies – which, as noted above, has traditionally been a source of pride and strength for Japan – and have reduced the supply of next-generation engineers needed to maintain strong creativity into the future.

The changing workplace culture and the deterioration of personal relationships

Changes in the working environment, such as the increase in working hours we discussed above, do not merely have negative effects on motivation and productivity in the short and medium-to-long term. Such changes also give rise to a variety of negative *secondary* effects. The vanishing of any leeway in engineers' ability to get their jobs done changes the personal relationship between one engineer and another within the workplace. Engineers deprived of the ability to spend time on their own personal activities of choice cannot hope to have any time – or any mental energy – left to focus on the work of their colleagues. As a result, positive interpersonal relationships in the workplace – relationships that had been based on friendship and a willingness to help each other out – begin to deteriorate. On top of this, pay-for-performance personnel systems place such high emphasis on short-term performance that anything not seen as contributing in the short term – including training or education not directly tied to immediate results, free and open workplace discussions, and the willingness to evaluate new ways of doing things – is considered detrimental to short-term results. This shift in focus inevitably modifies the culture and philosophy of the workplace. The extremely high proportion of survey respondents who agreed that 'the environment for training workers in the workplace is vanishing' (Table 5.7) is clear evidence of this changing workplace culture.

Diminishing motivation

The changes discussed in the preceding sections tend to reduce engineers' motivation toward their jobs and their organizations. When engineers are forced to work unwanted overtime hours, are unable to do their jobs to their own satisfaction due to time pressures, and are forced to work in an environment in which friendly mutual assistance between co-workers and a generally supportive workplace culture are rapidly becoming things of the past, it is only natural that those engineers will experience diminished regard for their organizations, diminished desire to contribute to their organizations' growth, and even diminished motivation to do their own work. In fact, such a loss of motivation is not the exclusive province of engineers, but is already becoming a reality across a wide variety of professions.

Figure 5.3 plots changes in job motivation among full employees in a variety of job descriptions in the electronics industry between 1994 and

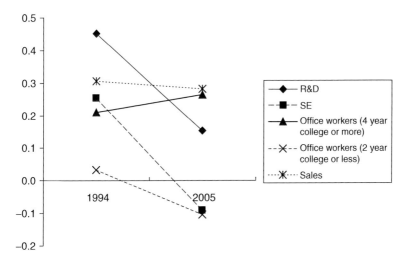

Figure 5.3   Changes in motivation to work

Source: Fujimoto and Nakata (2007), Table 6, Table A2.

2005. Here 'job motivation' is measured on a four-point scale ranging from lowest motivation to highest motivation; the results are controlled for factors that may be expected to influence work motivation, such as age and number of years in the workforce, as well as for personal characteristics such as gender, and the resulting data on job motivation are plotted, separately for separate job descriptions, with data points every two years. Four out of the five job descriptions compared here exhibited a decline in overall job motivation, with R&D engineers and systems engineers (SEs) exhibiting particularly steep declines. Similar patterns of decline are visible in data on organizational loyalty, and Fujimoto and Nakata (2007) have demonstrated that here too, engineers and systems engineers have exhibited particularly sharp declines in organizational loyalty. The high levels of motivation among engineers, which undergirded their traditionally high levels of achievement, are clearly becoming a thing of the past.

The medium-to-long-term deficit of young new engineers entering the workforce

As discussed above, changes in working conditions and in the workplace environment are beginning to have an impact beyond the confines of corporations, as demonstrated by the plummeting numbers of young Japanese people who aspire to become engineers. The general societal phenomenon of young people distancing themselves from technology is generally composed of two distinct components. One is the distaste of elementary and secondary school students for mathematics and science. As this distaste for the quantitative subjects grows, more and more students are prevented from advancing through technical subjects at the higher-education level. The second component is the avoidance of engineering professions at the job-selection stage. However, at least at the elementary and secondary education levels, the distaste for science and mathematics has not yet progressed to the point at which we need to be concerned. Nonetheless, the fraction of college students who aspire to major in technical departments (including science, mathematics, and engineering) has fallen rapidly over the past decade (see Figure 5.4).

On top of this is the fact that, even among students studying technical departments, the fraction of students who actually enter technical professions after graduation is decreasing. This *double* distancing of young people from the engineering professions will decrease Japan's supply of new engineering graduates in the near future.

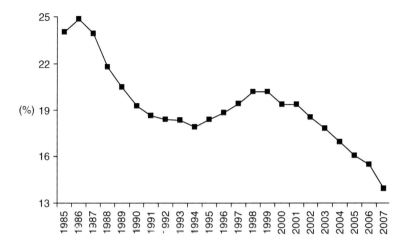

Figure 5.4   The fraction of all aspiring college students who aspire to major in science or engineering fields

Source: NISTEP (2008), Table 5–2-1 (A).

Is there a future for Japan's engineers? What we can do right now

No positive future for Japanese engineers can be realized simply by maintaining today's status quo. The four disturbing future trends we discussed above are only a subset of a larger set of transformations that we cannot deal with here. However, these four changes have already begun to have an impact, and their influence has accelerated over the past decade. Moreover, all of these trends are beginning to exhibit undesirable consequences, not only on engineers themselves but also on the organizations in which they work and on society as a whole. We must begin to take appropriate countermeasures. But what can engineers do? How can organizations change? What is society capable of?

Reasonable working hours: Toward an environment for continual learning and active human-resource investments in engineers

The pace of technological advancement will continue to accelerate in the coming years, and the education of engineers must accelerate along with it. To this end, on-the-job training (OJT) in the workplace, and off-the-job training (Off-JT) both in and out of the workplace, must be packaged together in appropriate combinations and provided to engineers. Equally importantly, the workplace environment itself must be conceived as an environment for continual learning, so that engineers – and their organizations – can derive the maximum possible benefit from the educational opportunities available. The first step in this direction is to establish reasonable working hours. This doesn't necessarily mean across-the-board reductions in working hours, but rather the creation of a system in which the needs and wishes of engineers are respected, and in which engineers themselves have at least partial discretion in determining their own working hours.

Improving conditions for women and middle-aged and senior engineers: Toward fair, performance-based treatment and compensation

By far the most effective and efficient remedy for the shortage of engineers is to make better use of female engineers, who, in the past, have too often seen their talents go underutilized, and who have abandoned the labor market in large numbers, thus constituting a strong and underutilized pool of potential applicants. Similarly, if middle-aged and senior engineers – whose numbers will only continue to increase in the coming years – can be activated to work at higher levels of motivation and ability than has been the case in the past, Japan's supply of engineers will be greatly improved. The first step in taking advantage of the talents of female, middle-aged, and senior engineers is to establish fair practices for workplace evaluations; the second step is then to establish fair policies for treatment and compensation based on those fair evaluation practices. The design of fair evaluation practices, and fair policies for treatment and compensation, is an urgent requirement for the future of Japanese engineering.

Teamwork evaluations: Toward a system for rewarding positive working styles

Even engineers cannot generate results on their own. Instead, results derive from teamwork with colleagues and from a supportive workplace culture. In this sense, the engineering workplace is a team environment, and performance is a measure of the productivity of the team as a whole. In view of this reality, it is important to evaluate both the performance of individual engineers and the teamwork of the groups in which they work; improving the balance between the two can make the workplace more productive and can allow each individual engineer to make greater contributions. Within the framework of a pay-for-performance personnel system, the targets of personnel evaluations must include both individual engineers and their working teams, and the importance of an appropriate workplace balance between the two must be emphasized.

Positioning short-term strategies within the context of long-term strategies: Toward management practices that make the best use of engineers

The various human-resource management policies we have proposed in the preceding sections are premised on the existence of a long-term managerial strategy. If the goal of management is simply to improve raw sales numbers in each accounting term, none of these three proposals will be anything more than an impediment to the attainment of short-term goals. Management does not succeed or fail on its policies for managing employees alone, but the converse is just as true: no manager who fails to extract the maximal possible contribution from each of his or her employees can be effective or efficient in attaining managerial objectives. In view of this fact, and in order to extract the maximal possible contribution from engineering employees, short-term managerial practices must be crafted with a clear long-term executive strategy in mind, and the relationship between short-term and long-term strategies must be carefully calibrated.

Taking the long view on labor negotiations: Toward more engineer-friendly labor unions

In the past, labor unions have taken as their mission to improve working conditions for union members, generally with 'working conditions' narrowly defined to include wages and working hours. However, as we have seen in this chapter, the motivation and performance of engineers are largely determined by the nature of their technologies, their jobs, and their workplaces; needless to say, motivation and performance are precisely the resources that enable an engineer's high level of self-actualization through work. In today's Japanese corporations, this fundamental relationship is rapidly disintegrating, under the withering onslaught of a continually changing external environment. Labor unions must redirect their negotiating powers: instead of striving only for traditional goals such as increased wages and reduced working hours, labor unions must apply their efforts and resources to negotiating benefits such as better job matching, better career development, and an improved workplace environment. Such a redirection is critical not only for Japanese engineers to continue to enjoy high levels of job satisfaction and self-actualization, but also for Japan as a nation to continue to enjoy the fruits of its engineers' boundless creativity. The transition toward more engineer-friendly labor unions will be a transition toward labor unions that better serve the very society in which engineers operate.

Notes

1. International comparison data exist only for numbers of researchers, not for numbers of engineers. However, the Japanese portion of the international OECD data used here was based on surveys of scientific and engineering researchers, where 'research' is broadly defined to include development activities within corporations. For this reason, to ensure maximal accuracy we have used the term 'researcher' in Table 5.2, but the population described by this term is nearly identical to the population described by the term 'engineer' throughout the rest of the text.
2. The ILO data that are available for international comparison consider only the broad category of 'all professional jobs', which includes engineering jobs. However, most professional jobs in the manufacturing sector are engineering or natural-science research positions, so we have used this alternative categorization here.
3. In practice, we computed a score for the first principal component identified by our principal component analysis of the four types of data, then used regression analysis to construct variables from which the influence of job description (basic research, design, development, and so on) and product area were eliminated.
4. In our analysis we set the significance level at 10 per cent.

References

Fujimoto, T. and Nakata, Y. (2007) 'Has Work Motivation among Japanese Workers Declined?', *Asian Business & Management*, 6 (S1): 57–88.
JEIU (2008) '*Koufukakachi gijutsusha no kyaria kaihatsu ni kansuru chousa kekka*' (Results of Career Development Survey of High-value-added Engineers), *Chousa Jiho* (Japanese Electrical and Electronic Information Union Survey Report), 374: p. 269 '*Kumiaiin chousa kekka shuukei hyou*' (Tabulation of Union Member Survey Results) and p. 323 '*Kanrishoku chousa kekka shuukei hyou*' (Tabulation of Manager Survey Results).
NISTEP (2008) *Kagaku gijutsu shihyou daigohan ni motoduku 2007 nen kaiteiban* (Digest of Japanese Science and Technology Indicators – Data Updated in 2007 for 5th edition), NISTEP (Japan's National Institute of Science and Technology Policy) *Chuosa Shiryo* (Research Material) 140.

6
Strategic Alliances in the Japanese Economy
Types, Critiques, Embeddedness, and Change
James R. Lincoln and Emily W. Choi

Introduction

This chapter reviews the role and consequences of strategic alliances in Japanese business. We are not aware of other research published in English that takes a similarly broad look at Japanese firms' embrace and utilization of strategic alliances. Some readers may take issue with this claim, pointing out that in fact an extensive literature addresses the cooperative customer–supplier relationships that are seen as an integral feature of Japan's 'lean production' model of manufacturing success (Dyer, 1996; Helper *et al.*, 2000; Liker and Choi, 2004). From our perspective, however, those vertical partnerships housed within the durable governance structures known as *keiretsu* are not strategic alliances in the usual sense of the term. Admittedly, alliances such as the *keiretsu* that form and persist for other reasons may at times take on strategic purpose. The bulk of our work here addresses the changing interplay between Japan's *keiretsu* networks and the strategic-alliance creation process in its domestic economy. Japan, of course, has been a major player in international strategic alliances, and we review the literature on those alliance patterns and how they have changed over time. However, the broad involvement of Japanese firms in alliances with foreign partners appears to have coincided with relatively little strategic-alliance activity at home, especially if we exclude government-led research consortia and the *keiretsu* themselves.

Our approach is less descriptive than analytical and critical. We wish to understand how Japanese strategic alliances reflect the structure and strategies both of individual Japanese firms and of the Japanese economy as a whole. Moreover, because of Japan's rapid ascent to the front ranks of global economic powers – and also, perhaps, because Japanese business and government have been conducted in ways that depart to some degree from Western norms – Japan has come in for a good deal of Western criticism. This is equally true for Japan's strategic alliances – especially the international ones – as for other facets of Japanese economic organization and behavior. We review some of those criticisms and attempt to assess their validity and origin. We then focus on one broad issue regarding Japanese domestic inter-firm alliances: the fact that, to a degree unhealthy for the Japanese economy in the long run, Japanese strategic partnerships have required embeddedness in a preexisting network infrastructure for their launch, persistence, and success. The scholarly literature has shown strategic alliances in other countries likewise utilizing this network infrastructure, particularly in the early stages of the alliance life cycle. But Japan is distinctive in the extent of its elaborate inter-organizational networks, which take the form of government-run consortia, trade associations, and *keiretsu* groupings. Building on the work of other authors who have addressed similar themes, we suggest that, while such network or community infrastructure once served a useful purpose, Japanese firms need to move beyond it – and we suggest that, according to our own empirical analysis of the Japanese electronics industry, Japanese firms have been doing just that: recent strategic alliances, and particularly technology-based alliances, are less embedded in *keiretsu* than was true of the alliances of the past.

Defining strategic alliances

Strategic alliances are difficult to define with precision. They may be said to include any cooperative and intentionally lasting partnership between two or more companies that has some express business purpose geared to improving the performance and competitiveness of the partner firms.

Strategic alliances can be divided between alliances aimed at R&D – cooperation in the creation or application of process or product technology – and alliances formed for other purposes.[1] Much if not most of the scholarly literature on strategic alliances addresses the R&D case.

Beyond the critical distinction between R&D partnerships and other types, strategic alliances serve a variety of purposes and take a variety of forms. They may be cost-sharing or economizing, as when two firms consolidate production or distribution. They may be skill-sharing or learning-based, as when one firm possesses expertise another needs

(Sakakibara, 2002). They may be synergy-producing, as when two or more firms possess distinct but complementary capabilities that interact in raising production or innovation. They may be asymmetric, as when one firm extracts knowledge from the other (for example, by licensing technology) or assists in gaining access to its distribution channels, or they may be symmetric, as when two or more firms commit equal resources to a venture and/or create dedicated boundary-spanning teams. An important distinction in the class of symmetric alliances is that between dissimilar partners possessed of complementary assets or capabilities and partners whose alliance mostly enlarges the pool of existing assets.

Most students of strategic alliance agree that the concept does not extend to the poles of Williamson's (1985) 'markets and hierarchies' continuum. That is, a merger or acquisition is not an alliance. By definition, if one firm is absorbed into another, such that its people and processes are subordinated to the second firm's authority hierarchy, a voluntary cooperative partnership no longer exists. Also excluded are pure exchange contracts in which one firm shifts assets – products or services – to another for a price or fee; in such agreements there is no provision for cooperation between the parties beyond a written contract specifying what is to be sold at what price and what recourse, legal or otherwise, is available to the parties in the event of default or defection.

Yet if the 'contract' fails to lay out in codified and closed form all the rights and obligations of the partners but is *implicit* and *relational* – a promise by the parties to trust and cooperate with one another to resolve problems along the way – it takes on the flavor of a strategic alliance (Macaulay, 1963). This is a particularly important consideration in the Japanese context, as Japanese purchase-supply contracts have been famously vague and short, necessitating privately ordered relational contracting as governance structure. Indeed, the prevalence of relational contracting in Japanese business has contributed substantially to scholarly interest in the roles of trust, commitment, and reciprocity in economic systems generally, even in the arm's-length and market-oriented 'Anglo-Saxon' West (Dore, 2000).

While companies may disdain explicit arm's-length contracts in favor of implicit and relational ones (more on this later), the presence of a formal contract in itself needs not imply the absence of cooperation. Hewlett Packard's successful strategic alliance with Cisco Systems involved frequent joint discussions, cross-functional and high-level buy-in, and other in-depth contact between employees of the two firms (Casciaro and Darwall, 2003). Participating managers reported that,

when a formal contract was signed, it provided a framework that facilitated, but did not substitute for, substantive cooperation.

Bona fide strategic alliances can and do vary in formal organization
and the autonomy of the partners. An equity joint venture, for example, is a corporate organization distinct from the parent firms that may
structure its activities and compete in markets in its own distinct ways.
Indeed, a strategic alliance is unlikely fully to acquire 'a life of its own'
without the embrace of legal devices of separate stock issuance, dedicated
management and board, etc. An important Japanese example is Fuji-
Xerox, a joint venture between Fuji Photo Film and Xerox Corporation,
which grew into a highly successful stand-alone business.

Japan's international alliance

Although our dominant concern in this chapter is with strategic alliances within the domestic Japanese economy and the role of *keiretsu*
and other network infrastructure in supporting them, such alliances
cannot be fully understood without some discussion of the many strategic tie-ups that Japanese companies have pursued with foreign corporate partners, particularly in Europe and the US. Table 6.1 reports data
from the CATI-MERIT Strategic Technology Partnership global database
maintained by Professor John Hagedoorn (2002) and his colleagues at
the University of Maastricht. This is the most complete compilation of
data on international and multi-sector technology alliances available.

Table 6.1   Domestic and international R&D strategic alliances
by period

	1980–1984	1985–1989	1990–2000
Domestic Alliances			
Europe	17.7	20.1	10
Japan	4.2	6.2	2
US	22.9	25.3	41
International Alliances			
Japan – Europe	6.5	5.7	4
Japan – US	17.6	11.7	8
Europe – US	22.1	22.5	26
All others	9	8.5	9
Total	100 %	100 %	100 %

Source: National Science Board (2002: 40).

Unfortunately, no comparable global database of non-R&D alliances exists. The CATI-MERIT data only concern privately funded alliances; government consortia and other public-funded cooperative ventures are excluded.

The table shows that, in the years 1980–1984, Japan's share of all strategic technology partnerships ('STPs' as the authors refer to them), at 24 per cent, was just 5 per cent less than that of all the European countries combined. Japan's contribution then declined to 17.4 per cent in the latter 1980s and to 12 per cent in the 1990s. A likely reason is the shift in the industrial composition of international alliances generally from consumer electronics and information technology – in which Japan was strong – to biotechnology, where Japan was weak. Probert (2006), however, suggests that the rate of participation of Japan's pharmaceutical companies in international biotech alliances is roughly equal to that of European pharmaceuticals if the smaller size of the Japanese companies is taken into account. A report using the same data for 1980–1994 by Narula and Hagedorn (1998) breaks down total recorded STP activity according to international and domestic partnerships and by separate countries. The US led with 4848 recorded STPs, followed by Japan with 1931. In Europe, the UK had 927, Germany 857, France 722, Netherlands 703, and Italy 421, with other European countries tallying 200 or fewer.

How do these alliances divide between international and domestic? First, international alliances make up 75 per cent or more of all alliances for every European country. Narula and Hagedorn suggest that smaller countries generally have more cross-border alliances, owing to the smaller size of their home markets and the greater availability of partners. It is also easier to form and manage international alliances in Europe, where, unlike Japan and the US, so many partner candidates are close at hand. The international alliance rate of the very large and geographically distant US, by contrast, was 41.3 per cent. On the other hand, Japan, despite being large and isolated as well, has the strategic-alliance distribution of a European country: 75 per cent of its alliances were with international partners. This high rate of external partnering no doubt reflects the Japanese economy's strong export orientation, but it also suggests that, despite an array of government and *keiretsu* supports, Japan's domestic technology alliances have been relatively few in number.

The (mostly Western) critique of Japanese strategic alliances

Although Japanese companies are perceived as being good at managing and working within networks, much criticism has been leveled at their participation in and use of strategic alliances – particularly international alliances, in which, as just noted, the country's profile has been high. Some of that criticism never stood up to scrutiny, and some of it is out of date. The complaints nonetheless shed light on the divergent paths that Japanese and Western companies have taken to the strategic-alliance process. It is thus useful to review the most prominent of the criticisms, which we do in the sections below.

Milking the partner

In the late 1980s and early 1990s, with Japanese economic power and Western resentment of it peaking, an oft-heard complaint was that Japanese companies' international alliances aimed at asymmetrically 'milking' the Western partner of knowledge while giving little in return. A much-cited piece by Hamel (1991) identified three reasons why the Japanese partner in an international strategic alliance learns the most: (1) intent – it is more concerned with learning; (2) transparency – it is better at keeping its own corporate processes opaque; and (3) absorptive capacity – it is more adept at assimilating and utilizing new knowledge. Hamel's evidence was qualitative and thus hard to verify, but his arguments rang true at the time.

One obvious reason that the Japanese firm is better positioned to learn from the partner than vice versa concerns language. The former, if imperfectly at times, will understand the partner's English, whereas the partner is highly unlikely to speak and read Japanese.[2] A second reason is the typical concentration of decision-making in the home office of the Japanese multinational firm. Many of the decisions that count will not be made locally and are thus hidden from the Western partner's view.[3]

Is one-sided milking of a strategic alliance necessarily a bad thing? In somewhat odd contrast with the critical tone of Hamel's 1991 piece, a paper the year before by Prahalad and Hamel (1990) put a positive spin on the Japanese proclivity to learn from foreign partners. Fast knowledge acquisition and utilization were cast as Japanese 'core competencies', evolved, perhaps, from the country's history since the early Meiji Era (the late 1800s) of copying Western nations to advance a national strategy of economic and military catch-up (Nonaka and Takeuchi, 1995; Westney, 1997). An influential theoretical piece by Cohen and Levinthal (1990) developed this argument in detail. These authors celebrated Japanese companies for their high levels of 'absorptive capacity'. The low specialization of functions within the Japanese firm, and the regular rotation of employees among them, facilitate internal learning – as, of course, do long-term employment, investments in training and mentorship, workforce commitment, and organizational cultures centered on team-work, quality, and continuous improvement (Lincoln and McBride, 1987; Lincoln and Nakata, 1997).[4]

Still, the evidence for the milking theory has been largely anecdotal and is doubtless colored to some degree by US and European resentment of the formidable competitive challenge Japanese companies mounted in the 1980s. One careful study did not support a key prediction from the theory, namely, that such asymmetric learning-based alliances would terminate once the 'milker' has drained the 'milkee's' knowledge pool. Hennart *et al.* (1999) found no difference in the life expectancies of Japanese and non-Japanese joint ventures. This, they conclude, testi-fies that the Japanese firm is no less committed than its partner to the venture's survival and success.

Too Dominant?

Another variation on the theme that Japanese companies in international alliances benefit disproportionately seems at first blush to be at odds with the milking critique, with its implication that the Japanese firm will walk away from a partnership after it has learned all it can. The complaint here is that Japanese firms tend to be too involved, too much in control, and, as a consequence, too well-rewarded by the proceeds. Hennart, Roehl and Zietlow (1999), however, see alliance control of that sort as a predict-able outgrowth of who learns the fastest and the most.

> *Value is appropriated in joint ventures when the venture is used to absorb the skills of the partner. The party that learns the fastest gets the upper hand in the venture and is able to renegotiate the terms of the venture in its favor.*

Turpin's (1993) review of prominent twentieth century joint ventures between large Japanese and Western firms agrees. He finds a general pat-tern of dominance by the Japanese side, but the fault, in his view, lies with the Western partner; had the Japanese firm behaved differently, the venture might well have failed. Furukawa's longstanding joint venture with Siemens, Borden's alliance with Meiji Dairy, and Sumitomo's part-nership with 3M are all cases cited by Turpin in which the Japanese firm was in the driver's seat and the alliance evolved down paths it favored. The Fuji-Xerox and NUMMI (GM-Toyota) cases, although not cited by Turpin, could be characterized similarly. In contrast to the pattern of Japanese international alliances in electronics, biotech, and other indus-tries, the Japanese partner in NUMMI – Toyota – was the teacher, and the Western partner, GM, was the pupil (Inkpen, 2005). Critics, particularly in NUMMI's early years, questioned GM's commitment to learning from the venture, but many of Toyota's lean production and supply chain management techniques eventually did filter through NUMMI to GM's North American and European operations. Similarly, Xerox was much in need of Fuji Photo Film's design and manufacturing capabilities in small copiers and integrated copier-fax-scanner technologies.

The reasons the Japanese partner 'got the upper hand' in such alliances had to do in part with the contrasts in management, organization, and culture that differentiate Japanese and Western firms. Immunity to shareholder pressures to maximize quarterly returns allowed the Japanese company to focus on long-term business expansion goals, which conflicted with the US company's characteristically short-term earnings orientation but ultimately served the alliance well (Inkpen, 1996). Likewise, the greater stability of the Japanese firm's managerial and technical workforce meant that, while Western executives came and went, the venture maintained continuity, including institutional memory, because the Japanese executives staying the same.

In high-tech fields, the international alliance partners pursued by Japanese corporations have often been small, entrepreneurial Western firms. The reasons have little to do with any Japanese propensity to prey on the innovativeness of the West. In cutting-edge science-based industries, Japanese companies generally lacked the basic research capabilities of their Western counterparts (Probert, 2006). As they acquired a stronger base of knowledge and experience, their international biotech alliances became focused less on one-sided learning and more on long-term, symmetrically cooperative relationships (Gassel and Pascha, 2000: 638)

Japanese firms in international alliances: Bad partners or bad press?

Japanese firms have been hugely active in international strategic alliances, many of which proved lasting ventures that at times outperformed the partners' separate businesses. Yet the perception became entrenched in the West that Japan's global alliances were more often than not asymmetric, designed to serve the interests of the Japanese firm at the expense of the partner, if not the alliance as a whole. The Japanese company was damned if it did and damned if it didn't – criticized for siphoning off knowledge while giving little in return and criticized for taking control of the alliance and steering it in ways it mostly chose.

We conclude that the behaviors of Japanese firms in international alliances targeted for such criticism are: (1) attributed mostly to anecdotal evidence; (2) when true, not out of the ordinary for any alliance partner, Japanese or other; and (3) occasionally attributable to bad or short-sighted management on the part of the (typically Western) partner, while good for the alliance in the long run.

Even so, there are reasons to believe that Japanese firms do at times struggle with their strategic alliances. Such partnerships are fragile affairs and are difficult to manage whatever the nationality of the partners. But Japanese firms have long been distinctive in the global economy for their strong corporate cultures, tight-knit employee communities, and centralized decision-making, which, when exacerbated by the language barrier, led to underutilization of, and limited cooperation with, foreign personnel (Lincoln and McBride, 1987; Lincoln *et al.*, 1995). Relative to North American-European alliances, where language and culture pose smaller obstacles to the cross-border meshing of people and processes, Japanese firms' global alliances have faced some distinctive challenges.

Japan's domestic alliances

We turn now to the question of Japan's domestic strategic alliances, that is partnerships composed only of Japanese firms. The principal question we address is the extent to which such alliances have been embedded in or supported by preexisting networks, principally the famous *keiretsu* business groupings, but also government and trade-association research consortia.

In contrast to their prominence as alliance partners on the international stage, Japanese companies have been less active in private sector strategic alliances at home. The MERIT-CATI data for 1984–1989 show Japan-specific alliances comprising just 6 per cent of the global total, which was 25.3 per cent intra-US and 20 per cent intra-European. As noted above, at 75 per cent, Japan's rate of international strategic technology partnerships is high for a country of its size and geographic isolation – much higher than the US and on a par with the smaller and geographically clustered European countries.

Indeed, our data on strategic alliances, discussed in detail below, show no increase in the rate of new R&D alliance formation in the domestic Japanese electronics industry between 1985 and 1998. International technology partnerships, as noted, have shifted since the 1990s from electronics and information technology to biotech. Given the low international profile of Japanese pharmaceuticals, one might expect the shift to be accompanied by a higher ratio of domestic to international Japanese STP's. Gassel and Pascha (2000) find this not so: most Japanese international alliances are of the market-positioning sort, and the development alliances that do occur are generally housed within government consortia. In their words:

> At a national level, Japanese firms often tend to refrain from provid-
> ing access to internal scientific resources and frequently regard joint
> government-sponsored R&D as unavoidable, but without major positive
> results expected.

In Japanese biotech, where venture capital and university scientists pursuing second or parallel careers as entrepreneurs have been limited (Darby and Zucker, 1999), research and commercialization have lagged behind the North American and European curves. In consequence, domestic alliances in the industry are few and far between, and, accord-ing to the data of Gassel and Pascha, a third of them are industry-university partnerships.

Government research consortia as strategic alliances

A distinctively Japanese form of technology alliance, occasioning much discussion and research, is the government-orchestrated R&D con-sortium, designed to bring together companies from one industry or technologically-related industries for cooperative research and develop-ment. The most famous such consortium was the VLSI project organ-ized by the Ministry of International Trade and Industry (MITI) in the 1970s (Sakakibara, 1993). Consortium-based cooperative R&D has drawn considerable attention in the economics of innovation (Branstetter and Sakakibara, 2002). In the heady years of the bubble economy – the late 1980s – the cooperative activities of Japanese firms via government con-sortia, *keiretsu*, and trade associations sparked concern in US policy circles over a less-than-level playing field. US anti-trust law, which at the time frowned on cooperative R&D as collusive and uncompetitive, was por-trayed as a hindrance to US competition with Japan whose government not only tolerated but actively promoted and supported industry cooper-ation in this and other areas (Kodama, 1992). Much writing by US policy scholars highlighted the disincentives to private sector R&D endemic to a highly competitive market economy. Corporate innovators with huge sunk costs in R&D have difficulty capturing returns on those invest-ments, as information spillovers enable competitors to copy and deploy the technology in competing products, thereby destroying the innova-tor's initial advantage in short order. Cooperative R&D was proposed as the solution. Cooperation would spread the costs of innovation across the members of the consortium and confine information spillovers.

The consortia were viewed by Japanese scholars and policy makers as a means of motivating (with government encouragement and incentives) and coordinating technology cooperation among competitor firms that would otherwise be resistant to partnering. Firms went along because of government inducements and the legitimacy gleaned from identification as a team player in a national competitiveness initiative (Darby and Zucker, 1999). Even then there were problems, some of them rooted in *keiretsu* alignments and divisions. In the 1970s, MITI was forced to divide the VLSI project into two distinct research laboratories in order to get firms from rival *keiretsu* to join (Fransman, 1990). The ministry faced similar difficulties in persuading electronics firms to work together in the Fifth Generation Computer Projects in the 1980s (Guillot *et al.*, 2000).

Research on the consortia nonetheless shows that they yielded tangible benefits in terms of higher rates of patenting by participant firms, both during and following the consortium (Sakakibara, 2002). Sakakibara's analysis further traces the firms' subsequent innovation upswings to the structure and content of the consortia, not merely to the government subsidies participants received.

The consortium model has been less prevalent and successful in biotech. Gassel and Pascha (2000) find Japanese pharmaceutical firms' commitment to the consortium process to be uneven and declining. Government and other funding diminished because the consortia failed to yield significant advances in innovation. Latecomer firms were happy enough to use them to access technology and other resources, but established firms in possession of proprietary technologies were deterred by the usual fears of knowledge spillovers. Unlike electronic technologies, in which many Japanese companies had previously achieved high levels of competence, the newness of global biotech and the lateness of Japan's entry into it meant that technological capability was unevenly distributed across Japanese pharmaceutical firms (Probert, 2006).

Alliances without consortia

Just after the peak of the bubble-era boom, an influential *Harvard Business Review* paper by Kodama (1992) heralded a wave of 'technological fusion' sweeping over Japanese industry. By this he meant the synergistic combination of (for example, electronic and mechanical) technologies through cooperative initiatives:

> ... *technology fusion grows out of long-term R&D ties with a variety of companies across many different industries. Investment in research consortia,*

120 James R. Lincoln and Emily W. Choi

joint ventures, and partnerships goes beyond tokenism. It is both reciprocal and substantial – all participating companies are on more or less equal footing in terms of responsibility for and reward from the investment.

The vehicles of technological fusion identified by Kodama included **(1)** the ministry-run consortia; **(2)** intra-*keiretsu* alliances (such as the collaboration of Sumitomo group companies in fiber optics); **(3)** Japanese companies' international learning (technology absorption) alliances, discussed above; *and*, finally, **(4)** the innovation efforts of individual firms, such as Sharp in LCDs. *Keiretsu* networks, like government consortia, he suggested, provided a 'safe environment' for R&D alliances, particularly of a cross-industry sort (which required less partnering with direct competitors). Both venues enabled interfirm research to proceed within a supportive and insulated community that prevented knowledge leaks to competitors, allowing member firms collectively to capture the returns to innovation efforts.

Intra-industry private-sector technology partnerships forged and sustained without embeddedness in consortia, *keiretsu*, trade associations, and other network infrastructure have been the relative exception in Japan. This pattern reflects the country's network-based industrial organization (Lincoln and Gerlach, 2004). If trust and cooperative give-and-take come easily to business partners who share a pre-existing tie, identity, supportive third-party network, and so on, then the *absence* of such network infrastructure implies an inter-organizational vacuum in which the trust and cooperation required for a *de novo* alliance are hard to bring about.

'If the Japanese knew how to write contracts,' a Japanese economist colleague said recently in semi-jest, 'they would have less trouble partnering with strangers.'[5] Indeed, the evidence that formal joint ventures comprise a smaller percentage of strategic alliance activity in Japan than in Europe or the US suggests that Japanese alliances are characterized by low degrees of legalism and formalism (Hagedoorn, 2002). As noted above, the rich literature on customer–supplier relations in Japanese producer-goods markets has been highly supportive of the idea that implicit and relational contracting had a larger hand in Japanese exchange and negotiation than was generally true of formal contracts (Dyer, 1996).

The trust and reciprocity so often attributed to Japanese transactions do not, however, circulate freely in the country's cultural 'ether', sparing every potential pair-up the opportunism, holdup, defection, and other market maladies that obstruct transactions in the West. Some alliances – specifically, those of firms affiliated with the same *keiretsu* – might have the features of the relational contracting model. Others, however, faced huge obstacles to partnering: loyalties to competing groups and other long-standing rivalries ruled out cooperative and productive exchange.

Exchange relations in the Japanese economy have been highly 'embedded,' to use a fashionable term, in preexisting networks or communities, which served as supportive infrastructure for stable partnerships possessed of few formal contractual features (Granovetter, 1985; Lincoln *et al.*, 1996; Uzzi, 1996). This was especially true of partnerships aimed at the creation and transfer of new knowledge. Kodama implied as much: his examples of 'technology fusion' alliances are mostly those of government research consortia, *keiretsu* groupings, and trade associations. One could add alliances embedded in regional enclaves such as Aichi Prefecture, Kyoto's high-tech corridor, and the textiles cluster in Nishiwaki studied by Ronald Dore (1983).

In addition to rules of participation that foster trust and discourage malfeasance, such communities provide a variety of supports and constraints: the transacting pair is not 'on its own', but is assisted, monitored, and constrained by a set of committed third parties. Another benefit to limiting technology partnerships to a company's preexisting network is that the knowledge generated and applied can be more tacit and inchoate (as opposed to codified and explicit), built into cultural routines, and thus hard for actors outside the network (for example, competitors) to absorb (Nonaka and Takeuchi, 1995). This is true more for the *keiretsu* than the government research consortia; true more for tighter-knit vertical *keiretsu* than the horizontal groups; and true more for process than product innovation.

An obvious obstacle to a firm venturing beyond its community or network to forge a free-standing alliance is the cost of the shared cultures and third-party supports forgone. Another is that, in an economy so riddled and segmented by networks, a firm that went searching for partners outside its network likely found itself linking into a rival network. If consortia and *keiretsu* functioned well to circulate yet contain innovative knowledge within a limited cluster of firms, they also helped to absorb and diffuse the information leaked from other clusters.

Figure 6.1 illustrates the point. Given Mitsubishi Electric's involvement in the Mitsubishi horizontal *keiretsu* network and Matsushita Electric's (now Panasonic) ties not only to its vertical *keiretsu* but to the Sumitomo horizontal group as well, knowledge spillovers from a strategic alliance between Mitsubishi Electric and Matsushita Electric would

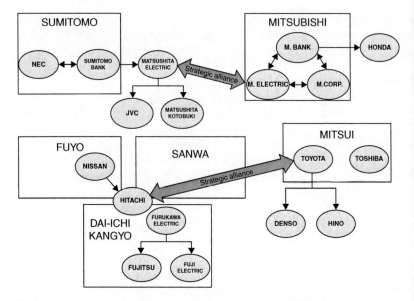

Figure 6.1 Strategic alliances connect horizontal and vertical *keiretsu*

Note: Firms within a rectangle are presidents' council members (Lincoln and Gerlach, 2004).

diffuse rapidly and broadly through their respective *keiretsu* networks. Similarly, a hypothetical alliance between Toyota and Hitachi risked knowledge leakage to the Toyota vertical group (no doubt a positive from Toyota's perspective), the Mitsui horizontal group, the Nissan vertical group, and, owing to Hitachi's unique status as an affiliate of the following three, the Fuyo, Sanwa, and DKB horizontal groups and their associated vertical *keiretsu* such as Furukawa (Gerlach, 1992).[6]

Keiretsu as infrastructure

We referred above to the role that Japan's famous *keiretsu* clusterings of stable inter-firm relations sometimes played in the strategic-alliance process. This section provides a more systematic treatment of that issue.

A consistent finding of strategic-alliance research is that firms choose, as partners for new alliances, companies with whom they have preexisting links of other sorts. One connection known to have a very strong effect in this regard is a prior strategic alliance. Firms often enter into new alliances with past partners. Some researchers interpret this pattern as a reflection of the trust, good will, and shared routines engendered by repeated partnering (Gulati, 1995). It may also reflect a kind of risk aversion or organizational inertia. Rather than investing in scouting out new partners, firms find it easier and safer to recycle old ones. For some purposes – smooth cooperation grounded in well-meshed processes and cultures – successive alliances with tried and true strategic allies may make sense. For other purposes – innovation of process and product technology – it may not.

Preexisting networks derived from boundary-spanning interpersonal contacts likewise serve as platform or infrastructure for new strategic alliances. Studies show that firms linked to one another via board interlocks and other professional and executive ties are more likely to enter into strategic alliances (Eisenhardt and Schoonhoven, 1996).

In the Japanese domestic economy the *keiretsu* constituted a preexisting network that supplied new strategic alliances with supportive infrastructure. The groups were a prominent institutional feature of the Japanese economic terrain to which enormous scholarly and journalistic attention has been paid (Lincoln and Gerlach, 2004). The word *keiretsu* translates as 'lineage' or 'hierarchy' and originally referred only to the vertical chains of suppliers and distributors organized around a large manufacturer such as Toyota, Nissan, Hitachi, NEC, or Nippon Steel. Over time, however, the term has come to refer as well to the diversified enterprise groups (*kigyo shuudan*) – horizontal *keiretsu*. Three of these – Mitsubishi, Sumitomo, and Mitsui – descended from the prewar *zaibatsu* conglomerates whose central holding companies were banned and executive ranks purged by the US Supreme Command of the Allied Powers (SCAP) immediately following World War II. Compared to the hierarchically structured vertical *keiretsu*, the horizontal groups were communities of relative equals, spearheaded by the triumvirate of a large commercial ('city') bank, a major trading company, and a heavy industry manufacturer.

Although the *keiretsu* are commonly characterized as 'groups', that term in any but the loosest sense is a misnomer here. The concept of group implies a sharp boundary delineating members and nonmembers. Both *keiretsu* types, however, were characterized by fuzzy and permeable boundaries – even, in the case of less cohesive groups, overlapping ones.

The prewar *zaibatsu*, on the other hand, were bona fide business groups of the sort now prevalent in developing economies and concerning which a large scholarly literature has recently grown up (Colpan *et al.*, 2010). Such groups take a distinct organizational form: majority ownership stakes in a few peak companies are held by a wealthy family enjoying close ties to the state. Those companies, in turn, own controlling shares in a second tier of firms, and so on down the hierarchy, such that relatively small family holdings at the apex of the pyramid convert into control of the whole. The prewar Japanese *zaibatsu* and *konzern* – predecessors of the vertical groups – took this form (Shimotani, 1991).

Like business groups in the developing world, the *zaibatsu* and the prewar vertical groups performed a number of functions in a Japanese economy whose fast development followed the Meiji restoration in 1868, which ended 265 years of Tokugawa feudalism (Caves and Uekusa, 1976). The vertical networks filled gaps in supply chains (Odaka *et al.*, 1988). The trading companies of the horizontal groups and the wholesalers and retailers of the vertical groups performed procurement and distribution functions. Intra-group lending by banks and insurance companies engendered 'internal capital markets' that filled gaps in Japan's underdeveloped corporate equity and debt markets. Furthermore, the risk sharing and pooling activities of the groups took over some of the functions of a merger-and-acquisition market for corporate control.

Much has been written about the contributions and liabilities of the *keiretsu* for the performance and competitive success of the Japanese economy (for a review, see Lincoln and Gerlach, 2004). The cooperative and flexible customer–supplier relations attributed to the vertical *keiretsu* are frequently contrasted with the arm's-length and adversarial pattern historically typical of US manufacturing (Helper and Sako, 1995). While an earlier generation of observers portrayed *keiretsu* suppliers as exploited and abused by their corporate customers, later scholars, armed with better evidence, concluded that manufacturers in the auto industry support and absorb the risks of their suppliers, buffering them from market volatility (Okamuro, 2001). A quantitative study by Branstetter (2000) furthermore reported convincing evidence of knowledge-sharing in the vertical *keiretsu*. Intra-group information spillovers enhanced the innovation performance of the member firms and, consequently, their financial performance as well.

Prior to the bursting of the asset bubble in 1991, and the decade-long financial crisis and recession/stagnation that ensued, the horizontal groups were widely praised for their stable cross-shareholdings, their interlocking directorates, and, especially, the monitoring and risk-sharing roles played by affiliate banks and trading companies. Such institutional arrangements were thought to overcome the corporate governance and management discipline problems then faced by the more market-oriented Anglo-American economies (Aoki and Dore, 1992; Nakatani, 1984; Thurow, 1992).

Were the *keiretsu* 'strategic' alliances?

A reasonable question is whether the *keiretsu* themselves should be cast as 'strategic alliances'. We think not, but, because the latter term has taken on so many meanings and is applied to such a range of inter-organizational forms, it is difficult to reach a firm conclusion. As compared with other kinds of partnerships and tie-ups, a *strategic* alliance is one created expressly for the purpose of advancing the partners' competitive strategies, better positioning them in supply chains and markets, enhancing their capabilities, and otherwise reducing their costs and increasing their earnings. Such a definition excludes both vertical as well as horizontal *keiretsu*, which came into being through a variety of idiosyncratic events and path-dependent processes, among them the decision by SCAP to break up the prewar *zaibatsu* conglomerates. Some *keiretsu* affiliates, like Denso in the Toyota vertical *keiretsu*, began life as spun-off divisions of the parent firm. Others, like Daihatsu, also a Toyota affiliate, and Akai Electric, of the Mitsubishi Group came into the orbit of a group through a financial rescue. No *keiretsu* came into being via a voluntary, rational decision-making process by independent firms aiming to collaborate in the pursuit of well-defined strategic goals (Porter *et al.*, 2000).

If not internally organized as strategic alliances, the *keiretsu* have nonetheless at times sought to achieve strategic goals. The vertical groups – hierarchical networks of suppliers and distributors under the direction of a major manufacturer – often developed, fabricated, assembled, and distributed products in unison, and thus behaved in some respects as coherent entities. Yet the vertical *keiretsu* firms also often went their own way, producing products and services that overlapped and competed. The loosely structured horizontal groups generally did not target strategic business goals or actions, although there were exceptions – a prominent one being the Mitsubishi Group's broad-based partnership with Germany's Daimler in the 1980s.

Risk-sharing is not a strategy

Indeed, an important but not strategic function long served by Japan's *keiretsu* groupings is that of risk-sharing and resource-shifting to ensure recovery from distress and the survival of affiliate firms (Nakatani, 1984). Over Japan's postwar history, *keiretsu* networks were mobilized to assist and turn around failing or otherwise troubled companies. Well-known cases are the Sumitomo bailout of Mazda, the Mitsubishi turnaround of Akai Electric, and the Mitsui restructuring of Mitsukoshi Department Store (Gerlach, 1992; Lincoln and Gerlach, 2004). In addition, there is abundant evidence, both anecdotal and quantitative, of the vertical manufacturing groups pooling risks (Asanuma and Kikutani, 1992; Okamuro, 2001). Large customers extended trade credits and set prices in order to manage the earnings of suppliers and distributors (Sheard, 1991). They also adjusted equity stakes and dispatched management and technical personnel to reorient leadership and otherwise help with restructuring.

The perception of risk-sharing activity as good or bad for the firms involved, and for the Japanese economy as a whole, has historically depended on whether Japan is doing well or poorly. In the 1960s, large-scale transfers of labor and assets from the fading industries of steel and shipbuilding to the burgeoning industries of automobiles and electronics were coordinated by the horizontal *keiretsu* with government assistance (Taira and Levine, 1985). Paul Sheard (1991), an astute observer of the Japanese economy, praised such private sector adjustments for their success in keeping the profile of the government, and the cost to taxpayers, low. Comparisons were made with the direct bailouts by the US government of Penn Central, Lockheed, the savings and loan industry in the 1980s, and Wall Street in 2008–2009. The consensus of the day was that these *keiretsu*- and bank-led adjustments enabled the Japanese economy to adapt to changing conditions while avoiding the wrenching adjustment shocks experienced by more market-driven economies. By the 1990s, however, the consensus view, especially in the West but increasingly in Japan as well, was that such chronic interventionism to keep failing firms afloat (as 'zombies' – walking dead), and thus in the process to sustain old networks and practices, was weakening the Japanese economy as a whole. Schumpeterian 'creative destruction' of the losing players and strategic allocation of resources to the winners were widely prescribed as Japan's best hope for restructuring its economy and pulling out of the slump (Katz, 1998).

It is also true – although not a topic on which there has been much research to date – that Japan's domestic strategic alliances themselves occasionally served as risk-sharing mechanisms (Sakakibara, 2002). The technology consortia led and overseen by MITI, and the many trade associations that bind Japanese firms together, were aimed not only at pooling the collective resources and capabilities of Japanese companies in the development of new technological solutions and product applications; they also lent a helping hand to corporate laggards unlikely to make it as innovators on their own. Many domestic alliance arrangements formed with an eye to assisting a less-than-sterling company to which one or more *keiretsu* affiliates had a long-standing commitment. Toyota's aforementioned 1967 bailout, and subsequent inclusion in its *keiretsu*, of minicar maker Daihatsu is a case in point, as, arguably, is Toyota's more recent move to increase its ownership and control of long-time *keiretsu* members Hino, Kanto, and (again) Daihatsu (Ahmadjian and Lincoln, 2001).

Of course, risk-pooling might be described as less a phenomenon of strong firms bailing out weak ones than a matter of *keiretsu* groups as a whole reorganizing so as to redistribute risks and resources to reduce costs and enhance collective performance. The recent reorganization of the seven companies of the Matsushita Group is reasonably framed as a traditional vertical *keiretsu* striving to transform itself into a strategic alliance (Lincoln and Shimotani, 2010). Like other realizations of the *keiretsu* form, the Matsushita Group was previously a set of companies (several of which were spin-offs of Matsushita Electric Industrial (MEI), the parent firm), each holding minority percentages of the others' stock and regularly exchanging executives and technical personnel. Yet the Matsushita companies maintained overlapping and competing product lines, R&D facilities, etc., and were managed independently. Following the top-to-bottom restructuring mounted by MEI President Kunio Nakamura in the early 2000s, they morphed into wholly-owned (with the exception of majority-owned JVC) MEI subsidiaries. Toyota engineered a similar conversion of most of its first-tier supply *keiretsu* into an integrated parent-and-subsidiary entity. Both parent firms justified the *de facto* takeovers of erstwhile *keiretsu* affiliates as a necessary response to an increasingly competitive global economic environment, which enabled tighter coordination and greater strategic focus of the groups (Ahmadjian and Lincoln, 2001).

The diminishing *keiretsu* role: A synopsis of research

This section reviews our recent research (see Choi and Lincoln, 2010; Lincoln and Guillot, 2010) on the changing role of vertical and horizontal *keiretsu* affiliations in the formation of new R&D and non-R&D alliances in the electronics industry, and their consequences for performance, from 1985 to 1998. This period of critical importance for the Japanese economy spanned the *endaka* slowdown (sparked by the Plaza Accord's revaluation of the yen), the 'bubble' recessionary era of rampant stock and real estate inflation, the post-bubble era brought on by the 1991–1992 collapse of the Nikkei index, the 1995–1996 recovery cut off by the 1997 Asian financial crisis, and, finally, the era of regulatory and corporate restructuring ushered in by the reform-minded Koizumi government. It also encompassed the unraveling of Japan's *keiretsu* networks – the horizontal groups, in particular, but to some degree the vertical manufacturing and distribution clusters as well. As the groups withered away, one might expect their infrastructural role in the creation of strategic alliances to have declined, and this, according to our data, is precisely what happened. However, the form and speed of the decline varied in interesting fashion with the *keiretsu* and strategic alliance types.

The principal findings are illustrated in Figure 6.2 and described below.

First, in the pre-bubble period (1985–1988), new strategic alliances were deeply embedded in horizontal as well as vertical networks. Strategic alliances, both R&D-based and otherwise, formed within, not across, *keiretsu* (whether horizontal or vertical) boundaries. This pre-bubble era, then, represented the old regime of 'Japan, Inc.'. Most of the structural attributes defining Japan's 'network economy' – *keiretsu*, main-bank dependence, ministry guidance, and Japan's distinctive labor market institutions of permanent employment, seniority-based compensation, enterprise unions, and the like – remained intact. In the second period, the bubble (1988–1990), the horizontal *keiretsu* effect on R&D alliances had altogether disappeared. A likely reason is that the bubble had hastened the dissolution of the *keiretsu*. With asset prices and business hubris skyrocketing, affiliate firms were straying from the *keiretsu* fold.[7] By the third period, the horizontal *keiretsu* effect on

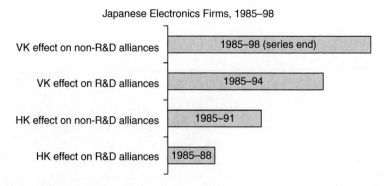

Figure 6.2   Observed durations of horizontal and vertical *keiretsu* effects on R&D and non-R&D alliances

non-R&D alliances had ceased to exist as well. The horizontal groups, battered by the financial crisis and the depressed stock market, were no longer providing protective umbrellas for strategic-alliance activity.

By the fourth period, a time during which the analysis of Lincoln and Gerlach (2004: Chapter 3) shows some rebound in *keiretsu* cohesion – an apparent 'circling of the wagons' in reaction to the troubled times and affiliate distress – the vertical group effect on the R&D alliance process was gone. Japan, it seems, had entered an era of R&D partnership in which *keiretsu* ties had no place. Yet the picture with respect to non-R&D alliances had suddenly reversed; new vertical-group alliances that lacked an innovation focus surged during this period. The vertical groups, it seemed, had resurfaced as platforms for alliance activity, but only of a particular type – namely, partnerships aimed at reducing production capacity, increasing economies of scale, and otherwise achieving cost reductions to shepherd member firms through the tough times.

Thus, despite their historical importance as infrastructural networks for the launch of new strategic alliances, by the late 1990s the horizontal groups were no longer performing that role. The vertical *keiretsu* continued to play the role, but only with respect to non-R&D alliances formed for cost-cutting and downsizing.

Chesbrough (2003) has argued that Japanese industry has long embraced a 'closed innovation' paradigm. Research and development activities were typically housed either within a firm or within a tight-knit cluster of firms such as a *keiretsu*, a government-sponsored research consortium, or a trade association (Schaede, 2008). The US and UK, in contrast, embraced the alternative 'open innovation' regime of abundant entrepreneurship and venture capital, wide-ranging, ever-shifting alliance activity, and churning merger and managerial labor markets. Our evidence on the declining embeddedness of R&D alliances in vertical as well as horizontal *keiretsu* in the late 1990s suggests that Japan was moving away from the closed innovation model and toward the open one.

What might be the reasons for such disembedding of strategic-alliance activity in the Japanese electronics and electrical machinery industries? The obvious one, suggested above, is that the *keiretsu* themselves were withering away, the horizontal groups first and most completely, the vertical groups second and to a lesser extent. Another reason is the substantially increased global integration of the Japanese economy. Firms operating abroad were constrained, sometimes by local content laws, to partner with foreign companies. Yet another factor was the shift of Japanese companies away from the old 'core competency' paradigm of leveraging existing assets for maximum growth and toward a new model of strategic positioning and value- and profit-maximization (Prahalad and Hamel, 1990; Schaede, 2008). Our evidence on the decay of the *keiretsu* effect in the late 1990s is consistent with the hypothesis that Japanese electronics firms' domestic networks were becoming more strategic, as partners were selected for their contribution to business goals and with less regard to *keiretsu* and other 'traditional' obligations. Relevant here is a finding, from another paper we have in draft, that Japanese electronics firms whose alliances lack or lose *keiretsu* affiliations became superior performers in profitability (return-on-assets) terms (Choi and Lincoln, 2010).

Do Japanese strategic alliances no longer require the support of pre-existing network infrastructure? A reasonable inference is that, with Japan's economic maturation – and specifically the reforms of Japan's corporate governance and financial reporting rules enacted in the late 1990s (Vogel, 2005) – Japanese corporations were both freer and better-prepared to enter into strategic tie-ups devoid of preexisting third-party network entanglements.

But of greatest interest to the question of network embeddedness is the following finding from our research. As the *keiretsu* effects on partner choice in new alliances waned, the effects of prior and third-party strategic alliance ties intensified. As the *keiretsu* network ceased to provide supportive infrastructure for new alliances, it appears, the prior alliance network to some degree took its place.

With the exception of the consolidation of alliances orchestrated by the vertical groups, then, strategic alliances in Japanese electronics were becoming less shaped and oriented by horizontal and vertical *keiretsu* ties. This was particularly true of R&D alliances, which had relinquished the 'security blanket' of *keiretsu* support at an earlier stage. The strategic-alliance process in this industry was thus increasingly embracing what Rtischev and Cole (2003) have called 'organizational discontinuity', a positioning that they believe Japan – and particularly its high-tech industries – needs more of. *Keiretsu* groupings, paralleling the internal structure and culture of the Japanese firm, provided a kind of community within which inter-firm trust, reciprocity, and knowledge-sharing flourished. But those communities were akin to islands in a choppy sea, such that sailing from one to another was difficult and hazardous to do. The dissolution of those communities has opened opportunities for interchange that will benefit Japan in years to come.

Conclusions

Japanese companies have been huge players in international strategic alliances, if less so in recent years as the industrial composition of global alliances shifted from consumer electronics and information technology to biotech, an area in which Japan lags behind the US and Europe. The participation of Japanese companies in international alliances has gotten highly mixed reviews. On the one hand, Japanese companies were seen, at least by Western partners and scholars, as adept but also self-interested learners. They were furthermore portrayed as capable and dedicated, if overly controlling, managers and stewards of the venture. Clearly, however, some of the criticism leveled at Japanese firms in international alliances stemmed from Western disgruntlement at Japanese competitive success in the 1980s, as well as from conflicting goals and communication difficulties, to which the Western side contributed as well.

As for strategic alliances in the domestic Japanese economy, the government-led cooperative research consortia have been particularly well studied and much discussed. These were often embraced reluctantly by the participants, but appear in the 1980s and early 1990s to have yielded returns in research and innovation productivity, both over the course of the alliance and after its conclusion, in the R&D efforts of the individual firms. The consortia have been less prevalent in recent years, partly due to the restructuring and downsizing in the late 1990s of the government ministries that directed them, but also because the consortium mechanism proved less adaptable to the biotech sector than to electronics and telecommunications.

Finally, based on the cooperative inter-firm relations famously attributed to Japan's vertical manufacturing *keiretsu* and, to a lesser degree, the looser horizontal enterprise groups, Japanese companies acquired an enviable reputation for 'relational capability' – the infusion of trust and reciprocity into customer and supplier transactions. But the *keiretsu*, especially the horizontal groups, are now largely gone, and, as the research reviewed here suggests, have ceased (apart from the capacity-reducing tie-ups of the late 1990s) to serve as platforms for the launch of new alliances. That, like the phasing out of consortia, seems a good thing, as it testifies that Japanese firms are forging more alliances with one another that are independent of the preexisting networks that both constrained and facilitated the process in the past. Those networks once worked well to advance R&D and other partnerships, but they reinforced what was an entrenched Japanese business tendency to shy away from partnerships, not only with rivals, but even with 'strangers'. Both as individual companies and in their inter-firm relationships, Japanese companies have become more strategic, choosing courses of action and partners less on the basis of commitment, reciprocity, and obligation and more with an eye to what is best for competitive success. This can only be a positive development for the Japanese economy as a whole.

Notes

1. A related distinction is that made by March (1991) between organizational activities that are directed at *exploitation* – performing as best one can with present resources and capabilities – and those aimed at *exploration* – acquiring new resources or learning new capabilities. The distinction is relevant to the topic at hand. Do Japanese companies attempt to make the most with present competencies, or do they identify opportunities and then seek out the competencies/resources needed to exploit them?
2. Even in continental Europe, the language of the Japanese joint venture workplace is apt to be English (Lincoln *et al.*, 1995).
3. Such home-office centralization is assigned some of the blame for Toyota's recent and deeply damaging spate of quality and safety failings in the US. Jim Lentz, President of Toyota Motor Sales USA, testified before Congress that he and other US executives of Toyota had no control over engineering, manufacturing, or safety matters in the US. The decision-making regarding all such issues was done in Japan (Chappell, 2010).
4. Japanese firms may be good at learning, but they are often faulted as weak on innovation, particularly of a fundamental or radical sort. Cole and Matsumiya (2007) argue that the Japanese manufacturing firm's culture of quality and strategy of incremental improvement, conducive as it clearly is to learning, limits the capacity to innovate. High and unwavering standards and an obsession with prevention over correction of errors foster rigidity and risk aversion that make fast response to discontinuous changes in markets and technology difficult to achieve.
5. Contracts in Japan are known to be short (less than 2 pages), in no standard format, vague on the obligations of the parties and the timing of activities, often drawn up without legal counsel, and with unclear provisions for legal recourse in the event of malfeasance or breach.
6. As of just a few years ago, Toyota, despite a sharply expanding need for electronic technology in its vehicles, refused to source from Hitachi. The reason was the latter firm's long-standing association with the Nissan Group (Ahmadjian and Lincoln, 2001).
7. Lincoln and Gerlach's (2004: Chapter 3) longitudinal cluster analysis of the Japanese inter-firm networks of trade, lending, director transfer, and equity ties found significant declines in the cohesion and definition of the groups over earlier periods.

References

Ahmadjian, C. L. and Lincoln, J. R. (2001) 'Keiretsu, Governance, and Learning: Case Studies in Change from the Japanese Automotive Industry', *Organization Science*, 12(6): 683–701.

Aoki, M. and Dore, R. P. (1992) *The Japanese Firm: Sources of Competitive Strength*, New York: Oxford University Press.

Asanuma, B. and Kikutani, T. (1992) 'Risk Absorption in Japanese Subcontracting: A Micro-econometric Study of the Automobile Industry', *Journal of the Japanese and International Economies*, 6(1): 1–29.

Branstetter, L. (2000) 'Vertical *Keiretsu* and Knowledge Spillovers in Japanese Manufacturing: An Empirical Assessment', *Journal of the Japanese and International Economies*, 14(2): 73–104.

Branstetter, L. and Sakakibara, M. (2002) 'When Do Research Consortia Work Well and Why? Evidence from Japanese Panel Data', *American Economic Review*, 92(1): 143–159.

Casciaro, T. and Darwall, C. (2003) 'The HP-Cisco Alliance (A)', Harvard Business School Case 9-403-120, April.

Caves, R. and Uekusa, M. (1976) *Industrial Organization in Japan*, Washington, DC: The Brookings Institution.

Chappell, L. (2010) 'Toyota's U.S.–Japan Disconnect: Americans Had Little Power to Respond to Safety Problems', *Automotive News*, 1 March.

Chesbrough, H. W. (2003) *Open Innovation: The New Imperative for Creating and Profiting from Technology*, Boston: Harvard Business Press.

Choi, E. W. and Lincoln, J. R. (2010) 'Categorical Diversity in Alliance Networks and Firm Performance', Unpublished Manuscript, UC Berkeley: Haas School of Business.

Cohen, W. M. and Levinthal, D. A. (1990) 'Absorptive Capacity: A New Perspective on Learning and Innovation', *Administrative Science Quarterly*, 35(1): 128–152.

Cole, R. E. and Matsumiya, T. (2007) 'Too Much of a Good Thing? Quality as an Impediment to Innovation', *California Management Review*, 50(1): 77–93.

Colpan, A., Hikino, T. and Lincoln, J. R. (eds) (2010) *The Oxford Handbook of Business Groups*, New York: Oxford University Press.

Darby, M. R. and Zucker, L. G. (1999) 'Local Academic Science Driving Organizational Change: The Adoption of Biotechnology by Japanese Firms', Cambridge, US, NBER Working Paper 7248, July.

Dore, R. P. (1983) 'Goodwill and the Spirit of Market Capitalism', *British Journal of Sociology*, 34: 459–482.

Dore, R. P. (2000) *Stock Market Capitalism: Welfare Capitalism: Japan and Germany versus the Anglo-Saxons*, Oxford: Oxford University Press.

Dyer, J. H. (1996) 'Specialized Networks as a Source of Competitive Advantage: Evidence from the Auto Industry', *Strategic Management Journal*, 17(2): 271–291.

Eisenhardt, K. and Schoonhoven, C. (1996) 'Resource-Based View of Strategic Alliances Formation: Strategic and Social Effects in Entrepreneurial Firms', *Organization Science*, 7(2): 136–150.

Fransman, M. (1990) *The Market and Beyond: Cooperation and Competition in Information Technology Development in the Japanese System*, New York: Cambridge University Press.

Gassel, K. and Pascha, W. (2000) 'Milking Partners or Symbiotic Know-how Enhancement? International versus National Alliances in Japan's Biotech Industry', *International Business Review*, 9(5): 625–640.

Gerlach, M. L. (1992) *Alliance Capitalism: The Social Organization of Japanese Business*, Berkeley: University of California Press.

Granovetter, M. (1985) 'Economic Action and Social Structure: The Problem of Embeddedness', *American Journal of Sociology*, 91(3): 481–510.

Guillot, D., Mowery, D., and Spencer, W. (2000) 'The Changing Structure of Government-Industry Research Partnerships in Japan', Paper Presented at the Administrative Science Association of Canada, Montreal, 7–11 July.

Gulati, R. (1995) 'Social Structure and Alliance Formation Patterns: A Longitudinal Analysis', *Administrative Science Quarterly*, 40(4): 619–652.

Hagedoorn, J. (2002) 'Inter-firm R&D Partnerships: An Overview of Major Trends and Patterns Since 1960', *Research Policy*, 31(4): 477–492.

Hamel, G. (1991) 'Competition for Competence and Inter-partner Learning within International Strategic Alliances', *Strategic Management Journal*, 12(S1): 83–104.

Helper, S. and Sako, M. (1995) 'Supplier Relations in Japan and the United States: Are They Converging?', *Sloan Management Review*, 36(3): 77–84.

Helper, S., MacDuffie, J., and Sabel, C. (2000) 'Pragmatic Collaborations: Advancing Knowledge while Controlling Opportunism', *Industrial and Corporate Change*, 9(3): 443–488.

Hennart, J., Roehl, T., and Zietlow, D. (1999) '"Trojan Horse" or "Workhorse?" The Evolution of US–Japanese Joint Ventures in the United States', *Strategic Management Journal*, 20(1): 15–29.

Inkpen, A. C. (1996) 'Creating Knowledge through Collaboration', *California Management Review*, 39(1): 123–140.

Inkpen, A. C. (2005) 'Learning through Alliances: GM and NUMMI', *California Management Review*, 47(4): 114–136.

Katz, R. (1998) *Japan: The System that Soured*, New York: M. E. Sharpe.

Kodama, F. (1992) 'Technology Fusion and the New R&D', *Harvard Business Review*, 70(4): 70–78.

Liker, J. Y. and Choi, T. (2004) 'Building Deep Supplier Relationships', *Harvard Business Review*, 82(12): 104–113.

Lincoln, J. R. and Gerlach, M. L. (2004) *Japan's Network Economy: Structure, Persistence, and Change*, New York: Cambridge University Press.

Lincoln, J. R. and Guillot, D. (2010) 'Business Groups, Networks, and Embeddedness: Innovation and Implementation Alliances in Japanese Electronics, 1985–1998', Unpublished Manuscript, UC Berkeley: Haas School of Business.

Lincoln, J. R. and McBride, K. (1987) 'Japanese Industrial Organization in Comparative Perspective', *Annual Review of Sociology*, 13: 289–312.

Lincoln, J. R. and Nakata, Y. (1997) 'The Transformation of the Japanese Employment System: Nature, Depth, and Origins', *Work and Occupations*, 24(1): 33–55.

Lincoln, J. R. and Shimotani, M. (2010) 'Business Groups in Postwar Japan: Whither the Keiretsu?', in A. Colpan, T. Hikino, and J. R. Lincoln (eds), *The Oxford Handbook of Business Groups*, New York: Oxford University Press.

Lincoln, J. R., Gerlach, M. L., and Ahmadjian, C. L. (1996) 'Keiretsu Networks and Corporate Performance in Japan', *American Sociological Review*, 61(Feb.): 67–88.

Lincoln, J. R., Kerbo, H. R., and Wittenhagen, E. (1995) 'Japanese Companies in Germany: A Case Study in Cross-cultural Management', *Industrial Relations*, 34(3): 417–440.

Macaulay, S. (1963) 'Non-contractual Relations in Business: A Preliminary Study', *American Sociological Review*, 28(1): 55–70.

March, J. G. (1991) 'Exploration and Exploitation in Organizational Learning', *Organization Science*, 2(1): 71–87.

Nakatani, I. (1984) 'The Economic Role of Financial Corporate Groupings', in M. Aoki (ed.), *The Economic Analysis of the Japanese Firm*, 227–258, North-Holland: Elsevier.

Narula, R. and Hagedoorn, J. (1998) 'Innovating through Strategic Alliances: Moving towards International Partnerships and Contractual Agreements', STEP Report R-05, STEP Group, Oslo, Norway.

National Science Board (2002) 'U.S. and International Research and Development: Funds and Alliances', in *Science and Engineering Indicators – 2002*, Chapter 4 (NSB-02–1), Arlington: National Science Foundation.

Nonaka, I. and Takeuchi, H. (1995) *The Knowledge-Creating Company: How Japanese Companies Create the Dynamics of Innovation*, New York: Oxford University Press.

Odaka, K., Ono, K., and Adachi, F. (1988) *The Automobile Industry in Japan: A Study of Ancillary Firm Development*, Tokyo: Kinokuniya.

Okamuro, H. (2001) 'Risk Sharing in the Supplier Relationship: New Evidence from the Japanese Automotive Industry', *Journal of Economic Behavior & Organization*, 45(4): 361–381.

Porter, M. E., Takeuchi, H., and Sakakibara, M. (2000) *Can Japan Compete?*, Basingstoke: Macmillan.

Prahalad, C. K. and Hamel, G. (1990) 'The Core Competence of the Corporation', *Harvard Business Review*, 68(3): 79–91.

Probert, J. (2006) 'Global Value Chains in the Pharmaceutical Industry', in D. H. Whittaker and R. E. Cole (eds), *Recovering from Success: Innovation and Technology Management in Japan*, 87–105, New York: Oxford University Press.

Rtischev, E. and Cole, R. E. (2003) 'The Role of Organizational Discontinuity in High Technology: Insights from a U.S.–Japan Comparison', in J. Bahnik (ed.), *Roadblocks on the Information Highway*, Lanham: Rowman & Littlefield Publishers.

Sakakibara, K. (1993) 'R&D Cooperation among Competitors: A Case Study of the VLS Semiconductor Research Project in Japan', *Journal of Engineering and Technology Management*, 10(4): 393–407.

Sakakibara, M. (2002) 'Formation of R&D Consortia: Industry and Company Effects', *Strategic Management Journal*, 23(11): 1033–1050.

Schaede, U. (2008) *Choose and Focus: Japan's Business Strategies in the 21st Century*, Ithaca: Cornell University Press.

Sheard, P. (1991) 'The Role of Firm Organization in the Adjustment of a Declining Industry in Japan: The Case of Aluminum', *Journal of the Japanese and International Economies*, 5(1): 14–40.

Shimotani, M. (1991) 'Corporate Groups and *Keiretsu* in Japan', *Japanese Yearbook on Business History*, 8: 3–22.

Taira, K. and Levine, S. (1985) 'Japan's Industrial Relations: A Social Compact Emerges', in H. Juris, M. Thompson, and W. Daniels (eds), *Industrial Relations in a Decade of Economic Change*, 247–300, Madison: Industrial Relations Research Association Series.

Thurow, L. C. (1992) *Head to Head: The Coming Economic Battle among Japan, Europe, and America*, New York: Morrow.

Turpin, D. (1993) 'Strategic Alliances with Japanese Firms: Myths and Realities', *Long Range Planning*, 26(4): 11–15.

Uzzi, B. (1996) 'The Sources and Consequences of Embeddedness for the Economic Performance of Organizations: The Network Effect', *American Sociological Review*, 61(4): 674–698.

Vogel, S. K. (2005) *Japan Remodeled: How Government and Industry and Reforming Japanese Capitalism*, Ithaca: Cornell University Press.

Westney, D. E. (1987) *Imitation and Innovation: The Transfer of Western Organizational Patterns to Meiji Japan*, Cambridge, MA: Harvard University Press.

Williamson, O. (1985) *The Economic Institutions of Capitalism*, New York: Free Press.

Williamson, O. (1996) *The Mechanisms of Governance*, New York: Oxford University Press.

7
R&D Management in Japanese Manufacturing Firms
Technology Trade, R&D Outsourcing, and Joint R&D

Akihiko Kawaura and Dai Miyamoto

Introduction

The collapse of the 'bubble economy' in the early 1990s plunged Japan's economy into an extended recession often termed the 'lost decade'.[1] In their efforts to survive the recession, Japanese companies demonstrated renewed interest in research and development (R&D) activities; this emphasis on innovation is of particular relevance in today's era of globalization, in which competition from emerging nations has become a pressing challenge in international markets. If Japanese firms are to avoid price competition from low-cost producers, they must shift their product portfolios toward innovative, high-value-added products, which in turn requires accelerating the creative and innovative dimensions of their product-development activities.

But such an emphasis on R&D is nothing new in Japan. As a nation not blessed with an abundance of natural resources, Japan has always invested in the creation of new knowledge; total R&D expenditures in 1985, to take just one example, amounted to some 8890 billion yen, or 2.77 per cent of GDP – a ratio which compares favorably to that of West Germany (2.84 per cent) and the US (2.72 per cent). The latest statistics indicate that Japanese R&D expenditures amount to some 3.3 per cent of GDP, with 1.1 per cent of Japanese employees engaged in R&D activities as of 2005. The OECD (2007) ranks these ratios as the third highest of all its member countries, trailing only Sweden and Finland.

Private-sector corporations have always been the principal players in Japan's innovation process. Some 60 per cent of R&D activities were conducted by such companies in the early 1980s; this fraction subsequently increased throughout the late 1980s and 1990s, climbing to 72.2 per cent in 2006.[2] This corporate dominance over Japanese innovation makes it critical for Japan's long-term growth that Japanese companies maintain successful R&D programs. But the resources devoted by Japanese companies to creative and innovative activities stagnated in the 1990s. First, total corporate R&D expenditures – which had expanded steadily throughout the 1980s – experienced their first decline in 1992, and continued to slide until 1994.[3] This period also marked a slowdown in the pace of Japan's long-term R&D expansion. In the years between 1980 and 1991, the average annual growth rate in real corporate R&D was 8.92 per cent; this plummeted to 3.38 per cent in the years between 1995 and 2006. Second, R&D spending per research employee peaked in 1992 and then proceeded to shrink steadily through 1995; not until 2006 did R&D spending per researcher recover to 1992 levels (based on constant prices) (see Figure 7.1). The poor financial performance of Japanese firms during the 'lost decade'

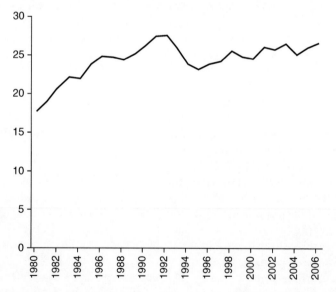

Figure 7.1   R&D spending by Japanese firms per research employee (million yen)

Source: Report on the Survey of Research and Development (Statistic Bureau, Ministry of Internal Affairs and Communications, Japan), various years.

was partly, but not entirely, responsible for these firms' failure to jump-start their innovation initiatives.

Faced with severe resource constraints, Japanese firms had no choice but to change their innovation strategies in the 1990s. Until that time, Japanese companies had preferred to keep most R&D programs in-house, and were hesitant to outsource research – both the inputs and the outputs of research – to external markets. In the past decade, however, attitudes have evolved – in the direction of greater R&D collaborations with outside organizations, including other firms, universities, and external research institutions – as Japanese firms discovered that utilizing such external innovation resources could alleviate R&D budget constraints, while simultaneously facilitating efficient allocation of internal R&D resources.

The objective of this chapter is to investigate the R&D management practices of Japanese firms in the context of those firms' relationships with other organizations. In view of the importance of manufacturing companies to the national economy, we focus our attention on the manufacturing sector. More specifically, we examine three particular areas of corporate activity: technology trade, R&D outsourcing, and joint R&D. In the following three sections, we consider each of these areas in turn, attempting in each case to identify whether or not Japanese manufacturers modified their behavior during the 1990s, and, if so, to explore the factors underlying those decisions.

Technology trade

Japanese companies have long imported technology from abroad. Indeed, such reliance on overseas technology – in the form of licensing agreements and appropriation of foreign expertise – was inevitable as long as Japan lagged technologically behind other industrialized countries during its years of recovery from the devastation of World War II. In 1980, Japanese firms paid some 239.5 billion yen, or 7.62 per cent of total R&D expenditures (3142 billion yen), for technology imports. As domestic corporate R&D programs expanded throughout the 1980s, this fraction declined, reaching 4.01 per cent in 1990 and remaining near 4 per cent thereafter.

As Japanese firms gained technological capabilities, they began to export technology, with those exports increasing steadily over the past quarter-century. Income from technology exports for all industries totaled 159.6 billion yen in 1980, and increased by an average annual rate of 10.95 per cent, climbing to 2378.2 billion yen in 2006.

If we consider the ratio of exports to imports, we see that technology exports stood at 66.6 per cent of imports in 1980; exports grew to equal imports for the first time in 1993, and then continued to grow faster than imports, with the export/import ratio reaching 3.37 by 2006 (Figure 7.2). Japanese companies have thus enjoyed a technology trade surplus since the mid-1990s.

A closer look at disaggregated trade data, however, reveals a somewhat different picture. First, a large percentage of all technology exports go to overseas subsidiaries of Japanese firms. Although relevant data are only available for the years 2002–2006, during this period some 70–76 per cent of exports were intra-group transactions, while intra-group imports amounted for only 10–17 per cent of total payments. This suggests that the overall technology trade surplus would be greatly reduced if we were to exclude trade within corporate groups, and, indeed, if we neglect intra-group trading, the ratio of technology exports to imports fluctuated between 0.888 and 1.031 during the years 2002–2006. Thus Japan's large technology-trade surplus is almost entirely the result of technology transfers within corporate groups.

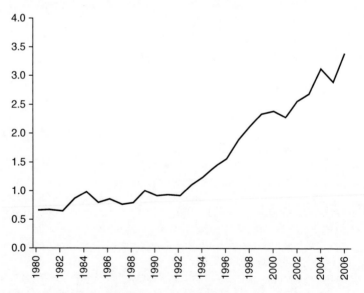

Figure 7.2   Ratio of the value of all Japanese technology exports to the value of all technology imports

Source: Report on the Survey of Research and Development (Statisfic Bureau, Ministry of Internal Affairs and Communications, Japan), various years.

Among individual industry sectors, the transportation equipment industry has seen a particularly substantial increase in technology exports. Exports in this sector grew by a factor of 57.2 between 1980 and 2006 (from 21.8 billion to 1246.8 billion yen), and this increase of 1225 billion yen accounted for more than half of the total increase in technology exports from all manufacturers during the same period (from 133.3 billion to 2322 billion yen).

Meanwhile, considering trade partners, we see a shift in primary export destination from Asia to North America during the mid-1990s, as shown in Figure 7.3. In 1985, the largest fraction of technology exports from Japan – 43.4 per cent – went to Asia, with only 25.1 per cent of exports bound for North America. The crossover occurred in 1997, in which year exports to North America grew by 67.5 per cent over 1996, while exports to Asia slumped by 16.7 per cent over the previous year. North America has remained the principal export destination ever since. On the other hand, the geographical origins of technology imports have been stable for many years.

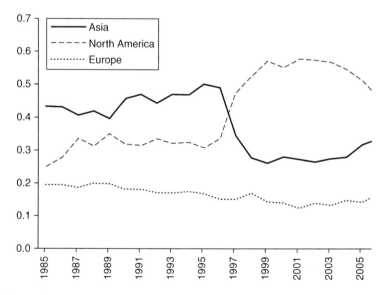

Figure 7.3 Fraction of technology exports going to Asia, Europe and North America

Source: Report on the Survey of Research and Development (Statistic Bureau, Ministry of Internal Affairs and Communications, Japan), various years.

These observations suggest that the expansion in foreign direct investment (FDI) by Japanese automakers in North American markets is responsible for the export surplus in the overall technology trade, with technology transfers among companies within automotive industry groups – primarily from the parent company in Japan to its North American affiliates – accounting for the bulk of the surplus. Thus Japan's technological competitiveness, which is supposedly reflected in the nation's overall technology trade surplus, is perhaps exaggerated. If we exclude intra-group technology trade, Japan continues to run a technology trade deficit *vis-à-vis* the US and European countries.

On the other hand, the increase in cross-border technology transfers within corporate groups might signal that Japanese companies have begun to seek ways to exploit their R&D resources more efficiently. The overseas operations of Japanese corporate groups have developed to such an extent that R&D activities, in addition to production and marketing, can now be conducted in host markets. Parent companies choose to promote the utilization of their own innovative technologies via overseas subsidiaries, because the sharing of technologies within the corporate group can facilitate effective and innovative cooperation among group companies. This, in turn, raises the productivity of overall R&D initiatives.

Assuming that these behavioral changes persist, it seems likely that technology trade within Japanese corporate groups will continue to expand. As overseas subsidiaries continue to grow and to accumulate innovative expertise, it seems quite possible that the direction of technology transfers might eventually reverse, and that technology imports, in the context of corporate group transactions, might eventually become commonplace. This will only further assist Japanese firms in optimizing the use of existing resources to realize new innovations.

R&D outsourcing

Technology trade consists of transactions in which the fruits of R&D activities – those which have proven to lead to new products or processes – are bought or sold. Companies can also utilize the innovative resources present in other organizations – including universities, research institutes, and even other companies – by 'outsourcing' R&D programs. Such R&D outsourcing exploits the R&D resources available on the open market, and hence can potentially reduce the cost of R&D programs, while allowing more efficient use of internal resources, which can be exclusively dedicated to in-house R&D projects.

Japanese firms traditionally adopted a *closed* model for inventive activities, entrusting the majority of their R&D efforts to their own employees. The 'lost decade', however, gave Japanese firms new incentives to pursue an *open* R&D model, in which firms actively seek opportunities to cooperate with outside organizations. Figure 7.4 demonstrates this trend by plotting the fraction of total corporate R&D expenditures that go toward external R&D activities.[4] This fraction hovered around 6–7 per cent throughout the 1980s and mid-1990s, but began to increase in the late 1990s, ultimately rising as high as 12 per cent in 2006.

This observation merits attention, as it represents a significant shift in inter-corporate relationships among Japanese companies. In the past, transactions with nonaffiliated firms were basically limited to simple buyer–seller relationships involving inputs such as raw materials, intermediate goods, and services. In emerging from the wreckage of the post-bubble 1990s recession, however, many Japanese companies began looking to partner with other companies as a means of optimizing their utilization of resources. The rise of R&D outsourcing exemplifies this trend, and a better understanding of this phenomenon could help us better appreciate the fledgling alliances among Japanese companies that we see today.

The analysis of R&D outsourcing in this section is based on data describing corporate-level R&D activities by Japanese manufacturers. The data are taken from the *Basic Survey of Japanese Business Structure*

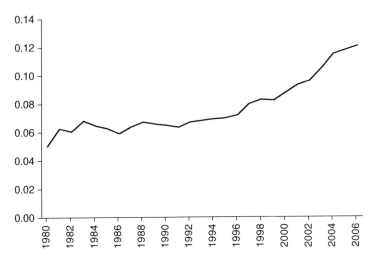

Figure 7.4   Fraction of corporate R&D expenditures disbursed for external R&D activities

Source: Report on the Survey of Research and Development (Statistic Bureau, Ministry of Internal Affairs and Communications, Japan), various years.

and Activities (*Kigyou Katsudou Kihon Chousa*), an annual survey conducted by Japan's Ministry of Economy, Trade and Industry (METI). The *Basic Survey* provides a comprehensive data set for a large number of firms, covering all firms with 50 or more employees and/or at least 30 million yen of paid-in capital.[5] The analysis in this study covers the period from 1995 to 2004, during which time the *Basic Survey* collected 63,571 observations from 11,665 different manufacturers.

We classify companies (and observations) into four categories (00, 01, 10, 11) depending on the nature of their R&D activities. Category 00 consists of firms which do not conduct *any* R&D activities. Category 01 contains firms which outsource all R&D, namely, firms which conduct only *external* R&D activities. The opposite of Category 01 is Category 10, which consists of firms which conduct only *in-house* R&D activities. Finally, companies which conduct both in-house and external R&D are designated as belonging to Category 11. As indicated in Table 7.1, about

Table 7.1   Categorization of firms during the sample period

Description	Number of firms	Fraction of total (%)	Notes		
Total Number of Firms	11,665	100.0			
Firms that remained in the same category throughout the sample period	8,895	76.3	Category 00	39	0.3%
			Category 01	239	2.0%
			Category 10	8,060	69.1%
			Category 11	557	4.8%
Firms that existed in two or more categories during the sample period	2,770	23.7	Two Categories	2,567	22.0%
			Three Categories	198	1.7%
			Four Categories	5	0.04%
			Categories 10&11	2,360	20.2%
			Categories 10&01	432	3.7%
			Categories 01&11	261	2.2%

Note: All percentages refer to fractions of the total number of companies (11,665).
The numbers of firms in the second sub-table in the third row add up to more than the total number of firms that existed in two or more categories (2,770), because some firms existed in three or four categories during the sample period.

three-quarters of all firms considered (8895 firms) remained in the same category throughout the entire sample period; of these firms, 39 firms belonged to Category 00, 239 firms belonged to Category 01, 8060 firms fell within Category 10, and 557 firms were designated Category 11. The remaining 2770 manufacturers made one or more category transitions during the sample period; of these, the largest group of companies (2360 firms) transitioned between Categories 10 and 11.

Table 7.2 tabulates the ratios of in-house and external R&D expenditures to sales for companies in each of our four categories. As is evident from the table, observations within categories 01 and 11 account for only around 18.5 per cent of all observations (11,734 out of 63,571), indicating that only a minority of Japanese manufacturers utilized external R&D resources during the period 1995–2004. Between these two categories, the average ratio of external R&D expenses to sales was higher for Category 01 firms than for Category 11 firms (0.9 per cent versus 0.6 per cent). In other words, firms that rely entirely on external R&D resources make more use of those resources than firms that conduct both in-house and external R&D. On the other hand, if we compare the ratio of in-house R&D expenditures to sales for firms in Categories 10 and 11, we see that the average Category 11 firm spent 3.3 per cent of total sales revenue on in-house R&D activities, a larger percentage than was spent by Category 10 firms, which conduct exclusively in-house

Table 7.2   Ratio of R&D expenditures to sales, by firm R&D category

Category	Sample size	R&D location	Mean	Std. Dev.
Total	63,571	internal	0.019	0.031
		external	0.001	0.011
Category 00 (No R&D)	206	N.A.	0.000	0.000
Category 01 (external R&D only)	1,514	external	0.009	0.017
Category 10 (internal R&D only)	51,631	internal	0.017	0.027
Category 11 (both internal and external R&D)	10,220	internal	0.033	0.046
		external	0.006	0.026

Note: The data in this table are pooled data for the 10-year period 1995–2004.

R&D. This suggests that extensive in-house R&D programs might lead firms to utilize external R&D resources.

Figure 7.5 plots the fractional population of each of our four R&D categories during the years sampled. As is clear from the graph, the distribution of firms across the four categories remained relatively stable throughout the sample period; firms in Categories 10 and 11 consistently accounted for the majority of the firms sampled, with a combined share of over 95 per cent. Although the fraction of firms in Category 10 diminished in the years 1998–2000, with a corresponding uptick in the fraction of Category 11 firms, those fractions reverted to their 1995–1997 levels in 2001–2004. In view of the fact that the average fraction of R&D activities conducted externally grew during the second half of the 1990s (as indicated in Figure 7.4), while the fraction of firms in Category 11 exhibited no corresponding growth, we conclude that individual firms in Category 11 must have increased their R&D outsourcing during those years. Indeed, the average ratio of external R&D to sales grew steadily for Category 11 firms during this period, which

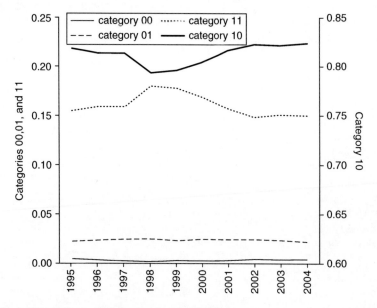

Figure 7.5   Shifts in distribution by R&D location

Source: Basic survey of Japnese business structure and activities (Ministry of Economy, Trade and Industry, Japan), various years.

led in turn to an increase in the overall fraction of R&D conducted externally.

We can thus summarize trends over the past decade in the R&D choices made by Japanese manufacturers as follows. In choosing between in-house and external R&D, most companies continue to rely most heavily on the former, but the latter has gradually gained in importance. This shift in emphasis is largely the result of more extensive use of outside R&D resources by Category 11 firms, and is not due to any large-scale migration of firms from Category 10 into Category 11.

The remainder of this section presents empirical analyses of Japanese corporate data. We first examine the factors that enter into the decision to engage in external R&D. We then investigate the degree to which firms utilize external R&D resources. The combination of these two analyses yields broad insight into corporate choices on R&D strategy: how firms decide whether or not to outsource R&D, and, if so, how much R&D to outsource.

Factors influencing the choice between in-house and external R&D

We first analyze a firm's decision to outsource its R&D activities. Taking firms in Category 10 (companies that engage only in internal R&D) as a reference group, we examine the factors that characterize companies that engage in both types of R&D (Category 11).[6] As the choice of whether or not to outsource R&D is a binary variable, we explore this issue with a probit model.

Among the variables that might affect R&D outsourcing decisions is the size of the firm, which we characterize by its number of employees. If the Schumpeterian hypothesis is correct, large firms should devote more resources to innovative activities.[7] As firms pursue R&D opportunities, they may begin to utilize outside resources once their size exceeds a certain threshold; this is captured by two dummy variables, *Size500* and *Size1000*, indicating companies with more than 500 and 1000 employees, respectively. Another explanatory variable is the intensity of R&D activities within the organization, which is characterized by the ratio of in-house R&D expenses to sales (*InternalR&D*). To the extent that firm behavior incorporates the 'learning' aspect of R&D, the relationship between internal R&D and external R&D is expected to be mutually complementary.[8] If this is the case, firms with large in-house R&D programs are more likely to conduct external R&D.

Also included among the factors influencing the decision to utilize external R&D resources are variables that reflect a firm's characteristics with regard to corporate groups.[9] Some 60 per cent of the companies in our data set of manufacturers have other firms within their corporate group; 30 per cent of firms have a parent company, and 15 per cent of firms are parent companies themselves. Hence, the majority of Japanese manufacturing companies belong to a corporate group network. Identifying innovation opportunities that lie outside of the firm requires extensive knowledge of other companies and research organizations, and the existence of a large corporate network should assist a company's decision to move forward with external R&D. In our analysis, two variables (*GroupFirm* and *GroupForeign*) characterize the impact of domestic and international networks within the corporate group. The former is the number of corporate group subsidiaries and affiliates a firm has, and the latter measures the fraction of overseas companies within the corporate group. The equity share owned by a firm's parent company (*ParentEquity*) describes the assistance a firm can expect to receive in terms of information on potential R&D sources.

The year in which a firm was established (*BirthYear*) is also included among the independent variables, allowing us to explore whether young firms or long-established companies are more likely to exploit outside innovation resources. One might hypothesize that young companies rely on outside R&D resources before establishing their own in-house innovation capacities.[10] Finally, industry dummy variables are introduced to account for the propensity of each individual industry to engage in external R&D. The machinery industry serves as a baseline for this characterization, since its average R&D intensity is close to the overall observed mean, and also because this industry has the largest number of observations of all industries.

In addition to variables describing the characteristics of firms, we use time dummy variables to examine changes in the factors underlying R&D outsourcing decisions during the sample period (1995–2004). The first three years serve as a baseline; the dummy variable *Year98–00* identifies the 1998–2000 sub-period, while the dummy variable *Year01–04* takes the value unity for observations in 2001–2004. These variables enter our regressions both as stand-alone explanatory variables and as terms that interact with the variables describing the characteristics of firms.

Results of a pooled regression, in terms of the marginal effects of the explanatory variables, with the Category 11 firm dummy variable taken as the dependent variable, are presented in the left portion of Table 7.3.[11] In the first version of the analysis, the time dummies (*Year98–00* and

Table 7.3 R&D outsourcing decisions and utilization rates

	Location decision (Probit model) Dependent variable: Category11 firms = 1				External R&D utilization (Tobit model) Dependent variable: Ratio of External R&D expenses to sales			
	dF/dx	Std. Err.	dF/dx	Std. Err.	Coef.	Std. Err.	Coef.	Std. Err.
Year98–00	0.0152	0.0038**	0.7159	0.5873	0.0010	0.3004**	0.0535	0.0545
Year01–04	-0.0122	0.0035**	-0.5985	0.3388	-0.0009	0.0006	-0.0209	0.0510
Size500	0.0735	0.0054**	0.0756	0.0095**	0.0055	0.0004**	0.0061	0.0008**
_y9800			0.0064	0.0112			-0.0006	0.0011
_y0104			-0.0109	0.0101			-0.0014	0.0011
Size1000	0.1999	0.0073**	0.1896	0.0125**	0.0123	0.0005**	0.0113	0.0008**
_y9800			0.0092	0.0124			0.0002	0.0011
_y0104			0.0096	0.0120			0.0018	0.0009*
Internal R&D	1.0053	0.0469**	1.0267	0.0870**	0.1940	0.0015**	0.1265	0.0081**
_y9800			0.0386	0.1143			0.0454	0.0082**
_y0104			-0.0915	0.1093			0.1116	0.0084**
Group Firm	1.1E-03	7.4E-05**	1.1E-03	1.3E-04**	5.4E-05	6.0E-06**	7.7E-05	1.1E-05**
_y9800			-2.7E-04	1.8E-04			-2.5E-05	1.6E-05
_y0104			2.8E-05	1.8E-04			-3.8E-05	1.4E-05**
Group Foreign	0.0387	0.0052**	0.0582	0.0099**	0.0025	0.0005**	0.0048	0.0010**
_y9800			-0.0183	0.0135			-0.0020	0.0013
_y0104			-0.0333	0.0126**			-0.0044	0.0013**
Parent Equity	2.3E-05	4.1E-06**	2.6E-05	7.4E-06**	1.7E-06	4.0E-07**	2.5E-06	7.4E-07**
_y9800			-4.7E-06	1.0E-05			-8.1E-07	1.0E-06
_y0104			-2.9E-06	9.8E-06			-1.1E-06	9.7E-07
Birth Year	5.4E-04	1.0E-04**	4.5E-04	2.2E-04*	8.2E-05	1.0E-05**	8.4E-05	2.2E-05**
_y9800			-2.8E-04	2.8E-04			-2.7E-05	2.8E-05
_y0104			4.0E-04	2.6E-04			9.6E-06	2.6E-05
Number of obs.	61,838		61,838		61,838		61,838	
Pseudo R2	0.1037		0.1043		0.0332		0.0344	
Log likelihood	-24,847		-24,830		10,891		11,051	

Notes: Both models are estimated with 10-year pooled data. Industry dummies are among the descriptive variables, although their estimates are not presented. _y9800 and _y0104 indicate interaction terms with the time dummy variables. The reference group for the location decision analysis (probit model) is the group of Category 11 firms. dF/dx indicates marginal effects. ** $p < 0.01$; * $p < 0.05$.

Year01–04) enter independently; the results are tabulated in the first column marked *dF/dx*. In this case, all the explanatory variables have the expected impact. Large firms have a greater tendency to engage in external R&D, while the presence of in-house R&D programs makes firms more likely to conduct external innovation activities. An extensive information network, implied by the existence of a large corporate group, provides greater opportunity to utilize outside innovation resources. Young companies are more likely to outsource R&D. The results for two time dummy variables are consistent with a rise and subsequent fall in the fraction of Category 11 firms during the sample period, as indicated in Figure 7.5.

The second column marked *dF/dx* in Table 7.3 tabulates results from a second version of the analysis, in which we include time-interaction terms for each explanatory variable. The effects of all independent variables remain the same, while the impact arising solely from the passage of time now vanishes. It is notable that, in this case, the fraction of overseas subsidiaries/affiliates in the corporate group (*GroupForeign*) has less impact toward the end of the sample period.

Factors influencing the extent of R&D outsourcing

Our analysis thus far has examined whether or not companies choose to engage in external R&D. The following empirical exercise augments this analysis by investigating the factors that influence the extent of a firm's R&D outsourcing. In this case the dependent variable is the ratio of external R&D expenditures to sales. As this variable is bounded below by zero, we may use a tobit model to estimate its relationship with the same set of explanatory variables adopted in the previous analysis.

Regression results are presented in the right half of Table 7.3. The results of these regressions essentially reproduce the findings of our probit model estimates for the attributes of Category 11 firms. The estimated influence of firm size supports our previous conclusion that large firms tend to make greater use of external R&D resources. Internal R&D efforts facilitate a firm's attempts to benefit from innovative resources that exist in other organizations. A firm's corporate group can stimulate the firm to use more outside R&D resources. Similarly, the influence of the variable characterizing the year of a firm's establishment again suggests that young firms not only choose to outsource R&D more frequently, but also make greater use of external R&D resources.

The results of the analysis including time-interaction terms (the second column labeled 'Coef' in Table 7.3) reveal that a variety of changes took place in these relationships at the turn of the twenty-first century. First, the tendency of large firms to use external resources grew stronger, albeit only marginally, toward the end of the sample period. Firms with large in-house R&D programs grew even more likely to exploit external resources. On the other hand, the relevance of the corporate group shifted in the opposite direction. The influence of the group as a whole was cut in half in the 2000s, while the influence of overseas corporate group members virtually disappeared altogether. Together with the results of our probit analysis, these observations suggest that Japanese firms benefited from corporate networks in their initial efforts to identify external R&D resources early in the sample period, but that the usefulness of the corporate group began to diminish as firms accumulated their own external R&D experience.

Joint R&D

Firms may also utilize external innovation resources by engaging in joint R&D programs with other companies. This form of innovation facilitates a sharing of the risks inherent in the innovation process. In this section, we investigate the factors underlying the decisions of Japanese manufacturers to pursue joint R&D activities, by conducting an analysis of firm-level data collected from the METI *Surveys*. Table 7.4 tabulates changes in joint R&D behavior in Japan in 1998, 2001, and

Table 7.4　Joint R&D activities in Japan: 1998–2004

Year	Sample size	Firms that conduct joint R&D			Partner firms		
		Num.	Ratio		Num.	Ratio	
	(a)	(b)	(b)/(a)	(c)	(d)	(d)/(b)	(e)
1998	2,479	943	0.380	0.054	2,826	3.00	2.12
2001	2,502	854	0.341	0.058	2,900	3.40	2.20
2004	2,280	702	0.308	0.044	2,543	3.62	2.56
Total	7,261	2,499	0.344	0.052	8,269	3.31	2.27

Note: Columns (c) and (e) indicate overseas joint R&D ratios.
Source: *Basic Survey of Japanese Business Structure and Activities* (Ministry of Economy, Trade and Industry of Japan).

2004 (our data are limited to these three years because the *Survey* gathered joint R&D information only in these three years). The number of companies that pursued joint R&D initiatives, (column **(b)**), as well as the fraction of all companies in the sample who pursued joint R&D initiatives (column **(b)/(a)**), both decreased over time. On the other hand, for the firms who did pursue joint R&D initiatives, the average number of partners increased (column **(d)/(b)**).

The following quantitative analysis examines the factors underlying decisions regarding joint R&D initiatives from two theoretical perspectives: the resource-dependence and the search-cost perspectives. The resource-dependence perspective maintains that inter-firm cooperation is motivated by the mutual desire of both firms to supplement innovation resources that are lacking in-house (Pfeffer and Salancik, 1978). This view predicts that the companies that engage in joint R&D are those that possess relatively abundant R&D resources; a company that lacks sufficient R&D resources does not conduct joint R&D, as it is unlikely to find other firms who would select it as an innovation partner.

The search-cost perspective provides an analytical framework that focuses on the search process.[12] In order to identify potential R&D partners, a company conducts a search process, including gathering information on the R&D resources of other companies and negotiating for joint R&D contracts. These search activities, however, cost companies. When the costs are large compared to the expected returns from joint R&D initiatives, companies may choose to subscribe to corporate networks to reduce them. Gulati (1998) and Ahuja (2000) found that the formation of joint business activities (including the selection of R&D partners) is strongly influenced by the networks to which a company belongs.

This potential link between corporate networks and joint R&D initiatives is of particular relevance in Japan, where a large number of corporate networks have existed for a long time. A company with many subsidiaries in a corporate group should enjoy lower search costs, as it can easily identify potential partners for joint R&D initiatives within its own corporate group, simply based on the information it routinely gathers from member companies. A parent company can also utilize its corporate group as an information-gathering network to help find suitable partners operating outside the group, assuming that its subsidiaries and affiliates in various markets have access to detailed information on local companies.

Subsidiaries and affiliates in Japanese corporate groups, on the other hand, may not enjoy the same access to information, and hence the same low search costs, as their corporate parent. Shimotani (1993) points out that many Japanese corporate groups are characterized by a hierarchical structure, where group firms other than the parent do not make important management decisions autonomously, and hence are restricted in their own R&D options as well. The search-cost perspective in the corporate group context would then predict that parent companies who have large corporate groups (particularly ones with overseas networks) should pursue joint R&D initiatives, while subsidiary group member companies, controlled by their parent company, have smaller joint R&D programs.

The predictions of the resource-dependence and search-cost perspectives are tested in the following with probit and tobit models. The dependent variable for the probit model is a dummy variable for companies that cooperate with at least one joint R&D partner. The dependent variable for the tobit regression is the number of R&D partners. To distinguish between domestic and overseas joint R&D initiatives, separate regressions are conducted for both cases. The explanatory variables are the same as those used for the R&D outsourcing analysis described in the last section.[13] The variables that isolate the effect of the progress of time are *Year01* and *Year04*, as the sample in this analysis contains only three data-points. Pooled data estimation results are tabulated in Tables 7.5(a) and 7.5(b).

The empirical results are broadly consistent with the resource-dependence perspective. Firms with higher ratios of internal R&D expenses to sales tend to pursue joint R&D initiatives and to have more R&D partners. The finding that larger companies are more likely to engage in joint R&D, and with a greater number of partners, also supports this viewpoint. Although these observations generally hold for both domestic and foreign research alliances, there are a few differences. The threshold above which firm size influences joint R&D decisions is higher for domestic ventures, as for domestic ventures only *Size1000* shows a significant effect, whereas for overseas ventures *Size500* also exhibits a positive influence on the scope of R&D alliances. The interaction between the impact of firm size and the time variables also suggest that the association between size and joint R&D initiatives is more straightforward for overseas ventures. The trend is always positive, with the impact greater in 2004 than in the earlier years. For domestic joint R&D initiatives, however, the impact of

Table 7.5(a) Factors influencing whether or not a company pursues *domestic* joint R&D initiatives (left half); factors influencing the extent of a company's utilization of *domestic* joint R&D initiatives (right half)

	Domestic joint R&D execution (Probit model) Dependent variable: Domestic joint R&D = 1				Domestic joint R&D utilization (Tobit model) Dependent variable: Number of domestic partners			
	dF/dx	Std.Err.	dF/dx	Std.Err.	Coef.	Std.Err.	Coef.	Std.Err.
Year01	-0.0193	0.0162	-0.0423	0.0575	-0.2962	0.7161	9.0235	9.2491
Year04	-0.0591	0.0166**	0.0842	2.1082	-1.6380	0.9506	2.6523	9.0494
Size500	-0.0195	0.0204	-0.0770	0.0335*	-0.7476	0.9222	-3.0665	1.5758*
_y01			0.0537	0.0505			1.7904	2.2019
_y04			0.1357	0.0519**			5.0570	2.2506*
Size1000	0.0675	0.0243**	-0.0073	0.0399	4.1936	0.9780**	0.3470	1.7214
_y01			0.1083	0.0583			2.3696	2.4044
_y04			0.1164	0.0594*			6.4031	2.4005**
Internal R&D	0.8132	0.2139**	0.8949	0.4373**	20.7434	7.7522**	33.0510	16.2534*
_y01			0.0012	0.5726			-2.1429	22.3626
_y04			-0.3306	0.5076			-19.1113	19.4250
Group Firm	0.0010	0.0003**	0.0015	0.0006*	0.0801	0.0103**	0.1528	0.0220**
_y01			-0.0008	0.0009			-0.0288	0.0324
_y04			-0.0007	0.0008			-0.1108	0.0255**
Group Foreign	0.0013	0.0238	-0.0702	0.0441	-0.2201	1.0570	-1.7859	1.9455
_y01			0.1154	0.0690			1.5689	2.6082
_y04			0.0827	0.0578			2.8711	2.5587
Parent Equity	-1.7E-05	1.9E-05	1.6E-05	3.4E-05	-0.0013	0.0009	-0.0001	0.0015
_y01			-3.2E-05	4.7E-05			-0.0001	0.0020
_y04			-6.9E-05	4.7E-05			-0.0018	0.0021
Birth Year	0.0010	0.0004*	0.0018	0.0008*	0.0141	0.0195	0.0359	0.0343
_y01			-0.0024	0.0011*			-0.0465	0.0473
_y04			-0.0001	0.0011			-0.0147	0.0463
Number of obs.	5,363		5,363		5,363		5,363	
Pseudo R2	0.0230		0.0274		0.0104		0.0119	
Log likelihood	-3,529.9		-3,514.0		-10,842		-10,825	

Note: Both models are estimated with 10-year pooled data. Industry dummies are among the explanatory variables, although their estimates are not presented. _y01 and _y04 indicate interactive terms with time dummies. dF/dx indicates marginal effects. ** $p < 0.01$; * $p < 0.05$.

Table 7.5(b) Factors influencing whether or not a company pursues *overseas* joint R&D initiatives (left half); factors influencing the extent of a company's utilization of *overseas* joint R&D initiatives (right half)

	Overseas joint R&D execution (Probit model) Dependent variable: Overseas joint R&D = 1				Overseas joint R&D utilization (Tobit model) Dependent variable: Number of overseas partners			
	dF/dx	Std. Err.	dF/dx	Std. Err.	Coef.	Std. Err.	Coef.	Std. Err.
Year01	0.0018	0.0068	0.0064	0.0157	0.3395	0.7193	12.1972	7.3010
Year04	-0.0171	0.0067**	0.0600	0.0611	-1.4297	0.7895	4.2821	6.3965
Size500	0.0286	0.0112**	0.0045	0.0152	2.3084	0.9162 *	0.4991	1.5670
_y01			0.0092	0.0228			0.5126	2.1960
_y04			0.0784	0.0414**			5.1404	2.2705*
Size1000	0.1188	0.0164**	0.0718	0.0239**	7.3238	0.8732**	5.1275	1.4646**
_y01			0.0151	0.0228			0.5503	2.0110
_y04			0.0657	0.0362*			5.0938	2.0752**
Internal R&D	0.2466	0.0730**	0.2683	0.1383*	34.4565	7.7090**	28.2769	14.0770*
_y01			0.0119	0.1896			5.6614	20.6998
_y04			-0.0404	0.1614			-0.3871	17.4186
Group Firm	0.0003	0.0001**	0.0005	0.0002**	0.0426	0.0069**	0.0528	0.0153**
_y01			0.0000	0.0002			0.0294	0.0220
_y04			-0.0003	0.0002			-0.0217	0.0173
Group Foreign	0.0352	0.0097**	0.0363	0.0160*	3.2307	1.0375**	3.5868	1.7482*
_y01			0.0056	0.0218			0.9757	2.3777
_y04			-0.0297	0.0234			-2.4300	2.5458
Parent Equity	-1.1E-05	8.7E-06	-1.6E-05	1.4E-05	-0.0011	0.0009	-0.0013	0.0016
_y01			2.1E-05	2.0E-05			0.0020	0.0022
_y04			-9.4E-06	2.2E-05			-0.0017	0.0024
Birth Year	0.0003	0.0002*	0.0009	0.0003**	0.0276	0.0198	0.0748	0.0346*
_y01			-0.0013	0.0004**			-0.1132	0.0475*
_y04			-0.0004	0.0004			-0.0233	0.0480
Number of obs.	5,312		5,312		5,363		5,363	
Pseudo R2	0.1418		0.1530		0.0872		0.0937	
Log likelihood	-1,176.5		-1,161.2		-2,138.3		-2,123.0	

Note: Both models are estimated with 10-year pooled data. Industry dummies are among the explanatory variables, although their estimates are not presented. _y01 and _y04 indicate interactive terms with time dummies. *dF/dx* indicates marginal effects. ** p < 0.01; * p < 0.05.

having more than 500 employees (*Size500*) is actually negative in the baseline year 1998, but changes sign, to a positive correlation, in the subsequent years. One possible explanation for this is that it is more costly to initiate a joint R&D-related initiative abroad than within Japan, and thus size matters to a greater extent for overseas joint R&D initiatives.

Among the variables that reflect the search-cost perspective, the size of the corporate group (*GroupFirm*) proves to be one of the factors determining whether or not a firm engages in joint R&D; this variable also determines the number of R&D partners. This is true for both domestic and overseas R&D partners. As we might have anticipated, the number of overseas companies in the corporate group (*GroupForeign*) is a factor influencing the decision to engage in overseas joint R&D initiatives, but not domestic joint R&D initiatives. Companies who lead corporate groups with many foreign members are more likely to engage in joint innovation initiatives with overseas partners. The equity share owned by the parent company (*ParentEquity*) is not related in a statistically significant way with either domestic or overseas joint R&D activities. This is consistent with the hypothesis that the parent company derives benefits from subsidiaries and affiliates within its corporate group, but not vice versa. These results suggest that joint R&D behavior among Japanese firms is consistent with both the resource-dependence and search-cost perspectives.

Conclusions

This chapter has examined R&D management in Japanese firms. Analysis of aggregate R&D data since 1980 indicates that corporate behavior shifted in the 1990s, when Japanese companies began to seek opportunities to combine their own in-house R&D efforts with external resources. Analyses of technology trade, R&D outsourcing, and joint R&D activities suggest that Japanese firms are trying to make the most efficient use of all available innovation resources.

Using detailed information on manufacturers during the period 1995–2004, we investigated manufacturers' utilization of external R&D resources in the 1990s. We conducted statistical analyses to answer two questions. First, did companies outsource R&D during this period, and, if so, to what extent? Second, what factors lie behind the decisions of Japanese firms to engage in joint R&D initiatives with other companies? These two analyses yield almost identical results. First, we found that in-house R&D activities facilitate outside R&D programs, implying that

R&D activities conducted internally and externally do not replace each other, but rather complement one another. This is consistent with the view that internal R&D nurtures a firm's ability to evaluate external R&D partners and to assimilate the fruits of externally available R&D resources. In addition, the magnitude of the impact of a company's internal R&D programs on the extent to which the company utilized external R&D resources grew larger as the sample period progressed. This may suggest that Japanese companies have attained higher levels of synergy between in-house and external R&D since the second half of the 1990s.

Second, the firms that exploit external R&D resources are primarily large firms, who find external R&D resources through their corporate group networks of subsidiaries and affiliates. Another interesting finding related to corporate groups is that a large equity stake share held by a parent company assists a subsidiary in outsourcing R&D, but not in pursuing joint R&D initiatives. This may arise from the greater information requirements that a firm has to meet before it can make a decision on a desirable joint R&D partner. This asymmetric role of parent companies in external R&D decisions is an area for further research.

Another important target for further inquiry is the small-firm sector not covered by METI's *Basic Survey*. This sector includes venture businesses, many of which are highly research-oriented. Investigation of the R&D behavior of these small companies, together with the insights obtained in the present study, will contribute to a better understanding of the R&D activities of Japanese companies.

Appendix

Appendix 7.1 Summary statistics of regression variables

Variable	# Obs.	Mean	Std. Dev.	Min	Max
Type 11 Company	61,849	0.165	0.371	0	1
External R&D	61,849	0.001	0.011	0.000	2.153
Size500	61,849	0.122	0.328	0	1
Size1000	61,849	0.114	0.317	0	1
Internal R&D	61,849	0.020	0.031	0.000	2.041
Group Firm	61,849	5.675	20.43	0	1,179
Group Foreign	61,849	0.151	0.285	0.000	1.000
Parent Equity	61,849	223.7	385.7	0	1,000
Birth Year	61,849	1958	15.83	1885	2,003

Continued

158   *Akihiko Kawaura and Dai Miyamoto*

Appendix 7.1   Continued

Variable	# Obs.	Mean	Std. Dev.	Min	Max
Domestic joint R&D	5,364	0.402	0.490	0	1
Overseas joint R&D	5,364	0.071	0.257	0	1
Domestic Partners	5,364	1.743	11.09	0	607
Overseas Partners	5,364	0.226	2.545	0	144
Size500	5,364	0.141	0.348	0	1
Size1000	5,364	0.151	0.358	0	1
Internal R&D	5,364	0.024	0.045	0.000	2.041
Group Firm	5,364	8.272	28.96	0	1,179
Group Foreign	5,364	0.190	0.303	0.000	1.000
Parent Equity	5,364	218.2	378.3	0	1,000
Birth Year	5,364	1956	17.38	1892	2,003

Notes

1. For analyses of the 'lost decade' in Japan, see, for example, Horioka (2006), Saxonhouse and Stern (2003), or Hayashi and Prescott (2002).
2. The source for the R&D data presented in this section is the *Report on the Survey of Research and Development* (various years) prepared by the Statistics Bureau of Japan's Ministry of Internal Affairs and Communications.
3. This statement is valid both in terms of nominal values and in terms of year-2000 constant prices.
4. The data plotted in Figure 7.4 are taken from the *Report on the Survey of Research and Development* (multiple years), which reports corporate R&D expenditures disbursed for both internal and external R&D activities, with the data aggregated by industry. The quantity plotted in Figure 7.4 is the percentage of total (internal and external) R&D expenditures devoted to external R&D.
5. Matsuura and Kiyota (2004) provide a detailed description of the data reported by METI's *Basic Survey*. Examples of studies using *Basic Survey* data to investigate corporate behavior include Fukao *et al.* (2005), a comparative study of foreign-owned and domestically owned firms.
6. We focus on firms in Categories 10 and 11 because these firms constitute the majority of the firms for which data are collected in the *Basic Survey of Japanese Business Structure and Activities*, as indicated in Figure 7.5.
7. For the Schumpeterian hypothesis, see Schumpeter (1950).
8. A reference on the 'learning' function of R&D activities is Cohen and Levinthal (1989). These authors explain that in-house R&D serves to improve a firm's capability to assimilate and exploit existing information, which is termed the firm's 'absorptive' or 'learning' capacity. When firms regard internal and external R&D operations as substitutes for one another, the choice between the two is primarily determined by the relative cost of each alternative. However, if the 'absorptive' capacity of in-house R&D is taken into account, then in-house R&D can enhance the potential benefits derived from external R&D. It then follows that external R&D utilization should increase in conjunction with in-house R&D efforts.

9. Firms within the corporate group include subsidiaries (firms in which a company has an ownership stake of 50–100 per cent) and affiliates (firms in which a company has an ownership stake of 25–50 per cent).

10. Examples of literature addressing the age of firms include Marshall (1920), which hypothesized that firm growth is negatively correlated with age. Jovanovic (1982) proposes the 'passive learning' model, which predicts an inverse relationship between growth and age, as a theoretical framework. Evans (1987a, 1987b) found that firm growth decreases with firm age and firm size, thus supporting the hypothesis of Jovanovic.

11. Summary statistics are in the top panel of the Appendix table. Results on industry dummy variables are not shown in Table 7.3, but are available from the authors upon request.

12. The search-cost perspective is often used in labor market analyses, especially in the context of job search. See, for example, Stigler (1962) and Mortensen (1986).

13. Summary statistics are in the bottom panel of the Appendix table.

References

Ahuja, G. (2000) 'Collaboration Networks, Structural Holes, and Innovation: A Longitudinal Study', *Administrative Science Quarterly*, 45(3): 425–455.

Cohen, W. M. and Levinthal, D. A. (1989) 'Innovation and Learning: The Two Faces of R&D', *Economic Journal*, 99(397): 569–596.

Evans, D. S. (1987a) 'The Relationship between Firm Growth, Size, and Age: Estimates for 100 Manufacturing Industries', *Journal of Industrial Economics*, 35(4): 567–581.

Evans, D. S. (1987b) 'Tests of Alternative Theories of Firm Growth', *Journal of Political Economy*, 95(4): 657–674.

Fukao, K., Ito, K., and Kwon, H. U. (2005) 'Do Out-In M&As Bring Higher TFP to Japan? An Empirical Analysis Based on Micro-data on Japanese Manufacturing Firms', *Journal of Japanese and International Economies*, 19(2): 272–301.

Gulati, R. (1998) 'Alliance and Networks', *Strategic Management Journal*, 19(4): 293–317.

Hayashi, F. and Prescott, E. C. (2002) 'The 1990s in Japan: A Lost Decade', *Review of Economic Dynamics*, 5(1): 206–235.

Horioka, C. Y. (2006) 'The Causes of Japan's "Lost Decade": The Role of Household Consumption', *Japan and the World Economy*, 18(4): 378–400.

Jovanovic, B. (1982) 'Selection and Evolution of Industry', *Econometrica*, 50(3): 649–670.

Marshall, A. (1920) *Principles of Economics: An Introductory Volume* (8th edition), London: Macmillan.

Matsuura, T. and Kiyota, K. (2004) '*Kigyo katsudo kihon chousa paneru deeta no sakusei-riyou ni tsuite*' (On the Creation and Usage of the Panel Data in the Basic Survey of Japanese Business Structure and Activities), Research Institute of Economy, Trade and Industry (RIETI) Policy Discussion Paper Series 04-P-004.

Mortensen, D. (1986) 'Job Search and Labor Market Analysis', in R. Layard and O. Ashenfelter (eds), *Handbook of Labor Economics*, II, 849–919, Amsterdam: North-Holland.

Organisation for Economic Co-operation and Development (2007), *Main Science and Technology Indicators*, Paris: OECD.

Pfeffer, J. and Salancik, G. R. (1978) *The External Control of Organizations: A Resource Dependence Perspective*, New York: Harper & Row.

Saxonhouse, G. R. and Stern, R. M. (2003) 'The Bubble and the Lost Decade', *The World Economy*, 26(3): 267–281.

Schumpeter, J. A. (1950) *Capitalism, Socialism, and Democracy* (3rd edition), New York: Harper & Brothers.

Shimotani, M. (1993) *Nihon no keiretsu to kigyou guruupu: sono rekishi to riron* (Keiretsu and Corporate Groups in Japan: History and Theory), Tokyo: Yuhikaku.

Stigler, G. (1962) 'Information in the Labor Market', *Journal of Political Economy*, 70(5) (Part 2: Investment in Human Beings): 94–105.

8
Foreign Direct Investment and Management in Japan
The Impact of Japanese Corporations' Foreign Direct Investment Strategies on Managerial Decisions and Corporate Performance in Japan: An Analysis Based on Corporate-Level Microdata

Jun Ma

Introduction

Foreign direct investment (FDI) by Japanese firms increased rapidly in the years following the Plaza Accord, and this trend spurred a number of studies investigating how FDI by Japanese companies affected Japan's domestic economy and industrial landscape. A significant fraction of these studies, including those by Fukao and Amano (1998), Fukao and Yuan (2006), and Horaguchi (1998a, 1998b) focused on the question of whether or not FDI was responsible for a 'hollowing out' of Japan's domestic manufacturing base. On the other hand, relatively few studies have addressed the question of how FDI impacted the corporate performance of Japanese firms. Kimura and Kiyota (2002) analyzed panel data from the *Basic Survey of Japanese Business Structure and Activities* (an annual survey conducted by Japan's Ministry of Economy, Trade, and Industry (METI)) and concluded that some companies – specifically, those who, in the 1990s, succeeded in responding to overseas competition by breaking free of domestic shackles and expanding into foreign countries – transformed themselves into more efficient organizations and were left better-equipped to adapt to changing economic conditions.

Previous studies that have considered the impact of a corporation's global activities on its manufacturing capabilities and innovativeness back in the home country seem, in all cases, to have arrived at one of two diametrically opposed conclusions. Some studies find that, when a corporation transfers its accumulated wealth of manufacturing technology and innovation capacity from the home country to overseas destinations, there is no corresponding growth in the new capabilities needed to make the most of the resources that remain in the home country, and the home country is left 'hollowed out'. Meanwhile, other studies find that corporations who expand overseas expose themselves to international competition, which forces them to become more efficient and to acquire new skills, ultimately allowing them to utilize the resources of the home country more effectively.

But perhaps the relationship between FDI and corporate performance is not so simple and straightforward. For one thing, corporations generally have not just a single objective, but a variety of objectives, for their FDI initiatives. Moreover, FDI tends to spur corporate restructuring in a number of areas, including organizational structure, facility investments, and research and development. *All* of these corporate activities are ultimately reflected in a corporation's bottom line.

In this chapter, we address some of the problems inherent in previous analyses of direct cause-and-effect relationships between FDI and corporate business conditions. By considering FDIs by Japanese firms over a period of approximately ten years, from the mid-1990s to the mid-2000s, and by paying particular attention to the specific mechanisms through which FDI impacted domestic corporate performance, we assess the influence of foreign investments on domestic corporate decision-making – including human-resource allocations, R&D activities, and inter-firm transactions – as well as on the corporate bottom line.

Previous studies and hypotheses

Many previous studies have attempted to assess the relationship between FDI and corporate behavior and performance, but the conclusions of these studies have not always been clear. For example, Grant (1987) conducted both static and dynamic analyses of manufacturing firms in England, found a positive correlation between corporate globalization and profits, and emphasized that overseas production contributed significantly to corporate sales and profits. In subsequent studies, Doukas and Travlos (1988) concluded that foreign investments by multinational corporations could increase corporate profits, while Waheed and Mathur (1995) similarly reported that geographical dispersion could benefit corporations in a variety of ways. Moreover, the work of Tallman and Li (1996) identified a weak but positive linear relationship between overseas activity and corporate financial performance.

Other studies, on the other hand, suggest that overseas investments are not always linked to improved corporate performance. Hitt *et al.* (1994) noted that, as corporations become more and more multinational, the increasing expense of transactions, together with the increasing cost of gathering, processing, and disseminating information, can cause profits to dwindle. In later work, Hitt *et al.* (1997) observed that, as corporations globalize, they consume an ever-wider spectrum of resources and must correspondingly master an ever-wider spectrum of corporate governance; when the combined strain exceeds a corporation's managerial capabilities, the added costs of transactions and information can overwhelm any increase in profits that the multinationalization might have brought about in the first place. Geringer *et al.* (1989), defining the degree of a corporation's internationalization to be the fraction of total sales due to overseas sales, suggest that the relationship between a corporation's degree of internationalization and its corporate performance is a nonlinear concave function. Daniels and Bracker (1989) report that, as long as the ratio of overseas sales to total sales – or the ratio of overseas assets to total assets – lies below 40–50 per cent, multinationalization has a positive impact on corporate performance, but that when this threshold is exceeded the impact on profits becomes less significant.

The broad dispersion of conclusions drawn by these prior studies testifies to the complicated relationship between corporate globalization and corporate performance. Grant (1987) pointed out that, in addition to the *direct* impact that overseas expansion has on corporate performance, other *indirect* effects, due to complementary relationships or conflicts that arise between corporate globalization initiatives and various other managerial activities, are of critical importance.

In this study, we consider not only the direct influences of FDI on corporate performance, but also the ways in which corporations can tie their overall performance to their overseas efforts, through effective, globally focused utilization of internal corporate resources and through efficient coordination and division of labor between FDI activities and business initiatives in the home country. Based on these observations, we attempt to analyze the impact of FDI on the corporate bottom line through the lens of a particular dynamic framework – namely, a consideration of the ways in which a Japanese corporation's choice of targets for FDI influences corporate behavior back in Japan, including human resources, technology development, and inter-firm transactions. Then, based on the results of our analysis, we investigate the impact of these managerial decisions on corporate financial performance.

In passing we note that Bartlett and Ghoshal (1989) conducted field research on nine multinational firms in three industries (home electronics, daily consumables, and communication devices), with particular focus on the characteristics of corporate structure and activity that differ based on overseas expansion objectives. These authors identified three distinct categories of managerial structure among corporations with overseas activities: a *multinational* model, a *global* model, and an *international* model. In corporations adhering to the *multinational* model, foreign subsidiaries are specifically designed to be able to respond sensitively to the unique features of the local environment in overseas destinations; decision-making authority is devolved to the subsidiaries, and the subsidiaries in the various foreign countries are thought of as independent business units. In corporations following the *global* model, on the other hand, overseas business units are thought of merely as stepping stones used to achieve global scale; the majority of the corporation's core competencies, authority, and decision-making powers remain concentrated at corporate headquarters, and the role of foreign subsidiaries is limited to producing and selling products that were developed at corporate headquarters. Finally, in corporations adopting the *international* model, although significant capabilities and authority are devolved to the subsidiaries, the foreign subsidiaries are nonetheless still thought of as extensions of corporate headquarters, which manages its subsidiaries through managerial planning and managerial structure. The parent company develops the core product technologies, and the subsidiaries turn these technologies into products can be locally produced.

Based on this logical framework, Bartlett and Ghoshal (1989) concluded that, in the 1980s, representative Japanese multinationals such as Matsushita, NEC, and Kao had adopted a *global* strategic model, utilizing new manufacturing technologies and pursuing global efficiencies of scale to stake out competitive positions in the world marketplace.

Inspired by the work of Bartlett and Ghoshal (1989), in this chapter we ask: What strategic business models did Japanese firms adopt for their overseas operations in the 1990s? If Japanese firms in the 1980s adopted a *global* strategic model, as suggested by Bartlett and Ghoshal (1989), we hypothesize that Japanese firms in the 1990s designed their FDI strategies to proceed in one of two general directions. Some firms preserved the *global* strategic model, while updating it to pursue even greater worldwide efficiencies of scale. Other firms, faced with the need to stay alive amidst ever-intensifying competition in wide swaths of the global marketplace, evolved from the traditional *global* strategic model toward an *international* strategic model.

Analytical models and data set

Analytical models

As a corporation expands into a new country or region, it necessarily adjusts its domestic managerial resources and business activities. The questions of which managerial resources must be brought from the home country in order to manufacture products overseas, and what kind of cooperative relationships can be struck with the domestic sector of the business back home, have different answers depending on the region and the objective of FDI.

For example, corporations that adopt a *global* strategic model attempt to pursue global-scale efficiencies by shifting production to low-cost regions – but maintaining high quality – while at the same time aggressively expanding into high-value-added regional markets. In order for such a strategy to succeed, the corporation must strengthen the capabilities of its corporate headquarters in the home country, while simultaneously maintaining a consistently closed model of product development at corporate headquarters, and aggressively pursuing a strategy of rationalization toward domestic subsidiaries and affiliates.

In contrast, corporations that adopt an *international* strategic model seek to realize a strategy of expanding globally based on a core set of technologies. In order for this strategy to succeed, the corporation must solve the problem of how to preserve the core competencies of its corporate headquarters while adapting to the unique conditions of regional markets. To this end, the scale of corporate headquarters in the home country must be kept to a minimum; the traditional closed model of product development must gradually evolve toward an open model, and domestic product manufacturing, based on core competencies, must be expanded; at the same time, development and manufacturing of peripheral products may be shifted to regional markets.

In this study, we use the following analytical model to describe the various strategic managerial decisions a corporation makes:

$$R_{i,t} = f\left(D_{i,t-1}, X_{i,t-1}\right) + \mu_{i,t} \tag{8.1}$$

where $R_{i,t}$ stands for any one of a variety of managerial decisions made by corporation i at time t, the quantities $\{D_{i,t-1}\}$ are dummy variables that describe the presence or absence of FDI (the creation of corporate subsidiaries) in various overseas regions at time $t-1$, and the quantities $\{X_{i,t-1}\}$ are control variables used to account for other influential factors.

Next, in assessing the impact of Japanese corporations' FDIs on corporate financial performance, we must keep in mind the dynamic and possibly time-delayed nature of the relationship between FDI and financial performance. To this end, we describe the impact of new FDIs in year $t-1$ on corporate financial performance in year $t+n$ ($n = 0, 1, 2, 3, \ldots$) according to a model of the form

$$V_{i,t+n} = f\left(\hat{R}_{i,t}, D_{i,t-1}, X_{i,t-1}\right) + \mu_{i,t} \tag{8.2}$$

Here $V_{i,t+n}$ denotes corporate added value[1] in year $t+n$, while $\hat{R}_{i,t}$, $D_{i,t-1}$, and $X_{i,t-1}$ denote various factors that impact corporate added value. As in model (8.1), the quantities $\{D_{i,t-1}\}$ are dummy variables that describe the presence or absence of FDI (the creation of corporate subsidiaries) in each region at time $t-1$. $\hat{R}_{i,t}$ is a fitted value for a variety of strategic managerial decisions made by the corporation in year t. This quantity allows us to account for managerial activities that were influenced by FDI, and the impact of those activities on corporate performance, within the context of a dynamic framework. In other words, we conduct a two-stage analysis, first using model (8.1) to predict a fitted value $\hat{R}_{i,t}$ for each of the corporate decision-making variables $R_{i,t}$, and then substituting these fitted values into equation (8.2) to analyze corporate added value. Finally, the variables $\{X_{i,t-1}\}$ in equation (8.2) are control variables that account for all other influential factors.

Data set

The analysis of this study is based on the analytical models described above together with microdata from the *Basic Survey of Japanese Business Structure and Activities* (*Kigyou Katsudou Kihon Chousa*), conducted by the METI annually since 1992. This is a designated statistical survey designed to collect basic data for use in crafting government policy relating to corporations, and provides a clear picture of the nature of corporate activities in Japan. The survey singles out three categories from Japan's list of standard industrial classifications, namely, categories D (mining), F (manufacturing), and I (wholesale and retail sales; bars and restaurants). Among corporations with offices in any of these three business areas, all companies with 50 or more employees and capital or investments of 30 million yen or more are targeted by the survey, yielding a total sample size of some 26,000 companies each year. The data items gathered by the survey include the following: (1) structure of the corporate entity and date of incorporation; (2) term of business and number of employees; (3) assets and liabilities, or capital and investments; (4) transactions with other companies and overseas entities; (5) research and development; (6) technologies possessed and status of transactions; (7) status of parent companies, subsidiary companies, and corporate affiliates. To conduct the analysis reported in this study, we created panel data by aggregating microdata from the *Basic Survey of Japanese Business Structure and Activities* since 1992 and tracking the corporate activity of individual companies over multiple years.

We now describe the primary variables that enter into our analysis.

Foreign-expansion dummy variables

First, the most important variables for the purposes of this study are the quantities collectively labeled $\{D_{i,t-1}\}$ in equations (8.1) and (8.2); these are binary dummy variables describing a corporation's choice of regions in which to make FDIs. We determine values for these variables as follows. First, we consider three possible target regions for investments, namely, Asia, Europe, and North America. We then introduce seven distinct foreign-expansion patterns, summarized in Table 8.1, to indicate the presence or absence of FDI (creation of corporate subsidiaries)[2] in the various regions in year *t–1*.

Figure 8.1 shows the fraction of corporations exhibiting each of these seven foreign expansion patterns (the number of corporations following each pattern divided by the total number of corporations) for the ten years from 1994 to 2003. The graph reveals that expanding only in Asia was the most common pattern during this ten-year period, while expanding in all three regions was the second-most common pattern; expanding only in Europe was the least common pattern.

Table 8.1 Foreign-expansion-pattern dummy variables (collectively denoted $\{D_{i,t-1}\}$ in equations (8.1) and (8.2))

Variable	Description	Meaning
$ASFDI_{i,\,t-1}$	Binary dummy variable denoting expansion into Asia only	= 1 if corporation i invested only in Asia during year $t-1$; =0 otherwise.
$EUFDI_{i,\,t-1}$	Binary dummy variable denoting expansion into Europe only	= 1 if corporation i invested only in Europe during year $t-1$; =0 otherwise.
$NAFDI_{i,\,t-1}$	Binary dummy variable denoting expansion into North America only	= 1 if corporation i invested only in North America during year $t-1$; =0 otherwise.
$AEFDI_{i,\,t-1}$	Binary dummy variable denoting expansion into both Asia and Europe	= 1 if corporation i invested in Asia and Europe during year $t-1$; =0 otherwise.
$ENFDI_{i,\,t-1}$	Binary dummy variable denoting expansion into both North America and Europe	= 1 if corporation i invested in Europe and North America during year $t-1$; =0 otherwise.
$ANFDI_{i,\,t-1}$	Binary dummy variable denoting expansion into both Asia and North America	= 1 if corporation i invested in Asia and North America during year $t-1$; =0 otherwise.
$AENFDI_{i,\,t-1}$	Binary dummy variable denoting expansion into all three regions (Asia, North America, and Europe) (1 or 0)	= 1 if corporation i invested in Asia, Europe, and North America during year $t-1$; =0 otherwise.

Managerial-decision variables

We next describe the variables we used to account for managerial activity in the home country. In this study, we use three measures to characterize managerial decision-making in the home country: personnel placements, research and development activities, and transactions between corporations. Each of these areas is described by multiple variables.

First, personnel placements are characterized by seven variables, as summarized in Table 8.2(a) (where, as before, the i and t subscripts label the corporation and the year in question, respectively).

Next, the four variables used to describe domestic R&D activities are described in Table 8.2(b).

Finally, the two variables used to describe inter-firm transactions are summarized in Table 8.2(c).

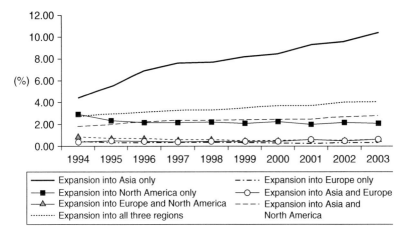

Figure 8.1 Fraction of foreign-expanding Japanese corporations adopting each of the seven possible foreign-expansion patterns between 1994 and 2003

Note: The fraction reported for each pattern is the number of companies adopting that pattern divided by the total number of companies that expanded overseas.

Control variables

Next, our model accounts for a variety of corporate attributes that may be expected to influence corporate management practices. These attributes are described by control variables, collectively denoted $\{X_{i,t-1}\}$ in equations (8.1) and (8.2) and described in the following tables.

First, we consider four control variables describing the attributes of corporation i in year $t–1$, as summarized in Table 8.3(a).

Next, we consider six control variables describing the regional dependence of the export and import behavior of corporation i in year $t–1$, as summarized in Table 8.3(b).

Quantities entering into equation (8.2)

Finally, we discuss the variables entering into equation (8.2).

First, the dependent variable $V_{i,t}$ (namely, LN-ADD-VULE$_{i,t}$) is the natural logarithm of corporate added value (defined as sales minus purchases) for corporation i in year t.

Next, the variables $D_{i,t-1}$ are the seven dummy variables indicating the presence or absence of new FDI (creation of subsidiaries) in year $t–1$, as described in Table 8.1.

The variables in equation (8.2) denote fitted values for managerial-decision variables in year t. The values inserted into equation (8.2) for these quantities are estimates obtained from equation (8.1) for

Table 8.2(a) Managerial-decision variables related to personnel allocations (collectively denoted $\{R_{i,t}\}$ in equations (8.1) and (8.2))

Variable	Description
$LNREG_{i,t}$	Natural logarithm of total number of regular employees
$L\text{-}REG\text{-}TOTAL_{i,t}$	Fraction of regular employees[a] who are full-time workers
$L\text{-}HF\text{-}TOTAL_{i,t}$	Fraction of all regular employees who work in functional departments at corporate headquarters
$L\text{-}HINTL\text{-}TOTAL_{i,t}$	Fraction of all regular employees who work in international business units at corporate headquarters
$L\text{-}RD\text{-}TOTAL_{i,t}$	Fraction of all regular employees who work in R&D (workers in R&D units at corporate headquarters or at corporate laboratories)
$L\text{-}HMFG\text{-}TOTAL_{i,t}$	Fraction of all regular employees who work in manufacturing divisions at corporate headquarters
$L\text{-}BDMFG\text{-}TOTAL_{i,t}$	Fraction of all regular employees who work in manufacturing divisions at locations other than corporate headquarters

Note: [a] The *Basic Survey of Japanese Business Structure and Activities* defines the term 'regular employees' to include (a) salaried executives, and (b) any worker, regardless of nominal designation (full employee, partial employee, part-time worker, and so on) who has been employed for over one month and who, in the most recent two months within the fiscal year in question or the most recent accounting period, worked 18 or more days. This includes most contractors to whom a corporation paid compensation. In this study, we have estimated the number of full-time workers by subtracting the number of part-time workers from the number of regular employees.

Table 8.2(b) Managerial-decision variables related to domestic R&D activities (collectively denoted $\{R_{i,t}\}$ in equations (8.1) and (8.2))

Variable	Description
$INRD_{i,t}$	Natural logarithm of R&D expenditure
$RD\text{-}SALE_{i,t}$	Ratio of R&D expenditures to sales
$RDSELF\text{-}SALE_{i,t}$	Ratio of in-house R&D expenditures to sales
$RDSELF\text{-}RDTOTAL_{i,t}$	Fraction of all R&D expenditures related to in-house R&D activities

a subset of eight of the managerial-decision variables described in Tables 8.2(a)–(c) above (namely, $P\text{-}L\text{-}HINTL\text{-}TOTAL_{i,t}$, $P\text{-}L\text{-}RD\text{-}TOTAL_{i,t}$, $P\text{-}L\text{-}HMFG\text{-}TOTAL_{i,t}$, $P\text{-}L\text{-}BDMFG\text{-}TOTAL_{i,t}$, $P\text{-}RD\text{-}SALE_{i,t}$, $P\text{-}RDSELF\text{-}RDTOTAL_{i,t}$, $P\text{-}TRSC\text{-}AFLT\text{-}SALE_{i,t}$, and $P\text{-}TRSC\text{-}AFLT\text{-}PCH_{i,t}$). (The

Table 8.2(c) Managerial-decision variables related to inter-firm transactions (collectively denoted $\{R_{i,t}\}$ in equations (8.1) and (8.2))

Variable	Description
$TRSC\text{-}AFLT\text{-}SALE_{i,t}$	Fraction of total sales due to sales to corporate affiliates[a]
$TRSC\text{-}AFLT\text{-}PCH_{i,t}$	Fraction of total purchases due to purchases from corporate affiliates

Note: [a] The term 'affiliate' here refers to any parent company, subsidiary company, or affiliated company of the company in question. Here a 'parent company' is a company that possesses more than 50 per cent voting rights in the company in question; a 'subsidiary company' is any company in which the company in question possesses more than 50 per cent voting rights; and an 'affiliated company' is a company in which the company in question possesses between 20 per cent and 50 per cent voting rights. However, overseas 'affiliated companies' are not included in these totals.

Table 8.3(a) Control variables describing corporate attributes (collectively denoted $\{X_{i,t-1}\}$ in equations (8.1) and (8.2))

Variable	Description
$AS\text{-}L_{i,t-1}$	Assets per employee (total value of assets/ number of full-time employees) (nominal value, unit: 10,000 yen)
$PRO\text{-}SALE_{i,t-1}$	Profit-to-sales ratio
$CAP\text{-}FR_{i,t-1}$	Ratio of foreign capital to company's overall capital in year
$F\text{-}AGE_{i,t}$	Age of firm

Table 8.3(b) Control variables describing regional dependence of corporate exports and imports (collectively denoted $\{X_{i,t-1}\}$ in equations (8.1) and (8.2))

Variable	Description
$ASEX_{i,t-1}$	Dollar-value fraction of all sales due to exports to Asia
$ASIM_{i,t-1}$	Dollar-value fraction of all purchases due to imports from Asia
$EUEX_{i,t-1}$	Dollar-value fraction of all sales due to exports to Europe
$EUIM_{i,t-1}$	Dollar-value fraction of all purchases due to imports from Europe
$NAEX_{i,t-1}$	Dollar-value fraction of all sales due to exports to North America
$NAIM_{i,t-1}$	Dollar-value fraction of all purchases due to imports from North America

Table 8.4 Statistical properties of variables

Variable	Sample Size	Average Value	Standard Deviation	Minimum	Maximum
$LN\text{-}ADD\text{-}VULE_{i,t}$	134,392	7.639	1.287	0.693	14.956
$AS\text{-}L_{i,t-1}$	121,159	0.298	0.338	0.000	33.169
$PRO\text{-}SALE_{i,t}$	134,655	0.022	0.226	−41.418	4.839
$RD\text{-}SALE_{i,t-1}$	109,860	0.010	0.023	0.000	0.898
$CAP\text{-}FR_{i,t}$	148,100	0.014	0.095	0.000	1.000
$F\text{-}AGE_{i,t}$	148,088	38.121	16.044	0.000	119.000
$ASFDI_{i,t-1}$	121,192	0.078	0.268	0.000	1.000
$EUFDI_{i,t-1}$	121,192	0.003	0.057	0.000	1.000
$NAFDI_{i,t-1}$	121,192	0.022	0.147	0.000	1.000
$AEFDI_{i,t-1}$	121,192	0.005	0.067	0.000	1.000
$ENFDI_{i,t-1}$	121,192	0.006	0.078	0.000	1.000
$ANFDI_{i,t-1}$	121,192	0.023	0.151	0.000	1.000
$AENFDI_{i,t-1}$	121,192	0.034	0.182	0.000	1.000
$ASEX_{i,t-1}$	109,860	0.016	0.059	0.000	1.000
$ASIM_{i,t-1}$	108,151	0.018	0.085	0.000	1.000
$EUEX_{i,t-1}$	109,860	0.005	0.027	0.000	0.981
$EUIM_{i,t-1}$	108,151	0.005	0.046	0.000	1.000
$NAEX_{i,t-1}$	109,860	0.008	0.039	0.000	1.000
$NAIM_{i,t-1}$	108,151	0.006	0.044	0.000	1.000
$LNREG_{i,t}$	148,077	5.057	0.997	1.609	11.317
$L\text{-}REG\text{-}TOTAL_{i,t}$	148,100	0.916	0.143	−0.759	1.000
$L\text{-}HF\text{-}TOTAL_{i,t}$	148,100	0.092	0.119	0.000	1.000
$L\text{-}HINTL\text{-}TOTAL_{i,t}$	148,100	0.003	0.012	0.000	1.000
$L\text{-}RD\text{-}TOTAL_{i,t}$	148,100	0.038	0.069	0.000	1.000
$L\text{-}HMFG\text{-}TOTAL_{i,t}$	148,100	0.393	0.346	0.000	1.023
$L\text{-}BDMFG\text{-}TOTAL_{i,t}$	148,100	0.280	0.329	0.000	1.000
$LNRD_{i,t}$	70,389	4.077	2.236	0.000	13.290
$RD\text{-}SALE_{i,t}$	134,663	0.010	0.027	0.000	4.194
$RDSELF\text{-}SALE_{i,t}$	134,663	0.009	0.023	0.000	2.041
$RDSELF\text{-}RDTOTAL_{i,t}$	70,389	0.946	0.187	0.000	1.000
$TRSC\text{-}AFLT\text{-}SALE_{i,t}$	108,863	0.244	0.375	0.000	1.000
$TRSC\text{-}AFLT\text{-}PCH_{i,t}$	77,987	0.180	0.2922	0.000	1.000

P- prefix added to the variable name denotes a fitted value for the variable in question.)

In addition, several control variables enter into equation (8.2): a two-digit industrial-category dummy variable,[3] the foreign-capital ratio (CAP-$FR_{i,t}$), the firm age (F-$AGE_{i,t}$), and the six variables measuring the fraction of total sales and purchases occupied by exports to and imports from Asia, Europe, and North America ($ASEX_{i,t}$, $ASIM_{i,t}$, $EUEX_{i,t}$, $EUIM_{i,t}$, $NAEX_{i,t}$, and $NAIM_{i,t}$).

The statistical properties of all variables used in our study are summarized in Table 8.4.

Results

The impact of FDI on corporate managerial activity in the home country

The predictions of equation (8.1) regarding the impact of FDI by Japanese firms on corporate managerial activity in Japan, including personnel placement, R&D activity, and inter-firm transactions, are presented in Tables 8.5–8.8. In the remainder of this section we discuss these results in detail.

The impact on domestic personnel allocations

We first consider the predictions of our model regarding the impact of FDI on the composition of the workforce in the home country (see Table 8.5). First, each of the seven dummy variables describing expansion into foreign countries is positively correlated, in a statistically significant way, with an increase in the number of full-time workers in the home country. Moreover, the correlation strengthens as the number of expansion regions increases. This indicates that FDI has a positive impact on the hiring of full-time workers within Japan, and that the magnitude of this impact grows as the regional breadth of overseas expansion grows. On the other hand, if we consider the fraction of regular employees who are full-time workers, we see that expansion into Asia alone, or expansion into Europe alone, is negatively correlated with this quantity, while the dummy variables for the other five patterns of overseas expansion are positively correlated with this quantity. Taken together, these two results suggest that, while FDI by Japanese corporations tends to increase hiring of full-time workers by those corporations within Japan, it is also true that, when corporations expand only into

Table 8.5 Conclusions of model regarding the impact of FDI on the composition of the domestic workforce (1)

	Natural logarithm of total number of regular employees	Fraction of all regular employees who are full employees	Fraction of all regular employees who work in functional departments at corporate headquarters
	$LNREG_{i,t}$	$L\text{-}REG\text{-}TOTAL_{i,t}$	$L\text{-}HF\text{-}TOTAL_{i,t}$
Lagged dependent variable	0.9664***	0.7884***	0.7058***
	(0.0008)	(0.0019)	(0.0022)
$AS\text{-}L_{i,t-1}$	0.0474***	0.0094***	0.0143***
	(0.0023)	(0.0009)	(0.0009)
$RD\text{-}SALE_{i,t-1}$	0.1030***	0.0399**	0.2247***
	(0.0300)	(0.0121)	(0.0131)
$PRO\text{-}SALE_{i,t-1}$	0.0249***	0.0007	0.0004
	(0.0028)	(0.0012)	(0.0014)
$CAP\text{-}FR_{i,t}$	0.0025	0.0064**	−0.0080***
	(0.0072)	(0.0029)	(0.0031)
$F\text{-}AGE_{i,t}$	−0.0004***	0.0001***	0.00002
	(0.0000)	(0.0000)	(0.00001)
$ASFDI_{i,t-1}$	0.0082***	−0.0031**	−0.0011
	(0.0024)	(0.0009)	(0.0010)
$EUFDI_{i,t-1}$	0.0229**	−0.0069*	0.0008
	(0.0104)	(0.0042)	(0.0046)
$NAFDI_{i,t-1}$	0.0182***	0.0002	−0.0018
	(0.0042)	(0.0017)	(0.0018)
$AEFDI_{i,t-1}$	0.0185**	0.0001	−0.0107***
	(0.0086)	(0.0034)	(0.0052)
$ENFDI_{i,t-1}$	0.0305***	−0.0002	−0.0078**
	(0.0081)	(0.0032)	(0.0034)
$ANFDI_{i,t-1}$	0.0272***	−0.0006	−0.0027
	(0.0043	(0.0017)	(0.0017)
$AENFDI_{i,t-1}$	0.0577***	0.0010	−0.0140***
	(0.0044)	(0.0016)	(0.0016)
$ASEX_{i,t-1}$	−0.0302***	0.0037	0.0339***
	(0.0108)	(0.0044)	(0.0048)
$ASIM_{i,t-1}$	−0.0202***	−0.0005	0.0245***
	(0.0070)	(0.0028)	(0.0032)

Continued

Table 8.5 Continued

	Natural logarithm of total number of regular employees	Fraction of all regular employees who are full employees	Fraction of all regular employees who work in functional departments at corporate headquarters
	$LNREG_{i,t}$	$L\text{-}REG\text{-}TOTAL_{i,t}$	$L\text{-}HF\text{-}TOTAL_{i,t}$
$EUEX_{i,t-1}$	0.0434	−0.0064	−0.0192*
	(0.0264)	(0.0106)	(0.0113)
$EUIM_{i,t-1}$	0.0045	0.0001**	−0.0207***
	(0.0137)	(0.0055)	(0.0060)
$NAEX_{i,t-1}$	0.0036	−0.0033	0.0359***
	(0.0182)	(0.0073)	(0.0079)
$NAIM_{i,t-1}$	0.0218*	0.0030	0.0060
	(0.0136)	(0.0055)	(0.0061)
CONS	0.1577***	0.1554***	0.0278***
	(0.0064)	(0.0025)	(0.0020)
Sample size	108,084	108,120	108,120
R^2	0.9741	0.7927	0.5251

Note: *** denotes statistical significance at the 1% level; ** denotes statistical significance at the 5% level; * denotes statistical significance at the 10% level.

Asia or only into Europe, non-full workers are hired at an even greater rate than are full-time workers.

For the next stage of our analysis, we group employees into various categories based on function. First, considering the fraction of all regular employees who work in functional departments at corporate headquarters (whom we label 'white-collar workers' in what follows), we see that four of the seven dummy variables were negatively correlated with this quantity in a statistically significant way (namely, expansion into Asia only, expansion into Europe only, expansion into both Europe and North America, and expansion into all three regions), while the correlations of the other three dummy variables with this quantity were not statistically significant. We next consider the fraction of all regular employees who work either in international business units

Table 8.6 Conclusions of model regarding the impact of FDI on the composition of the domestic workforce (2)

	Fraction of all regular employees working in international business units at corporate headquarters	Fraction of all regular employees who work in R&D divisions	Fraction of all regular employees who work in manufacturing divisions at corporate headquarters	Fraction of all regular employees who work in manufacturing divisions at locations other than corporate headquarters
	$L\text{-}HINTL\text{-}TOTAL_{i,t}$	$L\text{-}RD\text{-}TOTAL_{i,t}$	$L\text{-}HMFG\text{-}TOTAL_{i,t}$	$L\text{-}BDMFG\text{-}TOTAL_{i,t}$
Lagged dependent variable	0.2591***	0.7818***	0.7385***	0.8295***
	(0.0031)	(0.0020)	(0.0020)	(0.0017)
$AS\text{-}L_{i,t-1}$	0.0009***	0.0042***	−0.0305***	0.0034*
	(0.0002)	(0.0004)	(0.0024)	(0.0019)
$RD\text{-}SALE_{i,t-1}$	−0.0003	0.1856***	−0.2462***	−0.0111
	(0.0020)	(0.0061)	(0.0303)	(0.0250)
$PRO\text{-}SALE_{i,t-1}$	0.0003	0.0025***	−0.0042	0.0013
	(0.0002)	(0.0006)	(0.0028)	(0.002)
$CAP\text{-}FR_{i,t}$	−0.0008*	−0.0078	−0.0177**	0.0011
	(0.0005)	(0.0013)	(0.0073)	(0.0060)
$F\text{-}AGE_{i,t}$	0.0000***	0.0000	−0.0008***	0.0004***
	(0.0000)	(0.0000)	(0.00004)	(0.0001)
$ASFDI_{i,t-1}$	0.0020***	0.0009*	−0.0286***	0.0108***
	(0.0002)	(0.0005)	(0.0024)	(0.0020)
$EUFDI_{i,t-1}$	0.0033***	0.0037*	−0.0207	0.0104
	(0.0007)	(0.0020)	(0.0104)	(0.0086)
$NAFDI_{i,t-1}$	0.0020***	0.0023**	−0.0299***	0.0151***
	(0.0003)	(0.0008)	(0.0042)	(0.0035)
$AEFDI_{i,t-1}$	0.0033***	0.0059**	−0.0385***	0.0156**
	(0.0006)	(0.0017)	(0.0086)	(0.0071)
$ENFDI_{i,t-1}$	0.0034***	0.0020	−0.0233	0.0124*
	(0.0005)	(0.0015)	(0.0081)	(0.0066)
$ANFDI_{i,t-1}$	0.0036***	0.0054**:	−0.0418***	0.0153***
	(0.0003)	(0.0008)	(0.0042)	(0.0035)
$AENFDI_{i,t-1}$	0.0030***	0.0044***	−0.0432***	0.0185***
	(0.0003)	(0.0008)	(0.0041)	(0.0034)
$ASEX_{i,t-1}$	0.0142***	0.0084***	−0.0530***	0.0233*
	(0.0007)	(0.0021)	(0.0109)	(0.0090)
$ASIM_{i,t-1}$	0.0035***	0.0074***	−0.0170**	−0.0036
	(0.0005)	(0.0014)	(0.0071)	(0.0059)

Continued

Table 8.6 Continued

	Fraction of all regular employees working in international business units at corporate headquarters	Fraction of all regular employees who work in R&D divisions	Fraction of all regular employees who work in manufacturing divisions at corporate headquarters	Fraction of all regular employees who work in manufacturing divisions at locations other than corporate headquarters
	L-HINTL-TOTAL$_{i,t}$	L-RD-TOTAL$_{i,t}$	L-HMFG-TOTAL$_{i,t}$	L-BDMFG-TOTAL$_{i,t}$
EUEX$_{i,t-1}$	0.0276***	0.0103**	−0.0429	0.0159
	(0.0018)	(0.0051)	(0.0267)	(0.0220)
EUIM$_{i,t-1}$	0.0049***	0.0027	0.0521***	−0.0117
	(0.0009)	(0.0027)	(0.0138)	(0.0114)
NAEX$_{i,t-1}$	0.0087***	0.0176***	0.0207	0.0107
	(0.0012)	(0.0036)	(0.0138)	(0.0151)
NAIM$_{i,t-1}$	0.0041***	0.0027	−0.0675***	0.0266**
	(0.0008)	(0.0027)	(0.0137)	(0.0114)
CONS	0.0001	0.0015	0.1584***	0.0276***
	(0.0004)	(0.0009)	(0.0054)	(0.0043)
Sample size	108,120	108,120	108,120	108,120
R^2	0.2785	0.7682	0.7630	0.8254

Note: *** denotes statistical significance at the 1% level; ** denotes statistical significance at the 5% level; * denotes statistical significance at the 10% level.

or in R&D departments (Table 8.6). First, looking at the fraction of all regular employees who work in international business units at corporate headquarters, we see that all seven foreign-expansion-pattern dummy variables are positively correlated with this quantity in a statistically significant way. Next, looking at the fraction of all regular employees who work in R&D departments at corporate headquarters or research laboratories, we see that six of the seven foreign-expansion-pattern dummy variables are positively correlated with this quantity in a statistically significant way (the only exception being expansion into Europe and North America). Additionally, although not displayed in Table 8.6, we considered the fraction of all regular employees who work in accounting, general-affairs, and other similar departments at corporate headquarters; we found that six of the seven foreign-expansion-pattern dummy variables were negatively correlated with this quantity

Table 8.7 Conclusions of model regarding the impact of FDI on research and develop
ment and on inter-firm transactions (3)

	Natural logarithm of R&D Expenditures	Ratio of R&D Expenditures to Sales	Fraction of all R&D Expenditures Related to In-House R&D Activities	Ratio of In-House R&D Expenditures to Sales	Fraction of total sales due to sales to corporate affiliates	Fraction of total purchases due to purchases from corporate affiliates
	$LNRD_{i,t}$	$RD\text{-}SALE_{i,t}$	$RDSELF\text{-}RDTOTAL_{i,t}$	$RDSELF\text{-}SALE_{i,t}$	$TRSC\text{-}AFLT\text{-}SALE_{i,t}$	$TRSC\text{-}AFLT\text{-}PCH_{i,t}$
Lagged dependent variable	0.8407*** (0.0031)	0.7721*** (0.0024)	0.5396*** (0.0038)	0.5889*** (0.0117)	0.6878*** (0.0025)	0.5536*** (0.0029)
$AS\text{-}L_{i,t-1}$	0.1637*** (0.0154)	0.0008** (0.0002)	−0.0141*** (0.0026)	0.0005*** (0.0002)	0.0031 (0.0032)	0.0244*** (0.0031)
$RD\text{-}SALE_{i,t-1}$	−2.7253*** (0.1853)		−0.0769** (0.0268)	0.1614*** (0.0111)	−0.1279** (0.0431)	−0.1506** (0.0433)
$PRO\text{-}SALE_{i,t-1}$	0.0356* (0.0186)	0.0023*** (0.0003)	−0.0032 (0.0029)	0.0021*** (0.0003)	0.0062 (0.0039)	−0.0009 (0.0039)
$CAP\text{-}FR_{i,t}$	0.2233*** (0.0427)	0.0040*** (0.0006)	0.0060 (0.0071)	0.0030*** (0.0005)	−0.0099 (0.0103)	0.0701*** (0.0100)
$F\text{-}AGE_{i,t}$	0.0010*** (0.0003)	0.0001* (0.00005)	0.0004*** (0.0001)	0.0001*** (0.00002)	−0.0017*** (0.0001)	−0.0008*** (0.0001)
$ASFDI_{i,t-1}$	0.0908*** (0.0144)	0.0006*** (0.0001)	−0.0013 (0.0024)	0.0006*** (0.0002)	−0.0168** (0.0033)	0.0187*** (0.0032)
$EUFDI_{i,t-1}$	0.1856*** (0.0539)	0.0025*** (0.0009)	0.0012 (0.0088)	0.0028 (0.0008)	−0.0161 (0.0145)	0.0149 (0.0142)
$NAFDI_{i,t-1}$	0.1541*** (0.0238)	0.0025*** (0.0003)	−0.0041 (0.0039)	0.0024*** (0.0003)	−0.0261 (0.0058)	−0.0046 (0.0058)
$AEFDI_{i,t-1}$	0.2731*** (0.0444)	0.0040*** (0.0007)	−0.0159** (0.0073)	0.0039*** (0.0006)	−0.0128 (0.0116)	0.0377** (0.0112)
$ENFDI_{i,t-1}$	0.3969*** (0.0405)	0.0052*** (0.0006)	0.0035 (0.0067)	0.0050*** (0.0006)	−0.0020 (0.0107)	0.0283** (0.0103)
$ANFDI_{i,t-1}$	0.3033*** (0.0226)	0.0031*** (0.0003)	−0.0023 (0.0037)	0.0032*** (0.0003)	−0.0182** (0.0056)	0.0235*** (0.0054)
$AENFDI_{i,t-1}$	0.5549*** (0.0226)	0.0062*** (0.0003)	0.0037 (0.0037)	0.0062*** (0.0003)	0.0281*** (0.0053)	0.0680*** (0.0051)
$ASEX_{i,t-1}$	0.1730** (0.0668)	0.0034*** (0.0009)	−0.0017 (0.0111)	0.0038*** (0.0009)	−0.0780*** (0.0157)	−0.0289* (0.0153)
$ASIM_{i,t-1}$	−0.1012** (0.0434)	−0.0017*** (0.0006)	0.0064 (0.0071)	−0.0014*** (0.0006)	−0.0190* (0.0105)	0.0347*** (0.0101)
$EUEX_{i,t-1}$	0.2222 (0.1488)	0.0114** (0.0021)	0.0228 (0.0249)	0.0112** (0.0019)	−0.0504 (0.0387)	−0.0090 (0.0379)
$EUIM_{i,t-1}$	0.1791** (0.0812)	0.0043*** (0.0011)	−0.0297** (0.0134)	0.0015 (0.0010)	−0.0534*** (0.0205)	0.0582*** (0.0194)
$NAEX_{i,t-1}$	0.4113*** (0.1073)	0.0087*** (0.0015)	−0.0090 (0.0178)	0.0075*** (0.0013)	0.0063 (0.0267)	−0.0426* (0.0262)

Continued

Table 8.7 Continued

	Natural logarithm of R&D Expenditures	Ratio of R&D Expenditures to Sales	Fraction of all R&D Expenditures Related to In-House R&D Activities	Ratio of In-House R&D Expenditures to Sales	Fraction of total sales due to corporate affiliates	Fraction of total purchases due to purchases from corporate affiliates
	$LNRD_{i,t}$	$RD\text{-}SALE_{i,t}$	$RDSELF\text{-}RDTOTAL_{i,t}$	$RDSELF\text{-}SALE_{i,t}$	$TRSC\text{-}AFLT\text{-}SALE_{i,t}$	$TRSC\text{-}AFLT\text{-}PCH_{i,t}$
$NAIM_{i,t-1}$	0.1931***	−0.0018	0.0243*	0.0033***	−0.0733***	−0.0352*
	(0.0774)	(0.0011)	(0.0127)	(0.0010)	(0.0199)	(0.0193)
CONS	0.4244***	−0.0002	0.4305***	−0.0002	0.1500***	0.1137***
	(0.0455)	(0.0004)	(0.0087)	(0.0003)	(0.0073)	(0.0068)
Sample size	47,128	108,120	47,128	108,120	81,502	77,961
R^2	0.8879	0.6153	0.5310	0.6141	0.6448	0.4436

Note: *** denotes statistical significance at the 1% level; ** denotes statistical significance at the 5% level; * denotes statistical significance at the 10% level.

in a statistically significant way (the only exception being expansion into Europe alone).

We next consider the fraction of all regular employees who work in manufacturing divisions at corporate headquarters. We found that five of the seven foreign-expansion-pattern dummy variables were negatively correlated with this quantity in a statistically significant way (for expansions into Europe alone, or into Europe and North America, the correlations were not statistically significant). On the other hand, if we consider the fraction of all regular employees who work in manufacturing divisions at locations other than corporate headquarters (Table 8.7), we see that six of the seven foreign-expansion-pattern dummy variables were positively correlated with this quantity in a statistically significant way (for expansion into Europe alone, the correlation was not statistically significant.)

From these results of our analysis, we may draw the following conclusions. Although FDI by Japanese corporations did increase the number of full-time workers within Japan, it is not the case that all FDIs led to an increase in the number of workers in Japan. In addition, not all corporate divisions experienced an increase in the number of workers due to FDI. While expansions into Europe alone had an extremely small impact on hiring within Japan, expansions into Asia, or expansions into Asia together with one or both additional regions, had a significant impact on employment within Japan. Moreover, expansions into these regions resulted in an increased fraction of the Japanese domestic workforce working in R&D at corporate headquarters or research laboratories, or working on international business development at corporate headquarters. FDI tended to decrease the fraction of workers who worked in manufacturing divisions at corporate headquarters, but tended to *increase* the fraction of workers who worked in manufacturing divisions at locations other than corporate headquarters.

The impact on R&D activity

We next consider the impact of FDI on corporate research and development activity. Table 8.7 presents the predictions of our analysis regarding the impact of FDI on several quantities: total R&D expenditures at corporate headquarters in Japan, the ratio of R&D expenditures to sales, the ratio of *in-house* R&D expenditures to sales, and the fraction of all R&D expenditures related to in-house R&D expenditures.

Looking first at increases in total R&D expenditures, we see that all seven foreign-expansion-pattern dummy variables are positively correlated, in a statistically significant way, with this quantity. Expansion into Europe, and expansion into North America, are more strongly correlated with increased R&D expenditures than expansion into Asia. In addition, R&D expenditures increase as the number of regions into which a corporation expands increases; the maximal correlation between any foreign-expansion-pattern dummy variable and increased R&D expenditures is obtained for the case of expansion into all three regions (Asia, Europe, and North America).

Next, considering the ratio of R&D expenditures to sales, we see that five of the seven dummy variables (corresponding into expansion into North America, expansion into any two of the three regions, and expansion into all three regions) are positively correlated with this quantity in a statistically significant way. In addition, if we look at the ratio of in-house R&D expenditures to sales, we see that six of the seven dummy variables are positively correlated with this quantity in a statistically significant way (the only exception being expansion into Europe alone). On the other hand, when we consider the fraction of all R&D expenditures related to in-house R&D activities, we find that one of the foreign-expansion-pattern dummy variables (expansion into both Asia and Europe) is negatively correlated with this quantity in a statistically significant way, while the correlations for the other six foreign-expansion patterns were not statistically significant.

These results suggest the following conclusions. First, corporations that make FDIs tend to place greater emphasis on research and development, and this tendency grows stronger as corporations expand into a wider range of overseas regions. Next, corporations that expand into Europe and North America tend to place more emphasis on R&D than corporations that expand only in Asia. However, as we see from consideration of the fraction of R&D expenditures related to in-house R&D activities, companies that expand into both Europe and Asia (as compared to corporations that adopt other foreign-expansion patterns) are less insistent on conducting R&D activities in-house, and instead are willing to outsource R&D initiatives. A possible reason for this might be that corporations that expand into both Asia and Europe tend to have traveled further down the road toward an open R&D model.

The impact on transactions among corporations

Finally, we consider the impact of FDI on transactions among corporations. Table 8.7 presents the conclusions of our analysis regarding the impact of FDI on two quantities: the fraction of total sales due to sales to corporate affiliates, and the fraction of total purchases due to purchases from corporate affiliates.

First, looking at the fraction of total sales due to sales to corporate affiliates, we see that three of the seven foreign-expansion-pattern dummy variables (expansion into Asia only, expansion into Asia and North America, and expansion into all three regions) were correlated with this quantity in a statistically significant way. However, the *sign* of the correlation was not uniform: expansion into Asia only, and expansion into Asia and North America, were negatively correlated with this quantity, whereas expansion into all three regions was positively correlated with this quantity.

Next, looking at the fraction of total purchases due to purchases from corporate affiliates, we see that five of the seven foreign-expansion-pattern dummy variables (corresponding to expansion into Asia only, expansion into any two of the three regions, or expansion into all three regions) are positively correlated with this quantity in a statistically significant way, and moreover that the magnitude of the correlation increases as the number of foreign-expansion regions increases.

We might interpret these results as follows. When corporations expand into Asia and/or North America, they tend to outsource sales of their products to regional sales companies, whereas previously they might have sold products through corporate affiliates. However, when a corporation seeks to adopt a global sales strategy, including regions in Europe, the corporation seeks to realize economies of scale in its retail activities by establishing a marketing network for the full corporate group as a whole. In contrast, when we consider the purchase of raw materials and component parts, corporations that make FDIs tend to prefer to make purchases from corporate affiliates, with that preference growing stronger as the magnitude of FDI increases; the preference also grows stronger as corporations expand further into Asia, or as the breadth of regions in which the corporation invests widens. As a result, many Japanese manufacturing corporations that expand overseas (with the exception of some corporations who expand into Asia and/or North America) tend to rely increasingly on transactions within the corporate group, with the tendency growing more pronounced as the extent of corporate globalization advances.

The impact of FDI on the financial performance of domestic corporations

In the preceding analysis we have considered the impact of FDI on a corporation's managerial decisions. What is the corresponding impact of FDI, and the managerial decisions to which it leads, on the financial performance of domestic corporations? The answers to this question, as suggested by our analytical model, are tabulated in Table 8.8. The four columns in this table represent conclusions for various quantities in years t, $t+1$, $t+2$, and $t+3$.

Considering first the seven foreign-expansion-pattern dummy variables, we see from Table 8.8 that the values in year $t-1$ of all seven dummy variables are positively correlated, in a statistically significant way, with corporate added value in years t, $t+1$, and $t+2$; moreover, the magnitude of the correlation increases as the number of foreign-expansion regions increases. On the other hand, the correlation between foreign-expansion dummy variables in year $t-1$ and corporate added value in year $t+3$ was only statistically significant for three of the seven foreign-expansion patterns (expansion into Asia and Europe, expansion into Asia and North America, and expansion into all three regions), while the correlation between foreign-expansion dummy variables in year $t-1$ and corporate added value in year $t+4$ was not statistically significant for any of the seven foreign-expansion pattern dummy variables.

We next consider the impact of FDI-related managerial decisions on corporate added value. We first consider the impact of domestic personnel placements. If we look at the fraction of all regular employees who

Table 8.8   Conclusions of model regarding the impact of FDI on corporate added value

	Natural logarithm of corporate added value (year *t*)	Natural logarithm of corporate added value (year *t+1*)	Natural logarithm of corporate added value (year *t+2*)	Natural logarithm of corporate added value (year *t+3*)
LN-ADD-VULE$_{i,t-1}$	0.8699***	0.8836**	0.8940***	0.9526***
	(0.0025)	(0.0027)	(0.0046)	(0.0064)
CAP-FR$_{i,t}$	0.0650**	0.1431***	0.0633**	0.0315
	(0.0243)	(0.0285)	(0.0415)	(0.0505)
F-AGE$_{i,t}$	0.0007***	0.0005***	0.0004	0.0004
	(0.0002)	(0.0002)	(0.0003)	(0.0004)
P-L-HINTL-TOTAL$_{i,t}$	−1.8634***	−0.6667	−0.9709	0.4025
	(0.6448)	(0.7018)	(0.9164)	(1.2268)
P-L-RD-TOTAL$_{i,t}$	0.1021**	−0.0049	0.1265*	0.0464
	(0.0468)	(0.0532)	(0.0754)	(0.0918)
P-L-HMFG-TOTAL$_{i,t}$	−0.0864***	−0.1415***	−0.1028***	0.0085
	(0.0181)	(0.0201)	(0.0289)	(0.0346)
P-L-BDMFG-TOTAL$_{i,t}$	0.0413***	0.0241	−0.0116	0.0200
	(0.0159)	(0.0175)	(0.0253)	(0.0340)
P-RD-SALE$_{i,t}$	0.6955***	0.7267***	0.2783	0.0285
	(0.1312)	(0.1485)	(0.2014)	(0.2400)
P-RDSELF-RDTOTAL$_{i,t}$	−0.0134	0.0387	−0.0002	0.0328
	(0.0224)	(0.0257)	(0.0361)	(0.0438)
P-TRSC-AFLT-SALE$_{i,t}$	0.0970***	0.0703***	0.0075	0.0206
	(0.0121)	(0.0136)	(0.0190)	(0.0230)
P-TRSC-AFLT-PCH$_{i,t}$	−0.1191***	0.0263***	0.0257	−0.0211
	(0.0166)	(0.0092)	(0.0258)	(0.0307)
ASFDI$_{i,t-1}$	0.0508***	0.0640***	0.0536***	0.0200
	(0.0084)	(0.0092)	(0.0134)	(0.0162)
EUFDI$_{i,t-1}$	0.1395***	0.0943***	0.0634*	0.0807
	(0.0301)	(0.0347)	(0.0472)	(0.0547)
NAFDI$_{i,t-1}$	0.0872***	0.0997***	0.0504***	0.0235
	(0.0136)	(0.0155)	(0.0217)	(0.0259)
AEFDI$_{i,t-1}$	0.1071***	0.0945***	0.0628*	0.1516***
	(0.0248)	(0.0271)	(0.0376)	(0.0449)
ENFDI$_{i,t-1}$	0.1811***	0.1656***	0.1477***	0.0577
	(0.0230)	(0.0254)	(0.0352)	(0.0410)
ANFDI$_{i,t-1}$	0.1395***	0.1362***	0.1076***	0.0377***
	(0.0132)	(0.0142)	(0.0204)	(0.0244)
AENFDI$_{i,t-1}$	0.2603***	0.2362***	0.1943***	0.0842***
	(0.0136)	(0.0145)	(0.0212)	(0.0261)

Continued

184   *Jun Ma*

Table 8.8   Continued

	Natural logarithm of corporate added value (year t)	Natural logarithm of corporate added value (year $t+1$)	Natural logarithm of corporate added value (year $t+2$)	Natural logarithm of corporate added value (year $t+3$)
$ASEX_{i,t-1}$	−0.1608***	0.0738*	−0.0189	−0.1191*
	(0.0373)	(0.0427)	(0.0585)	(0.0711)
$ASIM_{i,t-1}$	0.1861***	−0.2097***	−0.1357***	−0.0624
	(0.0249)	(0.0300)	(0.0426)	(0.0529)
$EUEX_{i,t-1}$	0.0386	0.0925	0.1784	−0.1188
	(0.0860)	(0.0977)	(0.1384)	(0.1628)
$EUIM_{i,t-1}$	0.2258***	−0.1261***	−0.0291	−0.0529
	(0.0467)	(0.0532)	(0.0752)	(0.0920)
$NAEX_{i,t-1}$	0.1547***	−0.0528	−0.0508	0.1500
	(0.0606)	(0.0689)	(0.0998)	(0.1206)
$NAIM_{i,t-1}$	0.3255***	−0.1709***	0.0216	0.0100
	(0.0465)	(0.0540)	(0.0738)	(0.0887)
CONS	1.0222***	0.9244***	0.8813***	0.3050***
	(0.0398)	(0.0439)	(0.0670)	(0.0856)
Sample size	43,839	31,590	24,469	18,437
R^2	0.9258	0.9316	0.9050	0.8901

Note: *** denotes statistical significance at the 1% level; ** denotes statistical significance at the 5% level; * denotes statistical significance at the 10% level. Variables whose names contain the prefix P- refer to quantities obtained by inserting fitted values for the variables defined in Tables 8.2(a)–(c) into our analytical models.

work in international business units at corporate headquarters, we see that this quantity is negatively correlated with corporate added value in a statistically significant way in year t, but that the correlations in years $t+1$ and beyond are not statistically significant. The fraction of all regular employees who work in R&D divisions is positively correlated in a statistically significant way with corporate added value in years t and $t+2$, but the correlation in year $t+1$ is not statistically significant. The fraction of regular employees who work in manufacturing divisions at corporate headquarters is negatively correlated, in a statistically significant way, with corporate added value in years t, $t+1$, and $t+2$. On the other hand, the fraction of regular employees who work in manufacturing divisions at locations other than corporate headquarters is positively correlated, in a statistically significant way, with corporate added value in year *t*, but the correlations in later years are not statistically significant.

We next consider the impact of FDI-related R&D activities and inter-firm transactions. If we consider three quantities – the ratio of R&D expenditures to sales, the fraction of all sales due to sales to corporate affiliates, and the fraction of all purchases due to purchases from corporate affiliates – we find that all three quantities are correlated in a statistically significant way with corporate added value in years *t* and *t+1*, but that the correlations are not statistically significant in years *t+2* and beyond. The fraction of all purchases due to purchases from corporate affiliates is negatively correlated with corporate added value in year *t*, but positively correlated with corporate added value in year *t+1*. On the other hand, the fraction of R&D expenditures going toward in-house R&D activities was not correlated in a statistically significant way with corporate added value in any year.

We may interpret these results as follows. First, generally speaking, FDI contributes to corporate added value for two to three consecutive years, with the magnitude of the contribution increasing as the number of foreign-expansion regions increases. Next, managerial activity, including restructuring the domestic workforce, adjusting R&D expenditures, and rethinking inter-firm relationships, impacts corporate financial performance in two major ways. First, FDI tends to increase personnel and budgets in R&D divisions while simultaneously reducing the number of workers in manufacturing divisions; this generally makes a corporation more efficient overall and ultimately improves corporate financial performance. Second, particularly for Japanese corporations, FDI tends to stimulate inter-firm transaction activity, which, generally speaking, contributes to corporate added value. On the other hand, in view of our finding that the fraction of R&D expenditures related to in-house R&D activities was not correlated in a statistically significant way with corporate added value in any year, we cannot necessarily conclude that a 'closed', in-house model of R&D activity contributes to increasing corporate added value.

Conclusions

In the previous sections we have described a panel analysis we conducted, using corporate-level microdata, to assess the impact of FDI by Japanese corporations on the domestic managerial behavior of those corporations – including personnel allocations, R&D activities, and inter-firm transactions – as well as the relationship between FDI and corporate financial performance. In this final section we will attempt to draw conclusions from the results of our analysis.

First, since the 1990s, the FDI strategies pursued by Japanese corporations – particularly expansions into Asia and North America – have led to significant restructuring and downsizing of those corporations' domestic organizations. R&D activities, and work related to the development of international business operations, have been concentrated at corporate headquarters, while manufacturing activities have been moved to manufacturing divisions at locations other than corporate headquarters. As a result, corporate headquarters tended to see an increase in the number of employees working in international business development or in R&D, but a decrease in employees working in accounting or general-affairs departments. Meanwhile, the number of manufacturing employees at corporate headquarters decreased, but the number of manufacturing employees at locations other than corporate headquarters increased.

Next, FDI stimulated R&D efforts by Japanese corporations; the more overseas regions into which a corporation expanded, the more that corporation tended to emphasize R&D initiatives. In addition, corporations that expanded into Europe and/or North America tended to emphasize R&D initiatives more than corporations that expanded into Asia. On the other hand, most corporations that expanded overseas – with the exception of corporations that expanded into both Asia and Europe – did not actively pursue an outsourcing strategy for R&D.

Next, looking at Japanese corporations that traditionally would have sold products in Asia and North America via corporate affiliates, we found that FDI tended to cause these corporations to outsource their sales operations to local retail companies. However, when corporations expand into all three regions (Europe, Asia, and North America) and seek to pursue a global sales strategy, they seek to realize economies of scale in their retail activities by establishing a marketing network for the full corporate group as a whole. On the other hand, regarding purchases of raw materials and component parts, we found that, the more a corporation engages in FDI, the more it prefers to make purchases from corporate affiliates; moreover, we found that this preference grows stronger as a corporation expands further into Asia, or as the corporation expands into a wider range of global regions. Consequently, as the extent of a Japanese corporation's globalization increases, inter-firm transactions within the corporate group become more frequent.

To summarize all of these observations, we conclude that the international business strategies of Japanese corporations exhibit the following striking characteristics. The primary objective of FDI by Japanese corporations is the achievement of global-scale efficiencies, which are pursued by shifting manufacturing centers to lower-cost regions (but taking pains to ensure that high quality standards are maintained in the process), concentrating R&D activities at corporate headquarters, and actively expanding into high-value-added regional markets. In order to develop their businesses effectively on a global scale, Japanese firms strengthened the capabilities of their corporate headquarters in areas such as international business development and R&D, while simultaneously shifting manufacturing operations away from corporate headquarters, and building tighter relationships with domestic subsidiaries and affiliates – a managerial strategy we might label 'concentrate and select'.

Comparing these analytical conclusions with the observations of Bartlett and Ghoshal (1989) on the international business strategies of Japanese corporations in the 1980s, we find that the FDI strategies of most Japanese companies in the 1990s did not differ significantly from the strategies of the 1980s, with most companies adopting a *global* strategic model. However, we do begin to see a shift toward an *international* strategic model, including progress toward an open R&D model, particularly among companies that expanded into both Asia and Europe.

In response to the question of whether these types of global strategic models contribute to improvements in the bottom-line financial performance of Japanese corporations, we can draw the following conclusions. First, FDI does directly improve the financial performance of Japanese corporations, and the magnitude of that contribution increases as the range of foreign-expansion targets widens. Next, FDI tends to spur restructuring of domestic organizations, to clarify the roles of corporate headquarters and of corporate affiliates, and to concentrate strategic decision-making and R&D activities at corporate headquarters, while simultaneously encouraging the outsourcing of manufacturing operations to other corporate affiliates. Corporations who make FDIs tend to invest more human resources, and more material resources, in R&D initiatives, and tend to seek overall corporate efficiencies by conducting transactions with corporate affiliates wherever possible. These indirect influences of FDI may also be linked to improved corporate financial performance. On the other hand, the adoption of an in-house, 'closed' R&D model does not necessarily contribute to improved financial performance. As a result, the *global* strategic model that Japanese corporations consistently adopted from the 1980s through the first half of the 2000s did contribute in many ways to increasing corporate added value; on the other hand, in the future, in order for R&D initiatives to contribute more significantly to corporate added value, corporations will need to solve the important problem of how to move toward a more open R&D model.

In closing, we mention some questions that our study leaves for future work. In this study, we accounted for a corporation's FDI in a given region by using simple binary dummy variables that record whether or not the corporation had a presence in the given region. In reality, more detailed data would be needed to identify the full impact of FDI in a given region on corporate managerial activity and resources back in the home country: was the region a production center, a retail sales destination, a source for the purchase of raw materials and component parts, or all of the above? Related to this point is the fact that, in this study, we divided foreign expansion targets into three broad regions – Asia, Europe, and North America – whereas in practice the objectives and procedures for expanding into different subregions clearly differ based on the unique characteristics of each locale, even within the same larger region such as Asia or Europe. The *Basic Survey of Japanese Business Structure and Activities*, on which we relied in this study, does not provide information on corporations' objectives for making FDIs in various regions, and consequently in this study we were not able to consider such questions; in the future, more precise studies, based on more detailed data regarding corporate investments in overseas regions, are clearly needed.

Notes

1. To ensure the consistency of panel data from 1994 through 2003, we compute corporate added value as the difference between total sales and total purchases.
2. The *Basic Survey of Japanese Business Structure and Activities* tabulates the number of corporate subsidiaries in each year, but does not specifically ask corporations whether or not they created subsidiaries in any given year. Thus, to determine the numbers of corporate subsidiaries created in year $t-1$, we compared the number of corporate subsidiaries reported by the *Basic Survey* for year $t-1$ against the number reported for year $t-2$. In our analysis, it would have been possible to avoid using foreign-expansion-pattern dummy variables and instead to have considered the number of subsidiary companies established in each region. However, the number of subsidiaries created in a given region does not necessarily indicate a corporation's emphasis on FDI in

that region, and thus such a method would be highly susceptible to analytical bias. This is the reason behind our decision to use foreign-expansion-pattern dummy variables. We also note that the *Basic Survey* provides data only on the numbers of corporate subsidiaries within broadly defined regions (such as Asia, North America, and Europe), and does not provide any information on the characteristics of corporate subsidiaries, such as their objective, their scale, or their financial state.
3. The estimated coefficients for these variables are omitted due to lack of space.

References

Bartlett, C. and Ghoshal, S. (1989) *Managing Across Borders: The Transnational Solution*, Boston: Harvard Business School Press.

Daniels, J. D. and Bracker, J. (1989) 'Profit Performance: Do Foreign Operations Make a Difference?', *Management International Review*, 29(1): 46–56.

Doukas, J. and Travlos, N. (1988) 'Effect of Corporate Multinationalism on Shareholders' Wealth: Evidence From International Acquisitions', *Journal of Finance*, 43(5): 1161–1175.

Fukao, K. and Amano, T. (1998) *'Taigai chokusetsu toushi to seizougyoukai no "kuudouka"'* (Foreign Direct Investment and the 'Hollowing Out' of the Manufacturing Industry), *Economic Research* (Hitotsubashi University Institute for Economic Research), 49(3): 259–276.

Fukao, K. and Yuan, T. J. (2006) *'Nihon no kaigai chokusetsu toushi to kuudouka'* (Foreign Direct Investment and the Hollowing out of Japan'), in H. Itami, T. Fujimoto, T. Okazaki, H. Ito, and T. Numagami (eds), *Riidingusu: nihon no kigyou shisutemu, dai ni ki, dai go kan, kigyou to kankyou* (Readings: Japan's Corporate System, Term 2, Volume 5, Corporations and the Environment), 145–182, Tokyo: Yuhikaku.

Geringer, J. M., Beamish, P. W., and daCosta, R. C. (1989) 'Diversification Strategy and Internationalization: Implications for MNE Performance', *Strategic Management Journal*, 10(2): 109–119.

Grant, R. M. (1987) 'Multinationality and Performance of British Manufacturing Companies', *Journal of International Business Studies*, 18(3): 79–89.

Hitt, M., Hoskisson, R., and Ireland, R. (1994) 'A Mid-Range Theory of Interactive Effects of International and Product Diversification on Innovation and Performance', *Journal of Management*, 20(2): 297–326.

Hitt, M., Hoskisson, R., and Kim, H. (1997) 'International Diversification: Effects of Innovation and Firm Performance in Product-Diversified Firms', *Academy of Management Journal*, 40(4): 767–798.

Horaguchi, H. (1998a) *'Nihon no sangyou kuudouka – 1987 nen kara 93 nen no shuyou denki meekaa ni tsuite (jyou)'* (The Industrial Hollowing-out of Japan: The Major Electronics Manufacturers, 1987–1993, Part 1), in *Keiei Shirin* (The Hosei Journal of Business), 34(3): 113–123.

Horaguchi, H. (1998b) *'Nihon no sangyou kuudouka – 1987 nen kara 93 nen no shuyou denki meekaa ni tsuite (ge)'* (The Industrial Hollowing-out of Japan: The Major Electronics Manufacturers, 1987–1993, Part 2), *Keiei Shirin* (The Hosei Journal of Business), 34(4): 131–169.

Kimura, F. and Kiyota, K. (2002) *'Kigyou katsudou no guroobaruka to kigyou pafoomansu: "kigyou katsudou kihon chousa" ni motozuku bunseki'* (The Globalization of Corporate Activity and Corporate Performance – An Analysis Based on the *Basic Survey of Japanese Business Structure and Activitie*), *Keizai Toukei Kenkyuu* (Economic Statistics Research), 30(2): 1–12.

Sambhraya, R. B. (1995) 'The Combined Effect of International Diversification and Product Diversification Strategies on the Performance of U.S.-Based Multinational Corporations', *Management International Review*, 35(3): 197–218.

Tallman, S. and Li, J. (1996) 'Effects of International Diversity and Product Diversity on the Performance of Multinational Firms', *Academy of Management Journal*, 39: 179–196.

Waheed, A. and Mathur, I. (1995) 'Wealth Effects of Foreign Expansion by U.S. Banks', *Journal of Banking and Finance*, 19(5): 823–842.

9
Why Do Japanese Companies File Patents in China?
Empirical Findings from Japanese Firm-level Data

Yoshifumi Nakata and Xingyuan Zhang

Introduction

There is by now a large body of literature on the worldwide patenting boom, and especially on the particular upticks visible in the US since the mid-1980s and in Japan since the late 1980s.[1] However, due to the short history of the Chinese patent system, and to the weakness and inefficiency in protecting intellectual property rights (IPR), the dramatic surge in patenting in China has not received much attention thus far.

Hu and Jefferson (2006) shed light on China's recent patent explosion by analyzing a firm-level data set for Chinese enterprises and attempting to identify the factors accounting for China's patent boom. Their empirical results suggested that the increasing magnitude of foreign direct investment (FDI) at the industry level, corporate restructuring, and a shift toward more complex forms of industrial R&D were all factors behind the increasing propensity to patent. They also compared the patenting behavior of Chinese and foreign enterprises. Unfortunately, however, patenting by foreign enterprises was not investigated in their empirical analysis. As a result, it remains unclear why multinational enterprises (MNEs) patent in China, and what explains the recent uptick in patents filed in China by these MNEs.

As China has integrated into the global economy since the early 1980s, its inflows of FDI have risen dramatically, recently exceeding some US$50 billion per year.[2] Needless to say, MNEs have played a dominant role in investment in China. To increase and protect their market share, MNEs usually make effective use of IPR; this simple observation would seem to explain why MNEs devote so much time and energy to assembling patent portfolios in China.

However, as pointed out by Branstetter *et al.* (2006), the empirical evidence for a correlation between IPR and FDI is less clear. Several studies have analyzed the effects of IPR on FDI.[3] In a recent report, Branstetter *et al.* (2006) analyzed a firm-level data set of US MNEs that had invested in 12 countries and reported that MNEs respond to stronger IPR protections by increasing patent activities in countries that institute IPR reforms. However, this work did not directly analyze the impact of FDI on patenting behavior.

Some recent studies have focused on the remarkable expansion of overseas R&D undertaken by MNEs in recent years. Iwasa and Odagiri (2004) investigated two types of R&D conducted in the US by Japanese MNEs: *research-oriented* ('Type-R') R&D, and *local-support-oriented* or *adaptive* ('Type-S') R&D. The former refers to efforts to acquire and utilize advanced knowledge from overseas sites that would otherwise be unavailable in the home country, while the latter describes the process of adapting a company's existing technologies and products to the local conditions of the host country. This distinction between two types of overseas R&D has also been discussed by other studies, including Kuemmerle (1999), Granstrand (1999), Pearce (1999), and Le Bas and Sierra (2002). Using estimates for knowledge production functions, Iwasa and Odagiri found that the contribution of domestic and overseas R&D to inventions – as measured by the numbers of patents granted by the US Patent and Trademark Office (USPTO) – was highly significant, especially for firms conducting Type-R research.

In contrast, we might expect that overseas R&D in China, which is a less developed country than the US, would be focused on adaptive R&D efforts to enhance local sales by meeting local needs. However, Iwasa and Odagiri also reported that the proportion of inventions by Japanese firms operating abroad was small, even for those that had subsidiaries in the US. Most patent applications submitted to the USPTO were based on innovations developed entirely by parent companies in Japan, not by subsidiaries in the US.

Meanwhile, Chinese IPR laws – and methods of enforcing them – have been evolving with developments in trade, especially in patent-sensitive industries (Plasmans and Tan, 2004). The conventional wisdom regarding trade policy has been to assume that the degree of maturity of IPR laws and enforcement has significant impact on international trade flows. Within intensely competitive international markets, strengthening IPRs may broaden the market's interest in compensating MNEs for the costs of innovation, as long as these innovations are also protected abroad. Plasmans and Tan (2004) analyzed panel data estimates on China's bilateral trade with the US and with Japan, and found that strong IPRs augmented exports from the US to China, but had much less effect on Chinese imports from Japan.

Furthermore, as indicated in Branstetter *et al.* (2006), one of the potential motivations for a country to strengthen its IPRs is that such protections may induce foreign firms to produce and sell technologically advanced goods in that country. Branstetter *et al.* (2006) tested this hypothesis by analyzing the effects of IPR reforms in some developing countries on the royalty payments, and R&D expenditures, of US affiliates, as well as on the number, and the growth in the number, of patent filings by nonresidents in these countries. Their results showed that all of these quantities increased after IPR reforms.

As discussed above, patenting in China may be correlated with overseas R&D, FDI, and IPR reforms in China as well. In this work we focus primarily on the relationship between the patenting behavior of Japanese parent companies, their FDI activities, and Chinese IPR reforms; we exclude consideration of overseas R&D data due to difficulties in collecting these data at the firm level for the companies we study.[4] Using a firm-level data set of Japanese parent companies that owned one or more affiliates in China, and using a knowledge production function and dynamic panel analysis techniques, we analyze correlations between FDI, Chinese IPR reforms, and the patenting practices of Japanese companies.

Our main findings indicate that, the more FDI a Japanese parent firm commits to China in a given period, the more likely that firm is to apply for Chinese patents during that period. However, after China's second revision to its patent law in 2000, patenting by Japanese parent companies in China shifted in direction, and was increasing driven by the desire to obtain monopoly powers and collect royalties in the Chinese IPR market, rather than simply to protect against imitation products from local competitors. Our empirical results suggest that Japanese companies redirected their global innovation and IPR strategies in response to IPR reforms in China.

The remainder of this chapter is organized as follows. In the second section we briefly review the Chinese patent system and propose several hypotheses to explain the surge in Chinese patent applications by MNEs. The third section describes the analytical methods we used in our statistical analysis, the sources for our collection of Japanese firm-level data, and a discussion of our statistical results regarding the relationship between FDI, Chinese IPR reforms, and the patenting practices of Japanese MNEs. Finally, in the fourth section we present a summary and conclusions.

The patent explosion in China

The Chinese patent system

The Patent Law of the People's Republic of China was enacted in 1984 (the same year in which China signed the Paris Convention on the Protection of Industrial Property) and went into effect on 1 April 1985. This law establishes three types of innovations that may be patented in China: inventions, utility models, and designs. Any application for an invention or utility-model patent must be examined by China's State Intellectual Property Office (SIPO) on the basis of three criteria – novelty, inventiveness, and practical usefulness – while patent applications for designs need only pass an examination to determine whether or not the design in question is identical or similar to any other design patented or disclosed publicly in China or abroad. The 'inventiveness' requirement for the examination of patent applications is more stringent for inventions than for utility models, in that inventions are required to exhibit prominent substantive features and to represent notable progress in their field. In this way, Chinese patent law differs from that of other countries, in which the sole requirement for inventiveness is generally that an invention be non-obvious to one skilled in the relevant art.[5] In contrast to patents for inventions, patent rights for utility models and designs are based only on a preliminary examination if there are evident reasons for rejecting the applications.

As pointed out by Sun (2003) and by Hu and Jefferson (2006), the Chinese patent system incorporates some key features similar to those adopted in Japan and Europe. For example, priority in granting patents in China is based on the principle of 'first-to-file', rather than the principle of 'first-to-invent' used in the US. On the other hand, patent descriptions are to be disclosed 18 months after all patent applications have been filed with the SIPO. In contrast, patent applications in the US were only disclosed upon issuance until the year 2000.[6] In China, as in Japan, competitors who have substantially improved upon prior patented inventions or utility models can ask for compulsory licensing from the original inventor. Similarly, the original patent holders can ask for compulsory licensing of patented inventions and utility models whose designs are based on their own patented technologies. Also in common with Japan is the fact that, in China's examination request system, applicants have three years from the date of filing to decide whether or not to request an examination by the examiners of the SIPO.[7] Furthermore, Chinese patent law requires that foreign applicants use a Chinese domestic patent agency. This is quite similar to the practice in Japan, but different from that in the US, which allows a patent agency registered in the applicant's country of residence to file an application before the patent office does based on the principle of identical reciprocal privileges.[8]

The Chinese patent law has undergone three substantial revisions since 1984. The first revision, in 1992, enlarged the scope of patent protection to cover all technology fields, and extended the term of protection for imported patented products. This revision also extended the term of protection from 15 to 20 years for inventions, and from 8 to 10 years for utility model and design patents. In anticipation of China becoming a member of the World Trade Organization (WTO) and a signatory to the Agreement on Trade Related Aspects of Intellectual Property Rights (TRIPS), China made a second revision to its patent law, which went into effect in 2001. More recently, a third revision has been made; these latest revisions went into effect on 1 October 2009.

As pointed out by Liu (2002), the second revision made the Chinese patent law both more functional and more practical, because it provided, for the first time, specific procedures for determining the amount of compensation due in case of damage caused by infringement, as well as a prescription for initiating legal proceedings concerning infringement. Furthermore, over one thousand laws and regulations related to IPR were approved in the years around 2000. To cite just one example, China approved the PRC Administration Regulations of Technology Import and Export in 2001, providing a legal basis for technology trade by multinational enterprises in China.

The surge in patenting in China

According to data released by China's State Intellectual Property Office, the number of patent applications totaled 694,153 in 2007, with about 15 per cent of applications coming from foreign inventors. In 2000, applications by foreign inventors jumped by a factor of more than 7.9, and those by domestic inventors increased by a factor of 4.2. As indicated by Hu and Jefferson (2006), around this time there was also a noticeable shift in the patenting behavior of domestic and foreign inventors, and specifically in the types of patents – namely, inventions, utility models, or designs – for which they applied. By 2007, patent applications for inventions accounted for more than 85 per cent of all applications by foreign inventors, while this ratio was less than 26 per cent for local inventors.

Figures 9.1 and 9.2 plot patterns of growth in patent applications, and patents granted, for invention patents originating from four countries, namely, Japan, the US, the EU11 (treated here as a single nation), and

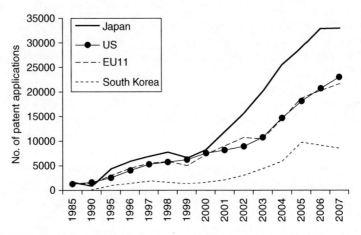

Figure 9.1   Growth of Chinese patent applications for foreign inventions
Source: SIPO (China's State Intellectual Property Office).

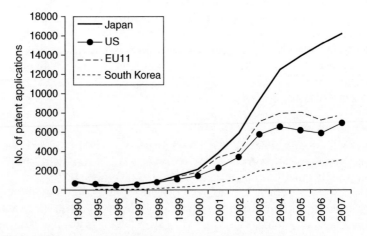

Figure 9.2   Growth of Chinese patent grants for foreign inventions
Source: SIPO (China's State Intellectual Property Office).

South Korea.[9] Together, these nations account for approximately 95 per cent of all foreign patent applications and foreign patents granted. All of these countries except South Korea began applying for patents on inventions in 1985, the year the Chinese patent law went into effect. However, the rates of growth in both patent applications and patents granted were sluggish until the early 1990s. All four countries exhibited a rapid surge in patenting beginning in the mid-1990s. For applications from Japan, South Korea, and the EU11, the surge in applications tapered off toward the end of the 1990s; in contrast, patent applications for inventions from the US exhibited sustained growth throughout the 1990s. All countries began accelerating applications for Chinese patents in 2000, with similar growth in the numbers of patents granted. Among the four nations, Japan exhibited a particularly steep increase in Chinese patent activity during the period 2000–2007; Japan's average growth rate during these years was 25 per cent for patent applications and 37 per cent for patents granted, significantly higher than the corresponding figures of 18 per cent and 29 per cent for the US and 19 per cent and 29 per cent for the EU11.

Evidence from Japanese MNEs

Each year the Chinese government releases a list of its Top 500 Foreign Investment Companies, with rankings determined by companies' total sales. Table 9.1 lists patent applications for inventions made by Japanese MNEs. These Japanese parent companies own one or more affiliates ranked among the Top 500 Foreign Investment Companies in China (2004).[10]

As indicated in the table, many MNEs, including Matsushita Electric Industrial, Mitsubishi Electric, Toshiba, Hitachi, and Sony, began applying for Chinese patents in 1985, when the Chinese patent law went into effect. However, the table also shows that other companies, including Toyota and Suzuki Motor Corporations and Kyocera Corporation, did not begin to file for Chinese patents until the early 1990s or later. This may be because these companies launched their Chinese business operations later than Matsushita, Mitsubishi Electric, Toshiba, or Hitachi. For example, Kyocera started business in China in 1996, and Toyota Motor in 1997. Because these firms delayed investing in China, they did not exhibit an uptick in patent applications for their inventions until the late 1990s.

The second important observation from Table 9.1 is that almost all Japanese MNEs have accelerated their patent applications for inventions since 2000. Although there was an earlier surge between 1995 to 1999, following the first amendment to China's patent law in 1993, the boom

Table 9.1 Patent applications for inventions in China by Japanese parent companies

Company	Starting Year[a]	1985–1989	1990–1994	1995–1999	2000–2003
Honda Motor	1992	12	102	617	1,328
Nissan Motor	1995	6	6	17	252
Mitsubishi Motors	1996	4	0	27	29
Matsushita Electric Industrial	1987	83	269	3,298	6,078
Sony	1993	167	276	2,201	2,992
Toyota Motor	1997	0	12	218	196
Suzuki Motor	1994	0	6	41	43
Mitsubishi Electric	1986	263	214	1,303	1,924
Sanyo Electric	1995	63	75	711	1,538
Isuzu Motors	1985	13	21	2	55
Toshiba	1987	198	252	296	1,410
Pioneer	1994	1	0	16	101
Sharp	1993	148	74	402	1,168
Hitachi	1989	513	347	1,321	1,420
Hitachi Construction Machinery	1996	1	3	62	82
Kyocera	1996	0	0	16	51
Seiko Epson	1998	21	50	665	2,050
Fujitsu General	1996	0	6	23	17
Rohm	1993	0	16	134	1,122
Sumitomo Metal Mining	1996	1	2	22	35

Note: [a] The first year of business in China.
Source: SIPO, Ministry of Commerce of the People's Republic of China, and the *Kaigai Shinshutsu Kigyou Souran* (2006).

in patenting after 2000 is even more remarkable. As discussed above, China made a second amendment to its patent law in 2000, and participated in the WTO in 2001. The acceleration in patenting activities by Japanese MNEs in China seems to coincide with these changes in the Chinese IPR environment.

Hypotheses

In this section we propose several hypotheses concerning the relationship between Chinese IPR reforms, FDI by Japanese MNEs, and the patenting practices of Japanese MNEs in China. In the following section we discuss statistical analyses conducted to assess the accuracy of these hypotheses.

As foreign firms broaden their manufacturing in China and increase their share of local production, they face increased risk that their technologies will be imitated by local competitors, and hence feel a stronger need to protect their IPR (Hu and Jefferson, 2006). Thus, patenting may play an important role as a legal weapon in the IPR strategies of MNEs that operate businesses in China.

However, in the absence of a truly international patent system, firms have to seek patent grants in each country in which they operate. Since obtaining these patent grants is not cost-free, MNEs have little incentive to devote time and effort to preparing and filing patent applications in jurisdictions where patent rights are weak (Branstetter *et al.*, 2006). When IPR reforms occur and patent laws are strengthened in host countries, MNEs have greater incentive to file patents for all technologies currently being used in these countries.

Furthermore, Branstetter *et al.* (2006) indicated that one of the potential benefits of strengthening IPRs is that such protections may motivate foreign firms to produce and sell technologically advanced goods in countries with stronger IPR systems. Related evidence can also be identified in China. Figure 9.3 plots the growth of technology trading in the Chinese technology market, as well as the growth in technology transfer from the US, Japan, and three European countries. In 2007,

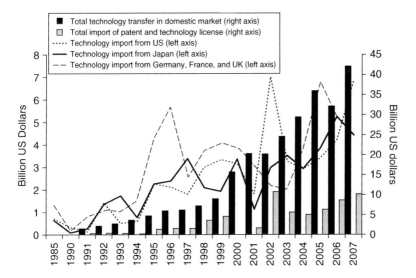

Figure 9.3 Growth of technology transfer in China

Source: China Statistical Yearbook on Science and Technology.

the total value of contracts in China's technology market amounted to US$42 billion, among which approximately one-quarter came from imports of patents and licenses from foreign countries. Since 2000, foreign countries seem to have accelerated technology transfers to China. As China strengthens its legal systems for protecting IPR, and as China's manufacturing industries become stronger, foreign companies will begin to feel the time to be ripe for reaping the benefits of patent licensing. For example, in 2002, Chinese DVD manufactures reached agreements with the so-called 6C patent licensing alliance, consisting of Hitachi, Matsushita, Toshiba, JVC, Mitsubishi, and Time Warner, and the 3C alliance, consisting of Phillips, Sony, and Pioneer, to pay US$4 and US$5, respectively, in royalties for every DVD player they export (see China Daily, 2004).

In view of these observations, we propose the following hypotheses.

Hypothesis 1: FDI, namely, the establishment of overseas affiliates by Japanese MNEs in China, has a positive impact on the patenting activities of those MNEs in China.

Hypothesis 2: Chinese IPR reforms since 2000 have stimulated the efforts of Japanese parent companies to file patents in China, because the reforms have made patents a more effective tool for protecting against imitations or other forms of infringement in local manufacturing.

Hypothesis 3: Japanese parent companies have accelerated their efforts to assemble IPR (or patent) portfolios in China because of their increasing desire to achieve monopoly power and collect royalties in the intensely competitive Chinese IPR market; this reflects an evolution in the global innovation and IPR strategies of Japanese MNEs in response to Chinese IPR reforms.

Cohen *et al.* (2002) distinguished between 'complex' and 'discrete' product industries on the basis of whether a new, commercialized product or process was comprised of numerous separately patentable elements versus a relatively small number of such elements. For example, as new drugs or chemicals in the US are typically comprised of a relatively small number of patentable elements, these may be characterized as 'discrete' products. In contrast, electronic products, such as semiconductors, tend to be comprised of a larger number of patentable elements, and would thus be considered 'complex' products. Thus, the complex product industries are those in which a single product can contain intellectual property covered by thousands of patents held by hundreds of patent holders.[11] Patent portfolios in such industries often play a defensive function, facilitating cross-licensing negotiations, rather than their traditional role of excluding competitors and securing the ownership of particular inventions.

Hu and Jefferson (2006) also reported that complex industries in China file more than three times as many patent applications as discrete industries. Cohen *et al.* (2002), however, argued that almost *all* products in Japan were complex, because Japanese patents encompass fewer claims, and those claims themselves tended to be interpreted more narrowly, generating more patents per product and, in turn, more widespread technological interdependence.

In view of these observations, we propose the following hypothesis.

Hypothesis 4: A company's FDI has different impacts on that company's Chinese patenting behavior depending on whether the company belongs to the complex or the discrete industry sector.

Blundell *et al.* (1995) represented the inherently dynamic and nonlinear process of technological innovation using a dynamic count model, in which feedback mechanisms establish a linkage between previous success in innovation and the production of new patents. In addition, the accumulation of experience and knowledge needed to translate, search for, and apply for patents influences a foreign company's abilities to file future patents in China. Indeed, translating, searching for, and applying for patents in China may seem a daunting prospect for many foreign companies seeking to protect their IPR. Yasui *et al.* (2007), in an analysis of questionnaires, also reported that mistranslations in Chinese patent documents may cause Japanese parent companies a great deal of trouble. Therefore, having IPR experts and experience in filing patents in China should give Japanese parent companies a clear competitive advantage when implementing their IPR strategies.

In view of these observations, we propose the following hypothesis.

Hypothesis 5: There are correlated dynamic effects in the patenting practices of Japanese parent companies in China.

Finally, as reported by Lee and Mansfield (1996), a country's IPR system influences the volume, and the structure, of FDI by MNEs from developed countries. If Chinese patenting practices can succeed in assuaging the fears of MNEs that Chinese patent protections are inadequate, the result might well be a corresponding increase in the volume of FDI, as well as a shift in the structure of that FDI. This possible reversal of causality – in which patenting influences FDI, instead of the other way around – must be carefully handled in our statistical analysis of the impact of FDI by MNEs on their patenting behavior in China.

Empirical analysis of Japanese firm-level data

The core of this chapter is an empirical analysis of the relationship between a Japanese parent company's patenting behavior and its FDI and technology transfer in China. We use panel data on Japanese MNEs to answer the following questions.

(1) How are FDI and technology transfer linked to patenting behavior?
(2) What impact have Chinese IPR reforms had on patenting behavior?
(3) Do experience and knowledge accumulated in China have any dynamic impact on the patenting behavior of Japanese parent companies?
(4) How do the answers to questions (1)–(3) differ if we account for endogeneity in our analytical models?

To answer questions (1) and (2), we define a knowledge production function to measure the impact of FDI on patenting, as in Iwasa and Odagiri (2004). To answer questions (3) and (4), we used the dynamic panel GMM technique proposed by Blundell and Bond (1998), which allows more detailed analysis of dynamic effects on patenting and the lag effects of FDI on patenting in China.

Patent production function

The key explanatory variables used in this chapter to estimate the impact of FDI on patenting behavior are AS_{it} – the total amount of capital of all new affiliates established in China by parent company i in year t – and a simpler dummy version of this variable, NA_{it}, which takes the value 1 if parent company i established one or more new affiliates in China in year t, and takes the value zero otherwise. The dependent variable in this analysis is NP_{it}, the number of patent applications for inventions made by parent company i in year t. Because MNEs make patent applications in China in order to protect the IPR of their advanced technologies and products from infringement or other pirating, as well as to adapt their technologies and products in response to the demands of the Chinese market, we expect that MNEs will make more patent applications in China when they decide to run their own corporate affiliates there. Therefore, the variables AS_{it} and NA_{it} capture information on important factors that may influence patenting behavior, as represented by the variable NP_{it}.

On the other hand, we also consider the increasing motivation of multinationals to collect royalties and the impact of this phenomenon

on patenting behavior. Because data on the volume of technology transfer between multinationals and domestic firms are not available at the
individual-firm level, we instead introduce a proxy variable, $License_{it}$,
which is a dummy variable taking the value 1 if parent company i
released news related to technology transfers in China in mainstream
Japanese newspapers[12] in year t. This definition is motivated by the
expectation that the frequency of news articles related to technology
transfer will be associated with the volume of actual technology transfer between Japanese parent companies and Chinese domestic firms.
Thus we expect *License* to be positively correlated with NP.

Analytical methods

We utilized the Negative Binomial Model with Random Effects, proposed by Hausman *et al.* (1984), to estimate our patent production function:

$$NP_{it}|\lambda_1 it \sim \text{Poisson}(\lambda_1 it)$$

Here λ_{it} includes observable factors x_{it}, with the functional form $\exp(x_{it}\beta)$,
and unobserved factors for firm-specific variables, δ_i, which are drawn
from a Gamma distribution, namely:

$$\lambda_{it} \sim \text{Gamma}(\exp(x_{it}\beta), \delta_i) \tag{9.1}$$

If the ratio $z_i = \delta_i/_{(1+\delta_i)}$, has a density function,

$$f(z) = [B(a,b)]^{-1} z^{a-1}(1-z)^{b-1},$$

where $B(a,b)$ is the beta function, then we have the likelihood function
for the Negative Binomial Model with Random Effects.[13] The parameter
β, which appears in the factor $\exp(x_{it}\beta)$ in Eq. (9.1), can be estimated by
maximum likelihood estimation (MLE).

The observable factors x_{it} affecting patent filing (NP_{it}) include the following variables.

(1) AS_{it}, NA_{it}, and $License_{it}$, factors related to FDI and technology transfer
activities by parent companies in China, as previously discussed. We
also examined whether or not RS_{it}, the ratio of shares held by new
affiliates of Japanese parent companies, would influence the patenting behavior of those companies in China. We assume that parent
companies with a higher ratio of shares would be more willing to

share advanced technologies with their Chinese affiliates; consequently, we expect these companies to file more patents to protect
their IPRs in China. Thus we expect that AS_{it}, NA_{it}, RS_{it}, and $License_{it}$
will all be positively correlated with patenting, as discussed in the
second section.

(2) log RD_{it}, the logarithm of R&D expenditures by parent company i in
year t. Griliches (1990) has shown that, in the conclusion emphasized
by Pakes and Griliches (1980), there is a strong relationship, across
firms and industries, between R&D investment and the number of
patents at the cross-sectional level. This relationship is almost contemporaneous, but with some lag effects, which are rather small and
not well estimated.[14] In this chapter we follow the tradition in the
literature (which was also observed by Iwasa and Odagiri (2004)) by
expecting a parent company's R&D investments to be positively correlated with that company's patenting efforts in China.

(3) ES_{it}, the export intensity of parent company i to China in year t.
Because statistics at the level of individual firms are only available
for exports to Asia as a whole, and not for exports to China alone, we
used statistics on exports to Asia as a whole, but adjusted these statistics using industry-wide statistics on the ratio of Chinese exports
to all Asian exports. The variable ES is computed by taking the ratio
of adjusted export sales to total sales. Strong IPRs in patents, trademarks, and copyrights should protect exporting firms against local
copying of products, thereby helping to increase the potential market for exporters. On the other hand, MacGarvie (2002) has demonstrated a positive relationship between exports and innovation in
French firms, implying that exporting may expand the opportunities for patenting, which is used as an indicator of innovations.

(4) log RD_{adapt}, where RD_{adapt} is defined as the product $RD \times ES$. We
use this quantity as a proxy variable to indicate the extent of *adaptive* R&D by Japanese parent companies – the work those companies
do to adapt their existing technologies and products to the local
Chinese market.

(5) PP_{it}, the propensity of parent company i to file patents in Japan,
defined as the ratio of the number of patent applications submitted
by the company to the Japan Patent Office (JPO) in year t to that
company's R&D expenditures in year t. As shown by Levin *et al.*
(1987) and by Cohen *et al.* (2002), only a fraction of a firm's innovations lead to patents, both in Japan and in the US. Cohen *et al.* (2002)
reported that, in Japan, patents appear to be relatively effective compared with other mechanisms for protecting IPR, such as secrecy,

lead time, complementary sales and services, and complementary manufacturing. These authors also showed that the average number of patent applications per million US$ of R&D expenditure was 2.8 in Japan, but only 0.6 in the US. One explanation for the greater number of patents filed per product in Japan is that Japanese companies use patents to protect market access via cross-licensing, leading to greater sharing of information, as occurs in complex product industries in the US. As discussed in the second section, there are some reasons to believe that the strategic uses of patents by Japanese parent companies in Japan might also be applicable to China. Thus, it is conceivable that a stronger propensity to patent by parent companies at home would be positively correlated with greater patenting activity in foreign countries.

(6) *Reform*, a dummy variable for the second revision of the Chinese patent law in 2000. We set *Reform* equal to 1 in the years after 2000 and 0 otherwise. We use this dummy variable to test *Hypotheses 2* and *3*, discussed in the second section.

Data sources

Data on Japanese parent companies' patent applications for inventions were taken from the SIPO in China. Data on R&D expenditures, export sales, and total sales were collected from the *Kigyo Katsudo Kihon Chosa* (the *Basic Survey of Japanese Business Structure and Activities*) conducted by the Ministry of International Trade and Industry (MITI).[15] Data on numbers of patent applications filed by parent companies with the JPO were obtained from a BIBin/CD–ROM published by NGB Corporation. Data on FDI were obtained from the *Multinational Enterprises Database* (or *Kaigai Shinshutsu Kigyou* File) published by Toyo Keizai Shinposha. This database includes data on the number of affiliates established in China by Japanese parent companies, their dates of establishment, their capitalization, and the ratio of shares held by the parent company.

Our data sample covers 436 Japanese parent companies during the period 1995 to 2003. For the variables describing total sales (*S*) and R&D expenditures (*RD*), we used simple linear interpolation to fill in some missing values. Table 9.2 presents descriptive statistics for the variables used in our empirical analysis.

Analytical results

Results for the full sample of Japanese parent companies are tabulated in Table 9.3. The estimated correlation coefficients were obtained from five regression equations differing only in the affiliate variables chosen,

Table 9.2 Descriptive statistics, 1995–2003 (N=436)

Variable	Mean	Stdev	Min	Median	Max
NP	15.7	80.7	0	0	2,108.0
NA	0.18	0.38	0	0	1.00
AS	217.9	1,845.2	0	0	87,853.7
RS	14.2	32.6	0	0	100.0
RD	10,962.8	40,100.7	5.8	1,854.5	527,359.0
S^a	240,094.7	642,011.9	2,818.0	74,064.0	9,104,792.0
EX	0.058	0.082	0.000	0.027	0.803
PP	0.026	0.042	0.000	0.015	0.623

Notes: Unit for *AS* is US$10 million; unit for *RD* and *S* is 1 billion Japanese yen.
[a] Total sales by Japanese parent companies.

namely, *NA*, *AS*, or *RS*, and the R&D variables, namely, log *RD* and log RD_{adj}.

The estimated coefficients for *AS*, listed in the second and fifth columns, are positive and statistically significant in all cases and fall within the range 0.023–0.030. The unit for *AS* is US$10,000. An elasticity of 0.023 thus implies that, on average, 2.6 Chinese patent applications were filed for every US$1 million of capital held by affiliates established in year *t*. The third and sixth columns show the estimated coefficients for *NA*, which are also all significantly significant, positive, and within the range 0.16–0.20. Since *NA* describes the activities of affiliates established in year *t*, these results imply that, in a given year, Japanese parent companies file an average of 0.18 application for new affiliates established in that year.

In addition to the FDI factors, the coefficients for *License* are positive and statistically significant in all five regressions, suggesting that technology transfer activities have a positive impact on patenting behavior by Japanese parent companies in China.

The coefficients estimated for *RS*, the ratio of shares held by Japanese parent companies in new affiliates they established, are also positive and statistically significant. Parent companies holding a higher ratio of shares in their joint-venture affiliates will file more patents in order to protect their IPRs in China.

The coefficient of log *RD*, which measures patent-R&D elasticity, describes the improvement in R&D productivity resulting from the filing of overseas patents by Japanese parent companies. Estimates for this coefficient are around 0.37 for the three types of regressions tabulated

Table 9.3 Estimated results for patent application

Variable	I	II	III	IV	V
AS	0.0233***			0.0305***	
	(3.69)			(4.42)	
NA		0.1579***			0.2024***
		(3.76)			(4.56)
RS			0.0017***		
			(3.73)		
License	0.2008**	0.1917**	0.1961**	0.2798**	0.2663**
	(2.36)	(2.24)	(2.27)	(2.49)	(2.36)
Log RD	0.3741***	0.3721***	0.3714***		
	(12.27)	(12.21)	(12.20)		
Log RD_{adapt}				1.0343***	1.0203***
				(6.72)	(6.62)
PP	3.4322***	3.4560***	3.4732***		
	(5.58)	(5.60)	(5.61)		
ES	9.3150***	9.2297***	9.2495***		
	(6.92)	(6.85)	(6.82)		
Reform	0.7890***	0.7850***	0.7834***	0.8025***	0.7975***
	(21.19)	(21.01)	(20.91)	(20.78)	(20.59)
Const	−3.2516***	−3.4066***	−3.3937***	0.2837***	0.066
	(−10.53)	(−11.25)	(−11.20)	(2.51)	(0.62)
a	0.8361***	0.8340***	0.8322***	0.6677***	0.6671***
	(13.11)	(13.11)	(13.12)	(13.88)	(13.88)
b	0.8137***	0.8079***	0.8031***	0.4519***	0.4503***
	(8.89)	(8.91)	(8.92)	(12.61)	(12.63)
No. of Obs.	3,488	3,488	3,488	3,488	3,488
Log Likelihood	−6,627.21	−6,626.86	−6,627.05	−6,689.23	−6,688.49

Notes:
1. The dependent variable is *NP*, namely, the number of patent applications. Industry dummies are included among the explanatory variables; their estimated coefficients are not shown in the table but are available upon request.
2. *denotes statistical significance at the 10% level.
**denotes statistical significance at the 5% level.
***denotes statistical significance at the 1% level.
3. Values in parentheses indicate student-t statistics.

in Table 9.3. We thus find an elasticity much smaller than that obtained by Iwasa and Odagiri (2004), who estimated the patent-R&D elasticity of Japanese firms filing patents in the US to be over 0.70.

The estimated coefficient for export intensity by the parent company (*ES*) is positive, statistically significant, and large in magnitude. This finding suggests that increased export intensity by parent companies tends to increase the number of patents filed in China. As expected, the coefficient of *PP*, namely, the patent propensity of the parent company, is positive and statistically significant for regressions I, II, and III. This suggests that affiliates are more likely to file patents in China when their parent companies have a stronger propensity to file patents in Japan.

Table 9.3 also shows that the coefficients for log RD_{adapt} are positive and statistically significant. The main purpose of adaptive R&D is to support marketing and sales by adapting products developed in Japan to suit local tastes and regulations. Consequently, adaptive R&D, defined as $RD \times ES$, may influence the patenting behavior of parent companies in China. Thus, our assumptions regarding adaptive R&D are supported by the estimated coefficients for log RD_{adapt}.

Finally, the coefficients of *Reform*, the dummy variable identifying the second revision of the Chinese patent law in 2000, are positive and statistically significant in all cases, implying that IPR reforms had a significant positive effect on patent applications by Japanese parent companies.

As discussed in the second section, if the responses of MNEs to IPR reforms are motivated solely by the desire of the MNE to protect against imitations, and if patenting in China is perceived as an effective legal weapon to this end, then we might expect that the number of patent applications would increase as new affiliates are established in China. On the other hand, if MNEs respond to IPR reforms based on their own IPR strategies, namely, building their patent portfolios, completing nets of patents, and collecting royalties in China, then the increase in patent applications might be expected to be related to an MNE's own global innovation and IPR strategies.

To assess which of these interpretations is borne out by statistical data, we use dummy variables to investigate the response of Japanese parent companies to IPR reforms in China. Table 9.4 presents the results of tests in which the coefficients for *AS* and *License* were measured together with the coefficients for each of these variables times *Reform*. In the full sample, the estimated coefficients for *AS* are statistically significant with magnitudes slightly larger than those in Table 9.3, while the coefficients of *License* are not statistically significant. However, the results for *AS* × *Reform* and *License* × *Reform* are precisely the opposite: the estimated coefficients for *License* × *Reform* are all *positive* and statistically significant (although not as large as in the second row), whereas the estimated coefficients for *AS* × *Reform* are all *negative*

Table 9.4 Impact of patent reforms on patent applications

Variable	Full Sample		Complex		Discrete	
AS	0.0781*** (10.67)	0.0782*** (10.60)	0.0712*** (6.90)		0.0819*** (7.92)	−0.794 (−0.89)
AS× Reform	−0.1141*** (−17.25)	−0.1162*** (−17.73)	−0.1058*** (−11.03)		−0.1327*** (−14.99)	
License	0.075 (0.56)	−0.033 (−0.24)	0.005 (0.03)			
License×Reform	0.257* (1.65)	0.6140*** (3.86)		0.5436*** (3.09)		1.509 (1.59)
Log RD	0.3438*** (11.23)	0.3678*** (12.41)	0.3039*** (8.07)	0.3183*** (8.47)	0.5480*** (10.03)	0.5351*** (10.15)
PP	3.5327*** (5.54)	3.1606*** (4.73)	1.5446** (2.32)	1.3374** (2.01)	3.2509** (2.60)	1.904 (1.31)
ES	11.024*** (8.08)	18.533*** (14.75)	12.435*** (8.06)	19.058*** (13.86)	4.2868 (1.48)	14.230*** (4.72)
Const	−2.7282*** (−8.75)	−3.4609*** (−11.89)	−3.3010*** (−6.79)	−3.4609*** (−11.89)	−4.1014*** (−7.92)	−4.6449*** (−9.45)
a	0.8056*** (13.15)	0.8007*** (13.18)	0.6738*** (10.20)	0.7933*** (13.09)	1.2009*** (7.87)	1.1193*** (7.60)
b	0.8200*** (8.73)	0.8130*** (8.78)	0.9151*** (6.76)	0.9776*** (8.22)	1.1324*** (4.79)	1.4270*** (4.28)
No. of Obs.	3,488	3,488	1,824	1,824	1,664	1,664
Log Like-lihood	−6,684.8	−6,834.48	−3,861.91	−3,917.39	−2,800.67	−2,903.41

Notes:
1. The dependent variable is NP, namely, the number of patent applications. Industry dummies are included among the explanatory variables; their estimated coefficients are not shown in the table but are available upon request.
2. * denotes statistical significance at the 10% level.
** denotes statistical significance at the 5% level.
*** denotes statistical significance at the 1% level.
3. Values in parentheses indicate student-t statistics.

and statistically significant. One possible interpretation of these results is that, in contrast to the years prior to 2000, in which MNEs focused their IPR strategies on protection against imitators, the increase in patent applications after 2000 was due to a spike in technology transfer from multinationals to Chinese affiliates, and thus reflects recent changes in the IPR strategies of MNEs in response to reforms in the Chinese patent system.

We continued our investigations into the response of MNEs to IPR reforms by dividing our corporate sample into subsamples for discrete and complex product industries, as the Chinese patenting practices of Japanese parent companies in each of these two industry categories might well be expected to differ.

Following Cohen *et al.* (2002), we classify industries such as foods, textile products, chemicals, drugs, metals and metal products as 'discrete' industries, while industries such as machinery, electrical and electronic equipment, transportation, and instruments are classified as 'complex' industries.

The results are tabulated in Table 9.4. The estimated coefficients for *AS* and *AS×Reform* exhibit patterns quite similar to those found in the full sample: the estimated coefficients for *AS* in both discrete and complex industries are positive and statistically significant, while those for *AS×Reform* are negative and statistically significant for both industry categories. For, *License×Reform*, on the other hand, the coefficient in the complex industry category is highly statistically significant, while the coefficient in the discrete industry category was not statistically significant. Patent portfolios in complex industries often serve to facilitate licensing or cross-licensing negotiations. Thus, our results may suggest that, in contrast to discrete industries – in which excluding competitors and protecting against imitation still plays a vital role – a strategic shift toward greater technology transfer became more conspicuous within Japanese companies in complex industries, especially after the second revision of Chinese patent law in 2000.

Cohen *et al.* (2002) argued that almost *all* products are complex in Japan, because Japanese patents encompass fewer claims, and those claims themselves tend to be interpreted more narrowly, generating more patents per product and, in turn, more widespread technological interdependence. Our findings seem to support their argument. However, we do see from Table 9.5 that the effects of the other explanatory variables on patenting behavior differ significantly in the two industry-group subsamples. For example, in discrete industries, the coefficient for the patent-R&D elasticity (log *RD*) is estimated at 0.54,

Table 9.5 Dynamic panel GMM estimates

Variable	I	II	I	II	I	II
NP/RD_{t-1}	0.8811*** (103.02)	0.7313*** (25.65)	0.8810*** (103.02)	0.7217*** (26.30)	0.8686*** (101.34)	0.6937*** (28.27)
NP/RD_{t-2}		0.3056*** (9.58)		0.3083*** (10.05)		0.3313*** (12.09)
AS_t	-0.0001 (-1.53)	0.0000 (-0.18)				
AS_{t-1}	-0.0001** (-2.40)	-0.0001** (-2.39)				
AS_{t-2}		0.0001*** (2.70)				
NA_t			-0.0001 (-1.53)	-0.0001 (-0.28)		
NA_{t-1}			-0.0001** (-2.40)	-0.0010* (-1.77)		
NA_{t-2}				0.0013*** (2.66)		
$License_t$					0.0020 (1.05)	0.0010 (0.50)
$License_{t-1}$					0.0054* (1.83)	0.0076** (2.27)
$License_{t-2}$						0.0206*** (3.82)
$\log RD_t$	-0.0010*** (-4.36)	-0.0013*** (-5.14)	-0.0010*** (-4.36)	-0.0012*** (-4.83)	-0.0011*** (-4.94)	-0.0013*** (-5.10)
$\log RD_{t-1}$	0.0010*** (4.69)	0.0010*** (4.53)	0.0010*** (4.69)	0.0009*** (4.24)	0.0010*** (4.73)	0.0010*** (4.57)
$\log RD_{t-2}$		0.0002** (2.02)		0.0002** (2.13)		0.0002 (1.45)
Sargan Test[a]	94.042[0.152]	86.729[0.234]	92.037[0.189]	86.538[0.238]	87.947[0.28]	87.288[0.221]
c1[b]	-1.638[0.101]	-2.094[0.036]	-1.644[0.100]	-2.144[0.035]	-1.625[0.104]	-1.836[0.066]
c2	1.038[0.299]	-0.094[0.925]	1.038[0.299]	-0.199[0.842]	1.020[0.308]	-0.842[0.400]

Notes:
1. The dependent variable is NP/RD_t, namely, the ratio of patent applications to R&D expenditures. The ratio of exports to total sales (of the parent company), and $\log RD$, are used as instruments.
2. *denotes statistical significance at the 10% level.
** denotes statistical significance at the 5% level.
***denotes statistical significance at the 1% level.
3. Values in parentheses indicate student-t statistics.
[a] Statistics for the over-identifying restrictions test and p-value.
[b] c1 and c2 are the p-values of the first- and second-order autocorrelations against the null of no serial correlations.

greatly exceeding the value of 0.31 obtained for complex industries. Also, in discrete industries, the parent company's propensity to patent (*PP*) seems somewhat irrelevant to patenting behavior in China, which is not the case in complex industries.

Dynamic panel GMM estimation

As discussed in the second section, correlated dynamic effects may be present in the patenting behavior of Japanese parent companies in China. We thus tested the influence that learning to patent, including cumulative patenting, had on patent applications by players in China.

In addition, in the analysis of the previous section, we treated FDI as exogenous, at least with regard to patenting behavior of Japanese parent companies in China. However, the relationship between FDI and patenting may in fact be endogenous: FDI and patenting may both be caused by one unobserved factor, or patenting, as a legal weapon, may encourage simultaneous FDI in China.

To address correlated dynamic effects and the endogeneity problem, we apply the dynamic panel GMM estimation techniques developed by Arellano and Bover (1995) and Blundell and Bond (1998) to obtain the following model patent production function incorporating FDI lag effects:

$$\left(\frac{NP}{RD}\right)_{it} = \alpha_0 + \sum_{k=1}^{p} \alpha_k \left(\frac{NP}{RD}\right)_{i,t-k}$$

$$+ \sum_{l=0}^{q} \beta_l \left(AS, NA, \text{ or License and logRD}\right)_{i,t-l} + u_{it}$$

$$(9.2)$$

where, as described above, *NP* is the number of patent applications for inventions made by the parent company in China, *RD* is the parent company's R&D expenditure, *AS* describes the capital used to establish new affiliates, *NA* is a dummy variable for new affiliates established, and *License* is a dummy variable for technology transfer activity by the parent company. Blundell and Bond (1998) proposed a linear GMM estimator (DPD-SYS) in which difference equations for individual values of *i* are combined with level equations for Eq. (9.2).

We began our estimates with *ARDL*(1,1) (namely, setting $p = 1$ and $q = 1$ in Eq. (9.2)). We found that, with these values of *p* and *q*, a serial correlation in u_{it} was present.[16] Thus, the data tabulated in Table 9.5 were obtained using *ARDL* (2,2), namely, with $p = 2$ and $q = 2$ in Eq. (9.2). For these values of *p* and *q*, various statistical tests of the GMM-SYS estimators, such as the Sargan test of the over-identifying restrictions on instruments, and tests against the null hypothesis of no first-order serial correlations in the first-differenced residuals, revealed no apparent problems.

The coefficients for the quantities NP/RD_{t-1} and NP/RD_{t-2} are positive and statistically significant, implying that the number of patent applications filed by Japanese parent companies is strongly correlated with patent-application behavior in previous periods. However, the magnitude of the coefficients is somewhat large, causing some stationary problems. This is likely due to the insufficient length of the time series covered in our sample.

The quantities NA_{t-1}, NA_{t-2}, AS_{t-1}, AS_{t-2}, $License_{t-1}$, and $License_{t-2}$ were all statistically significant against the null hypothesis. After controlling for endogeneity in the relationship between FDI (or technology transfer) and patenting by using GMM estimation and instrument techniques, the estimated effects of *License* (the dummy variable for technology transfer) seem to be more statistically significant than those for *AS* (the total capitalization of the new affiliates) or *NA* (the indicator variable for the establishment of new affiliates). Our results also confirm that there exists some lag structure in the effect of FDI and technology transfer on patent applications, particularly as measured with *License*.

Conclusions

In this chapter, we conducted statistical analyses on a set of firm-level data describing the Chinese patent application behavior of Japanese companies between 1995 and 2003. We examined the reasons companies applied for patents, and we assessed how those reasons changed over time; we attempted in particular to investigate the global innovation strategies of the companies in the sample and how those strategies were adapted to the local Chinese business environment. Our findings can be summarized as follows.

(1) Around the year 2000 there was a sudden uptick in patent applications by, and a corresponding uptick in patents granted to, Japanese companies operating subsidiaries in China.
(2) Among Japanese companies operating subsidiaries in China, those who make more direct investments in China in a given period are more likely to apply for Chinese patents during that period. These causal effects remain statistically significant even after controlling for endogeneity in this relationship.
(3) The Chinese patent law reform of 2000 had a significant positive impact on the number of patent applications filed by Japanese companies in China. Our findings also support the view that the surge in patent applications by Japanese companies resulted more from a strategic shift toward increasing technology transfer to China than

from a desire on the part of parent companies to protect their products against imitations from local competitors.

(4) The number of Chinese patent applications filed by Japanese companies is strongly correlated with the Chinese patent application behavior of those companies in previous years. Similarly, there is also some lag in the effect on local patent applications of direct investment and technology transfer to China.

(5) Adaptive R&D, conducted by Japanese companies seeking to adapt their products to the Chinese market, has had some influence on the patent practices of those companies in China, but the magnitude of this influence is much smaller than the corresponding influence found by Iwasa and Odagiri (2004) for Japanese firms applying for patents in the US.

(6) Among Japanese companies that engage in international trade with China, those with a higher fraction of all exports going to China file more applications for Chinese patents. Similarly, Japanese companies with greater propensity (relative to their R&D expenditures) to file patents in Japan tend also to exhibit greater propensity to file patents in China.

(7) If we group industries into two categories – 'complex' and 'discrete' industries, based on whether most new commercial products in an industry are comprised of multiple separately patentable elements versus just a few such elements – then we find no obvious differences between companies in the two categories regarding the impact of direct investment in China on local patenting activity in China. However, the impact of technology transfer on patenting behavior appears to be more significant for companies in complex industries than for companies in discrete industries.

In closing, we note that Japanese companies apply for local patent protection wherever they export or operate production facilities. These patent applications are motivated, among other factors, by a desire to defend products against imitations from local competitors, as well as by proactive technology transfers to local affiliates. In this chapter, based on our analysis of the patenting practices of Japanese companies in China, we demonstrated that Japanese companies exhibited a shift around the year 2000 in their primary motivation for applying for patents in China, and that this shift led to a dramatic surge in Japanese patent applications there. Although this uptick was facilitated by the patent law reform enacted by the Chinese government in 2000, it was also driven by a shift in Japanese companies' innovation/ IP strategies: *toward* increased technology transfer to China, and *away from* protecting products against imitations from local competitors. We believe that this is a manifestation of the capability of Japanese MNEs to adjust flexibly to global as well as local business environments. If Japanese companies evolved their global innovation/IP strategies around the year 2000, then we may expect this to be just one of many evolutions to come.

Notes

1. Kortum and Lerner (1998, 2003) attributed most of the recent growth in patenting to increased innovation and improved R&D management in the US. Kim and Marschke (2004) drew attention to certain industries, and to the particularly increased patent yields in the computing, electronics, and auto sectors. Hall and Ziedonis (2001) studied the US semiconductor industry, in which patents per R&D dollar have doubled over the last ten years. Branstetter and Sakakibara (2001) analyzed the relationship between the 1988 Japanese patent-law reforms and innovations. Cohen *et al.* (2002) compared the effects of pro-patent policies in Japan and the US.
2. See http://english.mofcom.gov.cn/, the website of the Ministry of Commerce of the People's Republic of China.
3. See Lee and Mansfield (1996), Maskus (1998), and Yang and Maskus (2001).
4. The *Multinational Enterprises Database* (*Kaigai Shinshutsu Kigyou* File), published by Toyo Keizai Shinposha, reports information related to R&D conducted by those Japanese MNEs in China for whom R&D is cited as one reason for entry into China. However, these data contained too many gaps to be useful for the analysis discussed in this chapter.
5. See Fai (2004).
6. See Cohen *et al.* (2002).
7. A 2001 amendment to Japan's patent law shortened the examination request time in Japan from seven years to three years, effective on 1 October 2001.
8. A third revision of the Chinese patent law was approved on 27 December 2008. This revision allows foreign applicants to entrust any legally formed patent agency in China to represent their patent applications.
9. The EU11 includes Germany, the UK, France, the Netherlands, Italy, Sweden, Finland, Belgium, Denmark, Austria, and Spain.
10. See http://english.mofcom.gov.cn/, the website of the Ministry of Commerce of the People's Republic of China.
11. See Hall and Ziedonis (2001).
12. In constructing this dummy variable we referred to the database of Nikkei Telecom, which allows searches for all news released in mainstream Japanese newspapers.
13. See Hausman *et al.* (1984: 927).
14. See Griliches (1990: 1674).
15. For details on data sources, see Nakata (2010).
16. According to Blundell and Bond (1998), it is essential to assume no serial correlations in u_{it} in Eq. (9.2) in order for the estimators to be consistent. If the disturbances, u_{it}, are not serially correlated, there should be evidence of

significant negative first-order serial correlations in the differenced residuals, and no evidence of second-order serial correlations in the differenced residuals.

References

Arellano, M. and Bover, O. (1995) 'Another Look at the Instrumental-variable Estimation of Error Components Models', *Journal of Econometrics*, 68(1): 29–52.

Blundell, R. and Bond, S. R. (1998) 'Initial Conditions and Moment Restrictions in Dynamic Panel Data Models', *Journal of Econometrics*, 87(1): 115–143.

Blundell, R., Griffith, R., and Van Reenan, J. (1995) 'Dynamic Count Models of Technological Innovation', *Economic Journal*; 105: 333–344.

Branstetter, L. G. and Sakakibara, M. (2001) 'Do Stronger Patents Induce More Innovation? Evidence from the 1998 Japanese Patent Law Reform', *Rand Journal of Economics*, 32(1): 77–100.

Branstetter, L. G., Fisman, R., and Foley, C. F. (2006) 'Do Stronger Intellectual Property Rights Increase International Technology Transfer? Empirical Evidence from U.S. Firm-Level Panel Data', *The Quarterly Journal of Economics*, 121(1): 321–349.

China Daily (2004) 'Enterprises Improving IPR Strategy', *China Daily*, 3 August 2004.

Cohen, W. M., Goto, A., Nagata, A., Nelson, R., and Walsh, J. (2002) 'R&D Spillovers, Patents and the Incentives to Innovate in Japan and the United States', *Research Policy*, 31(8–9): 1349–1367.

Fai, F. M. (2004) 'China's Growing Technological Capabilities: Opportunities and Threats for Foreign Multinational Enterprises', Paper presented to the Conference of International Association for Chinese Management Research, Beijing, 2004.

Granstrand, O. (1999) 'Internationalization of Corporate R&D: A Study of Japanese and Swedish Corporations', *Research Policy*, 28(2–3): 275–302.

Griliches, Z. (1990) 'Patent Statistics as Economic Indicators: A Survey', *Journal of Economic Literature*, 28(4): 1661–1707.

Hall, B. H. and Ziedonis, R. H. (2001) 'The Determinants of Patenting in the U.S. Semiconductor Industry, 1980–1994', *Rand Journal of Economics*, 32(1): 101–128.

Hausman, J., Hall, B. H., and Griliches, Z. (1984) 'Econometric Models for Count Data with an Application on the Patents–R&D Relationship', *Econometrica*, 52(4): 909–938.

Hu, A. G. and Jefferson, G. H. (2006) 'A Great Wall of Patents: What is Behind China's Recent Patent Explosion?', Mimeograph.

Iwasa, T. and Odagiri, H. (2004) 'Overseas R&D, Knowledge Sourcing, and Patenting: An Empirical Study of Japanese R&D Investment in the US', *Research Policy*, 33(5): 807–828.

Kim, J. and Marschke, G. (2004) 'Accounting for the Recent Surge in U.S. Patenting: Changes in R&D Expenditures, Patent Yields, and the High Tech Sector', *Economics of Innovation and New Technology*, 13(6): 543–558.

Kortum, S. and Lerner, J. (1998) 'Stronger Protection or Technological Revolution: What is Behind the Recent Surge in Patenting?', *Carnegie-Rochester Conference Series on Public Policy*, 48(1): 247–304.

Kortum, S. and Lerner, J. (2003) 'Unraveling the Patent Paradox', Paper presented to AEA Annual Meeting, Washington, DC, 2003.

Kuemmerle, W. (1999) 'Foreign Direct Investment in Industrial Research in the Pharmaceutical and Electronic Industries-Results from a Survey of Multinational Firms', *Research Policy*, 28(2–3): 179–193.

Le Bas, C. and Sierra, C. (2002) ' "Location Versus Home Country Advantage" in R&D Activities: Some Further Results on Multinationals' Locational Strategies', *Research Policy*, 31(4): 589–609.

Lee, J.-Y. and Mansfield, E. (1996) 'Intellectual Property Protection and U.S. Foreign Direct Investment', *The Review of Economics and Statistics*, 78(2): 181–186.

Levin, R. C., Klevorick, A. K., Nelson, R. R., and Winter, S. G. (1987) 'Appropriating the Returns from Industrial R&D', *Brookings Papers on Economic Activity*, 3: 783–820.

Liu, X. (2002) 'Changes and Prospects of Chinese Intellectual Property System on China's Participation in the WTO', *Patent Studies* (in Japanese), 34: 56–66.

MacGarvie, M. (2002) 'Do Firms Learn from International Trade? Evidence from Patent Citations and Micro Data', Mimeograph.

Maskus, K. E. (1998) 'The International Regulation of Intellectual Property', *weltwirtschaftliches archiv* (Review of World Economics), 134(2): 186–208.

Nakata, Y. (2010) 'Empirical Analysis of Japanese MNEs Patenting Behavior in China', *ITEC Working Paper Series* 10–09 (September), Doshisha University.

Pakes, A. and Griliches, Z. (1980) 'Patents and R&D at the Firm Level: A First Look', *Economics Letters*, 5: 377–381.

Pearce, R. D. (1999) 'Decentralised R&D and Strategic Competitiveness: Globalised Approaches to Generation and Use of Technology in Multinational Enterprises (MNEs)', *Research Policy*, 28(2–3): 157–178.

Plasmans, J. E. J. and Tan, J. (2004) 'Intellectual Property Rights and International Trade with China', Mimeograph.

Sun, Y. (2003) 'Determinants of Foreign Patents in China', *World Patent Information*, 25(1): 27–37.

Yang, G. and Maskus, K. E. (2001) 'Intellectual Property Rights and Licensing: An Econometric Investigation', *weltwirtschaftliches archiv* (Review of World Economics), 137(1): 58–79.

Yasui, A., Hiratsuka, M., and Nakajima, I. (2007) 'Japanese Companies' Intellectual Property Strategies to China', *Patent Studies* (in Japanese), 44: 17–23.

10
Changing Ownership and Governance Innovation
Japanese Enterprises in Transition
Asli M. Colpan, Takashi Hikino, and Toru Yoshikawa

Introduction

The corporate governance practices of large Japanese enterprises were a focus of controversy during and after the rapid rise of these enterprises to international prominence in the 1980s. The perception of Japanese governance mechanisms at that time stands out as the antipodal opposite of the current thrust for the 'global' standards. The popular view at the height of Japan's economic power was that top executives in Japan, with no distracting interventions from pesky shareholders, exercised their discretion to target long-term efficiency-enhancing goals, to the profit of employees, shareholders, and other stakeholders. According to this view, the agency costs of managerial autonomy should be adequately compensated by the knowledge capital accumulated in and utilized by salaried management. In the US, on the other hand – according to the conventional view at the time – shareholders pressured salaried managers to maximize short-term returns at the expense of their firms' economic health, thus ultimately harming the competitiveness of US industry in the 1980s.

But the bursting of the bubble economy in the early 1990s, and the subsequent arrival of the decade-long *Heisei* recession, have rendered this interpretation obsolete. Prevailing wisdom today holds that Japanese executive culture promoted excessive discretionary behavior on the part of professional managers (Watanabe and Yamamoto, 1992). Without effective monitoring by outside parties, such as shareholders or debt-holders, senior managers aimed to maximize firm growth, often in the form of excessive product diversification and/or overseas expansion. For top executives, the sheer size of the corporate empire, symbolizing the reach of those executives' dominion, remained more significant than profitability and shareholder return. Consequently, governance issues have recently been subject to renewed emphasis, and effective monitoring mechanisms that maximize shareholder value have been hotly debated and are gradually becoming institutionalized (Ahmadjian and Robbins, 2005; Gilson and Milhaupt, 2004).

Large Japanese firms since the early 1990s thus present an appropriate testing ground for various hypotheses related to agency and managerial theories of the firm. There are several reasons for this. First, starting around 1997, the Japanese government introduced a series of important legal and regulatory devices to usher in a new business environment in Japan, including the introduction of stock options, the establishment of the executive officer organization, and the legalization of pure holding companies (Milhaupt, 2003). Second, these regulatory changes were accelerated by an exogenous factor, namely, the Asian financial crisis that started in July 1997. This environmental shift, which further worsened the general business climate, forced Japanese executives to reorient their goals toward efficiency and profitability, rather than growth and size. Third, Japanese firms exhibit a curious blend of the conventional paradigm of managerial dominance with the emerging notion of shareholder orientation. The distinct institutional and economic environments that existed in Japan before and after 1997 thus serve to highlight the impacts of governance and of strategic factors on firm performance within the controlled macroeconomic conditions of a prolonged recession.

This chapter aims to examine and compare the effects of reformed governance and revised corporate strategies on firm performance – as measured by profitability – in the Japanese context. To this end, we begin in the second section with an overview of the paradigm shift in Japanese corporate governance in the 1990s. We then examine the impact on performance of changes in corporate governance, and the adoption of new growth strategies, both before and after the institutionalization of governance reforms around the year 1997. Our main concerns are, first, how much of the variance in the performance of Japanese firms can be attributed to the effects of governance factors emphasizing shareholder value, and how much resulted from strategic choices representing the sphere of managerial discretionary power? Second, given the evolution of institutional environments toward shareholder primacy, we are interested in understanding how much the new setting actually promoted the interest of shareholders. In other words, we aim to investigate whether corporate governance factors collectively explain more of the variance in firm performance due to rising interests in corporate governance and the commitment of shareholders to Japanese firms. Finally, we examine the impact of specific corporate governance measures on the financial outcome of individual firms.

Changing characteristics of ownership and governance

For decades after the end of World War II, the corporate governance of Japanese firms was characterized by a relationship-oriented model, based on the combination of stable institutional ownership and primarily main bank debt financing, with significant discretion left to professional management.[1] Beginning in the mid-1990s, however, this relational pattern began to evolve, for two reasons: a prolonged slump in the Japanese economy, and international pressures, mainly from US business interests (Hoshi and Kashyap, 2001; Miyajima and Aoki, 2002; Shimotani, 2006). The decade-long recession resulted in deteriorating corporate performance and a corresponding decline in share prices and dividend payments. As the financial misery of Japanese firms continued, many investors and observers began to pin the blame on the ineffectual corporate governance mechanisms of Japanese firms (Watanabe and Yamamoto, 1992). Amid a rising tide of public and international demand for the senior management of Japanese firms to deal with the weaknesses of Japanese corporate governance, Japanese managers belatedly started to pay greater attention to their governance practices. Meanwhile, stable investors, and particularly commercial banks, faced financial troubles themselves due to large numbers of non-performing loans. Portfolio investors, domestic and international, seeking capital and income gains bought shares sold by stable investors, and then imposed further pressure on corporations to reform governance practices and ultimately to improve financial performance (Colpan *et al.*, 2007).

The pressure to focus on shareholder value and corporate profitability mandated a fundamental shift in Japanese firms, from a relationship-based, stakeholder-oriented governance model toward a market-based, shareholder-oriented model. When a firm had tried to accommodate the interests of heterogeneous stakeholders, many of which may often be mutually incompatible, its management may be forced to choose a sub-optimal allocation of resources, thus diminishing profitability. In Japan's earlier corporate governance model, relationship-oriented investors had not aimed at maximizing return on their investment, and thus

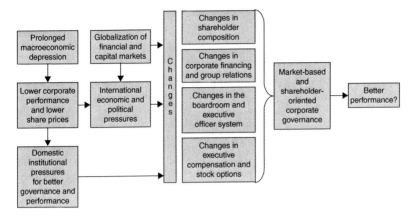

Figure 10.1 Structural change in Japanese corporate governance
Source: Adapted from Colpan *et al.* (2007).

did not impose significant pressure on top executives to improve firm performance (Charkham, 1994; Kester, 1991). However, as the interests and goals of stable shareholders evolved, and as ownership shifted toward international and performance-conscious domestic investors, it became necessary for many Japanese firms to move toward a more market-based model of corporate governance (see Figure 10.1).

Since the mid-1990s, when major legal reforms were introduced by the Japanese government in response to the new ownership environment, institutional changes in corporate governance practices have become something of a fashion for Japanese firms. In this context, changes in ownership constitute the most critical tool for forcing governance reforms, because shareholding represents the institutional and legal foundations on the basis of which governance mechanisms – such as the transparency and accountability of financial statements and the control and decision-making by the board of directors – are legitimized.

Changes in the composition of ownership of Japanese firms

Domestic financial institutions and non-financial firms have long dominated the ownership of large Japanese firms, often reflecting long-standing business relationships with partners known as 'stable' shareholders. Relationships between such shareholders are often characterized by reciprocal holdings, which imply an expression of goodwill (Clark, 1979) and function as an important instrument in transactional and historical ties (Gerlach, 1992). Thus, in these domestic shareholding relationships, the maximization of shareholder value was not necessary a primary goal (Phan and Yoshikawa, 2000; Sheard, 1994).

Changes in the capital markets and accounting rules, however, have exerted pressures toward change. The prolonged Japanese business slump since the early 1990s had a profound impact on conventional stable shareholdings (Shimotani, 2006). As new accounting rules were implemented in 1996 to make Japanese rules compatible with international standards, Japanese firms had to recalculate their investments in stockholdings from book value to market value. As the market value of shareholdings declined amid the poor business climate, companies attempted to minimize losses from their shareholdings, which eventually forced those companies to reduce their shareholdings in affiliated firms. In general, rising capital market pressures saddled corporations with mounting pressure to pay attention to the yield of their employed capital. Consequently, both stable ownership and reciprocal holdings have substantially declined over the past decade. According to figures from the NLI Research Institute (2004), stable shareholdings dropped from 45 per cent to 24 per cent, and reciprocal holdings declined from 18 per cent to 7 per cent during the period 1990–2003 (Colpan *et al.*, 2007).

A large number of the shares sold by these relationship-oriented investors were acquired by international investors or domestic but market-oriented institutions. Domestic pension funds and investment trusts have been gaining prominence in the Japanese capital markets ever since the mid-1990s (Fukao, 1999; Inoue, 1999). While they are not quite arm's-length players, such investors are surely more performance-conscious and given to seek higher returns on their holdings (Suto and Toshino, 2005). For international institutional investors, especially those from the US and Europe seeking to globalize their stock investments, the reduced prices of Japanese stocks after the burst of the bubble economy made those stocks much more attractive, and hence such portfolio investors have been increasing their holdings of Japanese stocks steadily since the 1990s (Miyajima and Kuroki, 2007). Thus, since the early 1990s, foreign ownership has risen from 4 per cent of all listed Japanese shares in 1990 to 22 per cent in 2004.[2] Many of these foreign investors look for higher investment returns based on more shareholder-oriented corporate governance models, while they hold only arm's-length relationships with the firms in which they invest (Jackson and Moerke, 2005; Yoshikawa and Phan, 2001). Figure 10.2 illustrates the changing ownership of Japanese

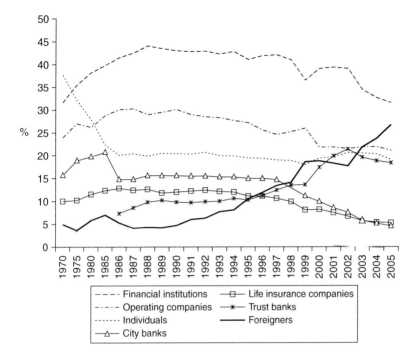

Figure 10.2   Change in ownership structure of Japanese firms
Source: Adapted from Colpan *et al.* (2007).

firms since 1970; both the long-term and recent trends described above
are visible in this graph (Colpan *et al.*, 2007).

These fundamental shifts in ownership structure mean that top
managers of Japanese firms now face strong pressure to accommodate
the needs of more return-oriented shareholders, such as foreign portfolio
investors, and domestic trust banks and pension funds. Foreign investors in particular demand that Japanese firms disclose more financial
information, since – in contrast to stable domestic shareholders – they
have no other means to gather such corporate information (Yoshikawa
and Linton, 2000). Understandably, those international institutional
investors pressure Japanese firms to adopt global standards of corporate disclosure and accountability (Useem, 1998). Hence, those Japanese
firms that have significant foreign ownership may have to place greater
focus on the interests of shareholders, while adopting global standards
for governance practices.

Executive shareholding among Japanese firms has also emerged and grown in consequence of the changes in shareholder composition and governance principles. The classic tenets of agency theory hold that corporate executives must own shares in the firms they manage in order to align their interests with those of general shareholders. Shareholdings by senior managers theoretically incorporate positive incentives to maximize shareholder value, rather than simply the size and sales of the company, because increased shareholder value leads directly to personal financial gains for those managers. Executive share ownership has thus become another factor that may cause Japanese managers to be more return-oriented (Colpan *et al.*, 2007).

Theory and hypotheses

Since the work of Jensen and Meckling (1976), most research on corporate governance has been grounded in a framework that focuses on the separation of ownership and control within an agency theory. This theory attempts to address the problems that arise in agency relationships when **(a)** the goals of the principal and the agent conflict, and **(b)** it is difficult or expensive for the principal to verify what the agent is actually doing (Eisenhardt, 1989). As residual risk bearers, shareholders have a claim to net cash flows – that is, to the cash remaining after expenses, including promised payments to agents or managers, are covered (Jensen and Meckling, 1976). In practice, however, decisions on the disbursement of cash flows are typically made by management. Thus, separation of residual risk-bearing from decision-management leads to systems that separate decision-management from decision-control.

Research based on agency theory finds that, whereas shareholders seek to maximize the return on their investment, managers seek to advance their own personal interests, some of which can be achieved by growth in the firm they manage (Marris, 1964). The larger the firm they manage, the greater their prestige and reputation. Also, since executive pay is generally positively correlated with firm size, managers have an economic incentive to expand the firm they manage, through increased market share, product diversification, foreign entry, acquisitions, or other growth strategies. However, size-oriented strategies do not necessarily lead to higher profitability and greater shareholder returns, and hence the interests of shareholders and managers may be in conflict. If managers are not effectively monitored, the firm may choose strategies that aim to promote size and growth but do not necessarily benefit shareholders.

In the Japanese context, the conventional wisdom has held that Japanese firms seek firm growth even at the cost of profitability. Two principal factors have been identified as the motivations for growth: *kigyou shuudan*, corporate groups, and *shuushin koyou*, lifetime employment. One critical reason for the tendency of senior Japanese managers to set growth and expansion as their primary goals is the characteristic ownership structure and control mechanism of Japanese firms. Many large Japanese firms belong to a corporate group, or *kigyou shuudan*, whose organizational characteristics include the complete-set principle and mutual ownership and mutual control (Miyazaki, 1980; Okumura, 1992). Because firms within a group ultimately own a substantial proportion of the shares of member firms, and because the salaried managers of each firm do not interfere, either independently or collectively, with the strategic decision-making of other companies, the managers of the individual firms effectively control their own firms. This Japanese version of the managerial enterprise has been considered the classic example of a growth orientation.

Another reason for the tendency of Japanese firms to seek growth is that the Japanese corporate system has traditionally placed greater emphasis on long-term employment relationships (Ahmadjian and Robinson, 2001; Cole, 1979). Long-term employment (also called 'lifetime' employment or *shuushin koyou*) has often been cited as a key factor underlying the success of Japanese corporations and the growth of Japanese industry (Aoki, 1990). In order to maintain this practice, it was essential that Japanese firms kept growing so that they could provide employment security and more positions for internal promotions.

These aspects of ownership, control, and employment encourage Japanese firms to seek strategies that aim to promote growth, regardless of their consequences on profitability. Thus, as long as these basic features remain intact, we expect that strategic factors should be a strong predictor of the variance in profitability of Japanese firms.

Nevertheless, observers of Japanese businesses suggest that the traditional emphasis on stakeholders – especially employees – and the relatively low priority given to shareholders' investment interests have gradually given way to a more shareholder-oriented approach to corporate governance of Japanese firms (Kikuchi, 1999; Yoshikawa and Phan, 2001). Since the late 1990s, Japanese firms have become increasingly exposed to pressure from foreign institutional shareholders – who, as mentioned above, are primarily investors from the US and Europe. Moreover, global competition has intensified in industry sectors in which Japanese firms once dominated during the 1980s. In addition, the prolonged poor corporate performance of Japanese firms during the 1990s has made the institutional environment more conducive to corporate governance reforms, through which salaried senior managers are forced to pay greater attention to the voice of shareholders and deliberately cater to their interests.

All these changes mean that corporate governance has directly and indirectly begun to play a more important role in Japanese firms since the second half of the 1990s. Because the new corporate governance movement emphasizes the enhancement of firm value and the maximization of investment returns for shareholders, we expect that corporate governance reforms should have had increasingly greater impact on shareholder returns as the 1990s progressed. If Japanese managers started to pay more attention to governance after 1997, governance factors should have a stronger effect on performance, both directly and through their interactions with strategies. We would thus expect that corporate governance factors explain more of the variance in profitability in the years after 1997 than was true before that year.

Aside from the relative explanatory power of governance and strategy variables as collective sets of two separate groups of factors, we would also expect that some other features of corporate governance, and especially block ownership, should have a positive influence on corporate financial performance. Block ownership increases shareholders' motivation and capacity to monitor the behavior of management (Hill and Snell, 1988). Increased stock holdings by financial institutions should also raise the effectiveness of corporate management, because those institutions, which not only own shares but also often function as the providers of debt financing, are assumed to possess higher capabilities for monitoring, as well as an increased focus on investment returns since the 1990s, as discussed above (Morck and Nakamura, 1999; Sheard, 1989). Foreign investors, in addition, presumably act to pressure management to establish profitability as its primary goal, since the main objective of such investors is to derive financial return from their shareholdings (Ahmadjian and Robbins, 2005; Yoshikawa et al., 2005). Stock ownership by management, in contrast, aligns the interests of the senior executives and general shareholders (Morck et al., 1988), and also encourages managers to equate shareholder value with their personal profit, so that financial yield will be highly appreciated.

We thus expect that each of the four ownership factors selected as independent explanatory variables describing governance features should have a significant positive impact on profitability. We further expect the impact of these governance factors to be more prominent in the years after 1997, when governance reforms opened up new opportunities for owners to influence corporate management and its financial performance.

Data and methodology

Sample

The sample in this study includes all the electronics companies listed on the first section of Japan's three largest stock exchanges: Tokyo, Osaka, and Nagoya. The electronics industry is chosen because it represents one of the most dynamic and successful industries in Japan. Electronics firms span the gamut of ownership and governance models, from firms operating under the conventional model of managerial dominance, to firms owned and managed by international investment funds. Moreover, the electronics industry encompasses both firms with single product categories and firms with widely diversified portfolios, and contains firms with no foreign operations as well as firms active in as many as 46 overseas national markets. Our study addresses the period from 1991 to 2002, which encompasses the entire duration of the prolonged *Heisei* recession. We deliberately choose this time period to coincide with the depressed yet stable macroeconomic climate that started in 1991 and ended around 2002, because recent studies have emphasized the significance of environmental factors that critically influence the dynamic relationships between specific strategic and governance measures and financial performance (Colpan and Hikino, 2005; Geringer *et al.*, 2000;Grant, 2002; Mayer and Whittington, 2003).

The majority of the statistical data was collected from three sources: **(a)** the *Yuuka Shouken Houkokusho* (*Report on Securities and Stocks*), the semi-annual reports filed by exchange-listed companies with the Ministry of Finance; **(b)** the Nikkei Needs Database, and **(c)** the *Yakuin Shikihou* (*Quarterly Reports on Corporate Executives*). We consistently use consolidated data, rather than data for parent companies only, as these data reflect comprehensive business activities under the unified strategic leadership of the entire company. However, whenever any substantial data were missing for any firm, that firm was removed from the sample. This meant that our original sample of 146 firms was reduced to 104 companies in our final analysis.[3]

Variables

Performance measures

We use accounting- and operating-based measures to define a firm's performance. Despite some criticisms of accounting-based measures, these measures are commonly used to assess strategic and managerial effectiveness. While the various measures of profitability are all significantly correlated (Robins and Wieserma, 1995), in this study we choose return on assets (ROA) as a measure of corporate profitability. The basic results of our analysis remain similar, but weaker, when we run the regressions using other measures of corporate profitability, such as return on equity or return on sales.

Strategy variables

Product diversity. We use a Herfindahl-type measure of product diversity, which takes into account both the number of segments in which the firm operates and the relative importance of each segment. This index of diversity is calculated as $1 - \sum_{i=1}^{N} (Si)^2$, where S_i is the share of a firm's total sales in 3-digit JSIC segment i and N is the number of JSIC (Standard Industrial Classification for Japan) industries in which the firm operates. The Herfindahl index is better suited than entropy measures for quantifying diversification and for representing a resource-based perspective (Robins and Wiersema, 1995).

International diversity. The extent of geographical operations is measured by the number of foreign countries in which a firm had operating subsidiaries. For the 104 firms in the sample, the number of host countries varied from 0 to 46 with a mean of 9.62. This measure is similar to that employed by Tallman and Li (1996).[4] The data were gathered from the annual *Kaigai Shinshutsu Kigyou Souran* (*Total Lists of Firms Operating Overseas*) and the quarterly *Kaisha Shikihou* (*Quarterly Report on Listed Companies*).

Capital intensity. We use the ratio of total assets to number of employees as a measure of capital intensity (Bettis, 1981). This measure represents the cumulative result of managerial commitment to capital investments.

Sales growth. We include sales growth to account for the common view of Japanese firms' emphasis on increasing market share and presence. This is measured by the percentage change in total sales from year to the next.

Ownership variables

Block ownership. This is the proportion of shares owned by the top ten largest shareholders; this quantity measures ownership concentration, which results in higher monitoring capacity.

Foreign ownership. This is the proportion of total shares held by foreign owners. This measure has been used reliably in past studies (Ahmadjian and Robinson, 2001; Yoshikawa *et al.*, 2005). The behavioral characteristics of international investors, in practice mostly US or European, are considered to differ from those of Japanese shareholders.

Financial ownership. This is the proportion of total shares held by Japanese financial institutions, including banks and insurance companies (Gedajlovic and Shapiro, 2002). Such institutions are assumed to possess higher monitoring capabilities than operating companies and individual investors.

Executive ownership. This is the proportion of total shares held by the members of the board and inside auditors. As the majority of Japanese board members are insiders (namely, senior executives), we treat the ownership by board members as executive ownership. Ownership by executives of shares of the firm they manage will encourage executives to promote shareholder value.

Control variables

We include several control variables in our regression models. Firm size is measured by total assets. Firm age is another firm-level control. The diversified business groups or *kigyou shuudan*, representing membership in one of the largest six financial groups, is an institutional-level control (Miyazaki, 1980; Morikawa, 1992). We include a dummy variable to control for any possible effects of this distinctive feature of the Japanese business environment. Average annual growth of industry shipments, represented by 3-digit JSIC sub-industry dummies, is an industry-level control.

Identification of strategic time periods

For two major reasons, we divide the time span of our analysis into two strategic time periods. First, the endogenous governance factors consist of the institutionalization of several shareholder-oriented policy measures in Japan, including the introduction of stock options, the establishment of an executive officer system, and the legalization of pure holding companies; all of these changes occurred in 1997. Second, the significance of that particular year is further highlighted by an exogenous macroeconomic factor, the Asian financial crisis, which began in July 1997 and thus provides a natural reason, based on secular trends of declines in real GDP, to divide our sample into two distinct time periods. We use prolonged periods, determined by exogenous and endogenous factors as just described, to assess the impact of fundamental and long-term strategic adjustments across different time periods.[5]

Our entire time span of 12 years can thus be conveniently divided into two distinct strategic time periods (STPs): 1991 to 1996 (STP1), and 1997 to 2002 (STP2). The first period is characterized by the economic slump that began in 1990, when the bubble economy of the second half of the 1980s came to an end with collapsing real estate prices and equity markets. Because many observers in business, government, and the press regarded these troubles as temporary, there was no systematic response in terms of strategic shifts and governance reforms. In the second period, after 1997, governance concerns took on critical significance in government policy-making as well as in business circles and financial markets, while the macroeconomic environment in Japan worsened further. Governance reforms, in particular, were then extensively institutionalized.

Methodology

We conducted multiple regression analyses to examine the effectiveness of corporate strategy and governance measures used by Japanese electronic firms since the 1990s. A panel data set was used for the analysis; time-series data, with figures in the panel, cover the period from 1991 to 2002. We used general linear square (GLS) models as an estimation technique.[6] Because the Hausman test indicated no significant systematic difference in the coefficients as computed from fixed-effects models and random-effects models, we have chosen to use random-effects models in our analysis.[7] We then decomposed the inter-firm variance in profit rates using F-tests to determine the relative significance of strategic, governance, and interaction factors.[8]

Statistical results

Table 10.1 presents descriptive statistics and correlation coefficients for our variables. As indicated in the table, there are no significant correlations among the variables. We next compute variance inflation factors (VIF) for each variable to check again for any possible problems. Because no single value of VIF is larger than 10 – which is taken as a rule-of-thumb value to detect serious multicollinearity – we can

Table 10.1 Pearson correlation coefficients

<table>
<tr><th></th><th colspan="12">Strategic time period 1 (STP1)</th></tr>
<tr><th></th><th>1</th><th>2</th><th>3</th><th>4</th><th>5</th><th>6</th><th>7</th><th>8</th><th>9</th><th>10</th><th>11</th><th>12</th></tr>
<tr><td>ROA</td><td>1.000</td><td></td><td></td><td></td><td></td><td></td><td></td><td></td><td></td><td></td><td></td><td></td></tr>
<tr><td>Firm age</td><td>-0.201</td><td>1.000</td><td></td><td></td><td></td><td></td><td></td><td></td><td></td><td></td><td></td><td></td></tr>
<tr><td>Firm size</td><td>-0.041</td><td>0.348</td><td>1.000</td><td></td><td></td><td></td><td></td><td></td><td></td><td></td><td></td><td></td></tr>
<tr><td>Kigyoshudan affiliation</td><td>-0.180</td><td>0.351</td><td>0.156</td><td>1.000</td><td></td><td></td><td></td><td></td><td></td><td></td><td></td><td></td></tr>
<tr><td>Industry growth</td><td>0.245</td><td>-0.098</td><td>-0.008</td><td>-0.029</td><td>1.000</td><td></td><td></td><td></td><td></td><td></td><td></td><td></td></tr>
<tr><td>Block ownership</td><td>-0.074</td><td>-0.274</td><td>-0.331</td><td>0.108</td><td>0.072</td><td>1.000</td><td></td><td></td><td></td><td></td><td></td><td></td></tr>
<tr><td>Foreign ownership</td><td>-0.031</td><td>-0.108</td><td>0.147</td><td>-0.136</td><td>0.103</td><td>0.095</td><td>1.000</td><td></td><td></td><td></td><td></td><td></td></tr>
<tr><td>Financial ownership</td><td>0.121</td><td>0.418</td><td>0.210</td><td>0.041</td><td>-0.145</td><td>-0.413</td><td>-0.026</td><td>1.000</td><td></td><td></td><td></td><td></td></tr>
<tr><td>Executive ownership</td><td>0.203</td><td>-0.471</td><td>-0.149</td><td>-0.381</td><td>0.114</td><td>0.376</td><td>-0.055</td><td>-0.403</td><td>1.000</td><td></td><td></td><td></td></tr>
<tr><td>Product diversity</td><td>-0.180</td><td>0.299</td><td>0.357</td><td>0.269</td><td>-0.089</td><td>-0.058</td><td>-0.126</td><td>0.031</td><td>-0.110</td><td>1.000</td><td></td><td></td></tr>
<tr><td>International diversity</td><td>0.023</td><td>0.108</td><td>0.434</td><td>0.150</td><td>0.055</td><td>-0.411</td><td>0.232</td><td>0.326</td><td>-0.198</td><td>0.207</td><td>1.000</td><td></td></tr>
<tr><td>Capital intensity</td><td>0.169</td><td>-0.227</td><td>0.261</td><td>-0.114</td><td>0.073</td><td>-0.195</td><td>0.221</td><td>0.053</td><td>-0.008</td><td>-0.099</td><td>0.325</td><td>1.000</td></tr>
<tr><td>Sales growth</td><td>0.402</td><td>-0.149</td><td>0.013</td><td>-0.014</td><td>0.359</td><td>-0.082</td><td>0.000</td><td>0.005</td><td>-0.002</td><td>-0.035</td><td>0.071</td><td>0.182</td></tr>
</table>

Continued

Table 10.1 Continued

		1	2	3	4	5	6	7	8	9	10	11	12
							Strategic time period 2 (STP2)						
ROA		1.000											
Firm age		−0.288	1.000										
Firm size		−0.091	0.326	1.000									
Kigyoshudan affiliation		−0.193	0.353	0.166	1.000								
Industry growth		0.177	−0.152	−0.087	−0.069	1.000							
Block ownership		0.091	−0.286	−0.264	0.170	0.034	1.000						
Foreign ownership		0.098	−0.153	0.314	−0.210	0.015	−0.078	1.000					
Financial ownership		0.137	0.274	0.204	0.016	−0.024	−0.361	0.175	1.000				
Executive ownership		0.249	−0.427	−0.135	−0.332	0.069	0.240	−0.084	−0.273	1.000			
Product diversity		−0.119	0.348	0.379	0.307	−0.032	−0.098	−0.119	0.120	−0.163	1.000		
International diversity		0.022	0.164	0.439	0.138	−0.042	−0.171	0.356	0.389	−0.172	0.271	1.000	
Capital intensity		0.266	−0.230	0.389	−0.073	0.003	−0.122	0.458	0.131	0.010	−0.082	0.361	1.000
Sales growth		0.421	−0.163	0.016	−0.026	0.348	0.114	0.097	0.051	0.127	−0.017	0.070	0.171

STP1, n=624;
STP2, n=624

Table 10.2 GLS regression results on ROA (STP1)[a]

	Dependent variable: ROA				
	1	2	3	4	5
Firm age	−0.047 (0.035)	−0.035 (0.036)	−0.004 (0.042)	−0.024 (0.038)	−0.020 (0.027)
Firm size	1.10E-07 (1.62E-07)	−6.87E-08 (1.63E-07)	−1.01E-07 (2.31E-07)	4.68E-09 (2.22E-07)	−6.92E-07** (1.94E-07)
Kigyoshudan affiliation	−1.470** (0.408)	−0.451 (0.448)	−0.342 (0.494)	0.103 (0.575)	−0.031 (0.651)
Industry growth	0.072** (0.017)	0.076** (0.017)	0.021† (0.012)	0.028* (0.012)	0.022* (0.011)
Governance variables					
Block ownership		−0.016 (0.024)		0.029 (0.049)	0.100* (0.039)
Foreign ownership		0.003 (0.045)		−0.026 (0.051)	−0.009 (0.037)
Financial ownership		0.083** (0.032)		0.102** (0.039)	0.103** (0.028)
Executive ownership		0.012** (0.032)		0.071 (0.108)	0.154 (0.100)
Strategy variables					
Product diversity			−1.997† (1.161)	−1.943† (1.112)	−1.924 (1.388)
International diversity			0.073 (0.373)	0.266 (0.373)	1.510** (0.576)
Capital intensity			0.015† (0.009)	0.015† (0.009)	0.033** (0.008)
Sales growth			0.116** (0.040)	0.124** (0.040)	0.130** (0.037)
Interactions					
Block ownership *Product diversity					0.521** (0.132)
Financial ownership *Product diversity					0.242* (0.114)
Foreign ownership *International diversity					0.085** (0.022)
Financial ownership *International diversity					−0.059** (0.021)
Executive ownership *International diversity					0.479** (0.153)

Continued

Table 10.2   Continued

	Dependent variable: ROA				
	1	2	3	4	5
Block ownership *Capital intensity					0.003** (0.001)
Foreign ownership *Capital intensity					0.001* (0.001)
Financial ownership *Capital intensity					0.001* (0.000)
R^2	0.095	0.120	0.269	0.294	0.464
Adjusted-R^2	0.089	0.108	0.250	0.267	0.413

[a]Unstandardized coefficients are shown, with standard errors in paranthesis
$n=624$
†$p<0.10$; *$p<0.05$; **$p<0.01$
Note: For interactive effects, only results with statistical significance are shown for the clarity of presentation.

Table 10. 3   GLS regression results on ROA (STP2)[a]

	Dependent variable: ROA				
	1	2	3	4	5
Firm age	−0.135** (0.033)	−0.097* (0.047)	−0.070** (0.025)	−0.080** (0.028)	−0.081** (0.026)
Firm size	1.66E-07 (1.78E-07)	2.53E-07 (2.61E-07)	−3.28E-07* (1.55E-07)	−1.88E-07 (1.54E-07)	2.07E-07 (2.29E-07)
Kigyoshudan affiliation	−0.893 (1.404)	−1.610 (1.877)	−1.310* (0.713)	−0.940 (0.896)	−7.92E-01 (0.765)
Industry growth	0.091** (0.027)	0.088** (0.026)	0.039* (0.020)	0.035* (0.018)	0.049* (0.021)
Governance variables					
Block ownership		0.130 (0.084)		−0.001 (0.025)	0.025 (0.022)
Foreign ownership		0.017 (0.088)		−0.056 (0.038)	−0.045 (0.038)
Financial ownership		0.061 (0.055)		0.061† (0.033)	0.066* (0.026)
Executive ownership		0.072 (0.108)		0.266* (0.109)	0.270** (0.102)

Continued

Table 10. 3 Continued

	1	2	3	4	5
		Dependent variable: ROA			
Strategy variables					
Product diversity			−2.123 (1.364)	−2.359 (1.819)	−3.731† (1.920)
International diversity			0.806 (0.706)	0.564 (0.702)	0.836 (0.575)
Capital intensity			0.014* (0.006)	0.017** (0.006)	0.021** (0.008)
Sales growth			0.130** (0.026)	0.129** (0.025)	0.136** (0.024)
Interactions					
Block ownership *Product diversity					0.250** (0.069)
Financial ownership *Product diversity					0.393** (0.133)
Financial ownership *International diversity					−0.134** (0.044)
Block ownership *Capital intensity					0.001† (0.000)
Executive ownership *Capital intensity					0.005** (0.002)
R^2	0.083	0.107	0.338	0.371	0.480
Adjusted-R^2	0.076	0.095	0.324	0.349	0.437

[a]Unstandardized coefficients are shown, with standard errors in paranthesis
$n = 624$
†$p<0.10$; *$p<0.05$; **$p<0.01$
Note: For interactive effects, only results with statistical significance are shown for the clarity of presentation.

say that collinearity does not appear to be a major problem for this study.

The results of our regression analyses are tabulated in Tables 10.2 and 10.3. Model 1 of the tables shows the base hypothesis with only control variables, while Models 2 and 3 are restricted models for governance and strategy effects. Model 4 presents the full regression model for both governance and strategy variables without interaction effects, while Model 5 incorporates the interaction effects. Based on the regression outcomes, we first examine the individual effects of independent variables before discussing variance decompositions.

The results show that, in general, only financial ownership can be singled out as a major factor that positively affects profitability on a consistent basis. Block ownership and financial ownership come out positive and statistically significant in STP1, and financial and executive ownership are positive and statistically significant in STP2. In addition to these findings, we observe several positive and significant interaction effects. In STP1, the most notable interactions (those with $p < 0.01$) are those between block ownership and product diversity, foreign ownership and international diversity, executive ownership and international diversity, and block ownership and capital intensity. In STP2, positive and statistically significant coefficients are obtained for the interactions between block ownership and product diversity, financial ownership and product diversity, and executive ownership and capital intensity. Meanwhile, foreign ownership exhibits almost no

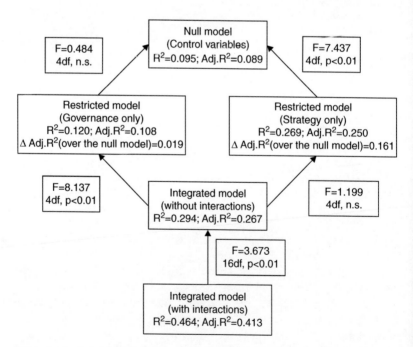

Figure 10.3 Relative influence of governance and strategy factors on ROA in STP1

significant impact at all, which is quite surprising given the reputed orientation of international – and particularly US – investors toward financial yields.

Figures 10.3 and 10.4 exhibit the explained variances of governance, strategic and interaction factors based on the specified regression models for STP1 and STP2, respectively. The figures illustrate the differences in the amount of explained variance as we impose a restriction by dropping interaction, governance, and strategy variables consecutively from the full model shown at the bottom of the figures. The F-tests near each arrow in the figures indicate the incremental or marginal contribution of the explanatory variables dropped in each case to the adjusted-R^2 of the original model.

Figure 10.3, for STP1, shows that the restricted model containing only governance variables offers no significant improvement over the null model ($F = 0.484$, 4df), whereas the strategy variables do bring significant increases in the coefficient of determination ($F = 7.437$,

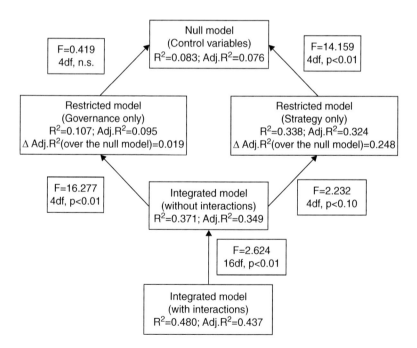

Figure 10.4 Relative influence of governance and strategy factors on ROA in STP2

4df, $p < 0.01$) over the null specification. The strategy model makes a similar contribution to the adjusted-R^2 in the presence of governance effects (15.9 versus 16.1 per cent). Governance variables again have no significant contributions to the integrated model (without interaction effects) in the presence of the strategy effects ($F = 1.199$, 4df). Interaction effects are highly significant as an incremental addition to the integrated model of strategy and governance without interaction terms ($F = 3.673$, 16df, $p < 0.01$).

The statistical significance of these results changes in STP2. Figure 10.4 illustrates that a restricted model with only governance variables remain insignificant over the base model in this period ($F = 0.419$, 4df). In sharp contrast, the strategy model's improvement over the null model is now even more significant (24.8 per cent, $F = 14.159$, 4df, $p < 0.01$ in STP2, as compared to 16.1 per cent, $F = 7.437$, 4df, $p < 0.01$ in STP1). The strategy model's contribution to the adjusted-R^2 in the presence of governance effects is also more statistically significant in this period (25.4 per cent, $F = 16.277$, 4df, $p < 0.01$). Governance variables, on the other hand, explain 2.5 per cent of variance in STP2, as compared to 1.7 per cent in STP1, in the presence of the strategy model. Thus the contribution of these variables remains low and grows marginally more significant. However, the interaction between governance and strategy factors accounts for less of the explained variance in STP2 than in STP1 (14.6 per cent in STP1 versus 8.8 per cent in STP2); the significance of the interaction declines from $F = 3.673$ in STP1 to $F = 2.624$ in STP2.

To analyze these results in a systematic fashion, in Table 10.4 we have tabulated the incremental contributions of the governance, strategy, and interaction effects to the adjusted-R^2. These results strongly suggest that strategy is significant on its own and in the presence of governance effects in both STP1 (16.1 per cent versus 15.9 per cent, respectively) and STP2 (24.8 per cent versus 25.4 per cent, respectively). The increasing significance of the strategy variables (see F-values and p-statistics in Table 10.4) also suggests that the strategy model's contribution to the explained variance increases from the first period to the second period. Governance, on the other hand, has no significant contributions alone in either STP1 or STP2. The contributions of governance in the presence of strategy effects are also marginal. In both periods, the interaction effects of corporate governance and strategy variables on profitability have the second highest explanatory power, after strategy effects (14.6 per cent and 8.8 per cent in STP1 and STP2, respectively). Table 10.4

Table 10.4   Incremental contribution of the explanatory variables

(Governance entering the regression analysis first)

		STP1				STP2		
Component	df	Incremental R^2	F-value	P	df	Incremental R^2	F-value	P
Control terms	4	0.089	1.028	n.s.	4	0.076	0.748	n.s.
Governance	4	0.019	0.484	n.s.	4	0.019	0.419	n.s.
Strategy	4	0.159	8.137	p<0.01	4	0.254	16.277	p<0.01
Interaction (governance*strategy)	16	0.146	3.673	p<0.01	16	0.088	2.624	p<0.01
Total model		0.413				0.437		
Error		0.587				0.563		

(Strategy entering the regression analysis first)

		STP1				STP2		
Component	df	Incremental R^2	F-value	P	df	Incremental R^2	F-value	P
Control terms	4	0.089	1.028	n.s.	4	0.076	0.748	n.s.
Strategy	4	0.161	7.437	p<0.01	4	0.248	14.159	p<0.01
Governance	4	0.017	1.199	n.s.	4	0.025	2.232	p<0.10
Interaction (governance*strategy)	16	0.146	3.673	p<0.01	16	0.088	2.624	p<0.01
Total model		0.413				0.437		
Error		0.587				0.563		

illustrates that interaction factors account for the almost equal, yet marginally smaller, amount of aggregate variance in profitability compared to the strategy model in STP1, while the relative significance of these factors declines significantly in the second strategic time period.

These results overall suggest the following conclusions. First, strategy factors are highly significant and account for around ten times as much of the profit variance as governance variables in both strategic time periods. Second, while governance factors have little or no direct impact on firm profitability, they do exhibit significant contributions to profitability when they interact with strategy. These interaction effects account for roughly as much variance as do the strategy factors alone in the first period, whereas the relative influence of the inter-action effects declines significantly in the second period. Ultimately, strategy becomes the dominant contributor to firm profitability in the second time period.

Conclusions and discussion

In this chapter we have attempted to examine and compare the chang-ing effects of corporate governance and growth strategy factors on the financial performance of Japanese electronics firms within the control-led macroeconomic setting of the prolonged recession of the 1990s. The depressed and still worsening business environment signifies two issues. First, shareholders' interests gradually became the center of managerial attention, as the agency cost of salaried management was recognized as a potential problem for the first time in the Japanese context. This was quite a change in a nation in which shareholders had long remained silent amid the prosperity of Japanese industry up to the late 1980s – an economic environment that allowed salaried top managers to exercise their discretionary power, while shareholders were more or less satis-fied with both income and capital gains. Second, with no exogenous demand-pull macroeconomic factors to raise profitability, the dimin-ished business climate provided an opportunity to identify the factors that genuinely contributed to financial performance and shareholder value. The Asian financial crisis, starting in July 1997, further deepened the profitability slump, ensuring that strategic factors – exemplified by resource allocation among competing projects – became a critical deter-minant of financial yields. These two forces – shareholders demanding better governance and management emphasizing strategic effective-ness – worked simultaneously to achieve higher profitability.

Our main findings regarding the effect of governance and strategy factors are interesting and surprising. Our ultimate conclusion is that governance factors, represented by the composition of ownership and also their interactions with strategy, have played a relatively weak role in influencing financial returns, even in the years after 1997, in which several legislative reforms designed to improve shareholder value were enacted and implemented in practice by Japanese firms. Theoretically, such a modified environment should be more conducive to the interest of shareholders, and, in view of the diminished financial performance of most Japanese firms, we would expect corporate governance factors to explain a larger portion of the variance in financial performance. And yet, paradoxically, our empirical results show that the total explanatory power of ownership factors actually *declined* after 1997. In other words, the profitability of Japanese firms was still predominantly determined by strategic choices representing managerial discretionary power, and these factors actually became even *more* prominent in the governance-oriented time period after 1997.

Our findings on the separate effects of individual ownership variables yield mixed results. Consistent with prior research, we found that ownership by financial institutions was positively related to firm performance in both time periods. This suggests that Japanese financial institutions continued to play a monitoring role during the 1990s, effectively demanding that the senior management of companies in which they invested work to improve financial performance. We also found that executive ownership was positively associated with firm performance, but only after 1997. We can interpret this as suggesting that the interests of executives and shareholders began to come into greater alignment in the second half of the 1990s, implying that this governance mechanism might have begun to kick in. Surprisingly, we did not find any positive relationship between foreign ownership and firm performance. One possible explanation for this puzzling result is that many relatively large and well-established Japanese electronics firms, in which foreign investors had preferred to invest, were not performing well during the 1990s. Hence, the original investment preferences of foreign investors may have influenced this finding.

These intriguing results necessitate a closer look. Our main concern on the relative explanatory power of the ownership factors after 1997 can possibly be elucidated from a few angles. We might hypothesize that senior Japanese managers became more profit-conscious as their firms began to face a depressed economic environment, and that those managers sensed implicit and sometimes explicit shareholder pressure, which led them to adjust their strategies in effective ways. Such competitive factors probably have much more direct impact – and also impose greater constraints on strategy – than do ownership factors. For example, senior managers may be more motivated to seek overseas sales due to poor demand in the domestic market, regardless of ownership and governance structure. Poor market conditions forced managers to reconsider their resource allocation decisions, with an eye toward greater profitability. As

Japanese executives could no longer afford *not* to seek financial return, those executives chose profit-maximizing strategies for their own reasons, with or without much influence from ownership and governance factors. Today's Japanese executives commit themselves to investment and administrative opportunities that particularly prioritize financial outcome, while deliberately cutting back on growth-oriented projects that may harm profitability. Growth in the size of the corporation then becomes a possibly constructive means of increasing profitability, but not the ultimate goal, as indicated by the positive and statistically significant value obtained for the sales growth variable.

Worsening macroeconomic environments after the Asian crisis of 1997 further altered the basic orientation of Japanese managers. Managers grew more concerned about difficult competitive environments after that year, primarily due to further deteriorating domestic economic conditions. Managers became acutely sensitive to the criticism they received for their incompetent performance, and further tailored their strategic choices in the direction of greater profitability. To the extent that managers successfully achieved this goal, we would expect the explanatory power of strategic variables to increase during the second strategic time period (STP2), even though governance consciousness was increasingly a focal issue for Japanese corporations during these years.

Nonetheless, it remains mystifying that governance variables do not collectively demonstrate any significant weights to influence profitability, even when those factors presumably became key points of discussion regarding corporate performance. This paradox may imply that either those governance devices remain ineffective, because they do not fit into the Japanese business and corporate context, or because their functions have still not matured enough to influence firm performance in significant ways. Alternatively, while new corporate governance devices may be adopted by many firms, their implementation may in reality be 'decoupled' from the original intent of those devices (Westphal and Zajac, 1998, 2001). Yet another possibility is that shareholders, including international investors, are now satisfied with the newfound managerial focus on profitability, and thus remain a largely invisible lobby, prepared to exercise their control and influence only in situations in which management commits to discretionary behavior that harms shareholder value. Satisfied or not, for whatever reason, domestic institutional shareholders may have remained relatively passive, and hence do not impose strong direct pressures on management (Colpan *et al.*, 2010).

Our observation of the limited and decreasing explanatory power of ownership factors must be tested further, within a more extensive framework that may include other governance measures. Our study employed all the ownership variables that represent the monitoring end of agency relationships. But the inclusion of variables related to *internal* monitoring mechanisms – such as the size and composition of the board, and the organizational and institutional arrangement of the management organization – will provide a more balanced picture of the influence of governance on performance.

Another possible direction for future research is to investigate the actual implementation of various reform measures for corporate governance. With corporate governance reforms receiving increased attention globally, firms in various countries have started to implement shareholder-oriented practices. However, prior research indicates that many of those practices produced only superficial changes and were actually decoupled from the original objectives (Fiss and Zajac, 2004). Thus reform measures do not always lead to substantive and effective changes in corporate governance. If many of the reform measures adopted by Japanese firms were of this type, then it would not be surprising that the rise of the shareholder-value orientation and the subsequent implementation of governance reform measures have not exercised a greater impact on firm performance.

Notes

1. This part draws on Colpan *et al.* (2007).
2. *Kabushiki Bunpu Chousa* (Stock distribution survey), 2004.
3. We verified that removing these companies did not lead to any sample bias in terms of the strategy or governance variables used in the study.
4. Tallman and Li (1996) suggest that country scope shows consistent positive relationships with accounting performance, even when controlling for variables such as industry growth and firm leverage, while the significant effects of another indicator, foreign sales ratio, seem to disappear when those control variables are added to the analysis. Other commonly used proxies for international diversity include foreign sales ratio or entropy measures based on weighted foreign sales (Grant *et al.*,1988; Hitt *et al.*, 1997), but these were not feasible using the data available to us for all enterprises.
5. Chung and Beamish (2005), for instance, also employ the Asian economic crisis as a natural dividing point between two distinct time periods in their research.
6. Generalized-least squares analysis is not sensitive to bias from heteroscedasticity and/or autocorrelation (Bergh and Holbein, 1997).
7. One methodological concern is the potential endogeneity of ownership and strategy variables. To check whether this issue poses a trouble, we followed the approach as in David *et al.* (2008). The results illustrated that our variables in concern did not create endogeneity problems.
8. This method of decomposing the inter-firm variance in performance rates is consistent with the procedures of previous studies (Hansen and Wernerfelt, 1989; Kotha and Nair, 1995; Schmalensee, 1985; Spanos *et al.*, 2004).

References

Ahmadjian, C. L. and Robinson, P. (2001) 'Safety in Numbers: Downsizing and the Deinstitutionalization of Permanent Employment in Japan', *Administrative Science Quarterly*, 46(4): 622–654.

Ahmadjian, C. L. and Robbins, G. E. (2005) 'A Clash of Capitalisms: Foreign Shareholders and Corporate Restructuring in 1990s Japan', *American Sociological Review*, 70(2): 451–471.

Aoki, M. (1990) 'Toward an Economic Model of the Japanese Firm', *Journal of Economic Literature*, 28: 1–27.

Bergh, D. D. and Holbein, G. F. (1997) 'Assessment and Redirection of Longitudinal Analysis: Demonstration with a Study of the Diversification and Divestiture Relationship', *Strategic Management Journal*, 18(7): 557–571.

Bettis, R. A. (1981) 'Performance Differences in Related and Unrelated Diversified Firms', *Strategic Management Journal*, 2(4): 379–393.

Charkham, J. (1994) *Keeping Good Company: A Study of Corporate Governance in Five Countries*, Oxford: Oxford University Press.

Chung, C. C. and Beamish, P. W. (2005) 'Investment Mode Strategy and Expatriate Strategy during Times of Economic Crisis', *Journal of International Management*, 11(3): 331–355.

Clark, R. (1979) *The Japanese Company*, New Haven: Yale University Press.

Cole, R. E. (1979) *Work, Mobility and Participation: A Comparative Study of American and Japanese Industry*, Berkeley: University of California Press.

Colpan, A. M. and Hikino, T. (2005). 'Changing Economic Environments, Evolving Diversification Strategies, and Differing Financial Performance: Japan's Largest Textile Firms, 1970-2001', *Industrial and Corporate Change*, 14: 897–940.

Colpan, A. M., Yoshikawa, T., Hikino T., and Miyoshi H. (2007) 'Japanese Corporate Governance: Structural Change and Financial Performance', *Asian Business & Management*, 6(S1): 89–113.

Colpan, A. M., Yoshikawa, T., Hikino, T., and Del Brio, E. (2010). 'Shareholder Heterogeneity and Conflicting Goals: Strategic Investments in the Japanese Electronics Industry', *Journal of Management Studies*, forthcoming.

David P., O'Brien J., Yoshikawa T., and Delios A. (2008) 'Do Shareholders or Stakeholders Appropriate the Rents from Corporate Diversification? The Influence of Ownership Structure', *Academy of Management Journal*, forthcoming.

Eisenhardt, K. M. (1989) 'Agency Theory: An Assessment and Review', *Academy of Management*, Review 14: 57–74.

Fiss, P. C. and Zajac, E. J. (2004) 'The Diffusion of Ideas: The (non) Adoption of a Shareholder Value Orientation among German Firms', *Administrative Science Quarterly*, 49(4): 501–534.

Fukao, M. (1999) 'Japanese Financial Instability and Weakness in the Corporate Governance Structure', *OECD Working Paper*, Paris.

Gedajlovic, E. and Shapiro, D. M. (2002) 'Ownership Structure and Firm Profitability in Japan', *Academy of Management Journal*, 45(2): 565–575.

Geringer, M. J., Tallman S., and Olsen, D. M. (2000) 'Product and International Diversification among Japanese Multinational Firms', *Strategic Management Journal*, 21: 51–80.

Gerlach, M. L. (1992) *Alliance Capitalism: The Social Organisation of Japanese Business*, Berkeley: University of California Press.

Gilson, R. J. and Milhaupt, C. J. (2004) 'Choice as Regulatory Reform: The Case of Japanese Corporate Governance', Columbia University Law School, Center for Law and Economic Studies, Working Paper 251.

Grant, R. M. (2002) 'Corporate Strategy: Managing Scope and Strategy Content', in A. Pettigrew, H. Thomas, and R. Whittington (eds), *Handbook of Strategy and Management*, 72–97, Sage: London.

Hansen, G. S. and Wernerfelt, B. (1989), 'Determinants of Firm Performance: The Relative Importance of Economic and Organizational Factors', *Strategic Management Journal*, 10: 399–411.

Hill, C. W. L. and Snell, S. A. (1988) 'External Control, Corporate Strategy, and Firm Performance in Research-intensive Industries', *Strategic Management Journal*, 9: 577–590.

Hitt, M. A., Hoskisson, R. E, and Kim, H. (1997) 'International Diversification: Effects on Innovation and Firm Performance in Product-Diversified Firms', *Academy of Management Journal*, 40(4): 767–798.

Hoshi, T. and Kashyap, A. (2001) *Corporate Financing and Governance in Japan*, Cambridge, MA: MIT Press.

Inoue, H. (1999) *The Accelerating Dissolution of Stock Cross-Holding*, Tokyo: NLI Research Institute.

Jackson, G. and Moerke, A. (2005) 'Continuity and Change in Corporate Governance: Comparing Germany and Japan', *Corporate Governance*, 13: 351–361.

Jensen, M. and Meckling, W. (1976) 'Theory of the Firm: Managerial Behavior, Agency Costs and Ownership Structure', *Journal of Financial Economics*, 3(4): 305–360.

Kester, W. C. (1991) *Japanese Takeovers: The Global Contest for Corporate Control*, Boston: Harvard Business School Press.

Kikuchi, M. (1999) *Kigyo kachi hyoka kakumei* (Revolution in Corporate Valuation), Tokyo: Toyo Keizai.

Kotha, S. and Nair, A. (1995) 'Strategy and Environment as Determinants of Performance: Evidence from the Japanese Machine Tool Industry', *Strategic Management Journal*, 16(7): 497–518.

Marris, R. (1964) *The Economic Theory of Managerial Capitalism*, London: Macmillan.

Mayer, M. and R. Whittington (2003) 'Diversification in Context: A Cross-national and Crosstemporal Extension', *Strategic Management Journal*, 24: 773–781.

Milhaupt, C. J. (2003) 'A Lost Decade for Japanese Corporate Governance Reform? What's Changed, What Hasn't, and Why', Columbia Law School, Center for Law and Economic Studies, Working Paper 234.

Miyajima, H. and Aoki, H. (2002) 'Changes in the J-type Firm: From Bank-centred Governance to Internal Governance', in J. Maswood, J. Graham, and H. Miyajima (eds), *Japan: Change and Continuity*, London: Routledge Curzon.

Miyajima, H. and Kuroki, F. (2007) 'The Unwinding of Cross-shareholding in Japan: Causes, Effects and Implications', in M. Aoki, G. Jackson, and H. Miyajima (eds), *Corporate Governance in Japan*, Oxford: Oxford University Press.

Miyazaki, Y. (1980) *Industry and Business in Japan*, White Plains: M. E. Sharp.

Morck, R. and Nakamura, M. (1999) 'Banks and Corporate Control in Japan', *Journal of Finance*, 54: 319–339.

Morck, R., Shleifer, A., and Vishny, R. W. (1988) 'Management Ownership and Market Valuation: An Empirical Analysis?', *Journal of Financial Economics*, 20: 293–315.

Morikawa, H. (1992) *Zaibatsu: The Rise and Fall of Family Enterprise Groups in Japan*, Tokyo: University of Tokyo Press.

NLI Research Institute (2004) '*Kabushiki mochiai jokyo chosa 2003*' (Cross-shareholdings Survey 2003), Tokyo: NLIRI (in Japanese).

Okumura, H. (2000) *Corporate Capitalism in Japan*, London: Palgrave Macmillan.

Phan, P. H. and Yoshikawa, T. (2000) 'Agency Theory and Japanese Corporate Governance', *Asia Pacific Journal of Management*, 17: 1–27.

Robins, J. A. and Wiersema, M. F. (1995) 'A Resource-Based Approach to the Multibusiness Firm: Empirical Analysis of Portfolio Interrelationships and Corporate Financial Performance', *Strategic Management Journal*, 16(4): 277–300.

Schmalensee, R. (1985) 'Do Markets Differ Much?', *American Economic Review*, 75(3): 341–351.

Sheard, P. (1989) 'The Main Bank System and Corporate Monitoring and Control in Japan', *Journal of 651 Economic Behavior and Organization*, 11: 399–422.

Shimotani, M. (2006) '*Mochikabu-kaisha no jidai: Nihon no kigyo-ketsugo*' (The Age of the Holding Company: Industrial Combination in Japan), Tokyo: Yuhikaku.

Spanos, Y., Zaralis, G., and Lioukas, S. (2004) 'Strategy and Industry Effects on Profitability: Evidence from Greece', *Strategic Management Journal*, 25(2): 139–165.

Suto, M. and Toshino, M. (2005) 'Behavioral Biases of Japanese Institutional Investors: Fund Management and *Corporate Governance*', Corporate Governance, 13: 466–477.

Tallman, S. and Li, J. (1996) 'Effects of International Diversity and Product Diversity on the Performance of Multinational Firms', *Academy of Management Journal*, 39(1): 179–196.

Useem, M. (1998) 'Corporate Leadership in a Globalising Equity Market', *Academy of Management Executive*, 12(4): 43–59.

Watanabe, S. and Yamamoto, I. (1992) 'Corporate Governance in Japan: Ways to Improve Low Profitability', *NRI Quarterly*, 1(3): 28–45.

Westphal, J. D. and Zajac, E. J. (1988) 'The Symbolic Management of Stockholders: Corporate Governance Reforms and Shareholder Rights', *Administrative Science Quarterly*, 43(1): 127–153.

Westphal, J. D. and Zajac, E. J. (2001) 'Decoupling Policy from Practice: The Case of Stock Repurchase Programs', *Administrative Science Quarterly*, 46(2): 202–228.

Yoshikawa, T. and Linton, J. (2000) 'The Applicability of North American Corporate Governance and Investor Relations Practice to Japanese Firms', *Journal of Asian Business*, 16: 1–24.

Yoshikawa, T. and Phan, P. H. (2001) 'Alternative Corporate Governance Systems in Japanese Firms: Implications for a Shift to Stockholder-Centered Corporate Governance', *Asia Pacific Journal of Management*, 18(2): 183–205.

Yoshikawa, T., Phan, P. H., and David, P. (2005) 'The Impact of Ownership Structure on Wage Intensity in Japanese Corporations', *Journal of Management*, 31(2): 278–300.

11
Why Do Japanese Companies Issue Stock Options?
Behind the Introduction of Stock Options in Japan: Theory of Shareholder Sovereignty vs. Theory of Managerial Sovereignty

Hiroaki Miyoshi and Takeo Nakao

Introduction

The two most significant changes to Japan's executive compensation system in recent years have been the introduction of stock options and the shift in executive salaries toward a performance-based pay system. Both initiatives were designed to promote shareholder-conscious management by strengthening the link between executive compensation and firm performance. A 1997 amendment to the Japanese Commercial Code paved the way for the full-scale introduction of stock options. Initially, firms could give stock options only to their own directors and employees; the numbers of shares that could be allocated to stock options was limited, and the options were required to vest within ten years. However, these restrictions were later abolished by an amendment to the Japanese Commercial Code in 2002, and by the end of August 2004 more than one-third of all publicly traded firms had introduced stock options (Tanaka, 2005)

In the US, numerous studies have investigated stock options (Bryant *et al.*, 2000; Gaver and Gaver,1993; Matsunaga,1995; Mehran,1995; Ryan and Wiggins,2001; Smith and Watts,1992; Yermack,1995, among others), but not all authors agree on the factors underlying the introduction of stock options. Yermack (1995), for example, argues that few agency theories have the descriptive power to explain observed patterns of CEO stock option awards. In Japan, several experimental studies have been conducted to identify the factors motivating the introduction of stock options (Kato *et al.*, 2005; Nagaoka, 2001, 2005; Otumasa, 2002; Uchida, 2004, 2006). Most of these studies support an incentive-based perspective to one degree or another. For instance, Kato *et al.* (2005) argue that the introduction of stock options in Japan is consistent with an incentive-based perspective, because option plans in Japan are more likely to be adopted by firms with more growth opportunities and less likely to be adopted by highly-leveraged firms or firms with extensive ownership of other corporations.

However, the incentive-based explanation for the decision of major Japanese firms to introduce stock options remains somewhat puzzling. Major firms listed in the first section of the Tokyo Stock Exchange have large numbers of shareholders, and the fraction of shares controlled by large shareholders is not particularly high. Such firms clearly enjoy a separation of ownership and management. In addition, it is quite common for a firm's board of directors – which is supposed to represent the profit of shareholders – to be comprised of top managers in the firm, since board and management functions are highly overlapping in Japanese business. Therefore, directors (to whom we refer below as 'managers'), including the board of directors, have broad discretion; moreover, it is reasonable to suspect that managers might prioritize maximizing their *own* utility over maximizing the profit of the firm. Indeed, the board of directors designs the stock option packages that the directors themselves receive, including the number of options granted, the exercise price, the waiting period, and the term of the options. Since directors themselves determine their own income, they might well choose to serve their own interests. On the other hand, for the issuance of stock options, an extraordinary resolution at a shareholders' meeting is required as long as it is an advantageous issuance. Thus the explanation suggested by incentive theory – that stock options are issued in order to maximize the profit of shareholders – cannot be rejected either. In other words, it is not clear whether stock options are introduced to maximize the profit of shareholders or the utility of managers.

We define the *theory of managerial sovereignty* to refer to the hypothesis that managers elect to introduce stock options in order to maximize their own utility. The alternative hypothesis – that shareholders choose to introduce stock options in order to enhance managerial incentives to improve corporate value and to reduce agency costs – we term the *theory of shareholder sovereignty.* In this chapter, we conduct empirical analyses to assess which of these two theories more accurately describes Japanese corporate behavior regarding the issuance of stock options.

The remainder of this chapter is organized as follows. In the second section we derive several predictions made by each of our two theories regarding corporate issuance of stock options. In the third section we describe a statistical analysis conducted to assess which theory makes more accurate predictions regarding the real world. In the fourth section, we present the results of our statistical analysis, and determine whether the actual observed patterns of Japanese corporate stock-option behavior are more accurately described by the theory of shareholder sovereignty or the theory of managerial sovereignty. Finally, in the fifth section we conclude and suggest directions for future work.

Predictions

Most previous studies of the introduction of stock options in Japan have followed the approach of Yermack (1995), analyzing the decision to introduce stock options, and the size of the stock-option packages introduced, by conducting statistical analyses in which the explanatory variables were taken to be variables describing agency costs and financial liquidity constraints. In contrast, in this work, we take our primary explanatory variables to be variables describing features and trends in the stock price of each firm.

In this section, we derive a number of predictions, made by each of the two theories discussed in the previous section, whose validity we will subsequently assess, by comparison with statistical data, in order to determine which of the theories more accurately describes observed corporate behavior. In our statistical analyses, we take the size of stock-option packages issued by firms as the dependent variable. Although detailed mathematical models are beyond the scope of this chapter, in general we can say that, in the shareholder-sovereignty model, managers calibrate the level of effort they exert in managing the company in order to maximize their own utility given the size of stock-option packages chosen by shareholders. Meanwhile, shareholders, anticipating this behavior from managers, set the size of stock-option packages in order to maximize their own profits. In contrast, in the theory of managerial sovereignty, managers set the value of all variables, including the size of stock-option packages issued; this is the single greatest difference between the theory of managerial sovereignty and the theory of shareholder sovereignty. Larger stock-option packages mean more profits for managers.

However, when stock-option packages grow larger, shareholders reap smaller profits, and managers face increased risk of being fired; indeed, it costs money for a company to issue stock options (the fair market value of the options), and, when managers exercise their stock options, the share price tends to decrease. The theory of managerial sovereignty predicts that managers will calibrate the size of stock-option packages in order to balance the utility they derive against their risk of dismissal.

We next derive a number of predictions made by our two theories regarding corporate decisions on stock options. We classify these predictions into three categories: (1) predictions made only by the theory of shareholder sovereignty, (2) predictions made only by the theory of managerial sovereignty, and (3) predictions made by both the theories of shareholder and managerial sovereignty.

Predictions made by the theory of shareholder sovereignty

The issuance of stock options entails certain costs – namely, the fair market value of the shares optioned. Moreover, the exercise of stock options by managers tends to decrease share prices. Thus, in situations in which managers can exercise their stock options without necessarily working any harder on behalf of the firm, we expect that shareholders will choose not to introduce stock options. Examples of such situations include (1) situations in which a firm's share price is trending upward and will increase in the near future irrespective of managerial behavior; (2) situations in which a firm's share price immediately prior to the issuance of stock options lies below the price expected based on long-term trends; and (3) situations in which a firm's share price is expected to change significantly on account of external factors (namely, factors other than managerial behavior). The theory of shareholder sovereignty predicts that, under such circumstances, the introduction of large stock-option packages is unlikely.

To summarize, the theory of shareholder sovereignty makes the following three predictions (the suffix 's' in the labeling of these predictions stands for 'shareholder sovereignty'):

P1s: When a firm's stock price is trending upward, that firm will issue *fewer* stock options.

P2s: When a firm's stock price immediately prior to the issuance of stock options lies below the price that would be expected based on long-term trends, the firm will issue *fewer* stock options.

P3s: When a firm's share price is expected to change significantly on account of external factors (namely, factors other than managerial behavior), the firm will issue *fewer* stock options.

Predictions made by the theory of managerial sovereignty

First, in direct contrast to the predictions of the theory of shareholder sovereignty, the theory of managerial sovereignty predicts *increased* issuance of stock options by each of the three types of firms just described, namely (1) firms whose share prices are trending upward, (2) firms whose share prices immediately prior to the issuance of stock options lie below the prices expected on the basis of long-term trends, and (3) firms whose share prices are expected to change significantly due to external factors. In short, the theory of managerial sovereignty makes the following three predictions (where the suffix '**m**' stands for 'managerial sovereignty'):

> *P1m*: When a firm's stock price is trending upward, that firm will issue *more* stock options.
> *P2m*: When a firm's stock price immediately prior to the issuance of stock options lies below the price that would be expected based on long-term trends, the firm will issue *more* stock options.
> *P3m*: When a firm's share price is expected to change significantly on account of external factors (namely, factors other than managerial behavior), the firm will issue *more* stock options.

Next, we consider the likelihood that a manager will be fired, as perceived by the manager himself. The most important factor influencing a manager's retention or dismissal is the difference between the profits realized by that manager and the profits that could be realized by a *potential* replacement manager. If an actual manager believes that his abilities are inferior to those of a potential replacement manager (namely, if the manager believes that shareholders deem his abilities inferior to those of a potential replacement), then that actual manager will anticipate his own dismissal. Now, the issuance of stock options *increases* a manager's risk of dismissal, because issuing stock options entails costs. Consequently, the utility (the income) a manager expects to derive from stock options will be limited, and hence the theory of managerial sovereignty would predict that the size of stock-option grants will be correspondingly limited.

A second important factor affecting the dismissal rate is the transaction cost of replacing an existing manager. Shareholders will seek to dismiss a manager, and replace her with a new manager, when the shareholders find that manager's performance to be inadequate. However, in modern exchange-listed Japanese firms, the ownership of stocks is widely distributed, and even the largest shareholders control a relatively small fraction of all outstanding shares. Consequently, in

252 Hiroaki Miyoshi and Takeo Nakao

order to dismiss an existing manager against his or her will, shareholders must either (a) win a proxy battle, or (b) buy up more than half of all outstanding shares via a take-over bid (TOB) or similar scheme. But both of these procedures entail huge costs for shareholders, including the cost of gathering information on existing and new managers, the cost of waging proxy battles, and the cost of combating opposition from other stakeholders – including employees – that may grow fierce when shareholders strongly assert their ownership rights. In addition, TOBs and similar schemes entail further costs, including increased acquisition prices and interest payments on borrowed capital. The greater the transaction cost, the less likely a manager will perceive his or her own dismissal to be, and hence the more utility the manager will expect to derive from stock-option income; the theory of managerial sovereignty then predicts that more stock options will be issued.

To summarize the preceding discussion, a consideration of managerial dismissal rates leads the theory of managerial sovereignty to make the following two predictions.

> *P4m*: When the performance of a firm's managers exceeds the performance expected from potential replacement managers, the firm will issue *more* stock options.
>
> *P5m*: When a firm has a large number of shareholders, the firm will issue *more* stock options.

We note that the largeness of shareholders (prediction P5m) implies large transaction costs. The theory of shareholder sovereignty does not necessarily make predictions P4m or P5m.

Predictions made by both theories

First, both theories predict that more stock options will be issued in situations in which the issuance of stock options has a significant influence on the firms' stock price (via the behavior of managers). Indeed, in such situations, managers understand that their efforts will lead to increased stock prices, which in turn will maximize their own profits; the more stock options issued, the harder managers will work and the more profits will result. On the other hand, in situations in which the efforts of managers cannot bring about immediate rises in stock prices, both theories predict that no stock options will be introduced; indeed, in such cases, the introduction of stock options will not motivate managers to work harder, as they will not expect to realize any capital gain from the stock options. Thus both the theory of shareholder sovereignty and the theory of managerial sovereignty predict a close linkage between profits, share prices, and the size of stock option packages.

Second, both theories predict that the size of stock-option packages will be larger in firms that experience liquidity constraints (Bryan *et al.*, 2000; Core and Guay, 2001; Matsunaga, 1995; Yermack, 1995). When there are significant profits and ample cash flows, managers can enjoy large cash payouts – in the form of executive salaries and bonuses – without being criticized by shareholders and other observers. However, when profits are limited and cash reserves for salaries and bonuses are depleted, it is less easy for managers to secure significant cash payouts. Thus, arguing on the basis of the theory of managerial sovereignty, we expect that, when profits are limited, managers will increase the size of stock-option packages in order to maximize their own profits. On the other hand, the theory of shareholder sovereignty also predicts that shareholders will increase the size of stock-option packages when profits are limited. Indeed, if total compensation for managers dwindles, the most competent managers are likely to leave the firms; to prevent such an exodus, shareholders will choose to compensate for reduced cash compensation by providing larger stock-option packages.

Third, both theories predict that more stock options will be issued when a high percentage of a firm's shares are held by foreign firms and/or individual investors. Let us first consider this point from the perspective of the theory of managerial sovereignty. As mentioned above, the likelihood that a manager will be fired, as perceived by the manager himself, plays an important role in the theory of managerial sovereignty. Another important factor influencing a manager's retention or dismissal is the composition of a firm's body of shareholders, and, in particular, whether corporate investors or individual investors control the majority of a firm's shares. To understand this phenomenon, we first note that the abilities and performance of new managers are always uncertain. Thus, even if the increase in profit expected to result from the replacement of a given manager equals the transaction cost of replacing that manager (by employing a new manager), nonetheless that manager may or may *not* be dismissed based on the risk-averseness of shareholders and the difference in risk premiums. For instance, if corporate investors, who tend to be less risk-averse than individual investors, control a significant fraction of a firm's shares, then we expect managers to be dismissed from that firm at higher rates. On the other hand, if individual investors, who tend to be more risk-averse than corporate investors, control a significant fraction of a firm's shares, then managers are less likely to be dismissed from that firm.

Thus, the theory of managerial sovereignty would predict that firms in which corporate investors are major shareholders should issue *fewer* stock options, while firms in which individual investors control a significant fraction of shares should issue *more* stock options. These ideas are also consistent with the observation that large shareholders have more incentive to bear the cost of monitoring managerial performance and can play an important role in disciplining management (see, for instance, Zeckhauser and Pound, 1990), while individual shareholders are often indifferent to the behavior of managers.

Aside from the composition of the body of shareholders, the theory of managerial sovereignty also attributes significance to the percentage of shares held by foreign firms, for two separate reasons. First, foreign firms, and particularly US corporate investors, tend to look favorably upon the issuance of stock options, simply because stock options are far more common in the US. Second, because foreign firms have limited ability to gather information on Japanese firms, they are particularly likely to have insufficient information on potential managers. Thus it is difficult for foreign corporate investors to replace an underperforming manager, even when those investors are clearly dissatisfied with the manager's abilities. These two observations suggest that, when foreign investors make up a significant fraction of a firm's shareholders, managers are less likely to anticipate their own dismissal, and the theory of managerial sovereignty thus predicts that the firm will issue more stock options.

Meanwhile, the theory of shareholder sovereignty also predicts that the fraction of shares held by individuals and/or foreign firms will impact a firm's issuance of stock options – and predicts that this impact will have the *same sign* as the impact predicted by the theory of managerial sovereignty. Indeed, a principal-agent relationship exists between shareholders and managers, and shareholders possess incomplete information pertaining to managers – that is, there exists an asymmetry of information between the two parties. The agency theory and the incentive view predict that, in order to induce managers to exert efforts to improve corporate value and to reduce agency costs, executive compensation must be sensitive to the performance of the firm. Stock options are thus characterized as a typical measure for linking executive compensation to firm performance. Generally, the level of asymmetry of information between shareholders and managers will be greater when the percentage of shareholdings by individuals and/or foreign firms is greater. Therefore, if individual investors and/or foreign firms are important shareholders in a firm, the theory of shareholder sovereignty suggests that more stock options will be issued.

Aggregating the above observations, there are four predictions that are made by both the theory of shareholder sovereignty and the theory of managerial sovereignty:

> *P6*: The stronger the relationship between a firm's profits and its share price, the larger the size of the stock-option packages it grants.
> *P7*: The lower a firm's profits, the greater the size of the stock-option packages it grants.
> *P8*: When a high percentage of a firm's shares are held by individual investors, the firm will issue more stock options.
> *P9*: When a high percentage of a firm's shares are held by foreign firms, the firm will issue more stock options.

To summarize, in this section we grouped a number of predictions regarding the size of stock-option packages into three categories: (1) predictions made only by the theory of shareholder sovereignty, (2) predictions made only by the theory of managerial sovereignty; and (3) predictions made by both the theory of shareholder sovereignty and the theory of managerial sovereignty. All of these predictions are summarized in Table 11.1.

Statistical analysis

In this section we describe the statistical models and the data set we used to assess the accuracy of the predictions described above.

Dependent variable

The dependent variable used in our analyses to characterize the size of stock-option packages is the number of stock options granted times the exercise price. This quantity accounts for the fact that the value of a stock-option package varies depending on the share price.

Explanatory variables

In this section we describe the explanatory variables used to assess the accuracy of each prediction.

First, to assess the accuracy of P1s and P1m, we must estimate the trajectory of the firm's share price. For this purpose we take time-series data on the share price of each firm as the dependent variable and the time as the explanatory variable. In cases where the estimated coefficient between share price and time was statistically significant, we use this estimated coefficient as the explanatory variable. In cases where the

Table 11.1 Predictions of the theories of shareholder and managerial sovereignty

Category	Prediction
Predictions made by the theory of shareholder sovereignty	P1s: When a firm's stock price is trending upward, the firm will issue *fewer* stock options.
	P2s: When a firm's stock price immediately prior to the issuance of stock options lies below the price that would be expected based on long-term trends, the firm will issue *fewer* stock options.
	P3s: When a firm's share price is expected to change significantly on account of external factors, the firm will issue *fewer* stock options.
Predictions made by the theory of managerial sovereignty	P1m: When a firm's stock price is trending upward, that firm will issue *more* stock options.
	P2m: When a firm's stock price immediately prior to the issuance of stock options lies below the price that would be expected based on long-term trends, the firm will issue *more* stock options.
	P3m: When a firm's share price is expected to change significantly on account of external factors, the firm will issue *more* stock options.
	P4m: When the performance of a firm's managers exceeds the performance expected from potential replacement managers, the firm will issue more stock options.
	P5m: When a firm has a large number of shareholders, the firm will issue more stock options.
Predictions made by both the theory of shareholder sovereignty and the theory of managerial sovereignty	P6: The stronger the relationship between a firm's profits and its share price, the larger the size of the stock-option packages it grants.
	P7: The lower a firm's profits, the greater the size of the stock-option packages it grants.
	P8: When a high percentage of a firm's shares are held by individual investors, the firm will issue more stock options.
	P9: When a high percentage of a firm's shares are held by foreign firms, the firm will issue more stock options.

estimated coefficient between share price and time was *not* statistically significant, we set the value of this explanatory variable to zero. If the theory of shareholder sovereignty accurately describes the introduction of stock options by Japanese firms, we expect that the estimated coefficient for this explanatory variable will be negative and statistically significant. On the other hand, if the theory of managerial sovereignty accurately describes the introduction of stock options by Japanese firms, then we expect the estimated coefficient for this explanatory variable to be positive and statistically significant.

Next, to assess the accuracy of P2s and P2m, we must quantity the extent to which a firm's share price exceeds or falls below the price we would expect based on long-term trends. For this purpose we define an explanatory variable that we term the 'trend discrepancy'. The trend discrepancy is the difference between a firm's actual share price and the share price expected based on long-term trends. If this quantity is large and negative, we expect the share price to rise in the near future. Thus, if the theory of shareholder sovereignty accurately describes the introduction of stock options by Japanese firms, we expect the estimated coefficient for this explanatory variable to be positive and statistically significant. On the other hand, if the theory of managerial sovereignty accurately describes the introduction of stock options by Japanese firms, we expect the estimated coefficient for this explanatory variable to be negative and statistically significant.

To assess the accuracy of P3s and P3m, we must quantify the anticipated change in a firm's future share price. When a firm's historical share price exhibits significant fluctuations, it seems likely that the future share price will be significantly affected by external factors. Thus, we take the standard deviation of the past share price as a measure of expected volatility in the future share price. If the theory of shareholder sovereignty accurately describes the introduction of stock options by Japanese firms, we expect the estimated coefficient for this explanatory variable to be negative and statistically significant. On the other hand, if the theory of managerial sovereignty accurately describes the introduction of stock options by Japanese firms, we expect the estimated coefficient for this explanatory variable to be positive and statistically significant.

To assess the accuracy of P4m, we must quantify the performance of existing managers relative to that of potential replacement managers, but this is difficult because the potential replacement managers are unspecified, and in any case it is difficult to quantify the ability of any manager, existing or potential. In this study we assume that potential replacement managers work in other firms within the same industry as the firm in question, and we quantify a manager's ability by looking at the market share controlled by the firm in which that manager works. If a firm enjoys a large share of its market, we assume that the abilities of that firm's managers exceed those of potential replacement managers. On the other hand, if a firm has small market share, we assume that potential replacement managers – managers at other firms in the same industry – have superior abilities.

To assess the accuracy of P5m, we take the total number of shareholders as the explanatory variable.

To assess the accuracy of prediction P6, we must quantify the relationship between profit and share price. To this end, we conduct a regression analysis, with share price as the dependent variable and corporate profit – and its rate of growth – as explanatory variables; we then take the resulting estimated coefficient as the explanatory variable.

To assess the accuracy of prediction P7, we use the profit of the firm as the explanatory variable.

To assess the accuracy of P8, we take the fraction of outstanding shares held by individual investors as the explanatory variable.

Finally, to assess the accuracy of P9, we take the fraction of outstanding shares held by foreign firms as the explanatory variable.

Control variables

In addition to the variables described above, various additional factors affect the size of stock-option packages; if we do not control for the influence of these factors, our estimates of the coefficients for explanatory variables will be biased. Thus we augment our statistical model with several control variables.

First, we introduce three control variables that directly affect the size of stock-option packages: the number of executives who are granted stock options, the sum of all executives' base pay, and the sum of all bonuses granted.

Next, we take the age of the corporation (the number of years that have elapsed since its establishment) and the growth rate of its industry sector as control variables influencing managerial income from stock options. Indeed, the rate of change in a firm's share price may be greater in new firms than in older firms, and may be greater in developing industries than in mature industries; the rate of change in a firm's share price clearly affects managerial income from stock options.

We also introduce several control variables related to the production function, and to the prices of a firm's products, as exogenous factors affecting a firm's profits – and thus, by the theory of shareholder sovereignty, the size of stock-option packages granted. As production-function-related control variables we use the capital equipment ratio, the export ratio, the labor productivity, and the fraction of all personnel expenditures taken up by expenditures for white-collar workers. The last of these variables measures the influence that employee ability can have on corporate performance. As for the prices of a firm's products, the following three factors are important determinants: whether or not the market concentration is high, whether the goods concerned are intermediate or final goods, and whether or not research and development is an important factor. As control variables measuring these quantities, we use the Herfindahl-Hirschman Index, the market concentration ratio, R&D expenditures (both in absolute terms and as a fraction of sales), and advertising expenditures (both in absolute terms and as a fraction of sales).

We also take the size of the corporation as a measure of the transaction cost involved in replacing an existing manager; this is an exogenous factor that influences managers' dismissal rates, and hence, by the theory of managerial sovereignty, the size of stock-option packages issued. We have already introduced the number of shareholders as an explanatory variable that accounts at least partially for transaction costs, but we can more accurately assess the influence of the number of shareholders by controlling for the size of the firm. In this study we use firm value as a measure of its size.

In addition to the control variables described above, we introduce a number of variables related to corporate profits, which, on the theory of shareholder sovereignty, should influence the size of stock-option packages. These variables include (1) the firm's total assets and ratio of debt to assets (which affect the interest rate at which the firm can borrow); and (2) the firm's wage rate, which affect its labor costs.

Data set

Here, we describe the statistical data set used to assess the accuracy of the predictions described above.

Sample

The companies analyzed in this work are manufacturing firms, listed in the first section of the Tokyo Stock Exchange, whose board of directors chose to issue stock options in 2003. From the set of all such firms, we excluded the following four categories of firms: **(1)** firms that grant stock options several times a year; **(2)** firms whose exercise price is not listed in our data sources; **(3)** firms which were unlisted either for a portion of the data-collection period (1997–2003) or for that entire period; and **(4)** firms that experienced mergers or corporate spin-offs, or who changed the month in which they settle their accounts. Furthermore, we restrict our analysis to firms for which financial data, share price data, and data related to stock options are consistently available throughout the sample period. After applying all of these considerations, we obtain a final sample size of 84 firms for the analyses reported in this chapter.

Data sources

Data regarding the details of stock-option contracts (including the number and price of stock options granted) for each firm were provided by Daiwa Securities SMBC Co. Ltd. In preparing financial data, we used 'NEEDS CD-ROM: Nikkei Corporate Financial Data' by Nikkei Needs (August 2006 Version). For share price data, we used 'The Stock Price CD-ROM' (2006 Version) from Toyo Keizai.

Summary

In this section we have described the dependent and independent variables in our analysis, the statistical sample we analyzed, and the sources of our statistical data. Table 11.2 summarizes the definitions, calculation procedures, and statistical properties of all dependent and independent variables in our study. (For explanatory and control variables that refer to data for a single year, we use values from the settlements of accounts for fiscal year 2002, since the dependent variable is as of 2003.) In addition, Table 11.3 summarizes the predictions of the two theories regarding the sign of the correlation between nine of the explanatory variables and the dependent variable (the size of stock-option packages issued), as anticipated based on the 12 predictions discussed above.

Results

We conducted least-squares regressions on the size of stock-option packages issued using the 9 explanatory variables and the 18 control variables described in the previous section (Model 1). We found statistically significance at the 10 per cent level for a total of 15 of these variables. To account for the possibility of multicollinearity among variables, we excluded variables with large p-values and repeated our analysis with 17 variables (Model 2). These results are presented in Table 11.4.

Noting that the adjusted R-squared for the results of Model 2 is 0.8361, we see that our model successfully accounts for the majority of the observed variations in the size of stock-option packages granted by the firms in our sample, thus establishing the validity of our analytical

Table 11.2 Definitions, calculation procedures, and statistical properties of dependent and independent variables

Variable	Definition	Calculation procedure	Mean	Variance
Dependent variable				
VALSO	Size of stock-option packages (unit: 100 million yen)	Number of stock options granted × Exercise price	104.308	258.903
Explanatory variables				
EQTR	Share price trend	We conducted a regression analysis on the logarithm of the share price at the beginning of each year (after adjusting for the number of stocks issued) with time taken as the explanatory variable. We take the annually averaged rate of change, which is the estimated coefficient for the time variable, as a measure of the share price trajectory for each firm. However, for firms whose p-value for the time variable exceeds 0.5, we set this quantity to zero. Our regression analysis was conducted over the period 1997–2003.	–2.350	11.201
DIF	Trend discrepancy (unit: yen)	We subtracted the expected share price (computed from our estimate of the share price trend) from the actual share price at the beginning of 2003.	–59.039	217.355
EQPDEV	Expected change in share price (unit: yen)	The standard deviation of the monthly share price (after adjusting for the number of shares issued) during the period January 1998–December 2002.	247.302	457.974

Continued

Table 11.2   Continued

Variable	Definition	Calculation procedure	Mean	Variance
MSH	Market share (%)	To calculate market share, we used the industrial classifications (small categories) defined by the 'NEEDS CD-ROM: Nikkei Corporate Financial Data' (Nikkei Needs).[a]	9.047	12.277
EQNUM	Logarithm of number of shareholders		9.416	1.213
COR	Correlation between profit and share price (%)	Using time-series data on sample firms during the sample period (1997–2003), we conducted the following regression analysis and used its determination coefficient: $\rho_{i,t} = a_{i1} + a_{i2}\pi_{i,t-1} + a_{i3}G\pi_{i,t}$ Here $\rho_{i,t}$ denotes the firm's share price at the beginning of year for the term t (after adjusting for the number of shares issued[b]), π_{it} denotes the firm's profit, and $G\pi_{it}$ denotes the percentage change in the firm's profit from one year to the next.	37.073	30.464
PROF	Profit (unit: 100 million yen)	Since this quantity fluctuates in time depending on the fiscal accounting period chosen by each firm, we used average profits over the interval 1997–2003.	32.659	138.534
HOMEQ	Percentage of shares held by individuals (%)	Number of shares held by individual and others / Total shares outstanding	27.290	14.673
FOREQ	Percentage of shares held by foreign firms (%)	Number of shares held by foreign firms / Total shares outstanding	12.684	12.950

Continued

Table 11.2 Continued

Variable	Definition	Calculation procedure	Mean	Variance
Control variables				
LEXEN	Logarithm of number of executives granted stock options	We used data provided by Daiwa Securities SMBC Co. Ltd. The numerical value of this variable is the logarithm of the number of executives receiving stock options times 100	236.095	651.858
FV	Firm value (Unit: 10 billion yen)	Share price at the end of the year 2002 × (number of shares issued at the end of FY2002 + number of shares issued at the end of FY2003)/ 2	27.911	55.300
YEARS	Years since corporation was established	The number of years between the year in which the company was first listed or traded over-the-counter (OTC) and the year 2003.[c]	34.845	7.434
INDGR	Industrial growth rate	Sales and operating revenue for each industrial classification (small category) in FY2003 / Sales and operating revenue in FY1997	0.920	0.164
LEXEY	Logarithm of sum of executive base pay and bonus	Executive base pay + executive bonus. The numerical value of this quantity is the logarithm of the sum of base pay plus bonus (in millions of yen) times 100.	299.440	191.686
KN	Capital equipment ratio (unit: 1 million yen)	Total capital/Number of employees	2.695	0.502
EXPOH	Export ratio (%)	Export sales and operating revenue / Total sales and operating revenue	18.210	20.467

Continued

Table 11.2   Continued

Variable	Definition	Calculation procedure	Mean	Variance
LP	Labor productivity (unit: 1 million yen)	(Ordinary gain + labor and welfare expenses (related to sales and general administrative expenses) + labor and welfare expenses (related to manufacturing statement)) / Number of employees	10.671	4.394
HRH	Ratio of personnel expenditure for white-collar workers (%)	Labor and welfare expenses (related to sales and general administrative expenses) / (Labor and welfare expenses (related to sales and general administrative expenses) + Labor and welfare expenses (in manufacturing statement))	42.561	21.978
HI	Herfindahl-Hirschman Index (%)	Calculated using market share	15.149	10.980
CR	Market concentration ratio (%)	Calculated using market share	58.855	21.525
RD	Ratio of research and development expenses to sales (%)	Research and development expenses / Sales and operating revenue	177.697	421.288
RDH	Research and development expenses (unit: 100 million yen)		5.130	4.253
AD	Ratio of advertising expenses to sales (%)	Advertising expenses / Sales and operating revenue	27.346	65.362
ADH	Advertising expenses (unit: 100 million yen)		0.944	1.599

Continued

Table 11.2 Continued

Variable	Definitions	Calculation Procedure	Mean	Variance
TA	Total assets (unit: 100 million yen)		40.162	74.465
DBTH	Debt ratio (%)	Total liabilities / Total assets	43.529	19.012
WG	Wage rate (unit: million yen)	(Labor and welfare expenses (related to retail and general administrative expenses) + labor and welfare expenses (related to manufacturing))/ Number of employees	8.132	1.527

Notes:
[a] For problems related to this method, see Nakao (2001: 77).
[b] To account for the possibility of stock splits, we multiplied the share price by the number of shares issued. Since the share price tends to vary depending on estimates for account settlements, we used share prices at the beginning of the accounting period. For example, we multiplied the share price at the beginning of 2000 by the number of shares at the end of fiscal year 2000.
[c] Data on the year a firm was first listed were taken from the 'NEEDS CD-ROM: Nikkei Corporate Financial Data' by Nikkei Needs. However, since this source only includes data from 1964 onward, firms that were listed prior to 1964 are recorded in our survey as having been listed in 1964.

Table 11.3 Expected signs of correlations between size of stock-option packages and explanatory variables

Variable	Relevant Prediction	Theory of Shareholder Sovereignty	Theory of Manager Sovereignty
Share price trend (*EQTR*)	P1s and P1m	−	+
Trend discrepancy (*DIF*)	P2s and P2m	+	−
Expected change in share price (*EQPDEV*)	P3s and P3m	−	+
Market share (*MSH*)	P4m		+
Number of shareholders (*EQNUM*)	P5m		+
Correlation between profit and share price (*COR*)	P6	+	+
Profit (*PROF*)	P7	−	−
Percentage of shares held by individuals (*HOMEQ*)	P8	+	+
Percentage of shares held by foreign firms (*FOREQ*)	P9	+	+

model. We now use the results of our analysis to determine which theory – the theory of shareholder sovereignty or the theory of managerial sovereignty – better describes the real world.

We first examine predictions P1s/P1m, P2s/P2m, and P3s/P3m, predictions made by both the theories of shareholder and managerial sov-

Table 11.4   Results of regressions on the size of stock-option packages

Variable	Relevant hypotheses	Model 1			Model 2		
		Coef.		t-value	Coef.		t-value
C		−395.133		−1.645	−419.459		−2.755
EQTR	P1s and P1m	−3.899	**	−2.261	−3.761	**	−2.551
DIF	P2s and P2m	0.326	**	2.765	0.254	**	3.427
EQPDEV	P3s and P3m	0.120	**	2.670	0.110	**	2.855
MSH	P4m	−2.564		−1.214			
EQNUM	P5m	3.744		0.165			
COR	P6	1.677	**	3.420	1.531	**	3.612
PROF	P7	−0.495	**	−2.529	−0.578	**	−3.848
HOMEQ	P8	−0.630		−0.494			
FOREQ	P9	1.253		0.581			
LEXEN		0.336	**	2.722	0.314	**	3.118
FV		5.446	**	7.917	5.288	**	9.795
YEARS		0.465		0.173			
INDGR		−70.183		−0.653			
LEXEY		0.449	**	2.079	0.479	**	2.506
KN		−35.736		−1.223	−33.470		−1.293
EXPOH		−0.622		−0.794			
LP		7.809		1.378	8.532	**	2.050
HRH		−1.847	*	−1.869	−1.658	**	−2.227
HI		−5.238	*	−1.739	−5.552	**	−2.258
CR		2.719	*	1.735	2.466	*	1.983
RD		0.058		0.652			

Continued

Table 11.4 Continued

Variable	Relevant hypotheses	Model 1			Model 2		
		Coef.		t-value	Coef.		t-value
RDH		−7.356	*	−1.692	−6.318	*	−1.834
AD		−1.183	*	−1.907	−0.905	*	−1.767
ADH		24.695	*	1.823	20.859	*	1.751
TA		−1.098	*	−1.920	−1.029	**	−3.026
DBTH		0.457		0.354			
WG		0.483		0.038			
R-squared		0.8779			0.8697		
Adjusted R-squared		0.8191			0.8361		

Note: * denotes statistical significance at the 10% level; ** denotes statistical significance at the 5% level.

ereignty in which the two theories arrive at opposite conclusions. The explanatory variables used to examine these three pairs of predictions are, respectively, the share price trend (*EQTR*), the trend discrepancy (*DIF*), and the expected change in share price (*EQPDEV*). It is evident from Table 11.4 that all variables are statistically significant; however, the firms that issued large (small) stock-option packages were those whose share price exhibited a downward (upward) long-term trend, but whose actual share price exceeded (fell below) the price expected on the basis of long-term trends, as well as those that exhibited large (small) fluctuations in stock price in the past. The signs of the observed correlation with both the share price trend and the trend discrepancy support the theory of shareholder sovereignty (predictions P1s and P2s), but the sign of the correlation with the change in expected share price is in accordance with the theory of managerial sovereignty (prediction P3m). Hence from these results we cannot conclusively identify which of the two theories better describes reality.

Thus we next examine the distribution of share price trends (*EQTR*) among the firms in our sample. Out of a total of 84 firms sampled, only 22 firms exhibited a positive (upward-trending) value for *EQTR*; 44 firms exhibited a downward-trend, while the remaining 22 firms did not exhibit any trend.

Meanwhile, technical analyses of share prices often invoke the notion of the 'golden cross'. This describes a situation in which the short-term trend in a stock price passes through the long-term trend, moving from a downward to an upward trend; under such conditions, the long-term trend shifts from a decline to an increase. Thus, in firms whose share price is at the golden cross, there must be a condition in which the share price trend is stable or downward, while the actual share price is in the neighborhood of, or above, the price predicted on the basis of the long-term trend. We examined the share price trends of firms exhibiting positive trend discrepancies. Of such firms, we found 20 firms with a downward share-price trend, 10 firms with a stable trend, and 4 firms with an upward trend. We also note that the share-price trend is stable or downward for a majority of firms sampled. We next conducted a least-squares regression analysis for the firms sampled, with the share price trend as the dependent variable and the fractional trend discrepancy (*DIFHI*) (the trend discrepancy divided by the share price) as the explanatory variable. This analysis yielded the following result:

$$EQTR = -3.06 - 14.25 DIFHI.$$

The sign of the coefficient of *DIFHI* is negative, and its t-value is –3.06; moreover, it is statistically significant at the 1 per cent level. These results imply that our sample included many firms whose share price is in the vicinity of the golden cross. Among the analytical results listed in Table 11.4, the fact that the estimated coefficient for the share-price trend (*EQTR*) is negative, while the estimated coefficient for the trend discrepancy (*DIF*) is positive, suggests that firms whose share price is at the golden cross tend to issue large stock-option packages. This provides strong support for the theory of managerial sovereignty, which predicts that, when share prices are expected to increase, managers will issue large stock-option packages. Combining this observation with the fact that the estimated coefficient for the expected share-price change (*EQPDEV*) is statistically significant and positive, we conclude that the results of our regression analysis overall support the theory of managerial sovereignty more than the theory of shareholder sovereignty.

Second, we note that our analysis found *neither* of the variables introduced by the theory of managerial sovereignty to describe managerial dismissal rates – neither the market share (*MSH*) nor the number of shareholders (*EQNUM*) – to be statistically significant.

Considering market share (*MSH*), we note that, since this variable reflects the competence of managers, the theory of managerial sovereignty predicts that the coefficient for this variable should be statistically significant and positive (prediction P4m). However, a common feature of Japanese industries is that transaction costs become large – for various reasons – when, for example, a large company attempts to acquire a relatively small company in the same industry. Similarly, in firms with small market share, the competence of managers may not necessarily be reflected in the firm's market share. These observations may explain the failure of our analysis to confirm a positive relation between market share and the size of stock-option packages issued.

Next, considering the number of shareholders (*EQNUM*), although we noted above that the number of shareholders tends to increase transaction costs (prediction P5m), the magnitude of this influence may not actually be very important. The largeness of shareholders implies the largeness of individual shareholders. However, in our analytical results, the estimated coefficient for the ratio of shares held by individuals (P8) also failed to be statistically significant, as we discuss later. Since individual shareholders can support both shareholders and managers through influence peddling, it is possible that none of the predictions will hold.

Third, we consider predictions P6, P7, P8, and P9, the four predictions made in common by both theories. Both the degree of correlation between profit and share price (*COR*, the explanatory variable we use to examine prediction P6) and the profit itself (*PROF*, the explanatory variable used to examine prediction P7) are correlated with the dependent variable in a statistically significant way, and with the signs of the coefficients as predicted by our theories. Thus we may conclude that, the stronger the relationship between a firm's profit and its share price, and/or the lower the firm's profits, the more stock options the firm will issue. However, because this result is predicted by both the theory of shareholder sovereignty and the theory of managerial sovereignty, it does not help us to determine which theory better describes the real world.

Next, in predictions P8 and P9, we suggested that the percentage of shares held by individuals and the percentage of shares held by foreign firms should have the same sign of impact on the scale of stock options in both theories. If individual investors and/or foreign firms are important shareholders, we might expect more stock options to be issued, due to high risk-averseness, to a lack of information regarding new managers (in the theory of managerial sovereignty), and to high information asymmetry between shareholders and managers (in the theory of shareholder sovereignty). But neither the estimated coefficient for the ratio of shares held by individuals (*HOMEQ*), nor the estimated coefficient for the ratio of shares held by foreign firms (*FOREQ*), was statistically significant.

The former of these observations – the lack of statistical significance for the percentage of shares held by individuals – may be attributed to two factors. One is that individual shareholders show a lack of interest in managerial behavior and do not consider the problem of information asymmetry. The other is that the likelihood that a manager will be dismissed, as perceived by the manager himself, does not only depend on the percentage of shares held by individuals or by corporate investors, but also depends significantly on the existence of specific important shareholders such as main banks.

Regarding the latter observation – the lack of statistical significance for the percentage of shares held by foreign firms – we can state that foreign firms have strong awareness of corporate governance and strong assertiveness regarding their rights as investors. These features have the effect of slowing down the introduction of large stock-option packages by managers when the degree of information asymmetry between shareholders and managers is lower. Thus, overall, the ratio of shares held by foreign firms should not affect the scale of stock options.

Conclusions

In this work, we conducted a series of analyses in order to clarify which of two entities – shareholders or managers – are primarily responsible for the issuance of stock options in Japanese firms. We identified 12 predictions and conducted regression analysis to assess the accuracy of these predictions. Our results suggest the following conclusions.

1. If a firm's share price exhibits a downward long-term trend, and if the firm's actual share price exceeds the price that would be expected on the basis of that trend, then the firm will issue more stock options. This result implies that firms whose share price is at the 'golden cross' will issue large stock-option packages, and this finding supports the theory of managerial sovereignty.
2. The greater the fluctuations in a firm's past stock price, the more stock options that firm will issue. This result supports the theory of managerial sovereignty.

Synthesizing these findings, we conclude that the theory of managerial sovereignty describes the introduction of stock options by

Japanese firms more accurately than the theory of shareholder sovereignty. Although stock options were ostensibly introduced to promote shareholder-conscious management by strengthening the link between executive compensation and firm performance, it seems highly likely that the issuance of stock options is superficial and serves merely to increase the utility of managers. Although we hope that this research contributes to the discussion regarding shareholder versus managerial sovereignty, further analysis is necessary, for two reasons. First, the analyses described in this chapter were limited to consideration of the scale of stock-option packages in 2003; a future analysis should extend over a longer time period. Indeed, it is possible that the theory of shareholder sovereignty was relevant in the early years of the stock-option phenomenon in Japan, but that the situation changed over time to hew closer to the viewpoint described by the theory of managerial sovereignty. This possibility could be identified by conducting an analysis spanning a number of years. Second, Japanese firms, which tend to exhibit a strong 'follow the leader' mentality, may choose to issue stock options, and may determine the size of the stock-option packages they issue, by examining the trends set by leading firms both inside and outside their industry and by mimicking the behavior of those firms. An analysis of such effects may yield further insight into the factors underlying the introduction of stock options in the Japanese context.

References

Bryan, S., Hwang, L., and Lilien, S. (2000) 'CEO Stock-based Compensation: An Empirical Analysis of Incentive-intensity, Relative Mix, and Economic Determinants', *Journal of Business*, 73(4): 661–693.

Core, J. and Guay, W. (2001) 'Stock Option Plans for Non-executive Employees', *Journal of Financial Economics*, 61(2): 253–287.

Gaver, J. J. and Gaver, K. M. (1993) 'Additional Evidence on the Association between the Investment Opportunity Set and Corporate Financing, Dividend, and Compensation Policies', *Journal of Accounting and Economics*, 16(1–3): 125–160.

Kato, H. K., Lemmon, M., Luo, M., and Schallheim, J. (2005) 'An Empirical Examination of the Costs and Benefits of Executive Stock Options: Evidence from Japan', *Journal of Financial Economics*, 78(2): 435–461.

Matsunaga, S. R. (1995) 'The Effects of Financial Reporting Costs on the Use of Employee Stock Options', *Accounting Review*, 70(1): 1–26.

Mehran, H. (1995) 'Executive Compensation Structure, Ownership, and Firm Performance', *Journal of Financial Economics*, 38(2): 163–184.

Nagaoka, S. (2001) '*Kigyo katsudo kihon chousa kara mita nihon kigyou ni yoru stock option no dounyu doukou*' (Adoption of Stock Options by Japanese Firms as Seen

272   *Hiroaki Miyoshi and Takeo Nakao*

from the Basic Survey on Business Structure and Activity), *Keizai Tokei Kenkyu,* 29(2): 35–51.

Nagaoka, S. (2005) 'Determinants of the Introduction of Stock Options by Japanese Firms: Analysis from Incentive and Selection Perspectives', *Journal of Business,* 78(6): 2289–2315.

Nakao, T. (2001) *'Rijyunritu kettei youin no toukeiteki bunseki: nihon no seizougyo 1985–1999'* (Empirical Analysis on the Determinants of Profitability of Japanese Manufacturing Firms 1985–1999), *The Doshisha University Economic Review,* 52(3): 63–102.

Otumasa, S. (2002) *'Stock option seido to keieisha incentive: Riron teki yosoku to keiken teki syouko'* (System of Stock Options and Management Incentives: Theoretical Prognosis and Empirical Evidences), *Journal of Hannan University* (Social Science), 37(4): 77–92.

Ryan, H. E. J. and Wiggins, R. A. (2001) 'The Influence of Firm- and Manager-specific Characteristics on the Structure of Executive Compensation', *Journal of Corporate Finance,* 7(2): 101–123.

Smith, C. W. J. and Watts, R. L. (1992) 'The Investment Opportunity Set and Corporate Financing, Dividend, and Compensation Policies', *Journal of Financial Economics,* 32(3): 263–292.

Tanaka, K. (2005) *'Nihon kigyo no stock option'* (Stock Options in Japan), *DIR Market Bulletin,* 3: 6–51.

Uchida, K. (2004) *'Nihon ni okeru stock option dounyu no kettei youin'* (Determinants of the Introduction of Stock Options in Japan), *Annual Report of Society for the Economic Studies for Securities,* 39: 74–77.

Uchida, K. (2006) 'Determinants of Stock Option Use by Japanese Companies', *Review of Financial Economics,* 15(3): 251–269.

Yermack, D. (1995) 'Do Corporations Award CEO Stock Options Effectively?', *Journal of Financial Economics,* 39(2 and 3): 237–269.

Zeckhauser, R. J. and Pound, J. (1990) 'Are Large Shareholders Effective Monitors? An Investigation of Share Ownership and Corporate Performance', in R. G. Hubbard (ed.), *Asymmetric Information, Corporate Finance, and Investment,* Chicago: University of Chicago Press.

12
Automotive Technology Policy in Japan

Masanobu Kii, Hiroaki Miyoshi, and Masayuki Sano

Introduction

By 2007, global production of automobiles had risen to around 73 million vehicles per year, and some 950 million vehicles were estimated to be on the world's roads. In every corner of the planet, the automobile has become an irreplaceable tool for economic activity and daily life. But the conveniences afforded by automobiles come with a number of serious problems, including traffic accidents, traffic congestion, and environmental pollution – problems that became increasingly evident as mass consumption of vehicles accelerated in the second half of the twentieth century, and for which comprehensive solutions have yet to be identified. On top of these concerns, the search for a response to the issue of global warming – a phenomenon which could well pose a threat to the continued existence of human civilization – has taken on urgent significance in today's world. As of 2007, CO_2 emissions from road transportation vehicles (originating from the burning of fuels) constituted some 16.7 per cent of total global emissions (IEA, 2009).

How must automotive policies evolve to meet these challenges? In this chapter, we will attempt to anticipate future directions in automotive policy-making, with particular focus on Japanese automotive technology policies designed to respond to the types of problems mentioned above. We begin in the second section with a survey of three areas of Japanese automotive technology policy – measures to improve safety, measures to reduce environmental pollution, and measures to reduce energy consumption and combat global warming – and we demonstrate that regulations played a critical role in advancing each of these initiatives. In the third section, we show that, in Japan, the process for determining regulatory standards was essentially identical to the commonly

273

employed industrial association–advisory committee system and we note that little has changed since the 1990s. In the fourth section, in an effort to contribute to the debate over the direction of future policies, we review the current state of global environmental problems, consider some technologies designed to address them, and present results of simulations conducted to assess the impact of widespread use of electric cars. Finally, in the fifth section, we use the results of our analyses (1) to argue for a shift in focus from regulatory policies toward economic incentives, and (2) to emphasize the importance of policies designed to stimulate broader adoption of new-energy vehicles.

Japanese automotive technology policy

The motorization of modern Japan began immediately after the 1964 Tokyo Olympics and has proceeded apace ever since, with the number of passenger vehicles owned first surpassing 10 million units in 1971. This ongoing motorization brings with it a range of associated societal problems, including traffic accidents and air pollution caused by vehicular emissions of exhaust gases. The state of these problems is significantly better today than in the past, but in the meantime a new problem – global warming – has emerged, with CO_2 emissions from automobiles identified as a major contributing factor. In this section we will review the history of Japanese automotive technology policy, from the early postwar period through the present day, with particular focus on three areas: safety measures, measures to reduce environmental pollution, and measures to reduce energy consumption and combat global warming.

Safety measures

Measures to promote automotive safety in Japan have proceeded in two general directions (Sano, 2008). First, the Road Vehicles Act imposes a number of standards designed to ensure the safety of vehicles, including restrictions on vehicle structure, installed equipment, passenger capacity, and maximum authorized freight mass; these standards are enforced primarily by periodic vehicle inspections. Next, the Road Traffic Act establishes safety guidelines relating to the use of vehicles, enforced by a licensing system and by traffic regulations. Among all of these safety measures, restrictions on vehicle design have been the most frequently updated; since their introduction in 1951, safety standards relating to the design of automobiles have been revised or expanded over 100 times, in response to changes in the frequency of traffic accidents and the severity of automotive pollution, the evolving traffic environment, and technological developments.

Let us look in particular at revisions that occurred during the 1990s. First, in the first half of the 1990s, the installation of anti-lock braking systems (ABS) was made mandatory, first for heavy-duty trucks and then for medium-duty trucks. Next, after a variety of safety measures failed to bring about a decline in the number of traffic fatalities, measures to ensure crash safety were strengthened. In 1993, new standards were imposed for passenger protection in the event of frontal crash, and frontal crash testing was made mandatory for all new vehicle designs. Crash safety standards were continually strengthened in the ensuing years, and new standards for passenger protection were introduced in 1999 to address rear-end crashes and in 2000 to address offset crashes. For the light-duty Japanese vehicles known as 'K-cars', a special provision was initially introduced to allow safety standards to be weaker than those for ordinary vehicles – in particular, the provision required that safety measures in K-cars be effective only for crash speeds up to 40km/h, not 50km/h as required for other vehicles. However, this measure was eliminated in April 1999, and since then crash tests for K-cars have been conducted at speeds up to 50km/h, as for other vehicles. To meet these enhanced standards, the regulated values for the total length and total width of the vehicle frame were enlarged.

Turning next to revisions to vehicle design standards that occurred in the 2000s, we note that the installation of speed limiters was made mandatory for heavy-duty trucks in 2001, and standards for the protection of pedestrians' skull and cranial regions were introduced in 2004. The former of these measures was designed to force large trucks to obey the legislated speed limit (80km/h) on highways and other expressways, and mandated the installation of devices that prohibit acceleration above 90km/h. The mandate went into effect for new trucks in 2003, and existing trucks were mandated to have the devices installed by 2006. The latter measure required that devices to assess the impact of a crash on a pedestrian's skull (skull impact sensors) be installed at several points on a car's front hood. By measuring the impact delivered to the skull impact sensors, the vehicle could be determined to be in compliance – or not – with regulations. This went into effect in 2005. The impetus for this revision to the safety standards was the observation that a large fraction of accidents involving pedestrians result in serious injury or death, with deaths in such accidents accounting for some 30 per cent of all traffic-related fatalities.

Measures to reduce air pollution

Measures to reduce vehicular emissions of exhaust gases in Japan fall into three categories: individual-vehicle regulations, vehicle-class regulations, and operating regulations. Individual-vehicle regulations operate by denying vehicle registration to any automobile whose exhaust gas concentration, as measured under certain fixed operating conditions, fails to meet established standards. These regulations correspond most closely to the vehicle-design regulations discussed in the preceding section, and are designed to ensure that only vehicles that satisfy certain exhaust gas performance standards are manufactured, imported, or sold. These regulations only apply to the registration of new vehicles, and are not applied to the registration of used vehicles or to vehicles already in use. The term 'vehicular exhaust gas regulations', in its narrow sense, refers to these types of regulations. On the other hand, vehicle-class regulations were introduced in 1992 with the establishment of the NOx law (Act on Reduction of Total Amount of Nitrogen Dioxide Originating from Automobiles in Designated Areas). These regulations establish certain geographic regions within which vehicles that fail to comply with exhaust gas emission standards cannot be registered as new vehicles, cannot have their registration transferred from other regions, and cannot have their registrations renewed. Finally, operating regulations establish restrictions on the operation of vehicles based on criteria such as vehicle type, vehicle purpose, fuel type, and exhaust gas performance; these regulations seek to mitigate air pollution in the vicinity of roads by cracking down on vehicles with inferior exhaust gas performance and alleviating traffic congestion. Note that, whereas vehicle-class regulations only apply to vehicles registered in certain regions, operating regulations apply to *any* vehicle that fails to meet emission standards, regardless of the region in which that vehicle is registered; this prevents the transfer of vehicles from regions with less stringent standards into regions with stronger standards.

In what follows we will focus on individual-vehicle regulations. Japan's automotive exhaust gas regulations cover carbon monoxide, total hydrocarbons, nitrogen oxides, particulate matter (PM), diesel smoke, and lead. These regulations began in earnest in 1972, when Japan's Ministry of the Environment established its 'Fiscal Year 1973 Regulatory Standards for Exhaust Gases', and have been strengthened almost every year since. Even in the relatively short period from the 1990s to the present day, the regulations have been tightened several times, from the 'short-term regulations' in 1994, to the 'long-term regulations' in 1999, to the 'new short-term regulations' in 2004, to the 'new long-term regulations' in 2005, and most recently the 'post-new-long-term regulations' in 2009. Looking at just one of these examples, the 'new long-term regulations' of 2005 revisited methods for testing exhaust gas emissions from both gasoline and diesel vehicles, implemented the world's most stringent standards on emissions (the 'new long-term regulations'), and aimed for overall reductions in automotive exhaust gas emissions. More specifically, the values for regulatory standards set by the 2005 regulations represented reductions (over the values set by the 'new short-term regulations') of (1) 55 per cent for nitrogen oxides and 55 per cent for hydrocarbons (for passenger cars) and (2) 85 per cent for particulate matter, 40 per cent for nitrogen oxides, and 80 per cent for hydrocarbons (for heavy-duty vehicles such as trucks and buses). The 'post-new-long-term regulations' of 2009 went even further: for exhaust gas emissions from diesel vehicles, the 2009 regulations mandated reductions in nitrogen oxides of 40–65 per cent, and reductions in particulate matter of 53–64 per cent, over the values set by the 'new-long-term regulations' of 2005.

Measures to reduce energy consumption and combat global warming

The amount of energy consumed, and the volume of CO_2 emitted, by an automobile is not determined exclusively by the fuel efficiency of the vehicle, but is also significantly influenced by other factors such as the vehicle's operating speed. For this reason, infrastructure facilities such as road installations can themselves be considered measures to reduce energy consumption and combat global warming. However, in this section we will restrict our attention to regulations on individual vehicle fuel efficiency, and will survey the history of government policy in this area.

The two oil shocks of the 1970s convinced Japan that large-scale improvements in energy efficiency would be critical for future economic development, and led in 1979 to the passage of the 'Act on the Rational Use of Energy' (sometimes abbreviated the 'energy-conservation law'). This legislation took gasoline-fueled passenger vehicles to be a particular target for vehicle fuel-efficiency standards, and the fuel-efficiency standard values enacted in 1979 (with a target of fiscal year 1985) were the first steps in this direction. Fuel-efficiency standards for gasoline-fueled passenger vehicles were updated in 1993 (with a target of fiscal year 2000), and new fuel-efficiency standards for gasoline-fueled cargo vehicles were introduced in 1996 (with a target of fiscal year 2003). However, the adoption in 1997 of the Kyoto

Protocol spurred a comprehensive revision of the energy-conservation law in 1998, leading ultimately to the introduction of the 'top-runner' scheme. Under this scheme, the energy-conservation law would single out certain high-energy-consumption products as 'special targets' for energy-conservation standards; these special targets would then be required to exhibit performance superior to that of the highest-performance product then available on the market. More specifically, under the 'top-runner' scheme, the energy-efficiency standard for products in a given category would first be set equal to the energy efficiency of the highest-performance product available on the market at that time. Then, based on expectations for technological developments and other factors, realistic predictions would be made regarding how much that level of energy efficiency could be expected to improve in the future, and these expectations would then set the standard for reduced energy consumption to be realized by the target date. Fuel-efficiency standards for automobiles under the top-runner scheme were gradually strengthened and progressively expanded to encompass wider and wider classes of vehicles. First, in 1999, fuel-efficiency standards were established for passenger cars (both gasoline and diesel vehicles) and small cargo vehicles; the target dates for these standards were fiscal year 2010 for gasoline vehicles and fiscal year 2005 for diesel vehicles. Next, in 2003, fuel-efficiency standards were established for LPG passenger cars (with a target date of fiscal year 2010); at this point, all passenger cars were subject to fuel-efficiency standards. Finally, fuel-efficiency standards for heavy-duty vehicles (such as trucks and buses) were first established in 2006 (with a target date of fiscal year 2015). Improving the fuel efficiency of heavy-duty vehicles is a critical component of the fight against global warming, but, for a variety of reasons – including the lack of any single accepted method for measuring fuel efficiency – fuel efficiency standards for heavy-duty vehicles had not been established before 2006, and heavy-duty vehicles were not designated as 'special targets' of the energy-conservation law. The 2006 revision to the energy-conservation law thus introduced the world's first fuel-efficiency standards for heavy-duty vehicles. Following on its heels, a 2007 revision to the law strengthened fuel-efficiency standards for passenger cars and small cargo vehicles (with a target date of 2015) and established fuel-efficiency standards for small buses. After this revision, *all* passenger and cargo vehicles were subject to fuel-efficiency standards. The details of the 2007 revision to the energy-conservation law require automobile manufacturers to achieve fuel efficiencies of at least 16.8km/L (10/15 mode) for passenger cars, 8.9km/L (10/15 mode) for small buses, and 15.2km/L (10/15 mode) for small cargo vehicles by the target date of fiscal year 2015. These numbers represent fuel-efficiency improvements of 23.5 per cent, 7.2 per cent, and 12.6 per cent, respectively, over the actual measured values from fiscal year 2004. In addition, the 2007 revision to the energy-conservation law mandated that vehicle fuel efficiency be measured using the 'JC08 mode', under which the testing conditions more closely approximate actual vehicular operating conditions. Fuel efficiencies measured in this new 'JC08 mode' are said to come in some 10 per cent lower than those measured in the older '10/15 mode'.

The process for determining regulatory standards

As discussed in the previous sections, regulatory standards have constituted the core of Japan's postwar automotive technology policy developments. Sano (2008) has conducted a detailed analysis of the decision-making process by which Japan's automotive technology standards are determined. According to this analysis, government work on automotive technology regulation is conducted by four agencies, starting with the Ministry of Land, Infrastructure, Transport, and Tourism. The specific details of government policies and regulations are proposed, discussed, and eventually adopted through an advisory committee system. This committee process allows for extremely tight cooperation between industry, academia, and government in determining the content of regulatory standards. The Japanese Automobile Manufacturer's Association (JAMA), an industrial association, also plays an important role in this process.

When the time comes to fix regulatory standards, the relevant government bodies consult an advisory committee regarding the target vehicle class, target date, and specific target values for the regulations. The advisory committee in turn convenes meetings of lower-level organizational units – including dedicated subcommittees and working groups – to answer specific questions. At this stage, the dedicated subcommittees and working groups gather technical experts (mainly from universities) and conduct extensive investigations, primarily focused on technological questions and including industry hearings, to prepare answers to the specific questions they are given. During this stage of the process, the dedicated subcommittees and working groups are in constant and close communication with the automobile industry, exchanging information in both directions; in addition, JAMA creates information portals to respond to inquiries, participate in hearings, and exchange information with the dedicated subcommittees and working groups. The responses obtained by the dedicated subcommittees and working groups are generally accepted largely as-is by the advisory committee as the official answers to the questions they were asked, and are eventually reflected in the automotive technology standards adopted.

The characteristic feature that stands out upon inspection of this decision-making process is that, by the time the government's regulatory standards go into effect, the automobile manufacturers have already had time to respond to any technological challenges that the standards might pose. Sano (2008) notes that, when the advisory committees and dedicated subcommittees conduct their deliberations, they pay extremely close attention to the current state of technological development, and seek to create standards that are finely calibrated to realistic expectations for how technology will have advanced by the time the standards go into effect.

Aoki (2001a, 2001b) refers to the attitude symbolized by 'no to specifics' – one of the institutional characteristics of Japan's political economy in protection of vested interests – as 'compartmentalized pluralism' or 'bureau pluralism'. In this system, 'business associations' exist atop the hierarchy of private organizations. Although the members of each business association compete with each other, they try to pursue their common interests together – as a unified front toward outside interests – by approaching the appropriate bureaus of relevant ministries or mobilizing the power of politicians. As with many of Japan's societal systems, the 'bureau pluralism' framework is considered to have fallen into dysfunction in the 1990s (Tsuru, 2002), but there is no doubt that the relationship between government and industry, and the business association–advisory committee system, have played an important role in preserving the efficacy of industrial policy. Business associations also play the important roles of aggregating the interests of individual corporations into a larger cohesive unit, achieving agreement throughout the industrial community, and serving as a portal for communication between government and industry (Okimoto, 1991); by mitigating the asymmetry in information that exists between any one corporation and the government, business associations have served to create more-effective government policy (Yonekura, 1993). This pattern is clearly visible in the particular case of the crafting and adoption of automotive technology policies, a process in which JAMA has played a critical role as a business association. Sano (2008) notes that the creation of fuel-efficiency standards under the top-runner scheme featured close collaboration between industry, government, and academia, both in determining the content of the regulation and in choosing the precise standard values, and did not differ in significant ways from the traditional process for determining the content of regulations. If we ask the underlying question of this book – *How did Japan's government and corporations change their organizations, strategies, and policies during the 'lost decade'?* – of the automobile industry, the best answer is that *while environmental and safety regulations were further strengthened, there was no substantive change to the business association–advisory committee system for determining regulatory standards.*

Automotive technology and the problem of global warming

In this section, with the aim of contributing to the ongoing debate over future policy directions, we review the status of the global warming problem and the technologies that have arisen to combat it. We then present the results of simulations conducted to assess the impact of more-widespread use of electric cars.

The global warming problem and the associated technological roadmap

As we saw in the second section, since 1960, measures to reduce emissions of NOx, PM, and other air pollutants have been a primary component of automotive technology policy, and advances in technologies to treat exhaust gases, as well as other factors, have contributed to a significant reduction in the volume of air pollutants emitted per mile traveled. Subsequently, in the 1990s, the problem of global warming began to attract attention, and increased fuel efficiency – as a means of reducing CO_2 emissions – became a prominent addition to the list of automotive technology policy objectives. However, in some cases, vehicles based on internal combustion engines (ICEs) with sophisticated processing of exhaust gases exhibit a *trade-off* between increased fuel efficiency and reduced exhaust gas emissions, and hence a desirable objective for the future is the simultaneous realization of a variety of efficiency-enhancement technologies together with strategies for reducing operating resistance. In the short term, technological advancements in ICE-based vehicles offer expectations of some moderate improvements in fuel efficiency while maintaining or improving on today's exhaust gas performance, but it seems possible that, in the medium to long term, the problem of global warming will demand CO_2 emission reductions far in excess of what can be realistically achieved merely by improving the efficiency of ICE-based vehicles. Instead, any comprehensive solution to the problem must unavoidably incorporate a shift from fossil fuels to electric power, hydrogen, and other alternative energy sources.

Let us now review the current state of the global warming problem and discuss the technology roadmap proposed by the International Energy Agency to address it. First, regarding the state of the global warming phenomenon, in the Fourth Assessment Report of the International Panel on Climate Change (IPCC), the IPCC's Third Working Group reviewed developments in global emission scenarios since the Third Assessment Report, and identified six categories of possible future scenarios describing the relationship between CO_2 emissions and rising average temperature in 2050 (as compared to 2000). Of these, scenario categories I and II have the lowest stabilization levels for the concentration of CO_2; according to these analyses, in order for the rise in average temperature to level off at a total increase of between 2.0 and 2.4°C since the time before the industrial revolution (scenario category I), CO_2 emissions would have to peak in 2015, then decrease by 2050 to 50–85 per cent of their 2000 levels. In order for the rise in average temperature to level off at an increase of between 2.4 and 2.8°C since the time before the industrial revolution (scenario category II), CO_2 emissions would have to peak in 2020, then decrease by 2050 to 30–60 per cent of their 2000 levels (Metz *et al.*, 2007). At the 2007 G8 Summit in Heiligendamm, the leaders of the G8 countries agreed to seriously consider methods for reducing global emissions of greenhouse gases by 50 per cent by 2050.

Turning next to the technology roadmap for combating global warming, the International Energy Agency has suggested technologies that must be realized in order to achieve either of two scenarios: the 'ACT Map' scenario, in which global emissions of CO_2 would return to their 2005 levels by 2050, and the 'BLUE Map' scenario, in which global emissions of CO_2 would be reduced by 50 per cent (over their 2005 levels) by 2050. Focusing on automobile-related technologies, in the ACT Map scenario, the majority of the reductions in energy consumption and CO_2 emissions realized within the transportation sector would come from major improvements in the energy efficiency of conventional vehicles and from increased market penetration of hybrid-electric vehicles (HEVs). This scenario also assumes that biofuels will play a role, principally as a replacement for gasoline to fuel cars. The BLUE Map scenario, on the other hand, requires that electric vehicles (EVs) and fuel-cell vehicles (FCVs) number some 1 billion units around the world by 2050; in this scenario, the transportation sector will require more investments than any other single sector. Electric batteries and hydrogen fuel cells are the main alternatives for cars, but, while it is difficult to judge whether or not either of these technologies – or some combination of these technologies – will become the most competitive alternative in the future, current estimates (even rather optimistic estimates) for technological progress and cost reductions in batteries and fuel cells still project the cost of EVs and FCVs at some US$6500 more than the cost of conventional vehicles in 2050 (IEA, 2008).

Projections for the spread of EVs

As emphasized by the IEA (2008), at present it is difficult for EVs and FCVs to gain significant traction in the general market. The reason for this is that the batteries and fuel cells that constitute the critical design elements of EVs and FCVs have not yet attained practical levels of performance or cost. In what follows, we present the results of simulations we have conducted to assess the impact of more-widespread use of EVs.

Analytical methods

We begin with battery supply curves taken from the work of Duvall and Alexander (2005). These authors used data (Anderman *et al.*, 2000) from BTAP (the California Battery Technical Advisory Panel), but also considered variations in the price of nickel to obtain supply curves based on reassessments of future prices, thereby yielding price predictions for PHEVs (plug-in hybrid-electric vehicles) and EVs. The supply curves used here estimate price per unit electrical storage capacity based on annual production volumes of batteries designed for use in EVs; in these curves, in contrast to typical supply curves, the price decreases as demand increases. On the other hand, the number of EVs sold depends on the price of batteries. Here we assume that consumers make decisions based on the total costs of conventional vehicles (CV) and EVs over the full period of ownership, and we model consumer decision-making activity using a logit model. This yields a demand curve, whose intersection with the supply curve determine the price and supply volume of batteries.

To simplify the conditions of our simulations, we put annual sales volume at 5 million units, assume that all consumers travel a total of 10,000 kilometers per year and own their vehicles for ten years, and assume a discount rate of 10 per cent, based on the investment decisions of private-sector corporations. On the other hand, based on the work of Weiss *et al.* (2000), we estimate the fuel efficiency and price of conventional vehicles at 1.543MJ/km and $19,400, respectively; we estimate the AC electric power efficiency of EVs at 0.544MJ/km, and we estimate the cost of an

EV, not including the battery, at \$15,960. (In the original work of Weiss
et al. (2000), the battery capacity was taken to be 50kWh, but here we
assume 30kWh. Then the total distance that may be traveled on one full
charge is approximately 230km.) We calculate the parameters of our logit
model based on the fraction of HEVs sold in Japan in 2004 together with
total costs over the full term of ownership. The conditions and parameters of our model are summarized in Table 12.1.

Table 12.1   Parameters used to simulate the impact of more-widespread use of
EVs

Item	Value	Notes
Supply curve for batteries used in EVs	Log $p = \alpha_0 + \alpha_1 \log N$ $\alpha_0 = 3.32$, $\alpha_1 = -0.168$	p: battery price N: number of units shipped annually *Source*: Duvall and Alexander (2005)
EV demand curve	$$\Pr_{EV} = \frac{\exp(\theta \cdot C_{EV})}{\exp(\theta \cdot C_{EV}) + \exp(\theta \cdot C_{CV})}$$ $\theta = 7.11 \times 10^{-4}$	C_{EV}, C_{CV}: Cost of EVs and CVs over the full term of ownership(\$) (θ is estimated from the probability of choosing an HEV in Japan)
Fuel Costs	Gasoline: US\$1.27/L = US \$0.039/MJ	Price (including tax) of gasoline in Japan (140 yen / L)
	Electric power: US \$0.091/kWh = US \$0.025/MJ	Overnight price of electric power in Japan (10 yen / kWh)
Number of units sold	5 million units / year	
Annual travel distance per vehicle	10,000 km	
Length of use	10 years	
Tax at time of purchase	10 %	
Discount rate	10 %	
Fuel efficiency	CV: 1.543MJ/km EV: 0.544MJ/km	US-FTP combined mode
Vehicle price	CV: US \$19,400 EV: US\$15,960 (excluding battery price)	*Source*: Weiss *et al.* (2000)

Note: US\$1 = 110 yen.

Estimates of growth in the use of EVs

Figure 12.1 shows battery supply and demand curves calculated under the assumptions discussed above. Here the solid lines plot EV demand *versus* battery price, while the dashed lines plot battery price *versus* EV sales volume. From the upper panel of Figure 12.1 we see that EV demand rises as battery price falls, while battery price falls as sales volume rises. The lower panel presents the same data in a log-log plot; although it is difficult to see in the upper panel, the curves intersect at two points, corresponding to battery prices of $180/kWh and $340/kWh. Supply and demand are equal at both of these points, but the point marked **A** in the figure corresponds to an unstable equilibrium; if the battery price rises higher than its value at point **A**, the sales volume will converge to zero, while if the price falls below the value at point **A** then sales will grow until equilibrium is attained at point **B**.

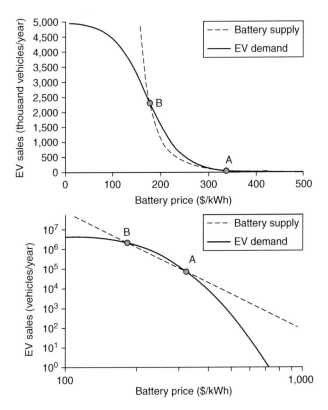

Figure 12.1　Relationship between battery price and EV sales volume ($\alpha_0 = 3.32$)

Figure 12.2 presents the same data as in Figure 12.1, but now calcu-lated using a 3 per cent larger value for the α_0 parameter in the expres-sion for the battery supply curve. In this case, there is no intersection between the curves even in the regime of high battery price; in such a situation there can be no supply–demand equilibrium, and EVs will not become widespread.

These results suggest two points to keep in mind in crafting government policy to promote the spread of EVs. One is that growth in the use of EVs is highly sensitive to the parameters that determine the supply curve, and will thus be heavily influenced by forecasts for battery price reductions due to mass-production effects. The results plotted in Figures 12.1 and 12.2 clearly demonstrate that small variations in battery price forecasts can entirely neutralize the impact of policies to promote EVs.

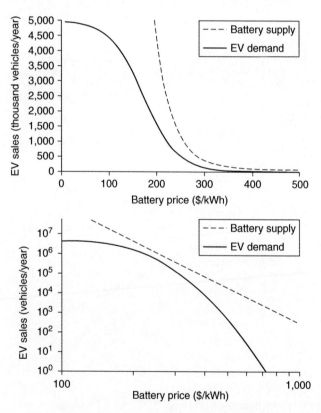

Figure 12.2 Relationship between battery price and EV sales volume (α_0=3.41)

A second point, also evident in the data plotted in Figure 12.1, concerns the adoption of any new technology: until production volume exceeds a certain threshold value, the new technology will not be widely adopted, but once production volumes exceed that threshold then mass-production effects quickly kick in, driving a decrease in the market price of the technology and its wider adoption. The goal of policies designed to promote the spread of new technologies must be to exceed this threshold value, and a cost-benefit analysis of these types of policies reveals that the optimal situation is one in which the price at point A (the threshold point) is relatively high, while the price at point B (the convergence point) is as low as possible. The supply curve parameters also have significant influence on this effect.

Figure 12.3 illustrates changes in the battery prices at points A and B as the two parameters in the supply curve are varied by ±10 per cent. The horizontal and vertical axes indicate the values of the α_0 and α_1 parameters, while the color indicates the battery price (brighter colors correspond to higher prices). The blacked-out region to the right of line C in each plot is the regime in which no intersection point (no supply–demand equilibrium) exists. (Line C is the equal-price curve, along which points A and B coincide.)

These figures indicate that, even if we consider only ±10 per cent variations in the parameter values, fully 44 per cent of the parameter space is blacked out; at parameter values falling anywhere within this region, use of EVs will not become widespread. As the parameter values decrease, the threshold price rises and the equilibrium price falls; in this case the difference between the threshold and equilibrium prices is large, and government policy has maximal impact. On the other hand, for parameter values lying near the vicinity of line C, the impact of government policies to promote the spread of the technology is minimal, even in cases where an equilibrium point exists. We thus see that small changes in parameter values can have a large influence on the efficacy of technology-promotion policies.

Note that, for production volumes in the range of 100,000 units per year or fewer, the battery supply curve we used in this study is based on corporate hearings and other sources and can be expected to predict prices with some degree of accuracy, but may be entirely unreliable for larger production volumes. In addition, although we have not included them within our analysis here, some uncertainties inevitably exist in demand-side models and in the assumptions and conditions we used to conduct our simulations, and these must not be ignored. Future work is necessary to incorporate these uncertainties into a more refined model.

288 *Masanobu Kii, Hiroaki Miyoshi and Masayuki Sano*

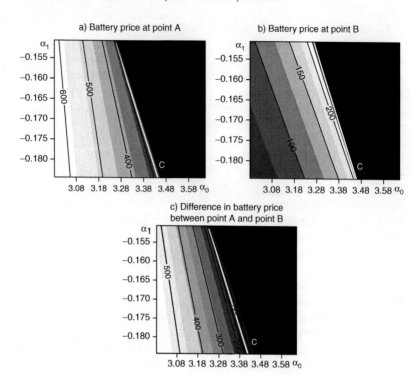

Figure 12.3 Sensitivity of battery price to changes in parameter values

Future directions for automotive technology

We began this chapter with a survey of Japanese automotive technology policies. We noted that these policies are generally crafted by a business association–advisory committee system, and that, in the years since the 1990s, regulatory standards have been strengthened several times, but the underlying system by which the regulations are adopted has remained largely unchanged. Next, we reviewed the present status of the global warming problem, and noted that, in order to realize the goal of halving CO_2 emissions by 2050, efficiency improvements to conventional vehicles alone will not suffice; instead, more widespread use of new-energy vehicles such as EVs and FCVs is an unavoidable requirement. Finally, we described simulations conducted to assess conditions necessary for the spread of EVs, and we observed that small changes in the values of price parameters can have significant influence on the efficacy of government policies to promote the spread of new technologies.

Based on these analyses, we would like to conclude this chapter by suggesting two directions for future automotive technology policies. The first is that, if we wish to mitigate the global warming crisis by stimulating the development of technology for – and more-widespread market availability of – new-energy vehicles, then taxes or incentives proportional to CO_2 emission volumes will be more effective tools than technical regulations. In April 2009, a new green tax system went into effect, under which automotive taxes, automobile acquisition taxes, and vehicle-weight taxes are reduced for HEVs and other vehicles that meet certain environmental standards. As a result, the climate for HEV sales grew more favorable; in the 2009 rankings for numbers of new vehicles sold, Toyota's Prius HEV was the leader in both registered vehicles and light motor vehicles. This is clear evidence of the effectiveness of economic incentives. Although we will not discuss it in detail here, the many new taxes and tax increases levied throughout the postwar period have left Japan's automobile-related tax structure resembling a crazy patchwork quilt. The entire automotive tax system should be reformed, and the resulting system should incorporate taxes or incentives proportional to CO_2 emissions to stimulate technological development and market availability of new-energy vehicles. In the rush to respond to the global warming crisis, it has become evident that large disparities exist among automakers' abilities to develop new-energy vehicles. If we attempt to respond to the crisis by imposing new regulations, these regulations would be crafted under the business association–advisory committee system: the regulatory standard levels would be calibrated to the base technological level expected to exist at the time the regulations go into effect, which would make it difficult in the future to achieve any sort of consensus; if economic incentives are strengthened, the system would gradually lose all substantive meaning.

The second direction we suggest is that, when it comes to new technologies such as electric vehicles and fuel cell vehicles, policies to promote the spread of technologies must always keep in mind the underlying technological uncertainties. In this chapter, we used batteries as a testing ground to analyze the impact of technological uncertainties arising from supply curves, and we demonstrated that small changes in pricing parameters can have a significant impact on the effectiveness of policies to promote the spread of technologies. Some voices call for policies to promote the spread of new technologies starting from whatever state currently exists in the market. For example, the Zero Emission Vehicle (ZEV) regulations enacted by California in

1995 required that EVs, FCVs, and other such vehicles account for 10 per cent of automobile manufacturers' total sales by 2003. However, no manufacturer had the technology to produce such vehicles at a price point that would allow their use to become widespread, and the regulations were eventually softened (and their deadlines extended) in 2003, and then softened again in 2008. (ZEV regulations were initially introduced in 1990; their weakening in 2008 represented the fifth time they were revised.) The lesson of this experience is that policies to promote new technologies must start by supporting and assisting technological innovation, and then proceed by stimulating the growth of those technologies within specific markets in which the relevant technologies can attain superiority; we must keep in mind that large-scale policy initiatives like California's ZEV regulations can ultimately wind up having absolutely no impact. Policies to promote the technologies of the future must reflect sufficient awareness of technological information and assessments of past policies.

References

Anderman, M., Kalhammer, F., and McArthur, D. (2000) 'Advanced Batteries for Electric Vehicles: An Assessment of Performance, Cost, and Availability', Prepared for State of California Air Resources Board, Sacramento, California.

Aoki, M. (2001a) *Toward a Comparative Institutional Analysis*, Cambridge, MA: MIT Press.

Aoki, M. (2001b) 'Beyond Bureau Pluralism', *Global Communication Platform*, Japanese Institute of Global Communications. Available at http://www.glocom.org/opinions/essays/200109_aoki_beyond/index.html (accessed 21 December 2009).

Duvall, M. and Alexander, M. (2005) 'Batteries for Electric Drive Vehicles – Status 2005: Performance, Durability, and Cost of Advanced Batteries for Electric, Hybrid Electric, and Plug-In Hybrid Electric Vehicles', *Technical Report*, Palo Alto: Electric Power Research Institute.

International Energy Agency (2008) *Energy Technology Perspectives 2008: Scenarios and Strategies to 2050*, Paris: OECD Publishing.

International Energy Agency (2009) *CO2 Emissions from Fuel Combustion*, Paris: OECD Publishing.

Metz, I. B., Davidson, O. R., Bosch, P. R., Dave, R., and Meyer, L.A. (eds) (2007) *Contribution of Working Group III to the Fourth Assessment Report of the Intergovernmental Panel on Climate Change, 2007*, Cambridge: Cambridge University Press.

Okimoto, D. (1991) *Tsuusanshou to haiteku sangyou – nihon no kyousouryoku wo umu mekanizumu* (Between MITI and the market: Japanese industrial policy for high technology), Tokyo: Simul Publishing Company.

Sano, M. (2008) '*Jidousha no gijutsu kakushin to gijutsu seisaku no keifu*' (The Genealogy of Technological Innovation in the Automotive Industry and

Government Technology Policies), in H. Miyoshi and M. Tanishita (eds), *Jidousha no gijutsu kakushin to keizai kousei* (Technological Innovation in the Automotive Industry and Economic Welfare), Tokyo: Hakuto-Shobo Publishing Company.

Tsuru, K. (2002) ' *"Shikirareta tagen shugi" saikou'* (Rethinking 'Bureaupluralism'), *Economics Review* 3, RIETI (Research Institute of Economy, Trade, and Industry, IAA).

Weiss, M. A., Heywood, J. B., Drake, E. M., Schafer, A., and AuYeung, F. F. (2000) *On the Road in 2020: A Life-Cycle Analysis of New Automobile Technologies*, MIT Energy Laboratory Report EL 00–003, Massachusetts Institute of Technology.

Yonekura, S. (1993) *'Gyoukai dantai no kinou'* (The Functions of Industrial Associations), in T. Okazaki and M. Okuno (eds), *Genzai nihon keizai shisutemu no genryuu* (The Japanese Economic System and its Historical Origins), Chapter 6, Tokyo: Nihon Keizai Shimbunsha.

13
Science and Technology Policy
Tateo Arimoto

Introduction

To examine the different ways in which innovations and technological changes are realized in different nations, a number of authors
(Freeman and Soete, 1997; Lundvall, 1992; Nelson, 1993) compared
various countries and proposed the concept of a 'national innovation
system' that forms separately in each country, grounded in that country's unique historical and cultural history and in its individual systems and markets. In a wide-ranging review, Fagerberg *et al.* (2004)
followed up on this idea, considering the concept of the innovation
system, the roles of industry, academia, and government, the relationship between elements such as human resources, capital, and intellectual property, and the impact of all of these factors on economic
growth and competitiveness.

Despite the existence of these research works, the rapid pace of globalization since the 1990s, and the 'once-in-a-century' global financial
and economic crisis of 2008, have mandated large-scale revisions to our
traditional ways of thinking about innovation systems and about the
concept of innovation itself.

In the roughly 100 years since Schumpeter (1912) first created the
theory of innovation, the theory has primarily developed around examples from the fields of management studies and practical corporate
management. In recent years, however, the domain of the theory has
expanded from corporate management to public policy. As we enter the
twenty-first century, the problems facing societies – globally, regionally,
nationally, and locally – continue to mount: global warming, deple-
tion of energy, water, food, and other resources, the spread of infectious diseases, poverty, terrorism, and more. Moreover, an unfortunate

consequence of globalization has been to increase the instability of the world's economic systems. To solve these problems, we need new ideas, new methods, and new rules – not just in corporate management, but in university management, public policy, and even in the very nature of citizens' lives – and hence the notion of innovation is garnering more and more attention as the twenty-first century progresses.

Meanwhile, turning our attention to the particular problems facing Japan, we find a number of crises demanding urgent responses: a diminishing population, an aging society, stagnant global competitiveness, and increasing societal unease. Moreover, the nation of Japan, having weathered the transition from its catch-up phase (which began some 150 years ago with an era of rapid modernization) to its status today as a global front-runner, now faces the possibility of a significant decline in its relative importance within the global economy: Japan must grapple with the possibility – as predicted by Goldman Sachs (2003) – that it will slide from its current rank as the world's second-largest economic powerhouse to a nation of only moderate economic significance in terms of gross GDP by 2050.

To address this daunting complex of problems amidst the new economic and societal realities of today's world, Japan needs to make a clean break with the catch-up phase of its past and adopt both a new national vision and a new set of societal values. At the same time, Japan needs to design a new innovation system, and a new framework for science and technology policy, to enable the nation to make the most effective use of its own homegrown knowledge and technology and to tie its international competitiveness to its societal values.

In this chapter, we begin with a historical survey of Japan's postwar scientific and technology policies. We then turn to a consideration of the Science and Technology Basic Law of 1995, reviewing the background behind the legislation, its significance, and its ramifications. Finally, we analyze the global trend away from science and technology policies and instead toward more *innovation*-focused policies, and we consider the future development of this transition.

A historical survey of science and technology policy in Japan

The institutionalization of science and technology in the postwar era

The structural edifice of modern science and technology was erected over a period of some 200 years, from the early nineteenth century to the present day, led primarily by Europe and the US. The Science Council of Japan (2005) has divided this history into three broad phases: the nineteenth century was the 'century of institutionalization' for science and technology, the twentieth century was the 'century of structuralization', and the twenty-first century will be the 'century of strategization'.

The 'structuralization' of science and technology in the twentieth century was led by the US after World War II. The bible of postwar science and technology policy, which eventually spread around the world, was *Science: The Endless Frontier*, a report prepared during the war at the request of President Roosevelt by Vannevar Bush, a central figure in the wartime mobilization of science and technology. The underlying premise of the report was that public investments in science and technology, and the establishment of comprehensive systems for research and development, were critical to secure a nation's security and defense needs, its economic power, and the well-being of its people even in peacetime; the report emphasized a 'linear model', which linked advancements in fundamental science to societal economic value, and called for the creation of institutions to stimulate and assist research. These recommendations led to the creation of several new institutions to conduct and assist research in the US, including the NSF, AEC, NASA, and DARPA, as well as a number of new fellowship programs designed to nurture and train young students. In Europe and Japan, the structuralization of science and technology proceeded through the 1960s and 1970s in conjunction with the recovery of national economies from the war. Among the consequences of this in Japan were the creation of various new institutions, including the Science Council of Japan, the Science and Technology Agency, the Agency for Industrial Science and Technology, and the Atomic Energy Commission, as well as a program to double the number of people trained in technical fields (Arimoto, 2006; Odagiri and Goto, 2005).

Thus, in the aftermath of World War II, the governments of nations around the world, led by the US, began to treat science and technology as important arenas for public policy; huge amounts of public investment were funneled into science and technology, and the 'structuralization' of science and technology proceeded in earnest. The subsequent deepening of the East–West Cold War only further accelerated the trend.

Technological trade friction between Japan and the US and the transformation in science and technology policy

The economic growth of Europe and Japan in the 1970s presented the US with the first glimpses of possible threats to its military and economic dominance; Ezra Vogel's *Japan as Number One* (Vogel, 1979) became a topic of anxious conversations from Washington, DC to Tokyo and everywhere in between. As US-Japan trade friction in the steel, automobile, and semiconductor sectors intensified in the 1980s, disputes spilled over into the scientific and technological arena, with the US vocally criticizing the economic policies, and the science and technology policies, of the Japanese government; phrases such as 'Japan, Inc.', 'industrial targeting policy', and 'free-riding on fundamental science' were commonly bandied about.

Broadly speaking, the innovation system that had been so successful for Japan until the 1970s consisted of borrowing technological ideas from advanced countries in Europe and the US, developing these ideas into competitive products – primarily through process innovation – and then exporting them. However, in view of the criticism that Japan was free-riding on fundamental research from the US, the continued success of this model seemed unlikely, and the emphasis of science and technology policy shifted toward basic research and product innovation. This led to a strengthening of capital systems oriented toward basic research, international personnel exchanges, and policies for making international contributions, and many corporations set up central research organizations focused on basic research. In addition, a large number of ameliorative measures were enacted during these years. For example, in the promising high-technology fields of supercomputers, space satellites, and analytical instruments, universities and national research laboratories were required to purchase US products. Such policies unquestionably weakened Japan's scientific, technological, and high-tech industrial foundations and planted seeds that would sprout into problems far into the future.

Meanwhile, long-term investments in education, in universities, and in scientific and technological foundations – and necessary initiatives to restructure them – lagged behind.

Throughout the postwar era, private-sector corporations had consistently been at the center of R&D investment activity in Japan, but, in the 1980s, public investments in universities and human-resource training dwindled to particularly anemic levels in comparison to the robust investments being made in the private sector. The paucity of public investment during this era clearly weakened the long-term foundations for basic research and education in Japan. The idea that private capital accumulated during periods of economic prosperity should be used to endow the essential facilities needed by universities and basic research institutions was briefly floated at the time, but, sadly, went nowhere.

Substantive initiatives in this direction had to wait for the 1990s and the passage of the Science and Technology Basic Law, as discussed in the next section.

World history is, in fact, replete with instances of trade friction, and technological friction, between advanced countries and developing nations. The fierce trade fracas that broke out in the late nineteenth and early twentieth centuries between the advanced nation of England and the emerging powers of the US and Germany is a classic example of this phenomenon. The British complained that the Americans and the Germans were stealing knowledge and technologies invented in England, then flooding the export markets with mass-produced products – thus pocketing profits that rightly belonged to England. In response, capitalists and academics in the US and Germany cooperated to make large investments in basic research, universities, and human-resource training – all areas in which both countries had previously been weak – thus laying the foundations of the scientific and technological powerhouse nations of today (Arimoto, 2009a). Japan's failure to digest this lesson in the 1980s was to be a major source of regret. As an aside, it is interesting to note that the nations boasting today's most impressive economic growth – China, India, and the world's natural-resource-producing nations – are all investing heavily in their own national foundations, including universities and human-resource training.

The enactment of the Science and Technology Basic Law

The end of the Cold War, the advent of the Internet and its spread around the world, the resulting intense global economic competition, and the entrenchment of globalization presaged major transformations in the science and technology policies that had existed previously. First, in the 1990s, US science and technology policies underwent a significant change in direction, moving from a primarily military-focused mindset to an viewpoint that emphasized economic growth. The 1993 cancellation of the Superconducting Super Collider particle-accelerator facility was symbolic of this 'military to civilian' shift.

Japan, until the 1980s, had achieved remarkable success with a model of borrowing technological ideas from foreign countries, turning these ideas into new products, and exporting those products to markets all over the world. In the 1990s, however, the structure of the world economic system changed in major ways; China rose to prominence as the 'world's factory', and Japan's innovation system fell into obsolescence.

Science and technology were seen as the saviors, widely saddled with enormous expectations for leading the nation out of its morass. Amidst severe trade friction with the world's advanced nations, criticisms about free-riding on basic research, and a series of shocks that threatened Japan's status as a nation of plenty, a consensus developed among the Japanese people that industrial competitiveness and quality-of-life improvements would have to be based on Japan's own basic research and knowledge. Such was the backdrop against which the Japanese Diet, by a unanimous vote, approved the Science and Technology Basic Law of 1995. The Basic Law would prove instrumental in pointing the way toward Japan's future.

The Science and Technology Basic Law and its significance

In this section, after first presenting an overview of the Science and Technology Basic Law enacted in 1995, we describe the system of Cabinet-approved Science and Technology Basic Plans mandated by the law, and discuss the significance of both the Basic Law and the Basic Plans.[1]

The Science and Technology Basic Law and the Science and Technology Basic Plans: An overview

An overview of the Science and Technology Basic Law

The Science and Technology Basic Law is intended to provide a core underlying framework for Japanese science and technology policy; in addition, the law is designed to form the backbone of a series of intense efforts to promote the development of science and technology within Japan, with the goal of making Japan a 'science-and-technology-creating-nation' in the twenty-first century. The law consists of the following four sets of provisions.

(1) Provisions regarding policies to promote science and technology.
(2) Provisions establishing responsibilities for public organizations to promote science and technology at both the national and local levels.
(3) A provision stating that Science and Technology Basic Plans are to be created, by the government, through panels convened by the Council for Science and Technology Policy. The provision also mandates that the government do its utmost to ensure that all necessary measures are taken to secure any funding required to implement the Science and Technology Basic Plans.
(4) A provision describing measures that will be the responsibility of the national government.

Science and Technology Basic Plans

The Science and Technology Basic Law requires the government to devise Science and Technology Basic Plans every five years beginning in 1996. The key provisions of the first Basic Plan (1996–2001), the Second Basic Plan (2001–2006), and the third Basic Plan (2006–2011) are as follows.

First, regarding the scale of the Plans, the government set aside 17 trillion yen for R&D investments during the first Basic Plan, and 24 trillion yen for the second Basic Plan, ensuring generous budgets for science and technology budgets relative to other government expenditures. In addition, the Plans did not merely increase budgets, but also introduced policies to define specific areas of emphasis, in response to occasional necessities arising on policy grounds. For example, the first Plan strengthened support for postdoctoral researchers and added some 10,000 new postdoctoral fellows, as well as introducing a tenure system for researchers in an attempt to increase the mobility of researchers and stimulate research activities. Similarly, the second Plan identified strategic investment targets (the promotion of basic research, as well as four areas in which national initiatives were deemed critical: life sciences, information and communications technology, nanotechnology and material sciences, and environmental sciences) and called for reforms in the science and technology system (a doubling of competitive research funding and stronger collaboration between industry, academia, and government).

The third Science and Technology Basic Plan set the total five-year budget for government R&D investments at 25 trillion yen, identified 62 research subfields as critical investment targets, and – for the first time – established performance goals in each subfield to be met by 2010. In addition, a number of the critical-investment subfields were singled out as 'core national technologies' worthy of long-term government emphasis.

A striking feature of the third Science and Technology Basic Plan is that it was the first Plan to propose *innovation* policies. Here, the term 'innovation policies' refers to science and technology policies that, rather than seeking to produce academic knowledge simply for its own sake, instead call for various stakeholders, such as industries, universities, and governments, to *connect* that knowledge to the creation of societal economic value. We will come back to this point later.

The significance of the Science and Technology Basic Law

The adoption of the Science and Technology Basic Law, and the succession of Science and Technology Basic Plans it mandated, have had a major impact on science and technology research in Japan, beginning in the mid-1990s and continuing through the present day. Large public investments were directed toward basic research conducted in an competitive environment, university facilities were improved, methods for the distribution of research funding and the subsequent assessment of results were modified, and large numbers of high-quality research papers and patents were produced.

On the other hand, many feel that conditions designed to stimulate competition in funding systems, university assessments, and other areas were introduced to an excessive extent, and that, as a result, researchers have too little time left to do research (NISTEP, 2009). Others have suggested that networks of researchers and engineers, which played such an important role in Japan's innovation system until the 1980s, were severed (Yoshikawa, 2007a). Some have criticized a shortage of investment in core operating expenses at universities, and in humanities and social sciences, while a number of voices have demanded the global liberation of personnel, research activities, and research funding (Sunami and Kurokawa, 2009).

Other authors have noted that the uniquely Japanese system of collaboration among universities, public institutions, and private-sector corporations, which was responsible for developing and implementing the miracles that symbolized Japan's high-growth era up until the 1980s – bullet trains, telephone and electronic communication networks, semiconductor technology, process engineering, and more – collapsed under the strain of US-Japan trade friction and the privatization of public institutions, and that no new system appropriate for a new era has yet emerged (Yoshikawa, 2007b).

Science and Technology Basic Plans calling for policy emphasis on the four critical areas mentioned above have been in effect for over ten years; meanwhile, at the same time, the importance of 'resolving problems' and 'merging disciplines' is routinely stressed. It is difficult to see how a policy framework that emphasizes four particular subfields, on the one hand, can coexist with a comprehensive system of research that transcends subfield boundaries and allows flexible support to researchers on the other hand; some authors have suggested that this inherent contradiction makes it impossible to direct sufficient investment and assistance toward the goals of 'resolving problems' and 'merging disciplines'. Resolving the incompatibilities between policies that operate at cross-purposes in this way must be seen as an urgent priority (Arimoto, 2009b).

Science and technology policy in the twenty-first century: Prospects and issues for the future

According to *The Economist*, in 2006, for the first time in well over 100 years, the combined GDP of the developing nations, including China, India, and Russia (all of which had been great economic powers before the first half of the nineteenth century), exceeded that of the world's seven most advanced nations, including Japan (The Economist, 2006).

On the other hand, as the twenty-first century progresses, the global instability of our economic systems is posing ever-more serious risks, as symbolized by the Lehman Brothers crisis. At the same time, a host of other global-scale problems are becoming more and more grave: global warming, shortages of energy, water, food, and other resources, the spread of infectious diseases, poverty, terrorism, and more.

The world that lies on the other side of these large-scale transformations in economic and societal systems will no doubt differ in significant ways from the world we know today, including both the values held dear by society and the structure of science and engineering. How do we go about shaping the post-crisis world and scientific enterprise? The answer to this question requires that we design a new innovation system without borders. In the following section, we discuss such a new system from three perspectives: a shift in emphasis from science and technology policies to innovation policies, innovation ecosystems, and the global innovation ecosystem.

From science and technology policy to innovation policy

In December 2004, the US Council on Competitiveness released a report entitled 'Innovate America' (also known as the 'Palmisano report') (Council on Competitiveness, 2005). The Palmisano report concludes that if the US is to continue to develop and grow in the twenty-first century, innovation must be the single most important driving force, and proposes measures in three areas – education personnel, research and development, and social infrastructure – designed to remake US society into an environment maximally conducive to innovation. Underlying the report is a strong sense of impending crisis regarding future US competitiveness amid the rapid rise of China and India; this fact makes the Palmisano report reminiscent of the Young report of the early 1980s, which called for industrial, academic, and governmental cooperation in the US to respond to the rise of Japan. The Young report ultimately led to the pro-patent policy and other changes in science and technology policy, motivated thoroughgoing international comparisons of technological abilities, and instigated a 'Buy American' campaign in high-tech fields such as supercomputers, space satellites, and analytical instruments.

Following on the heels of the Palmisano report, in 2005 the US National Academy of Science released its 'Augustine report' (National Academy of Sciences *et al.*, 2007), a document which could be fairly called a detailed blueprint for a new style of innovation. The report states that 'US advantages in the marketplace and in science and technology have begun to erode. A comprehensive and coordinated federal effort is urgently needed to bolster US competitiveness and pre-eminence in these areas.' The report focuses primarily on China and India as international competitors, and calls for a number of measures to strengthen US competitiveness against these challengers, including comprehensive science and math education at the elementary- and middle-school levels, stronger research in engineering and physical sciences, improved education in physical sciences at the high-school level, and the creation of an innovation ecosystem. The release of the Augustine report further intensified debate in Congress and ultimately led President Bush, in his 2006 State of the Union address, to announce an 'American Competitiveness Initiative' consisting of several proposals: a doubling, over ten years, of the budgets for the National Science Foundation (NSF), the Department of Energy (DOE), science bureaus, and the National Institute for Standards and Technology (NIST); making R&D tax cuts for industry permanent; and a dramatic strengthening in science and math education. The Obama administration has been accelerating these innovation policies, and has strengthened core initiatives, focusing primarily on climate change and environmental and energy issues – the so-called 'Green New Deal'. A report published by the new administration in September 2009, entitled 'A Strategy for American Innovation: Driving Towards Sustainable Growth and Quality Jobs' (Executive Office of the President, 2009), outlined a series of initiatives to connect scientific investment and knowledge to a revitalization of the US economy and employment situation.

The key thing to notice here is that, whereas traditional policies sought merely to stimulate science and technology, these new policy frameworks go further, seeking to stimulate the creation of concrete economic value through science and technology. We see here the very essence of the transition from *science and technology* policies to *innovation* policies.

The Palmisano report, and policies enacted in the US in the years after its release, stimulated unanimous responses from the European nations, Japan, China, India, and other countries, all of which followed suit by strengthening their own innovation policies. We thus find ourselves in an era of transformation, in which innovation policies are gradually replacing traditional science and technology policies.

Innovation ecosystems

In view of the rapid changes taking place in global institutions today, the design of new innovation systems must be an urgent public-policy consideration for all nations. Japan's third Science and Technology Basic Plan (2006–2011), which was the first legislation to introduce innovation policies in Japan, defined innovation as 'the fusing of scientific discoveries, technological inventions, and basic insight for the creation of new societal or economic value'.

In this section we will introduce the concept of the 'innovation ecosystem'. This concept was first proposed in the Palmisano report (Council on Competitiveness, 2004), which likened the process by which scientific knowledge provides a basis for realizing innovations to an ecosystem describing interconnections among living organisms. In the same way that ecosystems of living organisms participate in the process of evolution, new knowledge, new ideas, and new technologies similarly evolve, through interactions with various existing technologies, products, and ideas, and can only survive by adapting to the socio-economic conditions, systems, and regulations of the environment in which they are generated, eventually becoming institutionalized in society or brought to market, whereupon conditions proceed to adapt in turn. Moreover, innovations are the product of interactions among all participants in the innovation process, including universities, research institutions, private-sector corporations, investors, consumers, and the government. These societal systems are not fixed, static entities, but are constantly changing and evolving. The major goal for innovation policy is thus to establish economic and societal conditions and systems that ensure a high probability of stimulating innovation within short periods of time.

Figure 13.1 presents a schematic depiction of the general framework of an innovation ecosystem. This diagram was constructed, based on a large number of innovation case studies, by the Japan Science and Technology Agency's Center for Research and Development Strategy (CRDS), of which the author serves as vice-chairman (CRDS 2006, 2007).

As illustrated in Figure 13.1, the domain of basic research, fueled by the curiosity of scientists, constitutes the gateway into the innovation ecosystem. The critical point here is that scientific knowledge must be developed and stored in abundance and must be available in steady

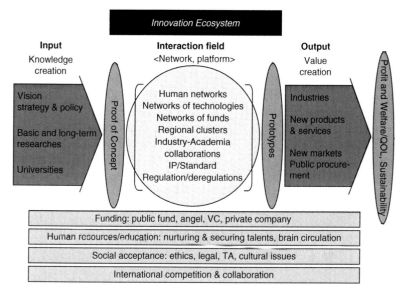

Figure 13.1 Schematic diagram of an *innovation ecosystem*
Source: CRDS (2007).

supply. In addition, activities at this stage must not be limited to the creation of knowledge and the production of research papers, but must also supply new concepts, and new ideas for technologies to implement those ideas in practice, to the next stage in the ecosystem (the interaction field).

At the output stage of Figure 13.1 lies the creation of value, represented by economic benefits or quality-of-life improvements realized by new products or services provided to markets and societies. In free-market economies, new technologies must capture their own market sectors by overcoming a variety of barriers to existing markets. Markets and societies are diverse and heterogeneous in both time and space, and technical innovations and investments – as well as technical management – must be well-adapted to that diversity. Moreover, policies and systems, such as government procurement programs and regulatory measures, must be put in place to guide markets and societies toward the acceptance of new technologies.

Between the input and output of Figure 13.1 lies the interaction field. This sector plays the critical role of receiving new concepts and new technologies from the input sector and delivering them to the output sector in the form of prototypes and test products. The interaction field is the most important domain in the science-and-technology-based innovation process. Proper formation, and long-term maintenance, of the interaction field can dramatically accelerate innovations and improve their probability of success. The interaction field is composed of a variety of people, organizations, technologies, information, capital, and systems, and must evolve appropriately over time.

As indicated at the bottom of Figure 13.1, a number of elements are critical at every stage of the innovation process: the provision of various forms of funding, both public and private; training, education, and retention of personnel; societal acceptance of new technologies, including ethical, legal and technological evaluation; and a culture capable of nourishing and encouraging the entrepreneurial spirit.

The global innovation ecosystem

We have described the creation of an innovation ecosystem as a project undertaken by an individual nation to strengthen its own competitiveness. But the globalization of the world economy, and the increasing seriousness of the worldwide environmental crisis and other global-scale problems, suggest that thinking of innovation systems as entities confined within national boundaries is an outdated and obsolete mindset.

In 2006, the author and others proposed the concept of the 'global innovation ecosystem' (GIES), and started a global conversation to develop the idea further.[2] As illustrated in Figure 13.2, the GIES is a *global-scale* innovation ecosystem that seeks to use science-and-technology-based innovations to find solutions to global-scale problems and to achieve sustained economic and societal growth. The GIES contains innovation interaction fields at the national, regional, and global levels; the interaction field at each level of the hierarchy is characterized by the following three elements, interoperating freely with one another: **(1)** science and technology, as well as markets and societies, working together in the interaction field; **(2)** the personnel, systems, and capital that are the fundamental constituent elements of the interaction field; and **(3)** public-sector and private-sector institutions working to calibrate those constituent elements. The system serves to create both economic and societal value – *economic value*, including growth and profits, led by private-sector institutions, and *societal value*, including social welfare and quality-of-life improvements, led by public-sector institutions – and in so doing to lead the way toward a regional- and global-scale international community in which economic values and societal values are compatible. These two sets of value systems must be interconnected in order for a global innovation system to be sustainable.[3]

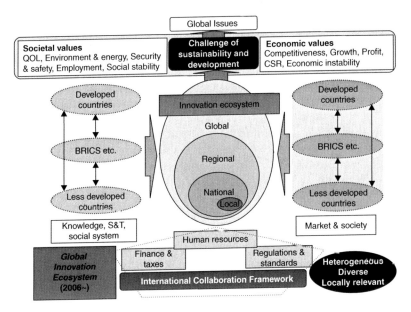

Figure 13.2 The global innovation ecosystem
Source: CRDS (2008a).

Conclusions: Toward an Asian research area

In this chapter, after reviewing the history of Japanese science and technology policy in the postwar era, we discussed the Science and Technology Basic Law that Japan enacted in 1995, and we examined the significance of this legislation. We then considered the worldwide trend in recent years of moving away from science and technology policy and toward innovation policy; we discussed the concepts of an 'innovation ecosystem', designed to foster sustainable innovation, and of a 'global innovation ecosystem', which could help to combat the problem of global warming and maintain ongoing economic and societal growth.

We would like to conclude this chapter by emphasizing the critical importance of international cooperation in a more integrated way (EC, 2009; Leshner and Turekian, 2009).

Notwithstanding the undeniable and significant progress of globalization, it nonetheless remains the case that the world is not simply flat, but rather teems with immeasurable diversity. This fact is of critical importance in constructing and coordinating innovation systems regionally and globally, which must be designed in a manner consistent with the unique historical, cultural, lifestyle, and market realities that exist in the nations and communities in which they operate. Looking at the economic structure of Asia, we find that, until the 1980s, a clearly hierarchical pattern of economic development existed, with Japan in the lead, the newly industrialized economies (NIEs) of Asia trailing behind, and the ASEAN nations, China, and India trailing further behind. Today, in contrast, we see a developing pattern of economic consolidation, in which cities and corporations enter into networks that transcend national boundaries (Nippon Keidanren, 2009; Slaughter, 2009). Meanwhile, the negative consequences of economic growth continue to worsen: environmental pollution, infectious diseases, natural disasters, and social inequality, to mention only a few. In view of this array of challenges and opportunities, if Asia is to enjoy sustained economic growth while simultaneously preserving the environment, we must have vigorous discussions of possible solutions and their societal implementation, grounded in investigations and analysis and resting on a strong scientific and technological platform; at the same time, we must invest in education, training, and cultural exchanges for the young students who will transform these hypothetical solutions into realities. To achieve concrete progress toward these objectives, the time has come to discuss the creation of an Asian Research Area (ARA) and a framework for its long-term sustained support (Commitee for Strategy for International Collaboration in Science and Technology, 2009).

Notes

1. In preparing this overview of the Science and Technology Basic Law and the Science and Technology Basic Plans, we referred to the website of the Japanese Ministry of Education, Culture, Sports, Science and Technology (MEXT) (http://www.mext. go.jp/english/index.htm). We accessed this site on 11 December 2009.
2. For details on GIES symposia conducted in 2007 and 2008, see the symposium websites: http://crds.jst.go.jp/GIES/archive/GIES2007/en/index.html and http://crds.jst.go.jp/GIES/archive/GIES2008/en/index.html.
3. This description is with reference to CRDS (2008b).

References

Arimoto, T. (2006) 'Innovation Policy for Japan in a New Era', in D. H. Whittaker and R. E. Cole (eds), *Recovering from Success: Innovation and Technology Management in Japan*, New York: Oxford University Press.

Arimoto, T.(2009a) '*Sekai no kagaku gijutsu taisei no henkan to nihon – juukyuuseiki, nijusseiki, soshite nijuuisseiki*' (The History of the World Science and Technology System and Japan – 19th, 20th and 21st Centuries), in Y. Takeyasu (ed.), *Kagaku gijutsu chosei seisaku shi* (The History of Science and Technology Agency), Tokyo: The Science News Ltd.

Arimoto, T (2009b) 'Commentary: Review on the Four Primary Priority Areas – Separation between Science and Technology, Interdisciplinary Approach/ Fusion of Areas, and Importance of Organizations', *Chemistry & Chemical Industry*, 62(1): 9–10. Available at http://www.chemistry.or.jp/kaimu/ronsetsu/ronsetsu0901-e.pdf (accessed 11 December 2009).

Committee for Strategy for International Collaboration in Science and Technology (2009) 'Toward an Asian Research Area – A Policy Proposal for International Collaboration in Science and Technology; An Interim Report', The Takeda Foundation, 15 December.

Council on Competitiveness (2005) *Innovate America:National Innovation Initiative Summit and Report*, Washington, DC: Council on Competitiveness. Available from http://www.compete.org/publications/detail/202/innovate-america (accessed 11 December 2009).

CRDS (Center for Research and Development Strategy) (2006) '*Kagaku gijutsu inobeeshon suishin no tame no national innovation ecosystem seisaku teigen no kentou*' (Discussion of Proposals for National Innovation Ecosystem Policies to Stimulate Scientific and Technological Innovation), April.

CRDS (2007) '*Senryaku puropoozaru: kagaku gijutsu inobeeshon no jitsugen ni muketa teigen – national innovation ecosystem no fukan to seisaku kadai*' (Strategic Proposal: A Recommendation for Achieving Scientific and Technological Innovation – The Long-Term View of a National Innovation Ecosystem and Related Policy Issues), CRDS-FY2006-SP-11. Available at http://crds.jst.go.jp/output/pdf/06sp11.pdf (accessed 11 December 2009).

CRDS (2008a) '*Chikyuu kibo no mondai kaiketsu ni muketa global innovation ecosystem no kouchiku: kankyou, enerugii, shokuryou, mizumondai*' (Architecting a Global Innovation Ecosystem as a Step Toward Resolving Global-Scale Problems: The Environment, Energy, Food, and Water), CRDS-FY2008-RR-02. Available at http://crds.jst.go.jp/output/pdf/08rr02.pdf (accessed 11 December 2009).

CRDS (2008b) '*Kagaku gijutu ni yoru chikyuu kibo mondai no kaiketsu ni mukete: global innovation ecosystem to asia keizai ken*' (Toward Science and Engineering Solutions of Global-Scale Problems: The Global Innovation Ecosystem and the Asian Economic Sphere), CRDS-FY2008-RR-02. Available at http://crds.jst.go.jp/output/pdf/08rr02.pdf (accessed 11 December 2009).

EC (2009) 'Global Governance of Science', *Report of the Expert Group on Global Governance of Science to the Science, Economy and Society Directorate, Directorate-General for Research, European Commission*, EUR 23616 EN.

The Economist (2006) 'Emerging Economies – Coming of Age', *The Economist*, 21 January.

Executive Office of the President, National Economic Council, Office of Science and Technology Policy (2009) 'A Strategy for American Innovation: Driving Towards Sustainable Growth and Quality Jobs'. Available at http://www.scribd.com/doc/20148775/Executive-Office-of-the-President (accessed 11 December 2009).

Fagerberg, J., Mowery, D. C., and Nelson, R. R. (eds) (2004) *The Oxford Handbook of Innovation* (Oxford Handbooks in Business & Management), New York: Oxford University Press.

Freeman, C. and Soete, L. (1997) *The Economics of Industrial Innovation* (3rd edition), Cambridge, MA: MIT Press.

Goldman Sachs (2003) 'Dreaming with BRICs: The Path to 2050', Goldman Sachs Global Economics Paper 99. Available at http://www2.goldmansachs.com/ideas/brics/book/99-dreaming.pdf (accessed 11 December 2009).

308   *Tateo Arimoto*

Leshner, A. I. and Turekian, V. (2009) 'Harmonizing Global Science', *Science*, 326(5959): 1459 (11 December).

Lundvall, B. (ed.) (1992) *National Systems of Innovation: Toward a Theory of Innovation and Interactive Learning*, London: Pinter Publishers.

National Academy of Sciences, National Academy of Engineering, Institute of Medicine (2007) *Rising Above The Gathering Storm: Energizing and Employing America for a Brighter Economic Future*, Washington, DC: National Academies Press.

Nelson, R. R. (ed.) (1993) *National Innovation Systems: A Comparative Analysis*, New York: Oxford University Press.

Nippon Keidanren (2009) '*Higashi ajia keizai sougou no arikata ni kansuru kangaekata – keizai renkei nettowaaku no kouchiku wo tsuujite, higashi ajia no shourai wo souzou suru*' (How to Think About the State of Economic Consolidation in East Asia by Creating the Future of East Asia by Designing Economic Collaboration Networks), 20 January. Available at http://www.keidanren.or.jp/japanese/policy/2009/006/index.html (accessed 11 December 2009).

NISTEP (Japan's National Institute of Science and Technology Policy) (2009) '*Kagaku gijutsu shisutemu no kadai ni kansuru daihyouteki kenkyuusha, yuushikisha no ishiki teiten chousa*' (On Issues in the Science and Technology System: A Fixed-Point Survey of Representative Researchers and Key Individuals), NISTEP 114 (March).

Odagiri, H. and Goto, A. (1996) *Technology and Industrial Development in Japan: Building Capabilities by Learning, Innovation and Public Policy*, New York: Oxford University Press.

Science Council of Japan, Science and Technology Basic Plan Review Committee (2005) '*Kagaku gijutsu kihon keikaku ni okeru juuyou kadai ni kansuru teigen*' (Recommendations Regarding Critical Issues Concerning Science and Technology Basic Plans), 2 February. Available at http://www.scj.go.jp/ja/info/kohyo/pdf/kohyo-19-te1022-2.pdf (accessed 11 December 2009).

Schumpeter, J. (1912) *Theorie der wirtschaftlichen entwicklung* (Theory of Economic Development), Leipzig: Verlag von Dunkel & Humbolt.

Slaughter, A. (2009) 'America's Edge – Power in the Networked Century', *Foreign Affairs*, January/February. Available at http://www.foreignaffairs.com/articles/63722/anne-marie-slaughter/americas-edge (accessed 11 December 2009).

Sunami, A. and Kurokawa, K. (2009) 'Recession Watch: No Time for Nationalism', *Nature* 457(19 February): 960–961.

Vogel, E. F. (1979) *Japan as Number One: Lessons for America*, Cambridge, MA: Harvard University Press.

Yoshikawa, H. (2007a) 'Science-based Innovation', Presentation at REE Asia 2007 Conference, 20–22 June at Korea Advanced Institute of Science and Technology (KAIST) in Daejeon.

Yoshikawa, H. (2007b) 'Higher Education, Innovation and Entrepreneurship', Presentation at UNU/UNESCO International Conference of 'Pathways Towards a Shared Future: Changing Roles of Higher Education in a Globalized World', 29–30 August at United Nations University in Tokyo.

Index

Accenture, 44, 45
ACT Map scenario, 282
agency costs, 218
agency theory, 224, 248, 254
air pollution, measures to reduce, 276–7
AMD, 35
anti-locking braking systems (ABS), 275
antitrust laws, 17, 118
Apache, 53
ASET, 34
Asia, economic consolidation in, 306
Asian financial crisis, 219, 242
Asian Research Area (ARA), 306
Asuka, 34
Augustine report, 301
automobiles, problems caused by, 273, 274
automotive industry, 142
automotive technology policy, 10–11, 273–90
    air pollution measures, 276–7
    future directions for, 288–90
    global warming and, 273, 274, 277–9, 281–8
    process for determining, 279–81
    safety measures, 274–5

base pay, 32, 71, 72, 75
Basic Survey of Japanese Business Structure and Activities, 3, 166–7, 188n2
'best-in-class', 4, 92
block ownership, 226, 229, 236
BLUE Map scenario, 282–3
board of directors, 248
bonuses, 32–3
'bubble economy', 1, 137, 218, 222
bureau pluralism, 280
business failures, 26
business environment, changes in, 219

business relationships
    see also keiretsu
    long-term, 4, 5, 49, 53, 221

capital intensity, 228
Chief Information Officer (CIO), 59
China
    FDI inflows, 191–2, 193
    intellectual property rights in, 192–3, 199–200
    manufacturing outsourcing to, 33–4
    offshore design centers in, 34, 35
    rise of, 296
    start-ups in, 22
Chinese patents, 8–9, 191–215
    by Japanese MNEs, 197–214
    surge in, 195–7, 213–14
    system for, 194–5
Cisco Systems, 111
closed innovation paradigm, 129
cloud computing, 66
CO2 emissions, 281–2, 288–9
compartmentalized pluralism, 280
complex product industries, 200–1
computer industry, early development of, 46–9
contingent governance, 9
contracts, 111, 120, 132n5
cooperative ventures, 24, 25
corporate divisions, 23–4
corporate governance, 218–20
    contingent governance, 9
    evolution of Japanese, 2, 9–10, 220–4, 226
    market-based model of, 73–5, 221
    profitability and, 230–43
    relationship-based, stakeholder-oriented model of, 220–1, 225–6
    role of, 226
    shareholder-oriented, 222–3
    study data and methodology, 227–30

corporate governance – *continued*
  study results, 230–40
  theory and hypotheses on,
    224–7
corporate groups, 225
corporate headquarters, R&D
    concentrated in, 8
corporate performance
  governance and, 219–20, 230–43
  impact of FDI on, 161–4, 166,
    182–5, 187
crash safety standards, 275
credit crunch, 18–19
customized software, 55–61

discretionary labor, 80, 82, 86n3
domestic alliances, 6–7, 117–22,
    126–7
dynamic random-access memory
    (DRAM), 15, 18, 19, 20

electric vehicles (EVs), 10–11, 282–8,
    289–90
electronics industry
  corporate governance in, 227
  human-resource management in,
    79–84
  issues facing, 84–5
Elpida, 32, 35
emerging companies
  see also start-ups
  paths for, 23–6
  support for, 27
employee classifications, 71, 75–8, 82
employee evaluations, 71, 72, 75,
    106–7
employee morale, 12, 32–3
employees
  regular vs. nonregular, 76–7, 81–4
  roles of, 71, 75
energy consumption, measures to
    reduce, 277–9
engineering innovativeness, 6
engineering innovativeness
    determination model, 94–100
engineers, *see* Japanese engineers
enterprise software industry, 41–67
executive compensation, 247
  see also stock options

executive officer organization, 219
executive ownership, 236–7
executive shareholding, 224
executive structure, 229

fabless business model, 23
Fab Solutions, 24–5
factory models, of software
    development, 49–52
FDI, *see* foreign direct investment
    (FDI)
financial ownership, 229, 236
financial sector, evolution of
    Japanese, 2
foreign direct investment (FDI), 8
  in China, 191–2, 193
  impact on financial performance,
    161–4, 166, 182–5, 187
  impact on inter-firm transactions,
    178, 181, 184–5, 186
  impact on personnel allocations,
    173–9, 182, 185
  impact on R&D, 178–80, 184–7
  intellectual property rights and,
    192
  Japanese firms strategies of, 8
  managerial decisions and, 161–81
  patenting practices and, 8–9,
    201–14
  research on, 162–5
foreign expansion patterns, 167–8,
    169
foreign investors, 226
foreign ownership, 229, 236, 237
foreign subsidiaries, 164
foundries, 18, 23, 35
France, 93
fuel-cell vehicles (FCVs), 282–3, 288,
    289–90
fuel-efficiency standards, 277–81
Fujitsu, 15, 35, 45, 46, 48

General Motors (GM), 115–16
Germany, 91, 93, 137, 296
global competition, in semiconductor
    industry, 17–18
global financial crisis, 292
global innovation ecosystem (GIES),
    11, 304–5

globalization, 296
  consequences of, 293
  Japanese responses to, 2
global strategic model, 164–5, 187
global warming, 10–11, 273, 274,
    277–9, 281–8
governance, of Japanese firms,
    220–244
government policies
  industrial technology policy, 10–11
  science and technology policy, 11
government research consortia, 118–22
Great Depression, 1

Hashimoto cabinet, 2
Heisei recession, 218, 227
Herfindahl-Hirschman Index, 259
Hewlett Packard, 67, 111
high-commitment HRM system,
    27–32, 36
high-innovation HRM systems, 28–32
high-tech companies, 2
Hitachi, 15, 35, 46, 49, 86n4
human-resource management, 5–6,
    14–15, 31–3, 70–87
  comparison between US and Japan,
    73–8
  in electronics industry, 79–84
  evolution of Japanese, 31–3, 70–87
  high-commitment, 27–32, 36
  high-innovation, 28–32
  in Japan, 14–15, 70–87
  Japanese engineers and, 107
  performance-based pay, 32–3
  performance management and,
    79–84
  in semiconductor industry, 36
  in US, 73–5, 77–8
hybrid electric vehicles (HEVs), 289

IBM, 4, 15, 44, 46–50, 57–8, 62, 66–7
import protection, 15
incentive theory, 248
incubators, 27
independent spin-out model, 24–5
independent start-ups, 24, 25, 26
India
  outsourcing to, 34
  rise of, 296

indirect hiring, 81–2, 85
industrial technology policy, 10–11
influence peddling, 269
information service firms, 44
information systems, methods of
    building, 54–6
information technology, 41
  deployment and migration in
    Japanese firms, 53–4
innovation, 88
  closed innovation paradigm, 129
  Japanese engineers and, 91–4
  national innovation system, 292
  open innovation paradigm, 7
  process innovation, 295
  product innovation, 295
  start-ups and, 22–3
  theory of, 292–3
innovation ecosystems, 11, 302–5
innovation policy, 300–2
Intel, 17, 18, 19
intellectual property rights, 191–3,
    199–200
intellectual property strategies, 8–9
inter-corporate relationships, 6–7
inter-firm transactions, impact of FDI
    on, 178, 181, 184–5, 186
internal combustion engines (ICEs),
    281–2
international alliances, 112–17
international diversity, 228
International Panel on Climate
    Change (IPCC), 282
international strategic model, 164–5,
    187
Internet, 296
inter-organizational networks, 110
interpersonal relationships, in
    workplace, 102–3
intra-industry alliances, 120–1
investment
  see also foreign direct investment
    (FDI)
  decline in, 18–19
  in human resources, 105–6
  in IT, 18, 66
  public, in science and technology,
    11, 294–5
  in R&D, 119–22

investment trusts, 222

Japanese Automobile Manufacturer's
    Association (JAMA), 279–80
Japanese banking crisis, 2
Japanese engineers, 5–6, 88–108
    countermeasures for improving
        conditions of, 105–8
    deficit of new, 104–5
    education and training for, 88
    factors enhancing performance of,
        98–100
    female, 106
    future trend affecting, 100–5
    innovativeness of, 88, 91–100
    labor unions and, 107–8
    motivation of, 88–9, 103–4
    pay-for-performance systems and,
        88–9, 106
    teamwork evaluations for, 106–7
    work environment of, 89–90,
        101–3, 105–6
Japanese software industry, 4–5,
    41–67
    compared with US, 41–3
    system integration market, 43–6
Java, 53
job motivation, of Japanese engineers,
    103–4
joint R&D programs, 151–6

keiretsu, 43, 48, 49, 61, 67, 109,
    119–31
    diminishing role of, 127–30
    vs. strategic alliances, 125–7

labor market
    mobility, 32–3
    norms, 27–31
    semiconductor industry and, 36
labor productivity, of Japanese
    engineers, 93–4
labor unions, 107–8
Latin America, in 1980s, 1
legal reforms, 221
lifetime employment, 225
Linux, 53
long-term employment, 225
lost decade

in Japan, 1–2, 137, 138–9, 218
    meaning of term, 1

mainframe computing, 43, 52, 53–4
management strategies, 8–9
managerial autonomy, 218, 248
managerial decisions
    analytical model and data set for,
        165–72
    FDI strategies and, 161–81
managerial enterprise, 225
manufacturing centers, 8
manufacturing outsourcing, 33–4,
    162
market-driven personnel systems,
    72–3
Matsushita Electric, 121–2
Matsushita Group, 127
MegaChips, 25
memory chips, 15, 16, 18–20
meritocratic management, 72
Microsoft, 62
milking theory, of Japanese strategic
    alliances, 114–15
Mirai, 34
Mitsubishi, 35, 49, 121–2
multinational enterprises (MNEs),
    Chinese patents and, 191–2,
        197–214
multinational strategic model, 164
Mu Solutions, 23–4

national innovation system, 292
NEC, 16, 17, 32, 35, 46, 48, 49
new companies, *see* start-ups
new-energy vehicles, 11
NOx law, 276
NUMMI, 115–16

open architecture, 52–4
open innovation paradigm, 7
Open Source Systems (OSS), 53
Oracle, 62, 67
organizational performance
    management systems, 5
organizational structures, in
    electronics industry, 79–80
outsourcing
    manufacturing, 162

outsourcing – *continued*
R&D, 7–8, 142–51
in semiconductor industry, 33–4
ownership structure, 225
block ownership, 229, 236
changes in composition of, for
Japanese firms, 221–4
executive ownership, 236–7
executive structure, 229
financial ownership, 229, 236
financial performance and, 230–43
foreign ownership, 229, 236, 237

packaged software, 54–5, 62–6
Palmisano report, 300, 301–2
partnership networks, 120–1
patents, 91–3
Chinese, 8–9, 191–215
FDI and, 201–14
pay
base, 32, 71, 72, 75
performance-based, 5, 32–3, 71, 72,
85, 88–9, 106, 247
seniority-based, 72
pension funds, 222
performance-based pay, 5, 32–3, 71,
72, 85, 88–9, 106, 247
performance evaluations, 71, 72, 75,
106–7
performance management, 73–5,
79–84
performance measures, 228
personal computers, 19
personnel allocations, impact of FDI
on domestic, 173–9, 182, 185
personnel development, 84
personnel evaluations, 71, 72, 75,
106–7
personnel management, *see* human-
resource management
personnel systems
see also human-resource
management
evolution of, 70–8
market-driven, 72–3
pharmaceutical industry, 113
Plaza Accord (1985), 17, 161
PostgresSQL, 53
process innovation, 295

product diversity, 228, 236
product innovation, 295
profitability, 219, 220–1, 225, 226

quality-first mentality, 52

regulatory standards, 10, 219, 273–4
for automotive industry, 274–9
process for determining, 279–81
relational management, 48
Renesas, 32, 34, 35
research and development (R&D), 7–8
adaptive, 192
closed, 8, 129, 187
concentrate in corporate
headquarters, 8
consortia, 118–22
environment for, 88
expenditures on, 137–9
external, 7–8, 142–51
impact of FDI on, 178–80, 184–7
in-house, 144–50
investment in, 295–6
joint, 151–6
joint, in semiconductor industry,
34–5
local-support-oriented, 192
management, 137–59
open, 143, 180, 187
outsourcing, 7–8, 142–51
private sector, 137–8
research-oriented, 192
in semiconductor industry, 22–3
resource-dependence perspective,
152–3, 156
retention issues, 84–5
return on assets (ROA), 9, 237
risk-sharing, 125–7
role-based employee classifications,
75–8, 82

safety measures, in automotive
industry, 274–81
Samsung, 17, 18, 25
SAP, 62
Science and Technology Basic Law, 11
enactment of, 296–7
overview of, 297–8
significance of, 298–9

Science and Technology Basic Plan, 302
science and technology policy, 11, 292–306
  historical survey of Japanese, 293–7
  innovation policy and, 300–2
  postwar era, 293–4
  in twenty-first century, 300–5
Science: The Endless Frontier, 294
search-cost perspective, 152–3, 156
Selete, 34
SEMATECH, 17
semiconductor industry, 3–4, 14–38
  changes in industry leadership, 16
  domestic market and, 19–21
  excess capacity in, 36
  fabless business model, 23
  global competitors in, 17–18
  government support of, 15
  home substitution index for semiconductor sales, 20–1
  human-resource management in, 27–33, 36
  outsourcing in, 33–4
  reasons for decline of Japanese, 18–27
  research and development in, 34–5
  restructuring and reform in Japanese, 14, 33–7
  rise of Japanese, 15–17
  start-ups in, 21–7
  US, 15–19, 22
Semiconductor Industry Association (SIA), 17
seniority-based pay, 72
shareholder orientation, 219
shareholders, 218
shareholder value, 220–1, 222, 224, 226
Silicon Valley model, 24, 25–6
software, 41
  customized, 55–61
  packaged, 54–5, 62–6
Software Engineering Institute (SEI), 51
software engineers, 31, 63
software factories, 4, 49–52
software industry, 4–5, 41–67
  customization, 56–61

early development of, 46–9
factory models of software development, 49–52
Japan, 41–3, 51–67
methods of building information systems, 54–6
open architecture, 52–4
system integration market, 43–6, 56–61
US, 41–3, 55–8, 62–3
Sony, 35
South Korea, 17–19, 92
Spansion, 35
start-ups, 14
  independent, 24, 25, 26
  lack of support for, in Japan, 21–7
  paths for new, 23–6
  support for, 27
  US, 18
State Intellectual Property Office (SIPO), 194–5
stockholder interests, 9
stock options, 9–10, 219, 247–71
strategic alliances, 6–7, 109–32
  see also keiretsu
  critique of Japanese, 113–17
  defining, 110–12
  domestic, 117–22, 126–7
  government research consortia as, 118–22
  international, 112–17
subsidiaries, 23–4, 164
Sun Microsystems, 53, 67
System Development Corporation (SDC), 50–1
system integration market, 43–6, 56–61
system integration services, 42

Taiwan, 18–19, 22
technological change, 88
technological revolution, 14
technology fusion, 119–20, 121
technology policy, *see* automotive technology policy; science and technology policy
technology trade, 139–42
technology transfer, 15
Texas Instruments, 15, 16, 19

Index 315

theory of managerial sovereignty, 10, 248–58, 267–71
theory of shareholder sovereignty, 248–50, 251–7, 267, 271
THine Electronics, 25
Toshiba, 16, 32, 34, 35, 49
Toyota, 115–16, 132n3, 132n6
trade friction, US-Japan, 294–6
trade partners, 141
transportation equipment industry, 141
TSMC, 18

UMC, 18
United Kingdom, 1, 93
United States
  competitiveness of, 300–2
  computer industry in, 46–7
  corporate governance in, 218
  after Great Depression, 1
  human-resource management in, 73–5, 77–8
  innovation policies, 301
  labor market mobility in, 32–3
  labor market norms in, 27–31
  semiconductor industry in, 15–19, 22
  software industry, 41–3, 49–51, 55–8, 62–3
  start-ups in, 22
  system integration market, 43, 44

technological trade friction
  between Japan and, 294–6
US Council on Competitiveness, 300
US government policy, semiconductor industry and, 17
US Patent and Trademark Office (USPTO), 192

vehicle design standards, 275
vertical business model, 4–5, 17
vertical markets, in software industry, 41, 47–9, 65
vertical partnerships, 53, 109, 121–31

wage management, 73–4, 76–8, 82
women
  engineers, 106
  in labor force, 76
work environment, for Japanese engineers, 89–90, 101–3
work hours, 89–90, 101–2, 105–6
work-life balance, 84, 87n7, 89–90, 101
workplace culture, 102–3
World War II, 294

Young report, 300

zaibatsu, 123–4
Zero Emission Vehicle (ZEV) regulations, 289–90